The Saints of the Anglican Calendar

Kathleen Jones was an editorial consultant to the new *Butler's Lives of the Saints* (Burns & Oates) and edited two volumes in the series. She is the author of *Women Saints*, also published by Burns & Oates.

She is Emeritus Professor of Social Policy in the University of York and was a member of the Archbishops' Commissions on Church and State, and on Marriage, and of the General Synod of the Church of England. She lives in York.

The Saints of the Anglican Calendar

Kathleen Jones

CANTERBURY
PRESS
Norwich

First published in 2000 by The Canterbury Press Norwich
(a publishing imprint of Hymns Ancient & Modern Limited
a registered charity)
St Mary's Works, St Mary's Plain
Norwich, Norfolk NR3 3BH

British Library Cataloguing in Publication Data

A catalogue record for this book is available
from the British Library

ISBN 1-85311-375-1

Typeset by Regent Typesetting, London
Printed in Great Britain by
Biddles Ltd, Guildford and King's Lynn

Contents

Introduction

Nearly five hundred years after the Reformation, the Church of England is coming to a fuller appreciation of the saints through the *Common Worship* Calendar. This calendar includes not only the feast days of familiar saints such as the Apostles and the patrons of England, Ireland, Scotland and Wales, but also well over a hundred 'Lesser Festivals' and nearly as many 'Commemorations'. Some are Celtic or Anglo-Saxon, their traditions previously all but forgotten. Some are mediaeval Englishmen and women. Some are post-Reformation Anglicans who helped to establish a Church both Protestant and Catholic. Some are twentieth-century people such as William Temple and Evelyn Underhill. Some are Christians from overseas, like the martyrs of Uganda and Papua New Guinea. Some are members of other Churches – they include John Henry Newman and the Curé d'Ars, an Indian Sádhu or holy man, two Russian Orthodox monks, the Quaker George Fox, John and Charles Wesley, and William and Catherine Booth of the Salvation Army.

This is an important development in the life of the Anglican Church. These people represent a 'great cloud of witnesses' (Hebrews 12:1) who have contributed to our understanding of our faith: not perfect people, sinners like the rest of us, but people who have faced up to the problems of living the Christian life, often in conditions of great pain and difficulty. We have a legacy of 2000 years of Christian values in the lives of the saints – and in a world where Christian values are attacked on all sides, we need to draw on it. Why the revival of this tradition took so long, and how it came about, require some preliminary explanation.

In the ancient and mediaeval worlds, most Christians were unlettered. The lives of the saints were their folk-history, passed on by word of mouth. Soldiers on campaign told stories of their saints back home. Merchants and travellers recounted heroic martyrdoms round camp fires in the desert or across Europe. Sailors swapped yarns about saints on deck under the Mediterranean stars. Pilgrims visited their shrines, and hoped for healing or insight. The saints maintained popular culture, providing drama and human interest and stories of violence for generations which knew nothing of television 'soaps' or the Internet.

Inevitably the stories became embroidered and sometimes muddled. Saints were often credited with supernatural marvels and improbable miracles; but their lives had the merit of *personalizing* theology – bringing the great issues of Christian living down to the human level, and providing models for others to follow.

When the monasteries developed, monks wrote down the stories of the saints in their careful Latin. Some of them were credulous, some of them were poor copyists, and most of them were more interested in telling an edifying story with a moral than in recording historical facts. Errors multiplied: so did superstition and commercialism. As the Middle East fell to the Ottoman Empire, relics were transported to Europe to provide a focus for devotion in new churches: the Crusaders brought back many devotions to saints, including that to St George, who may have been a Cappadocian and was certainly not an English-man. In Rome, boxes of bones with dubious attributions were sold for large sums to the pious. Parties of monks were sent out to take their saint's bones on tour on fund-raising expeditions. Pilgrimage centres prospered on specious accounts of past marvels and promises of future blessings.

In the Roman Catholic Church, the Society of Bollandists, a group of Jesuit scholars, began work in the seventeenth century, trying to distinguish between a *vita fide*, or reliable life, a *vita suspecta*, and a *vita fabulorum plena*. Many have been found to be *fabulorum plena*, and the work of critical hagiography – disentangling the facts from centuries of accretions – is still going on.

In England, the legacy of the saints had been almost wiped out by that time. The Vikings destroyed much of the heritage of the Celtic Church in the North. Lanfranc, William the Conqueror's archbishop of Canterbury, set a Commission to replacing traditional Anglo-Saxon saints with Continental imports; Henry VIII abolished the monasteries, with the loss of many shrines and documents; and Cromwell's New Model Army took to slicing the heads off saints' statues, shatter-ing stained glass windows with their pikes, and scattering the contents of tombs. The reputed bones of St Frideswide of Oxford were deliberately mixed with those of a woman supporter of Zwingli so that people could no longer visit her shrine.

After centuries of religious hatred and sectarian warfare, the Church of England came to balance and toleration at the end of the seventeenth century. The Calendar of the 1662 *Book of Common Prayer* preserved the commemoration of the apostles and the patron saints and some others, including the great Latin Fathers of the Church; but for over three hundred years, the Church of England was so wary of the excesses of the past that it made no additions and no revisions to the list. The 1928 Prayer Book proposed a fuller Calendar, but was not accepted by parliament. While the extended list, together with the 'Commons' for martyrs and bishops, was used in some churches, it had no official status.

When the General Synod of the Church of England came to consider the publication of the *Alternative Service Book* in the 1970s, the issues were raised again. Some names were added to the ASB Calendar in 1978, but the matter clearly required extensive study and discussion. The Synod's Liturgical Commission set to work. In 1996, two reports from the Revision Committee on their proposals were debated in full Synod. They recommended a new Calendar, which included many English names from both before and after the Reformation, some names from other parts of the Anglican Communion, and, in a remarkable ecumenical attempt to heal old controversies, names which cut across the divisions between the Churches and the bitterness of centuries of misunderstanding.

These proposals were authorized at the July 1996 session of the General Synod. The new *Common Worship* Calendar came into use in Advent 1997, and prescribes ways in which the people whose names are included may be celebrated in liturgical worship. The operative word is 'may'; honouring the saints is an aid to devotion for some Anglicans, but is not enjoined upon all.

Anglican procedures are not the same as Roman Catholic procedures for beatification and canonization (see appendix). Though the people included may be referred to collectively as 'saints', the *Common Worship* Calendar does not refer to 'Saint A' or 'Saint B' individually; and like other Calendars of saints, it has no pretensions to exclusiveness. There have been many people through the Christian centuries whose spiritual qualities have gone unrecognized. Because of persistent inequalities in human society, calendars and martyrologies have inevitably over-represented scholars, noblemen and senior clergy, and they contain the names of far more men than women because of women's historic 'invisibility'. Ultimately, the names of the saints are known only to God: we can only celebrate those we know about.

In 1997, Brother Tristam SSF, a member of the Liturgical Commission and the Revision Committee of General Synod, compiled *Exciting Holiness*, a book of collects, psalms and Bible readings to accompany the *Common Worship* Calendar. This was followed in 1998 by Robert Atwell's *Celebrating the Saints*, containing appropriate daily spiritual readings. These pioneer studies contain brief biographical notes. The present study complements them by giving fuller biographies, together with source-notes for further reading. I should like to record my gratitude to both authors; also to the Very Revd Michael Perham, Provost of Derby, who was kind enough to encourage me in this project and set me on the right track; and to Paul Burns, managing editor of *Butler's Lives of the Saints*, who caused me to learn most of what I know about saints.

General Synod Papers GS1161Y (May 1996) and GS1161A (July 1996); The Lectionary according to the *Common Worship* Calendar 2000. Richard Symonds, *Far Above Rubies* (1993), pp. 1–20, describes the discussions preceding the adoption of the *Common Worship* Calendar; Brother Tristam, SSF, *Exciting Holiness* (1997, repr. 2000); Robert Atwell, *Celebrating the Saints* (1997, repr. 2000). Biblical quotations are taken from the New Revised Standard Version of the New Testament (anglicized edition) 1989, 1995.

Abbreviations

AA.SS.	*Acta Sanctorum,* 64 vols, Rome, Paris, and Antwerp, 1643–1940. (Page and volume numbers vary slightly in diferent editions.)
Anal.Boll.	*Analecta Bollandiana,* Brussels, monthly from 1882.
A.S.C.	G. N. Garmonsway, trans. and ed., *The Anglo-Saxon Chronicle,* 1972.
Attwater	Donald Attwater, *Saints of the East,* 1962.
Bede, *H.E.*	Bede, *Ecclesiastical History of the English People,* trans. Leo Sherley-Price, rev. R. E. Latham, with minor works trans. D. H. Farmer, 1955, rev. 1990.
Bridge Builders	H. A. L. Rice, *The Bridge Builders,* 1961.
Butler	*Butler's Lives of the Saints,* revised edition, 12 vols, 1995–2000. Various editors.
Cantuar	Edward Carpenter, *Cantuar: the Archbishops of Canterbury in their Office,* 1971.
Chandler	Andrew Chandler, ed., *The Terrible Alternative: Christian martyrdom in the Twentieth Century,* 1998.
D.A.C.L.	*Dictionnaire d'archéologie chrétienne et de liturgie,* Paris, 1907–53.
Delehaye	H. Delehaye, *Étude sur le légendier romain,* Société des Bollandistes, Brussels, 1936.
D.H.G.E.	*Dictionnaire d'histoire et de géographie ecclésiastique,* Paris, 1912.

Dict. Spir.	*Dictionnaire de spiritualité*, 16 vols, Paris, 1912.
D.N.B.	*Dictionary of National Biography*, 1885–.
D.T.C.	*Dictionnaire de théologie catholique*, 15 vols, Paris, 1903–50.
Early Christian Fathers	Cyril C. Richardson et al., trans. and ed., *The Early Christian Fathers*, Philadelphia, 1953.
Eddius Stephanus	Eddius Stephanus, *Life of Bishop Wilfrid*, ed. B. Colgrave, 1927, paperback edn, 1985.
E.E.T.S.	Early English Text Society.
Eusebius, *H.E.*	Eusebius of Caesarea, *The History of the Church from Christ to Constantine*, trans. G. A. Williamson, rev. and ed. A. Louth, 1965.
Far Above Rubies	Richard Symonds, *Far Above Rubies*, Leominster, 1973.
Foxe	*Foxe's Book of Martyrs*, ed. and abridged G. A. Williamson (1965) from John Foxe, *Acts and Monuments* (1694).
Golden Legend	Jacobus de Voragine, *The Golden Legend*, ed. W. G. Ryan, 2 vols, Princeton edn, 1993.
Great Christians	R. S. Forman, ed., *Great Christians*, 1933.
H.E.	*Historia Ecclesiastica*
Hieronymianum	H. Delehaye, *Commentarius Perpetuus in Martyrologium Hieronymianum* (*AA.SS.* vol. 64), 1940.
Irish Saints	D. Pochin Mould, *The Irish Saints*, Dublin and London, 1964.
Later Christian Fathers	H. Bettenson, trans. and ed., *The Later Christian Fathers*, 1970, paperback edn, 1972.

Levinson	W. Levinson, *England and the Continent in the Eighth Century,* 1946.
Lightfoot	J. B. Lightfoot, ed. and trans., *The Apostolic Fathers,* 1891, ed. J. Harmer, 1898.
Loane	Marcus L. Loane, *Masters of the English Reformation,* 1954, repr. 1956.
L.S.S.	W. M. Metcalfe, trans., *Ancient Lives of Scottish Saints,* 1895).
Mayr-Harting	H. Mayr-Harting, *The Coming of Christianity to Anglo-Saxon England,* 1972.
Men.E.W.	R. Stanton, *A Menology of England and Wales,* 1892.
N.C.E.	*The New Catholic Encyclopaedia,* 14 vols, New York, 1967.
N.L.A.	C. Horstmann, ed., *Nova Legenda Anglie,* 2 vols, 1901.
N.P.N.F.	P. Schaff and H. Wace, eds, *The Nicene and Post-Nicene Christian Fathers,* 2nd series, Grand Rapids, Michigan, 1887–1900, repr. 1979.
O.C.B.	B. M. Metzger and M. D. Coogan, eds, *The Oxford Companion to the Bible,* New York, 1993.
O.D.S.	D. H. Farmer, ed., *The Oxford Dictionary of Saints,* 3rd edn, 1992.
P.B.	F. Guérin, ed., *Vies des saints des Petits Bollandistes,* Paris, 1880.
P.L.	J. P. Migne, ed., *Patrologia Latina,* 221 vols, Paris, 1844–64.
Powicke	Maurice Powicke, *The Thirteenth Century,* Oxford History of England, 2nd edn, 1961, repr. 1992.
R.S.	Rolls Series, *Rerum Britannicum medii aevi*

	scriptores, H.M. Stationery Office, London, 1858–.
Stenton	F. M. Stenton, *Anglo-Saxon England*, Oxford History of England, 3rd edn, 1971.
Stock	E. Stock, *History of the Church Missionary Society*, vol. 1, 1899.
Twentieth Century	Bro. Kenneth, C.G.A, *Saints of the Twentieth Century*, Oxford, 1976.
Victorian Church	Owen Chadwick, *The Victorian Church*, 1966, 3rd edn, 1971.
Western Fathers,	F. R. Hoare, trans. and ed., *The Western Fathers*, 1933, rev. edn, New York, 1954.

Notes

i. in the following text, an asterisk * before a name indicates that the person concerned has a full entry elsewhere in the Calendar.

ii. the category of celebration for individuals whom the Church honours is indicated after the name, as follows: **Festival;** L.F. (Lesser Festival); *Commem.* (Commemoration).

iii. Works cited in the notes by author and date without a title are lives or biographies of the subject.

January

2. Basil the Great (*c*.329–79) and Gregory of Nazianzus (*c*.329–89) [L.F.]

Basil and Gregory Nazianzen both came from illustrious Christian families in Asia Minor. Basil's parents are both recognized as saints in the Eastern Church, and among his nine brothers and sisters were *Gregory of Nyssa and *Macrina. Gregory's father was bishop of Nazianzus.

The two met in Athens as students, and became close friends. Both were drawn to the religious life, but they were of very different temperaments: Basil was sociable, and an organizer, while Gregory was quieter and more contemplative. When their student days were over, Basil taught rhetoric and law for a time, and then embarked on a study tour of monasteries, visiting Syria, Palestine, Egypt and Mesopotamia. He came back with a wide knowledge of monasticism, and settled at Pontus, just across the river from where his mother and Macrina had a community for women. He discarded the Egyptian pattern of monasticism, in which monks lived as solitary ascetics, meeting only for worship and certain meals, and introduced a communal régime in which they lived and worked together. His Rule survives in nearly all the monastic establishments of the Eastern Church. It was known to *Benedict, and so entered the Western monastic tradition.

Gregory meanwhile had stayed in Nazianzus, acting as assistant to his father the bishop. He remained there until Basil, having spent five years setting up his first monastery, wanted to experience life as a hermit, and he joined him for a period of about two years. Then Basil went to Caesarea, to work with Bishop Eusebius, who was taking his stand on the doctrinal formulations of the Council of Nicaea (325). Gregory went back to assist his father. They were both under-studying aged bishops, but in different cities.

Eusebius was defending orthodox Christian belief against the Arian emperor, Valens. The Arians were a powerful body in the Eastern Church who held that Christ was created by God the Father, and was not consubstantial or co-eternal with him (see *Athanasius). When Eusebius died, Basil was elected archbishop in his place. Valens tried to weaken his position by splitting the archdiocese, creating a second archdiocese based on Tyana. Basil went to great efforts to have Gregory elected archbishop, so that they could work together; but Gregory's father was still alive, and Gregory felt that it was his first duty to support him at Nazianzus. Basil put pressure on Gregory, and actually had him consecrated, but Gregory never went to Tyana. When his father finally died, he became bishop of Nazianzus in his place.

This battle of wills left its mark on their friendship. Basil became a creative and energetic administrator. He set up the *Basiliad*, an institution for the needy in the suburbs of Caesarea which included a hospital, a hostel and a leprosarium, and became a model for Christian charity. He dispensed justice, he provided what would now be called rehabilitation programmes for thieves and prostitutes, and he preached daily to great crowds. His pastoral concern made him much loved, and gave him great power.

Gregory's life followed a quieter course. In 375, his health broke down, and he retired into solitude for five years. Then he was asked to go to Constantinople, where the patriarch was an Arian, and someone was needed to preach the orthodox faith. Gregory, poor, worn and prematurely aged, took on the task. He lodged in a house owned by relatives, and converted it into a church called the *Anastasis*, meaning that there would be a new dawn for the orthodox faith. There he preached a series of celebrated sermons on the Trinity, which led to his title of Gregory the Theologian. The Arian threat ended with the death of the emperor Valens in 378, and his successor, Theodosius, banished the Arian patriarch and appointed Gregory in his place. It was as patriarch of Constantinople that Gregory preached a moving valedictory sermon at Basil's funeral in the following year.

Theodosius called the bishops together at the Council of Constantinople, and Gregory Nazianzen worked with Gregory of Nyssa, Basil's younger brother. The two were responsible for producing a key definition of the nature of the Holy Spirit, which ran, 'We believe in the Holy Spirit, the Lord and Giver of life, who proceeds from the Father, who together with the Father and the Son is worshipped and glorified'. This was enough to settle the controversy at the time, though it fell short of 'proceeding from the Father and the Son', the formulation of the Roman Church. This was to be the major issue in the schism between the Eastern and Western Churches in the eleventh century.

Gregory's uncertain health made it necessary for him to retire from Constantinople, but the main doctrinal battles had been won. He lived a quiet contemplative life in his final years, writing religious poetry and the *De Vita Sua*, which is the main source of information about his life.

Basil: *AA.SS.,* June, 3, pp. 295–436; E. F. Morison, *St Basil and his Rule* (1912); W. K. Lowther Clarke, *St Basil the Great: a Study in Monasticism* (1913) and *The Ascetic Works of St Basil* (1925); G. L. Prestige, *St Basil the Great and Apollinaris of Laodicea* (1936); M. M. Fox, *The Life and Times of St Basil* (1939); Attwater, pp. 26–46, *Butler*, Jan., pp. 13–15. Works: *De Spiritu Sanctu* and *Letters* in *N.P.N.F.*, 8. *Later Christian Fathers*, pp. 59–98.

Gregory: *AA.SS.*, Jan., 1, pp. 21–31; A. Benoît (1885); P. Gallay (1943); R. R. Ruether, (1969); *Butler*, Jan., pp. 16–19. *Letters* in *N.P.N.F.*, 8. *Later Christian Fathers*, pp. 99–128.

Seraphim of Sarov (1759–1835)   *[Commem.]*

Seraphim, who came from Kursk, entered the monastery at Sarov, near Moscow, where the régime was very harsh. The monks fasted completely on Wednesdays and Fridays, ate only one meal on other days of the week, and were vegetarians, living largely on the food they were able to grow for themselves during the summer months. There must have been long periods during the bitter Russian winters in which they were reduced to bread and root vegetables. Seraphim's health broke down as a result of the poor diet, long hours of liturgical worship and study, and manual work in the bakehouse and the carpenter's shop. He was bedridden for three years, and had visions of the *Virgin Mary and the apostles. When he recovered, he made an altar of cypress wood for the monastery chapel in thanksgiving. He became a priest in 1793.

Seraphim was greatly attached to his abbot, and when the abbot died, he asked permission to go and live as a hermit. He lived in the woods about two hours' journey from the monastery, cutting his own wood and baking his own bread (tasks for which his labour in the monastery had well prepared him) and growing his own vegetables.

He cared for wild animals such as foxes and birds, and was said to make friends with wolves and bears. On one occasion, brigands attacked him with his own axe. He managed to crawl back to the monastery, and was cared for there, but his spine must have been damaged. Thereafter, he was bent, and he walked with a stick.

In 1807, the abbot died, and so great was Seraphim's reputation for holiness that he was asked to become abbot. He refused, and, mourning this second abbot, he returned to his solitude and went through 'the trial of silence', not speaking for three years. Then he went back to the monastery, where he lived in a bare cell without a bed. As if he had had his fill of silence, he devoted himself to looking after visitors and ministering to the nuns in the nearby community of Divelev.

Seraphim died in his cell, his face turned towards an ikon of the Virgin Mary, his clothes singed by a candle he held at the moment of death. His teaching was recorded in his lifetime by Nicholas Motovilov. He emphasized the importance of combining prayer with service to others and manual labour, and his mysticism has become well known in the Western Church as an example of Orthodox asceticism and spirituality.

C. de Grunwald, *Saints of Russia* (1960); V. Zander, *St Seraphim of Sarov* (1975); L. Gorainov, *The Message of St Seraphim* (1973); O.D.S., pp. 430–1.

Samuel Azariah Vedanayagam (1874–1945)   [*Commem.*]

Thomas Vedanayagam was an Anglican village priest in south India. His son Samuel became an evangelist at the age of nineteen, and secretary for the YMCA in the whole of south India in his twenties. He combined administrative ability with a conviction that the Church must develop indigenous leadership. In 1909, he was ordained priest and took charge of the mission station at Dornakal, in a remote corner of the state of Hyderabad. His aim was to develop a well-educated Indian clergy able to communicate with the villagers in a predominantly rural economy. He had a particular concern for the Untouchables, then still the lowest caste in a rigid caste system: he gave them dignity as human beings, and the assurance that they were equal with others in the sight of God. Many of his social concerns were similar to those of his contemporary, Mahatma Gandhi.

In 1913, he was consecrated assistant bishop in the diocese of

Madras, and began to make a notable contribution to the work of the World Council of Churches. His views were always strongly ecumenical. Like many Christians in the developing countries, he was impatient of the distinctions between High and Low Church, SPG and CMS, which seemed so important to English missionaries. He made a powerful speech on the need for Christian unity at the Lambeth Conference in 1930. His religious sympathies went wider – to the other faiths of India; and his great cathedral of the Most Glorious Epiphany at Dornakal is a sermon in stone, blending traditional Christian architecture with Hindu and Moslem architecture.

Bishop Samuel was one of the leaders in the movement for a united Church of South India. He died two years before that was finally achieved in 1947.

C. Graham, *Azariah of Dornakal* (1946); J. Z. Hodge, *Bishop Azariah of Dornakal* (1946).

10. William Laud (1573–1685)   [*Commem.*]

Laud, the son of a clothier in Reading, had a brilliant career at Oxford in the reign of James I, where he came into collision with Calvinist theologians. At one point, he was called before the vice-chancellor for expressing 'popish opinions'. As president of St John's College, he became the leader of the 'Arminians', or High Church party. King James I supported him: he became dean of Gloucester in 1616, chancellor of the University of Oxford in 1620, and bishop of St David's in 1621; but it was in the reign of James's successor, *Charles I, that he came to great authority in the Church of England. In 1626, he became bishop of Bath and Wells, in 1628 bishop of London and a privy councillor, and in 1633, archbishop of Canterbury.

Laud was opposed to the Calvinistic practices which were being introduced into the Anglican Church, and attempted to impose uniformity. He limited ordination, with certain exceptions, to men who were about to take up parish work, thereby infuriating the Puritan preachers who were proposing to travel the countryside at will. He instituted a detailed visitation of the dioceses to enforce conformity in church observance. In particular, church authorities were instructed to remove the altar (or communion table) from the centre of the church, and to place it at the east end, where it would serve as a focus for worship.

Laud considered the change a simple matter of reverence, but it roused great hostility among the Puritans, who considered it Romish and superstitious. John Milton said that the altar was being 'pageanted about like a dreadful idol'.

In the spirit of the Elizabethan Settlement, Laud was not concerned to control people's minds. He proposed to control their behaviour, and to keep the balance between Rome and Geneva. He supported Charles I as governor of the Church; but as the king came into increasing conflict with parliament, Laud inevitably became identified with the political rule of Thomas Wentworth, Earl Strafford. As a member of the court of Star Chamber, Laud assented to the sentencing of the Puritan William Prynne in 1634 and 1637. Prynne, who preached furiously against royal despotism and ecclesiastical autocracy, was mutilated by losing his ears on the pillory and being branded with the letters 'SL' for 'Seditious Libel'. Prynne maintained that the brands stood for 'Stigmata Laudis'. There were widespread mob protests on his behalf.

The crisis in the Church came with the notorious 'et cetera oath'. This required the clergy to swear 'not to alter the government of the Church by archbishops, deans and archdeacons *et cetera*'. Many refused, pointing out that the oath required unconditional and perpetual obedience to unspecified authorities.

In November 1640, the Long Parliament met for the first time. Both Strafford and Laud were arrested and impeached for treason. The king was powerless to save them. Strafford was executed, and Laud watched him go to his death. His own ordeal continued until 1644, when he was attaindered on a charge of 'attempting to alter religion as by law established, and to subvert the rights of Parliament'. He was condemned and beheaded at the age of seventy-two.

H. Trevor-Roper (1940, repr. 1962); Charles Carlton (1987); William Prynne, *Hidden Works of Darkenes* (1645) and *Canterburie's Doom* (1646). Works pub. 1847–53 in the Oxford Library of Anglo-Catholic Theology. *A Summarie of Devotions* (first pub. 1647) is the best known.

11. Mary Slessor of Calabar (1848–1915)   *[Commem.]*

Mary, the second of seven children, was born in Aberdeen, where her father was a shoemaker. Under the pressure of poverty and unemployment, the family moved to Dundee to work in the textile mills, and at the age of eleven, young Mary was working in the weaving sheds. Her father began to drink heavily – Mary was to say later that coping with him in his violent, Saturday night moods was good preparation for working with the drunken tribes of the Calabar. Her mother and the children went through great hardship. Four of the children died young, and when Mary's father died, she became the chief support of her mother and two younger sisters.

They were Presbyterians. Mary said later, 'We would as soon have thought of going to the moon as of being absent from a service.' The Presbyterian Church had missions in India, China, Japan and Africa, and at home, the Slessor children played missionaries. Mary was fascinated by what she heard of the Calabar Mission in Nigeria, founded in 1846 – a small but heroic attempt to bring Christian values to an area of swamps, rivers and forests where the people were said to be 'the most degraded in Africa'. At least part of the degradation was due to the coming of white traders, who bought slaves from the Calabar tribes and paid them in gin or rum. The tribes were in a constant state of warfare with each other. Mary and her brother John knew all about the problems of the Calabar from reading the *Missionary Record*, and he hoped to become a missionary there; but John died, and Mary, after much prayer, felt called to offer her services in his place. She worked twelve hours a day in the ceaseless din of the weaving sheds, attended night school, and attended Bible classes. When her sisters were at last in secure jobs and her mother settled, she volunteered. She was accepted, given three months' special training in Edinburgh – 'too bookish and insufficiently practical', said Mary – and reached the mission at Duke Town in September 1878 at the age of thirty. Her salary was £60 a year, and she sent most of it home to her mother and sisters.

Mary was just five feet tall, with red hair. She communicated with the people of the Calabar as simply and directly as with the mill girls of Dundee. She picked up Efik, the lingua franca of the area. She taught in the Mission school, and she made trips to the out-stations by river and on foot, learning how the people lived, preaching the gospel, providing simple medicines and talking to the chiefs. Long before the anthropologists came, she discovered that the people of the region had a very complex society with its own customs and conventions. After two years in the main mission, she moved to take charge of the station at Old Town, which was an outpost, and then to work with the Okoyong, a Bantu tribe at the junction of the Cross and Calabar

Rivers. 'I am going to a new tribe up-country', she wrote home, 'a fierce, cruel people, and everyone tells me that they will kill me. But I don't fear any hurt – only to combat their savage customs will require courage and firmness on my part.' Among these customs were ritual sacrifice, trial by ordeal, and twin-murder. Twins were regarded with abhorrence, since it was held that the second child must be the result of intercourse with the devil. The child was ritually killed, and the mother became an outcast.

Mary sailed into this unhealthy, fever-ridden area in a canoe on a river infested with crocodiles. She occupied a simple wattle-and-mud hut, and lived as simply as the local people. Most of them had never seen a white woman before, and she was jostled, poked and prodded by curious hands; but they accepted her. She confronted the chiefs, made friends with the women, and taught the children. Before long, she had a refuge, mostly composed of rejected twins. People brought their problems to her, and she was often told 'Run, Ma! Run!' to save victims of the ordeal, prevent a palaver leading to armed warfare, or to save a runaway slave or a sick child's life. In 1891, she was appointed as the British agent for the Okoyong, and became the magistrate for the district. She is said to have beaten one recalcitrant chief over the head with an umbrella. When she went home on furlough, she would not talk of the dangers and the dramas. She preached the gospel and the need for mission as simply as when she was a girl: all for Christ. She did not believe in large missions and elaborate buildings. 'Raw heathen', she maintained, needed one-to-one contact and simple structures like their own mud huts.

Mary died at Itu in Nigeria soon after the outbreak of the First World War, and thousands came to mourn and see the body of *Eka kpukru owo*, 'Everybody's mother'.

W. R. Livingstone, *Mary Slessor of Calabar, Pioneer Missionary* (1916). Hugh Goldie, *Calabar and its Mission* (1901); *Far Above Rubies*, pp. 212–24; *Twentieth Century*, pp. 77–80. Some of Mary Slessor's letters and diaries are kept in the Dundee City Museum and the Dundee Public Library.

12. Benedict Biscop (c.628–90)   [Commem.]

Benedict Biscop set out with *Wilfrid of Ripon for Rome in 653. They were both young noblemen from Northumbria, and they met at the court of King Erconberta of Kent when Wilfrid was eighteen or nineteen, and Biscop in his early twenties. They travelled together as far as Lyons. Wilfrid stayed there with Bishop Annemundus, while Biscop went on to Rome.

Bede describes how Biscop made this pilgrimage and how he went back to Rome to escort King Egfrith's son Alcfrith in 665, but he says nothing of what happened to him between these dates. We know from other sources that Biscop spent most of his time in Frankish monasteries, and at least two years in the great monastery of Lérins, off the southern coast of France (now opposite Cannes), where St Patrick himself had reputedly been a monk before going to Ireland. Lérins was changing from an association of hermits in single cells to a community of monks who worked and prayed together on Benedictine lines. Biscop was admitted as a monk, and presumably took the name of the founder of the Benedictine Order. He must have learned much of the problems involved in the transition from one way of monastic life to the other. He developed an impressive knowledge of the Benedictine Rule and monastic practices. He evidently missed the Synod of Whitby in 664, and the bitterness and acrimony which accompanied the English Church's sudden move to Latinization; but he was very well equipped to deal with the problems which occurred afterwards.

He was in Rome again when Pope Vitalian commissioned the Greek monk *Theodore of Tarsus as archbishop of Canterbury in 668, and he was the obvious choice to accompany Theodore to England on his mission. They took a year on the journey, staying at monastic houses, and when they finally reached Canterbury, Theodore showed his gratitude by appointing Benedict abbot of the monastery of St Peter and St Paul (later St Augustine's). After two years at Canterbury, Benedict went back to Rome, where the Pope gave him permission to found a monastery in Northumbria, granting him special privileges to ensure its independence against both temporal and spiritual overlords. Then he began to collect books, paintings, and other objects for the monastery in Northumbria. He had learned on the Continent how churches and monasteries could be enriched with these aids to learning and devotion. When he returned home, King Egfrith gave him seventy hides of land at the mouth of the river Wear, and the monastery became known as Monkwearmouth. Builders, stonemasons, glaziers and other craftsmen were brought over from France.

In all, Benedict made six journeys to Rome, and more to the Frankish monasteries. The books which he brought – eventually for other monasteries as well as his own, and not merely by the cart-load but in convoys of carts – included patristic texts, commentaries on the scriptures, books of prayers and books on monastic practices. There were pictures of the *Virgin Mary and the apostles and of scenes from the Gospels, relics of the apostles and martyrs, sacred vessels and vestments, silks, tapestries, and ivories. He also brought with him Abbot John the Chanter, the chief precentor from St Peter's, Rome, who taught Gregorian chant. Monks from other monasteries flocked to Monkwearmouth to learn the intricacies of plainsong. One of the young entrants to Benedict's monastery school was the seven-year-old *Bede.

Benedict taught the virtues of the Benedictine Rule – stability, obedience and democratic monastic government. In the last three years of his life, he was stricken by paralysis. When he was dying, he called his monks together and urged them to follow the Rule which he had given them. 'For,' he said, 'you cannot suppose that it was my own untaught heart which dictated this rule for you. I learnt it from seventeen monasteries which I saw in my travels and most approved of, and I copied these institutions thence for your benefit.' He commanded that the 'large and noble library' which he had built up should be kept intact and neither neglected nor dispersed. It was later to form the background to Bede's own work.

Bede, *The Lives of the Holy Abbots of Weremouth and Jarrow*, in *The Historical Works of the Venerable Bede*, trans. J. A. Giles (1845), pp. 83–102; Bede, *H.E.*, bk 4, chs 18, 19, autobiographical note; *D.C.B.*, 1, p. 309; *D.N.B.*, 2, pp. 214–16; *N.C.E.*, pp. 2, 281–2. Mayr-Harting, pp.153–4, 156–7.

Aelred of Hexham (1110–67)   [L.F.]

Aelred (or Ailred) had a good education in the monastic school at Durham, and joined the court of King David of Scotland, taking responsibility for organizing the king's household; but he was attracted to the monastic life, particularly that of the Cistercian Order which developed under the rule of *Bernard of Clairvaux.

Bernard made an English foundation at Rievaulx, north of York, in 1132, sending his secretary, William, to be the first abbot. Aelred joined the community two years later. His combination of administrative and political skills must have been very valuable to the growing community. In 1142, he was sent as envoy to Rome in the matter of the disputed election of archbishop William of York. This was the occasion on which William's appointment was set aside, though he was later restored to office. Aelred became master of novices at Rievaulx, and then in 1143, abbot of a small daughter house at Revesby, Yorks. Four years later, he became abbot of Rievaulx.

Under his rule, the harsh régime laid down by Bernard of Clairvaux was somewhat mitigated. He was a gentle and humane man. Under his guidance, the monastery grew to become the largest in England, with 150 choir monks and 500 lay brothers. Aelred was still managing a large mediaeval establishment. It was a sizeable enterprise, with sheep-farming (since the land proved unsuitable for crops), flax-growing, and its own foundry and tannery.

The best known of Aelred's writings are his treatise on Spiritual Friendship, in which he drew on the thought of Augustine and also on Cicero's *De Amicitia*, and the *Speculum Caritas* or 'Mirror of Charity'. He wrote biographies of the saints of Hexham, and adapted a life of Edward the Confessor by Osbert of Clare.

Aelred made five other foundations from Rievaulx, some in Scotland and some in England, and despite very poor health (he was troubled with gall-stones or kidney stones, and a painful complaint which may have been gout) he travelled repeatedly to visit them. Towards the end of his life, Aelred had to spent much of his time in the monastery infirmary. His disciple Walter Daniel, in his biography, describes how the monks would visit him in groups, asking his counsel and his blessing, and how great was the grief at his passing.

F. M. Powicke, ed., *The Life of Ailred of Rievaulx by Walter Daniel* (1950); modern Lives by A. Squire (1969) and J. P. McGuire (1995); M. Talbot, *Christian Friendship* (1942); G. Webb and A. Walter, *The Mirror of Charity* (1962); *Butler*, Jan., pp. 81–3. *N.L.A.*, 1, pp. 41–6, 2, pp. 544–52.

13. Hilary of Poitiers (*c.*315–365) [L.F.]

Hilary was a native of Poitiers in western France, the son of a noble family. He had a good classical education and became a public orator. He married, and had a daughter named Afra. In the wake of the formulation of the Nicene Creed in 325, he became interested in Christian doctrine. He embarked on a long period of study, and came to the conclusion that there was one God, and that Jesus Christ was both human and divine. He was much impressed by the Prologue to St John's Gospel, and the formulation that 'when all things began, the

Word [*Logos* to someone with his classical background] already was
. . . the Word was with God at the beginning, and through him all
things came to be'.

He was baptized in 350, and became a champion of the orthodox
position agreed at Nicaea against the Arians. He became bishop of
Poitiers by popular demand in 353. While *Athanasius contended
with the Arians in the Eastern Church, Hilary took a similar stand in
the Western Church. He managed to avoid confrontation with the
Arian emperor Constantius until 356, but at the Council of Béziers in
that year, he refused to condemn Athanasius, and was exiled to Asia
Minor for four years. He wrote his great works on the Trinity and on
Synods there. When he was permitted to return to Poitiers, he was
joined by *Martin of Tours, the ex-Army officer who had become one
of his disciples.

Hilary summoned a synod of Gallic bishops in 361, and they
accepted the Nicene Creed. Both *Jerome and *Augustine praise
Hilary as 'the Athanasius of the West', and Jerome described him as
'the trumpet of the Latins against the Arians'. When he died in 368,
Martin became his successor.

Hilary's feast day commences the spring term in the law courts and
at universities, traditionally known as the Hilary term.

AA.SS., Jan, 1, pp. 64–85 includes a Life by Venantius Fortunatus. Biographies by
A. Largent (1902); P. Galtier (1960). See also an evaluation by M. H. Williams in
the *Journal of Ecclesiastical History*, 42 (1991), pp. 202–17. N.C.E. 6, pp.
1114–16; *Later Christian Fathers*, pp. 48–57. Works in P.L., vols 9 and 10; Eng.
trans. in N.P.N.F., 9; *De Trinitate*, trans. and ed. S. McKenna (1954).

Kentigern (Mungo) (d. ?603)   [*Commem.*]

Many legends tell of the ministry of Kentigern as a monk and bishop in
Strathclyde and Cumbria. These seem to have survived as oral history
for some five hundred years before they were written down, for there
are no written sources earlier than the eleventh and twelfth centuries,
and there is no evidence that earlier sources existed. Kentigern was
clearly a powerful figure remembered with much affection. He became
part of the folklore of the area, and many improbable marvels are
accredited to him.

His mother is said to have been the daughter of Loth, tribal king of the Lothians. She became pregnant, and would not name her suitor, so her father ordered her to be hurled from a cliff-top on the southern bank of the Firth of Forth. Somehow, she survived, and was cast off in a coracle which drifted up the Forth on the current to Culross, where her child was born. Kentigern was brought up by a hermit named Serf (Servanus) who lived in that area, and who called him Mungo, or 'darling' in the local tongue. He grew up to become a monk in the Celtic tradition, and a great evangelist of the Strathclyde area, being consecrated bishop by an Irish bishop.

At one point in his life, he was forced into exile during a persecution of Christians. He is thought to have travelled to *St David's great monastery of Menevia in Wales, and to have gone north to Hoddam (Dumfries) and Glasgow. There is a story that he met *Columba shortly before the latter's death in 597, and exchanged pastoral staffs with him.

Kentigern/Mungo is honoured as the patron saint of Glasgow, and his shrine is in St Mungo's cathedral in that city.

A. P. Forbes, *The Lives of St Ninian and St Kentigern* (1874); *L.S.S.* has the Life by Goscelin or Jocelyn of Furness, pp. 175–80; K. H. Jackson, 'Sources for the Life of St Kentigern', in N. K. Chadwick, ed., *Studies in the Early British Church* (1958), pp. 273–357; *D.N.B.*, 11, pp. 26–7; *Butler*, Jan., pp. 91–2.

George Fox (1624–91)   [*Commem.*]

Fox's *Journal* has had such immense influence that recent Quaker historians have been at pains to show that Quakerism was not a one-man movement: the emergence of the quiet people as a recognized sect was essentially democratic, and has many other notable figures; but Fox, who took his message to the Midlands and the North of England through the years of Cromwell's Commonwealth and the reign of Charles II, surviving calumny, mob fury, beatings and repeated imprisonment, remains an outstanding figure.

Fox owed nothing to theological study, and little to a knowledge of religious history. All we know of his family is that they were Puritans. His father, Christopher, was called 'Righteous Christer' by his neighbours, and his mother was 'of the stock of the Martyrs'. George was taught to read his Bible, and was noted as a child for 'gravity and staidness of spirit'. His father was a weaver in Drayton-le-Clay, now

Fenny Drayton, in Leicestershire. There was some talk of making the boy a priest, but he was apprenticed to a neighbour who dealt in cattle and wool, with shoe-making as a sideline.

When he was twenty-one, he tells his readers, 'At the command of God, I brake off all familiarity or fellowship with young or old.' He began to travel in search of answers to his religious questions. He went to London and talked to clergy: one told him to take tobacco (which he detested) and to sing psalms. He came to the conclusion that 'being bred at Oxford and Cambridge did not qualify a man to be a minister of Christ', and that God did not dwell in temples made with hands. He walked 'mournfully' about the Peak District of Derbyshire, fasting and insistently asking questions. After a time, he 'regarded the priests less and looked more to the dissenting people'.

In 1647, he attended a meeting of Baptists near Mansfield, and he says that the Lord opened his mouth. He 'saw the Light, and all was manifest'. He began to preach with power, and people 'came from far and near' to hear him, 'as a young man that had a discerning spirit'. Out of the cauldron of dissenting ideas bubbling in Cromwellian England, he and the other 'Friends of Truth', as they called themselves, fashioned a distinctive set of beliefs. They believed that the True Light would enlighten those who waited on the Spirit. They were opposed to any institutional structure for religion – churches, priests or formal liturgy. They refused to pay tithes, to swear oaths, to recognize titles or honours, or to bear arms. They dressed soberly, and used the biblical 'thee' and 'thou' in their conversation.

These principles led them into direct public confrontation. The Quakers interrupted services in what they called 'steeple-houses', refused to pay their tithes, and the men refused to doff their hats to gentry, clergy, or magistrates. They were taken from church to court, wore their hats in court, and refused to take the oath. They were charged with blasphemy, sedition, riot and other offences. At Lichfield, Fox marched through the streets crying 'Woe to the bloody city of Lichfield'; at 'Beverley steeple-house,' he cried to the preacher, 'Come down, thou deceiver' because the preacher promised his congregation the water of life freely, and charged them £300 a year in tithes for it.

The Presbyterians and the Baptists called the Friends 'Quakers' in derision, because they shook with the force of the Spirit. They adopted the name themselves; and their numbers multiplied, chiefly in the provinces. There was little opposition at the national level to their activities, for they were no threat to either Commonwealth or kingdom: George Fox met Cromwell in 1655, when he had been consigned to the Marshalsea Prison. The Lord Protector of England listened to his peroration, said it was 'very good and true', and had tears in his eyes when he set the Quaker free. They had regular quarterly meetings and monthly meetings in many parts of England, but these were usually held in rural areas, because they were still being assailed by 'men with pitchforks and flails and staffs'. After the new religious settlement – the Act of Supremacy of 1662 and the institution of the revised Prayer Book – the persecution became stronger, and they suffered very badly in the lower courts.

The movement was spreading abroad – in the English colonies in North America, in the West Indies, in the Netherlands and in Germany. George Fox went to visit these groups of Friends, who were able to worship in a more free environment than English Quakers. He was in his mid-sixties when the 'Glorious Revolution' of 1688 took place, and the Toleration Act of 1689 at last put an end to persecution (though there was still the awkward matter of tithes). He died in London in 1691, and his *Journal* became an inspiration to a new and more peaceful generation of Quakers.

George Fox: the Journal, ed. and intro. Nigel Smith, Penguin Classics edn. (1997); W. C. Braithwaite, *The Beginnings of Quakerism* (1959); M. Mullett, ed., *New Light on George Fox* (1991); H. Larry Ingle, *First Among Friends: George Fox and the Creation of Quakerism* (1994).

17. Antony of Egypt (?251–?356)   [L.F.]

If Antony did not actually reach the advanced age of a hundred and five which is credited to him, he lived a very long and fruitful life, first as a solitary in Upper Egypt and later as a counsellor and leader of the Desert Fathers. He was not the first of his kind: *Jerome insists that 'the first to enter the road' of solitude and asceticism was Paul of Thebes, and possibly there were even earlier Christian ascetics, for when the imperial persecutions reached Alexandria, both men and women left the cities and went out into the sparsely populated regions. Antony's pre-eminent position as the father of desert monasticism comes from the quality of his contribution to the movement, and from the biography written by *Athanasius of Alexandria, who knew him personally and wrote within a year of his death.

Antony was the son of wealthy land-owning parents in the city of Coma in Upper Egypt. They died before he reached the age of twenty, and when he heard Christ's injunction, 'Sell all thou hast and give to the poor', he put it into practice. He gave some of the family estates to neighbours, sold others and gave the money to the needy of the city, and spent a time as the disciple of a local hermit. Then he moved out to a disued cemetery on the Outer Mountain at Pispir, on the banks of the Nile, where he lived alone for thirteen years. After that, he looked for an even more remote spot, and went into the Arabian desert, where he lived for a period of twenty years. The stories of demons and tempters who appeared to him during this period may owe more to Arabian traditions of *djinni* and *afreets*, or to local superstition, than to Antony's personal experiences.

By this time, Antony must have been in his early or mid-forties. His first long period of solitary communion with God was over, and he founded two monasteries on the pattern later common in the Upper Thebaïd: groups of hermits living in single cells in minimal association with one another. He went to Alexandria in 311 to help the Christian community during a period of persecution, and then retreated again to live in solitude with a disciple named Macarius; but other monks came to join them, and there were constant visitors, seeking counsel. Antony saw those who could benefit from spiritual advice, and delegated the others to Macarius.

He was far from idle, even in his extreme old age. He believed in physical labour, and laboured in what must have been a rather unproductive garden; he wove mats from rushes; he visited at least one of his monasteries regularly, and he went to Alexandria at the invitation of the bishops to preach against the Arians.

Antony was asked by a philosopher how he could be happy when he was deprived of the comfort of books. He replied, 'My book, philosopher, is the nature of created things, and as often as I have a mind to read the words of God, it is at my hand.' His letters include quotations from Plato and Origen; and if he wrote no books, we have his letters, and his disciples collected his words, which reached the Western Church through the Sayings of the Fathers. Antony said, 'Fish, if they tarry on dry land, die; even so monks that tarry outside their cell or abide with men of the world fall away from their vow of quiet. As a fish must return to the sea, so must we to our cell.' He said, 'Who sits in solitude and is quiet hath escaped from three wars: hearing, speaking, seeing: yet one thing shall he continually battle: that is, his own heart.'

The work of the Desert Fathers was well-known in Rome and Jerusalem by the end of the fourth century, and Athanasius' *Life* of Antony had a lasting influence on Western monasticism.

Life and Letters in *P.L.*, 73, pp. 125–70; Eng. trans. in R. T. Mayor, *Ancient Christian Writers*, vol. 10 (1950). See also D. Chatty, ed., *The Letters of Saint Antony the Great* (1975); T. Merton, *The Wisdom of the Desert* (1960); H. Waddell, *The Desert Fathers* (1936, repr. 1962); *Butler*, Jan., pp. 116–20; Mayr-Harting, pp. 237–9.

Charles Gore (1853–1932) [Commem.]

In the last quarter of the nineteenth century, the Christian Socialist movement, founded by Charles Kingsley and *F. D. Maurice, became 'a nursery of bishops'. None was more influential than the Oxford scholar Charles Gore. He became vice-principal of Cuddesdon theological college at the age of twenty-seven. When *Dr Pusey died, a memorial fund in his memory led to the founding of Pusey House as a new centre for theological teaching and research, and Gore became its first principal when he was only thirty. He had an outstanding intelligence, he was good with students, and he had a very clear commitment to moderate Anglo-Catholicism and to social justice. Though the conservative camp regarded him as dangerously High Church and dangerously liberal, he was a leader for a new age.

In 1887, Gore founded the Society of the Resurrection, a fellowship of Anglican priests committed to a rule not unlike that of the Oratorians (see *Philip Neri). They were committed to regular prayer, simplicity of life and a vow of celibacy, to be annually renewed. This led in 1892 to the Community of the Resurrection, which was originally based at Pusey House, and six years later became established at Mirfield.

Gore's editorship of *Lux Mundi* (1882), a collection of essays on biblical criticism, brought him into a storm of controversy. Though Christians had sought to interpret the Bible through the ages, what was then called 'the higher criticism' was new; and Gore himself wrote an article on *kenosis,* the doctrine that Christ, during his earthly life, must have been subject to the limitations of knowledge and insight appropriate to the understanding of his own day. His main area of study was Christology, the person and nature of Christ. His Bampton Lectures, also in 1899, expressed his personal devotion to Christ, and attracted very large audiences. When he published *The Sermon on the Mount* (1896) and *The Body of Christ* (1901), he was attacked by both extreme Anglo-Catholics and extreme Protestants for views which are now in the middle ground of Anglican theology.

His consecration as bishop of Worcester in 1902 attracted vociferous objections from the 'Kensitites'. He thought that the diocesan structure he inherited was out-dated: the Worcester diocese then included the whole of the Birmingham area, and he threw his energies into the creation of a separate diocese of Birmingham, contributing £10,000, a legacy from his mother, to the fund himself. In 1905 he moved to the new diocese as its first bishop. Industrial radicalism was closer to his sympathies than the traditionalism of the rural areas.

In 1911, he became bishop of Oxford. Commentators generally regard his eight years at Oxford as a difficult period of his life. He never liked administration, and said that being a bishop was 'a dog's life'. Even in the university, there were problems: though Gore was theologically progressive, he could not accept the new modernist ideas, which involved the denial of the Virgin Birth, the physical resurrection of Jesus, and the miracles. He remained a moderate Anglo-Catholic, devoted to making sense of the industrial age.

Gore retired from his diocese in 1919 at the age of sixty-six, and entered on the most productive period of his life: he wrote on world peace, the League of Nations, industrial order, Church unity, biblical scholarship and other causes close to his heart. He lived in his 'beloved hovel' near All Saints', Margaret Street in London, rejoicing that he no longer had to occupy a vast and draughty palace. He went about on public transport, and dispensed with a secretary by taking to correspondence by postcard, like George Bernard Shaw. Many organizations he did not want to address received a postcard simply saying 'Sorry – can't'; but he threw himself into his own causes. He was involved in the foundation of the Industrial Christian Fellowship, in the Oxford Mission to Calcutta and the Universities' Mission to Central Africa. He took part in the celebrated Malines conversations with the Roman Catholic Church in 1923, and made an extensive tour of the Eastern Orthodox Church. He undertook the immense labour of editing *A New Commentary on Holy Scripture*, known to generations of theological students as 'Gore's commentary'; and he influenced a whole generation of younger men, including *William Temple, who said of him, 'Though I have had many tutors in Christ, he was perhaps above all others my father.'

Charles Gore's memorial plaque in the Community chapel at Mirfield says simply 'Carolus Gore – Episcopus – Fundator'.

G. L. Prestige (1935); A. R. Vidler, 'Charles Gore and Liberal Catholicism' in *Essays in Liberality* (1957); J. Carpenter, *Gore, a Study in Liberal Catholic Thought* (1960); Michael Ramsey, *From Gore to Temple* (1960); *Bridge Builders*, pp. 158–89; J. C. Masterman in *Great Christians*, pp. 211–22. Gore's own writings include *Lux Mundi* (1898); *Belief in God* (1921); *Belief in Christ* (1922); *The Holy Spirit and the Church* (1924); and *A New Commentary on Holy Scripture* (1928).

19. Wulfstan (*c.*1009–95)   [L.F]

Wulfstan was a Benedictine monk who became bishop of Worcester, and held his post through the turmoil in the Church which followed the Norman Conquest. He was educated in the abbey schools at Evesham and Peterborough, and at the age of about twenty-four, he entered the household of the bishop of Worcester. He was ordained priest, and although he was offered a wealthy living, he chose to become a monk in the small cathedral priory. There he became successively master of the boys, cantor, sacristan and, about 1050, prior. At that time, there were only twelve monks, but Wulfstan reorganized their finances and improved their observance of the Benedictine Rule.

In 1063, Wulfstan became bishop of Worcester. *King Edward the Confessor approved the appointment. As a bishop, he was thorough and hard-working. He made systematic visitations to all parts of his diocese, as few bishops then did; he preached vigorously, and gave counsel.

During his brief year as king, Harold Godwinson sent Wulfstan to Northumbria to secure support for his rule. The mission was unsuccessful: the Danes were already challenging Harold's rule in the north. In 1066, the Norman Conquest took place, and Wulfstan was one of the first of the bishops to make his submission to William the Conqueror. Despite his Saxon heritage, he already had strong links with Benedictine houses on the Continent. Whether his acceptance of the Norman rule was a matter of political and religious conviction or a matter of coming to terms with the inevitable, he kept his diocese free from upheaval in a period when the transition from Saxon to Norman led to many ecclesiastical changes.

In his later years, Wulfstan rebuilt Worcester cathedral, which had been destroyed in a Danish invasion in 1041 – though little remains of his work. He seems to have had a serene temperament. He stayed healthy, he worked hard, and he fulfilled his duties conscientiously. He had a reputation for being humble, abstemious and generous. He lived to the remarkable age of eighty-seven, and was bishop of Worcester for thirty-two years. After his death, he was held in much affection. William Rufus covered his tomb with gold and silver, and many pilgrims came to Worcester to honour him with his predecessor *Oswald.

A Life by Wulfstan's chaplain, Coleman, now lost, was the basis of a Life by William of Malmesbury: Eng. trans. J. H. F. Piele (1934); J. H. Newman (1901); J. Wharton (1933); W. J. Lamb (1933); D. H. Farmer, 'Two Biographies by William of Malmesbury', in T. A. Dorey , ed., *Latin Biography* (1967), pp. 157–76.

20. Richard Rolle (d. 1349)   *[Commem.]*

Richard came from Thornton-le-dale, near Pickering in Yorkshire. His family was probably not wealthy, since he was sponsored at Oxford by the archdeacon of Durham; but he left university before taking his degree, and literally ran away from home to be a hermit, wearing a sort of habit made out of his father's rain-hood and two of his sister's tunics.

It was the eve of the Feast of the Assumption. Richard went to the local church, and occupied the pew of the lady of the manor. When she arrived at the church, he appeared rapt in prayer, and she would not allow the servants to move him. At Mass on the following day, after the Gospel, he preached a sermon of great power and beauty. The constable of Pickering Castle took him home for a meal, gave him more suitable clothes for his habit, and found him a place to live.

In this way, Richard began a life-long career as a hermit. There is no firm evidence that he was ever licensed as a hermit or ordained, though a French commentator, Dom Maurice Noettinger, came to the conclusion that he must have been a priest because he spoke of receiving the Saviour's Blood. In Richard's day, the laity only communicated in one kind, if at all. He was a prickly character. His comments on the clergy and monks were scathing. He was often rude to visitors, and uncouth towards women, whom he frequently offended. He was apt to disagree with his patrons. Yet, there must have been a certain cachet attached to having a hermit on one's land, for he moved several times, and he never seems to have lacked for a patron.

Richard needed his solitude. His contemplative life, the result of penances and extreme asceticism, was richly rewarding. He writes of his mystical experiences in terms of *calor*, *dulcor* and *canor*. *Calor*, heat, must have been particularly significant in the bleak Yorkshire winters. His best-known work is *The Fire of Love*, and he says that the fire was so strong in him that he actually felt his chest to see if it was alight. *Dulcor*, sweetness, was also significant when one recalls that there was no sugar or confectionery in England in his time: the only sweet substance available was honey. *Canor*, melody, was the song of the 'perfect souls' who 'companied with angels'. He invokes God, 'O honeyed flame, sweeter than all sweet, delightful beyond all creation', and he describes the 'spiritual song which bursts out from that inner fire'.

Richard was a poet, and a prolific writer. He wrote his works in Latin, English and sometimes Northumbrian dialect, pouring out his vision of the heavenly life beyond the bonds of earth, rejecting the world and all that passed for worldly wisdom. There has been some debate over whether he was a true mystic, or primarily a man of letters. In the Western tradition at least, mysticism is usually accompanied by experiences of desolation, isolation from God, and painful striving towards unattainable perfection. Richard's writing has been described by commentators as 'exuberant' and 'buoyant'; and it is highly emotional. Though Richard wrote of charity as 'the queen of virtues, the loveliest star of all', there is no indication that he practised it towards his fellow humans at least until the last years of his life, when he directed a small community of Cistercian nuns at Hampole, near Doncaster. Perhaps, as Clifford Wolters comments, 'his early bark was worse than his mellow bite'. The nuns must have been greatly impressed by his holiness, because they subsequently compiled a series of nine lessons, known as the *Legenda*, for his feast day when he should be made a saint. In Yorkshire, he became well known as 'St Richard, Hermit'.

F. M. Comper's *Life* includes an account compiled by the nuns of Hampole. For other biographical material, see C. Horstmann, *Yorkshire Writers* (1895) on

Richard Rolle and his successors, and the introduction to C. Wolters, *The Fire of Love*, Penguin Classics edn (1972). *Selected Works*, trans. and ed. G. C. Heseltine (1930); H. E. Allen (1931); J. C. Hassell (1963).

21. Agnes (?292–305)   [L.F.]

Agnes is the most celebrated of the virgin martyrs of Rome. She was only twelve or thirteen years old when she refused to sacrifice to the Roman gods, and was executed in the Piazza Navona, where the church of Sant' Agnese in Agone now stands. Her death is said to have occurred in the final weeks of the persecutions of Diocletian, which began with an edict in February 303, and lasted less than two years: her traditional date of death is 21 January, so the year was probably 305. Her parents set up a marble tomb for her on a family burial plot along the via Nomentana, about two miles outside Rome, and the church of Sant' Agnesi fuori le Mura (without the walls) stands on the same site today.

The story of Agnes is exceptionally well attested. *Ambrose marvelled at her courage in his *De Virginibus,* written about 377, and *Jerome, before the end of the fourth century, cited her as an outstanding example of virginity and martyrdom. Jerome was for three years secretary to Pope Damasus, and the inscription which Damasus wrote for Agnes is still extant. This epitaph was re-discovered in her church on the via Nomentana in 1728, when the flooring was being restored.

About the year 400, Prudentius composed his imaginative poem to Agnes, telling how she went to her execution, singing a hymn to God. In his version, she sings, 'Eternal sovereign, open to me the gates of heaven; O Christ, call my soul to come . . . it is a virgin soul, sacrificed to the Father.' Then he tells how 'Her soul, set free, leapt into the air, and was escorted on its dazzling way by angels.'

From that time, the legends began to grow. When Cardinal Jacobus de Voragine wrote the *Golden Legend* in the fourteenth century, the popular version of the story was that the prefect of Rome himself desired to marry Agnes, and promised her 'diamonds and great riches if she would consent to be his wife'. When she refused, she was stripped and taken to a brothel, but her hair grew at once to cover her, and an angel appeared before her with a tunic.

Popular legends of this kind often became attached to stories of the early martyrs of the Church. All that can be said for certain is that

Agnes was very young, and that she died as a Christian virgin. Great efforts have been made to validate her relics, most recently in 1901, and the weight of evidence is impressive. Some commentators regard her as an archetype – a symbol and memorial of the many virgins who died in the persecutions, rather than an individual girl; but her example has inspired devotion and affection through the centuries. She is the subject of paintings by Duccio, Fra Angelico, Tintoretto and other Renaissance artists, and of many mediaeval rood paintings and stained glass windows. Her name derives from the Greek *agneia*, white or pure, and not from *agnus*, a lamb, but she is often depicted with a lamb in her arms or at her feet as a symbol of innocence and purity.

Ambrose, Sermon 48, P.L., 17, pp. 701–6; Ambrose, *De Virginibus*, 1, 2, N.P.N.F., 10; Jerome, Letter 22 to Eustochium, N.P.N.F., 6, pp. 22–41; Prudentius, *Peristephanon* 14; *Golden Legend*, 1, pp. 101–4; D.A.C.L., 1, pp. 905–18 contains a resumé of Agnes's life: cols 918–65 provide detailed archaeological evidence, with illustrations; F. Jubaru, *Sainte Agnès de la Voie Nomentane d'après les nouvelles recherches* (1907) and *Sainte Agnès vierge et martyre* (1909); Life: L. André-Delastre, trans. R. Sheed (1963); Delehaye, p. 85.

22. Vincent of Saragossa (d. ?304) [Commem.]

Vincent is the protomartyr of Spain. He was a relative of Valerius, bishop of Saragossa, which lies in Aragon, north-east of Madrid. Valerius taught him the faith, and he became a deacon, well trained in the Christian faith. They were both arrested during the persecutions of Diocletian and Maximian in 304. Valerius is said to have had a speech impediment, and it was Vincent who testified to their faith, eloquently and without fear. The Roman governor of Spain was Dacian, who ruled with great cruelty. Vincent was cast into prison and systematically ill-treated to force him to sacrifice to the Roman gods. The accounts say that he was semi-starved, kept in the stocks, burned and tortured, and he died under his sufferings.

Prudentius knew the story, and it may have been he who took it to Rome. He was there in the year 400, gathering material for his poems on Christian martyrs, and his *Peristephanon* includes poems on both Vincent and *Agnes, who died in the same persecution. Prudentius was capable of considerable poetic licence, but he was close enough to the events to have the outlines of the story right. *Augustine knew the story of Vincent, and preached a sermon about his martyr-dom.

Vincent is one of the ten patron saints represented on the frieze surrounding the tomb of King Henry VII in Westminster Abbey. The ten names were specified in his will, and Vincent is shown between *Edward the Confessor and *Anne, mother of the *Virgin Mary. Henry claimed the English throne through his mother, Lady Margaret Beaufort, from John of Gaunt, whose second wife was Constance, daughter of Pedro the Cruel, king of Castile.

Prudentius, *Peristephanon*, book 5; Augustine's sermon is in *P.L.*, 38, pp. 1252–68, and summarized in *Anal.Boll.*, 1 (1882), pp. 259–62; *AA.SS.*, Jan., 2, pp. 393–414; L. de Laeger, *S. Vincent de Saragosse* (1917); *Butler*, Jan., pp. 144–5; W. Sinclair, *The Chapels Royal* (1912), pp. 69–70.

24. Francis de Sales (1567–1622)   [L.F.]

Francis de Sales was born in his family's château at Thorens, near Annecy. His father expected him to seek a military career; but when he went to Paris with his tutor, he studied rhetoric, philosophy and theo-logy. During that time, he went through a deep spiritual crisis: he encountered the Calvinist doctrine of predestination, and was appalled at the thought that, if he was not one of the elect, no amount of prayer and good works could save his soul. Eventually he decided very sensibly that even if he was not destined to praise God through all eternity, he could at least love God during his time on earth.

After studying canon law in Padua, he was ordained, and became provost of Geneva in 1693. The title was an empty one, for *Calvin had turned the city of Geneva into a Protestant theocratic state. The bishop, elderly and ailing, was an exile in Annecy, and the scattered population of the mountainous rural areas, faced with the rival claims of Rome and Geneva, had for the most part given up religious obser-vance altogether.

Francis began the arduous work of reclaiming the region. He travelled alone in remote valleys where there were still wolves and bands of outlaws. Parishes were established, and he found priests to serve them. He was always gentle and sensitive in his approach to others, holding that more could be done 'through love and charity than through severity and harshness'.

In 1598, Francis was sent to Rome as an emissary for his bishop. While he was there, he faced a searching theological examination by three of the great men of the Vatican: Cardinal Baronius, Cardinal Borghese (later Pope Paul V) and the future Cardinal Bellarmine, who all approved him. He went back to Annecy to attend to the ever-increasing administration of the Geneva diocese, and in 1601 was sent on a mission to Paris. There he met Henry IV, who had decided that 'Paris was worth a Mass', and had become a Catholic on his accession in 1589. The king was so impressed by the devout and gentle persuasion of 'Monsieur de Genève', as Francis had become known, that he offered him a wealthy bishopric in France. Francis said that he already had a poor wife, and he could not desert her for a rich one. He was consecrated as bishop of Geneva in 1602.

By this time, the diocese contained 450 parishes. The Council of Trent had proposed a number of reforms to strengthen Church discipline and re-order parish life, so Francis applied himself to the work of reform, peacefully and patiently teaching and improving public worship and the cure of souls. Francis excelled as a spiritual director, and kept in touch by letter with the many people who sought his counsel. He was accustomed to write twenty or thirty letters a day, demonstrating an intuitive understanding of human problems and his correspondents' search for God in the circumstances of their own lives. He had a particular insight into the spiritual needs of women who were drawn to the religious life, including Angélique Arnaud, abbess of Port-Royal, and Jane Frances de Chantal, who founded the Order of the Visitation.

Francis made many journeys – to Paris, to Turin, to Avignon, to Lyons – and crowds came to hear him preach; but he stayed away from Rome. He had no desire for a cardinal's hat, and when the pope summoned him, he pleaded 'lack of means, the difficulty of travel, and the care of the diocese itself'. He was very ill during his last months at Annecy, and when a nun asked him for a final word of counsel, he took a piece of paper and wrote HUMILITY three times. He died on 28 December 1622.

His life was set in a time and a place of fierce theological controversy, but Francis remained calm, balanced, and eminently sensible in his decisions and the advice he offered. He said that devotion was the 'spiritual sugar' which took away bitterness – 'the poor person's discontent, the rich man's smugness, the loneliness of the oppressed, the conceit of the successful, the sadness of one who lives alone and the dissipation of one who lives in society'. Of his writings, the *Treatise on the Love of God* and the *Introduction to a Devout Life* have become spiritual classics.

J. P. Camus (6 vols, 1639–41, Eng. trans. 1952); F. Trochu (2 vols, Paris, 1946); H. Burton (2 vols, 1925); M. de la Bédoyère (1960). Works: Annecy edn, Eng. trans. H. B. Mackay et al. (6 vols, 1883–1908). *Introduction to the Devout Life*, trans. A. Ross (1952), M. Day (1956). *Spiritual Maxims*, trans. and ed. C. J. Kelley (1954).

26. Timothy and Titus, Companions of Paul   [*Commem.*]

When *Paul and *Barnabas separated, Paul took Silas as a companion, and went to Lystra in Asia Minor, where he found another colleague in Timothy, the son of a Jewish mother and a Greek father. Timothy's grandmother, Lois, and his mother, Eunice, had taught him the Jewish scriptures from early childhood (2 Timothy 1:5; 3:15). The great debate over whether Christian men should be circumcised in the Jewish tradition was still raging, and Timothy was circumcised 'out of consideration for the Jews who lived in those parts, for they knew his father was a Greek' (Acts 16:1–3). The three went on to Macedonia together, and carried out a mission at Philippi, which was a Roman colony.

By the time Paul wrote his Letters to the Corinthians, probably in the year 57, Timothy was visiting the Christian communities in Greece on his behalf. Paul calls him 'my loyal child in the faith'. Much later, when Timothy is working in Corinth, Paul calls him 'my beloved child' (2 Timothy 1:2). They were working together when the Letters to the Philippians, the Colossians and the Thessalonians were written. Though Paul signs these letters, they are sent jointly from 'Paul and Timothy, servants in Jesus Christ', Paul and 'our brother Timothy', 'Paul, Silvanus and Timothy'.

The two Letters to Timothy are believed to have been written when Timothy was in Ephesus. Both are letters of practical instructions on the administration of the church at Ephesus: how to order the Christian community, the qualities required of a leader or *episcopos* (this word did not yet have the full force of 'bishop'), how to employ and pay the elders, how to treat widows (evidently with great caution if they were under sixty years of age). In the second letter, Paul is in prison, and conscious of his own imminent death. He says, 'I have fought the good fight. I have finished the race. I have kept faith' (2 Timothy 4:6–7); but he expects to see Timothy shortly, telling him, 'Get Mark and bring him with you', and to bring his cloak, his books and his parchments. To Timothy, he says, 'Continue in what you have learned and firmly believed, knowing from whom you learned it' (2 Timothy 3:10–14).

According to Eusebius of Caesarea, Timothy became bishop of Ephesus. The *Acts of Timothy* were written at Ephesus in the fourth or fifth century, but may be based on an older account. Though there are obvious accretions, they are generally conceded to have a basis of historical fact. They record that Timothy was killed at Ephesus during a festival to Dionysius, when each man carried a statue of the god, and a club to smite down infidels.

In his Letter to the Galatians, Paul recalls how he went to Jerusalem fourteen years after his conversion with Barnabas, 'taking Titus with us'. This suggests that Titus was a junior colleague, whereas Barnabas was an old and trusted partner in mission. Like Timothy, Titus was a Greek, but this time the apostles in Jerusalem did not insist that he should be circumcised (Galatians 2:3–6).

Paul writes to the Corinthians to exhort them to be generous in giving to less fortunate Christians, since they are a rich community, and says, 'We have asked Titus to visit you.' Titus is eager to do this – 'more eager than ever, he is going to you of his own accord'. As with Timothy, Paul gives his disciple his full support: 'If there is any question about Titus, he is my partner and my associate in dealing with you' (2 Corinthians 8:17 and 23).

We learn in 2 Timothy 4:10 that Titus has been sent to Dalmatia, but by the time of the single Letter to Titus, he is in Crete, and apparently experiencing a very difficult ministry. There is some doubt about the authenticity of this Letter, which may not be Pauline. The writer knows the church in Crete. He tells Titus that he will have to cope with rebellious people, idle talkers and deceivers. He has a low opinion of Cretans: 'It was one of their prophets who said "Cretans are always liars, vicious brutes, lazy gluttons." That testimony is true' (Titus 1:10–16).

Titus evidently stayed the course with this unpromising apostolate, and Eusebius tells us that he became bishop of Crete.

Eusebius, *H.E.*, 3, ch. 4; *Butler*, Jan., pp. 178–9; *N.C.E.*, 14, pp. 167 and 181; *O.D.S.*, pp. 167 and 467–8. Commentary: J. M. Basse, *1 Timothy, 2 Timothy, Titus* (Nashville, Tennessee, 1946).

28. Thomas Aquinas (1225–74)   [L.F.]

In the Fine Arts Museum at Seville, there is a celebrated painting of the Apotheosis of St Thomas Aquinas by Zurburán: the great 'angelic doctor' ascends into heaven in front of his pupils, an open book in one hand, still teaching, teaching, teaching. Theologian, philosopher and perpetual student, he made a tremendous impact on Christian thought.

Thomas was born in the castle at Rocca Secca, near Aquino, between Rome and Naples. He was educated at the great Benedictine monastery of Monte Cassino until he was thirteen, and then sent to study in the University of Naples for five years. At this time, Christian, Arabic and Jewish scholars were able to work together in Naples, and he was able to study many sources of philosophy, including the works of Aristotle.

While he was a student, he was attracted to the Dominican Order, which combined scholarship with poverty. His family were dismayed: as a Benedictine, this brilliant young man could have expected a great career in the Church, but the Dominicans were mendicants and socially unacceptable. Thomas joined the Dominicans in spite of family opposition, but was kidnapped by his brothers, and held in a tower at the castle of Rocca Secca for over a year.

When he regained his freedom, the Dominicans sent him to Saint-Jacques in Paris, where their scholars worked on reconciling the thought of Aristotle to the Christian faith, using Arabic and Jewish commentaries to increase their understanding of Aristotle's *Ethics*. From there he went to the *studium generale* in Cologne, where he worked under Albert the Great. Albert, sometime bishop of Regensburg, is credited with the foundation of the scholastic system which Thomas was to develop and elaborate. He said of Thomas that 'the lowing of this dumb ox would be heard all over the world'. It seems that Thomas was a large man, and silent except when he had something to say. There is a story that on one occasion when he was dining with the pious King Louis IX of France, he sat wrapped in abstraction throughout the meal until he banged the table with his fist, and announced 'That settles the Manichaean heresy!' The king was not offended, but sent a clerk to take note of his observations.

Thomas had a great deal to say, and most of it is still available in academic libraries: his two major works are the massive *Summa contra Gentiles* and the equally massive *Summa Theologica*. In the former, he applies deductive reasoning to the existence of God, the creation, and Christian revelation. This work is directed at people who did not accept Christian orthodoxy: Greek classical philosophers, Moslems, Jews and various heretical sects. The *Summa Theologica* is a statement of Christian orthodoxy for Christians. It also employs deductive reasoning, dealing successively with God and creation, morality, and Christ and the sacraments. Thomas's method was to divide each topic into questions, raise objections against the argument he wished to propose, elaborate the argument, and deal with the questions one by one. Each argument is numbered, which makes reference easy when his system is understood: thus ST 2a, 2e, 34, 2, ad 1 means the *Summa Theologica, secunda secundae* (i.e. the second part of the second book), question 34, second reply to the first objection. The work is enormously thorough, totally logical (given the acceptance of Christian revelation) and entirely intellectual. Unlike the Franciscans, the Dominicans had no place in their thinking for emotional understanding: will and intellect demanded the subjugation of human affections and impulses.

Thomas also wrote many other works, including philosophical commentaries on Aristotle, Boethius, Pseudo-Dionysius and Peter Lombard; the *Questiones disputatae*, which deals with the nature of truth, power and evil; and extensive biblical commentaries (though he knew neither Greek nor Hebrew, and had to work from translations). His teaching career was spent largely in Paris, in Naples and in Rome, where he was appointed to the Roman Curia.

Thomist thought has become part of the intellectual equipment of Christendom. It came from his own prayer life and spiritual experience, mediated through a remarkable mental power; but what began as a liberation in Christian thinking eventually became a restriction. In the early twentieth century, it acquired such ascendancy that the 1917 Code of Canon Law required all schools and colleges to teach philosophy and theology 'according to the method, teaching and principles of the Doctor Angelicus'. It was not until the second Vatican Council that this restriction was officially lifted, and the way was cleared for new philosophical and theological thinking.

AA.SS., Mar., 1, pp. 655–74 contains contemporary Lives by two of his pupils. Complete works in many editions (25 or 26 volumes). Eng. trans. of the *Summa Theologica* (22 vols, 1912–26); the *Summa contra Gentiles* (5 vols, 1928–9); *Basic Writings of St Thomas* (2 vols, 1945). Modern commentaries by F. C. Copleston, *Aquinas*, Penguin Philosophy Series (1955); E. Gilson, *Le Thomisme* (1944, Eng.

trans. *St Thomas Aquinas*, 1957); R. Barron, *Thomas Aquinas: Spiritual Master* (1995).

30. Charles I (Charles Stuart) (1600–49)   [L.F.]

The trial and execution of Charles I still rouse passionate debate. Was he, as his supporters maintained, a defender of the rights of Church and people? Or was he, as his accusers charged, a despot who had violated the people's trust?

Historians have put forward varying explanations for the bitter divisions which caused the English Civil War, and the death of some 160,000 men. Some have emphasized the constitutional issues relating to the supremacy of King or the House of Commons. Some have stressed fiscal issues – the protracted struggle over Ship Money and other forms of taxation. Some have seen the war as a class struggle between two élites. More recently, there has been a return to the view that the central issues were religious, and so wide in their implications that conflict was almost unavoidable.

When Charles I raised his standard in 1642, the doctrines of *Martin Luther and *Jean Calvin had swept northern Europe, while southern Europe kept its allegiance to the papacy. The Gunpowder Plot had been defeated less than forty years earlier, and people over sixty could remember the Spanish Armada. In Ireland, there was a Roman Catholic rebellion. In Scotland, the Presbyterians were intransigent. James I managed to keep these contradictory elements in balance, and to maintain the Elizabethan Settlement. His son Charles, more devout but more rigid in his views, was unable to do so. There is no doubt that Charles believed in the Settlement. He told parliament in 1641 that 'nowhere on earth could be found a Church that professed the true religion with more purity of doctrine than the Church of England, and he would maintain it, not only against Papists, but against separatists'.

Charles was the second son of James I and Anne of Denmark. He was a sickly child, and he stammered all his life. He became king in 1625, and married Henrietta Maria of France in the same year. The marriage contract gave the queen the right to practise her own Roman Catholic faith, and to bring up the children until the age of thirteen. Charles's strong attachment to his wife and children – he sacrificed *Laud and Strafford to save them from a Whitehall mob – increased the Puritan suspicion that he was himself a Roman Catholic.

Charles believed implicitly in the Divine Right of Kings. 'I must avow that I owe the account of my actions to God alone,' he told parliament in 1629 – and he proceeded to rule without parliament for eleven years. At his trial, he denied the authority of the court, saying, 'A king cannot be tried by any superior jurisdiction.' From the scaffold – when he must be presumed to have been speaking the bleakest and most fundamental of his beliefs – he said that the people had no claim to a voice in government. 'A subject and a sovereign are clean different things.'

Possibly he was carried away by the enthusiasms of Strafford, who wanted to make him 'the most absolute prince in Christendom', and Laud, who wanted to root out Calvinism. The King could not save them, and their deaths did not save the King.

Charles stood firmly for episcopacy. He defended the principles of the Prayer Book and the spiritual jurisdiction of Anglican bishops. It was a difficult and dangerous position to take. In London, the clergy were being attacked, with cries of 'There goes a Jesuit, a Baal priest, an Abbey-lubber, one of Canterburie's whelps,' and the surplices were torn from their backs.

Both Charles I and his accusers sincerely believed that they were defending the rights and liberties of the people, and both believed that they were doing God's work. Oliver Cromwell prayed and read his Bible, being, it is said, much moved by the story of Gideon, who overthrew the King of the Midianites (Judges 6–8) and the injunction in Psalm 149 to bind kings with chains and their nobles with fetters of iron. At his trial, Charles conducted himself with great coolness and dignity, denying the competence of the court and describing its proceedings as 'a mockery and a scorn'. He was accused of being a tyrant, a traitor, a murderer and an implacable enemy of the people. The trial was certainly a charade – the president of the court was an obscure judge from the Welsh borders because no High Court judge would agree to preside; more than half the judges did not attend; and signatures to the warrant of execution were extorted by threats.

In his last speech (muffled by the beating of drums, so that only those close to him could hear) Charles said: 'I am the martyr of the people. I have a good cause. I have a gracious God. I will say no more.' He died bravely. When the axe fell, a great groan went up from the crowd. Eleven years later, the monarchy, the House of Lords and the Church were restored under his son, Charles II.

The Trial and Execution of King Charles I: facsimile copy of contemporary accounts, Scolar Press, Leeds, 1966; G. E. Aylmer, *The Personal Rule of Charles I*, Historical Association, London, 1989; C. V. Wedgwood, *The Trial of Charles I* (1964); *D.N.B.*, 4, pp. 67–84; Godfrey Davis, *The Early Stuarts*, The Oxford History of England (2nd edn, 1959, repr. 1991), chs 4—6.

31. John Bosco (1815–88)   [Commem.]

The work of John Bosco, founder of the Salesian Order, has to be seen against the background of the society in which he lived. He was born in Piedmont, Italy, in the year of the Battle of Waterloo. He worked in the slums of Turin through the years of the *Risorgimento* and the unification of Italy, through a time of social dislocation due to the growth of industrialization.

John was the son of a peasant farmer who died when he was only two years old. His mother brought him up in great poverty, and when he went to the seminary of Chieri at the age of sixteen, he had to wear charity clothes and shoes. He was ordained priest in 1841, and was sent to study at the theological college in Turin. There he came under the influence of Father Joseph Cafasso, a lecturer in moral theology, who persuaded him not to become an overseas missionary, but to seek a vocation nearer home. There was great poverty and widespread unemployment in Turin, and homeless children were roaming the streets, becoming involved in vice and crime. Don Cafasso introduced Don Bosco to the poor, and also to wealthy patrons, and he started a house named the Oratory where boys could be kept from bad influences and taught the elements of religious faith.

The boys needed work, so Don Bosco started workshops: first one for shoemakers and tailors, then a bookbindery, a joiner's shop, a printing press and an iron foundry. By 1862, he had some six hundred pupils living in his houses, and another six hundred attending daily. Other priests came to help him, and formed the nucleus of a religious community named after *Francis de Sales and established in 1854.

Opposition came from several different quarters. The government of Piedmont was anti-clerical; traditionalist clergy, including the archbishop of Turin, found the work objectionably innovative; while revolutionary clergy, of whom there were many, found it lacking in political content. Don Bosco simply went on working, meeting the immediate needs, dedicating himself wholly to his boys.

The system spread to other parts of Italy, to the rest of western Europe, to Canada and the United States, and to Australia. Don Bosco's disregard for advanced education and wider questions of political justice continued to attract criticism, but his motto was 'We go straight to the poor', and his insistence on the immediate relief of the needs of poor people earned respect. Today there are some 2,000 Salesian communities in 113 different countries, running primary schools, technical colleges and hospitals.

When Don Bosco died early in 1888, forty thousand people filed past his coffin to pay their respects, and in 1934, a national public holiday was declared in Italy in his honour.

L. C. Sheppard (1957); Peter Lappin, *Give Me Souls! Life of Don Bosco* (1957); W. R. Ainsworth (1988, repr. 1995). John Bosco, *Memoirs of the Oratory* (Eng. trans. 1984).

February

1. Brigid of Kildare (c.452–c.524)   [Commem.]

Brigid, also known as Bridget or Bride, is second only to *Patrick as a
patron saint of Ireland. She was born in a village some five miles from
the great abbey of Kildare, became a nun, and was eventually abbess of
the double monastery. Like *Hilda of Whitby, she was responsible for
the administration of both the men's community and the women's
community, and so great was her influence that it was later said that
she had been created a bishop. This is extremely unlikely but the story
reflects the esteem in which the Irish held her.

    Ireland in Brigid's day was a land of Celts and Viking invaders, and
the great abbey at Kildare must have stood as a bulwark of the
Christian faith against superstition and paganism; but as was often the
case, the Church built upon existing religious ceremonies rather than
opposing them. The Druids worshipped a goddess named Brigg, the
goddess of knowledge and wisdom and of fire. Her festival, on the
same day as Brigid's feast day, celebrated the coming of spring. Like
Patrick, Brigid is associated with the fire of the Holy Spirit: the nuns of
Kildare abbey kept a perpetual fire in the abbey for centuries in her
memory, and her emblem includes a flame. The four-armed cross of
reeds or straw, the *Crosóg Brigde*, was believed to protect houses from
burning down. These crosses are still made in Ireland, and displayed
on the eve of her feast.

    Brigid is the subject of many stories of kindness and mercy: she heals
the sick, reconciles the unhappily married, takes a blessing into the
homes of the poor, and sings runes to the cows so that they give freely
of their milk. She is called 'Mary of the Gael', and in one hymn 'Brigid,
excellent woman / Golden, sparkling flame'. *The Irish Saints* gives
examples of special prayers invoking Bridgid which were current in
Wales, the Western Isles and St. Gael in Switzerland, as well as in
Ireland.

The devotion to Brigid was taken to Europe by Irish pilgrims. There is a church bearing her dedication in Piacenza, where there was an Irish bishop in the ninth century, and other dedications were to be found in mediaeval times in the Low Countries, the Rhine valley and Brittany. Monsignor Guérin, the compiler of the *Vies des saints des Petits Bollandistes*, published in 1880, mentions a pilgrimage at Fosses, in Brittany, where loaves blessed in Brigid's name were still used to touch the sick on her feast day.

The Lives of Brigid are of relatively late composition, and many folk-tales became interweaved with the oral traditions. She becomes confused with the *Virgin Mary, with the Druidic goddess who preceded her, and with the Viking goddess Brigantia. Many miracles are attributed to her.

St Bride's church, Fleet Street, known as 'the journalists' church', is dedicated in her name.

AA.SS., Feb., 1, pp. 99–185. Modern Lives by A. Knowles (1927); A. Curtayne (1931, new edn 1954); F. O'Briain (1938); D. Pochin Mould (1964). See also *N.L.A.*, 1, pp. 153–60; *D.H.G.E.*, 10, 717–18; *Butler*, Feb., pp. 1–5.

3. Anskar (*c*.801–65)   [L.F.]

Anskar was born in Amiens. He studied at the monastic school of Corbie in that city, and after some years as a monk, he was sent to Corvey in Westphalia (known as 'New Corbie') to carry out apostolic work on a Scandinavian mission. An early mission to the Danes depended on patronage from the king of the Franks, and when this was withdrawn, the mission failed. He worked in Sweden with limited success, and then became abbot of Corvey and in 832, bishop of Hamburg.

For thirteen years, he sponsored and took part in missions to Norway, Sweden and Denmark. He was a powerful preacher, and made many converts, but the decline of Frankish power and the increasing raids by the Vikings on Christian settlements meant that the work was always difficult and frequently unrewarding. In 842, Vikings from Norway overran Hamburg. Anskar was consecrated archbishop of Bremen, which was united with the see of Hamburg, and given a general jurisdiction over the three very pagan Scandinavian countries. He continued to operate mission stations in Denmark and Sweden, and founded schools. He worked hard to release slaves from the

Vikings, and to help the poor. His personal life was ascetic: he wore a hair shirt, and fasted on bread and water for long periods.

Anskar's work in Sweden achieved very little that was lasting. A century and a half later, *Sigfrid had to begin again there; but Anskar had greater success in North Germany and in Denmark. He is the patron saint of Denmark. He died in Bremen, and was buried there.

AA.SS., Feb., 1, pp. 395–450 contains the *Vita Anskarii* by Anskar's successor, Rembert, Eng. trans. C. H. Robinson (1931). Modern Lives by E. de Moreau (1930); P. Oppenheim (1931). See also C. J. A. Opperman, *English Missionaries in Sweden and Finland* (1937), pp. 38–45; *P.B.*, 2, pp. 230–6; *O.D.S.*, p. 24; *Butler*, Feb., pp. 35–7.

4. Gilbert of Sempringham (c.1083–1189)   [Commem.]

Gilbert has the distinction of being the only English founder of a monastic Order. His father was a Norman nobleman named Joscelin. Gilbert was unable to bear arms because he suffered from a physical deformity, and he became a scholar.

His father gave him two livings – the churches of Sempringham and West Torrington in Lancashire; but Gilbert was only in minor Orders (as all scholars were). He appointed a priest for the two parishes, and lived in considerable poverty in Sempringham vicarage, giving the revenues of West Torrington to the poor. In 1122, the bishop of Lincoln, Robert Bloet, gave him a post as a clerk in his household. Robert Bloet's successor, Alexander, also employed him, and ordained him as a priest, offering him a rich archdeaconry; but he refused this. He spent something like ten years in the episcopal household before returning to Sempringham on the death of his father.

When Gilbert inherited his father's estates, he recruited a group of seven devout young women, and gave them a house near the church where they could live the religious life on the Benedictine pattern. This involved seclusion from the outside world, and on the advice of the Cistercian abbot of Rievaulx, he also recruited lay sisters, and later lay brothers, who could carry out heavy tasks and till the land to support them. The foundation developed, and in 1147, Gilbert travelled to Cîteaux to ask that the Cistercian Order should take over jurisdiction. Pope Eugenius III, who had been a monk at Cîteaux, was there at the time, attending the chapter; but he and Bernard of Clairvaux decided that affiliation would be inappropriate. While the lay brothers followed the Rule of Cîteaux, the nuns followed the Benedictine Rule; and the Cistercians may not have been ready to make a foundation in England, as they had recently taken over jurisdiction of the Order of Savignac. Bernard helped Gilbert to draw up a constitution for what was originally called the Sempringham Order, and the Pope appointed Gilbert as the first abbot.

Gilbert subsequently recruited priest-canons on the Augustinian model, so that his Order was an amalgam of three distinct monastic traditions. The nuns were the strongest part of the Order, the canons providing spiritual direction for them, and the lay brothers physical support. More houses were set up, chiefly in Lincolnshire and Yorkshire. Gilbert travelled from one to the other, a modest and retiring supervisor who would help in building work, carpentry or copying manuscripts. He lived a very austere life, wearing a hair shirt and keeping many vigils.

The Order, which had become known as the Gilbertines, helped Archbishop Thomas Becket to escape the wrath of Henry II in 1163, when he was forced to flee to the Continent. Becket took shelter in Gilbertine houses, and went in disguise as a Sempringham lay brother. Gilbert was summoned by the king, but was subsequently pardoned, and the Order was spared. It grew steadily on its idiosyncratic English pattern. In all Gilbert founded thirteen monasteries, of which nine were double monasteries and only four restricted to men. There were some 1500 members of the Order at the time of his death.

He is said to have lived to the age of a hundred and six. In his old age, much of the management of the Order was delegated to Roger of Malton.

The Gilbertine Order continued to spread after his death. In all, there were twenty-five monasteries in England and one in Scotland at the time of the dissolution of the monasteries by Henry VIII. The Order died out, but is remembered as the only distinctively English contribution to the history of Latin monasticism.

Life by John Capgrave in the *Bulletin of the John Rylands Library*, 55 (1972–3, pp. 112–87; *E.E.T.S* (1910); *Men.E.W.*, pp. 52–3; R. Foreville, *The Book of St Gilbert* (1986); B. Golding, *Gilbert of Sempringham and the Gilbertine Order* (1995); *N.C.E.*, 6, pp. 481–2; *Butler*, Feb., pp. 41–3.

6. The Martyrs of Japan (1597–1638)   [*Commem.*]

When *Francis Xavier left Japan in 1551, he had made something like a thousand converts. In the next few years, the Jesuits came from Portugal and then from Spain in force to run a large-scale missionary enterprise. They were intelligent missionaries: they respected the Japanese culture as they came to understand it, learned the Japanese language, and attempted to convert the rulers. At that time, the emperor was largely a figure-head, and the real power lay in the hands of the *daimyos*, or provincial rulers. The Jesuits also engaged with the *Samurai*, the warrior caste, and with Buddhist abbots and monks. They trained indigenous leaders – Japanese priests and catechists. Though Pope Gregory XIII had given the exclusive right to carry out missions in Japan to the Jesuits, his successor, Sixtus V, approved Franciscan missions in addition. The Franciscans had carried out extensive missionary work in the Philippines, where they had met many Japanese and were familiar with Japanese culture.

For a time, the missions prospered, and a separate Japanese diocese was set up; but the work of the missionaries was dependent on the favour of the civil power. In 1587, a military dictatorship or shogunate was set up under the Emperor Hideyoshi, and an edict was issued expelling the missionaries. This did not, apparently, take immediate effect: in 1588, an apostolic visitor, Father Alessandro Valignano, instituted two seminaries, and there were said to be about 150,000 converts; but suspicion about the foreigners and their impact on Japanese society grew with their success. As the Portuguese vied with the Spaniards and the Jesuits vied with the Franciscans, the Emperor Hideyoshi came to believe that both Spain and Portgual were bent on conquest, and that the missionaries were only the first wave of foreign aggression. In February 1597, the first of the martyrdoms of Nagasaki took place, in which twenty-five Christians were mutilated, led through the town, fastened to crosses and killed with lance-thrusts. Six of them were Franciscan missionaries, three were Japanese Jesuits, and the rest Japanese catechists apart from one Korean. Nagasaki was the major port used for sea traffic between Japan and India, and the centre of the missionaries' work; but the barbarous death of these Christians did not discourage the missionaries or their followers: the Dominicans and the Augustinian canons sent missions, and there were many fresh conversions.

Hideyoshi died in 1598, and for a time there was fighting among the warlords. Eventually Tokugawa Ieyasu set up a military dynasty which was to last through to the Meiji Restoration in 1865. At first the new emperor was favourable to the Christian missions, but as traffic with the European nations increased, and Dutch Calvinists made their appearance, he decided to be rid of them all. An edict of banishment was issued in 1614, and the Japanese were told that anyone who accepted Christianity or even dealt with Christians would be burned alive.

Some missionaries defied the ban. There were sporadic persecutions until 1617, when a hundred Christians were executed at a site between Nagasaki and Omura. In 1619, there were five more executions at Nagasaki, and in 1622, twenty-two missionaries were killed by being burned over a slow fire, while thirty Japanese converts were beheaded. The increasing use of agonizingly slow methods of death for the Europeans seems to have been caused by a desire that they should reject their faith and thus lose public esteem rather than by a love of torture for its own sake; but nearly all the missionaries stood firm.

In 1623, it was decreed that all Japanese should declare their religious adherence once a year. From 1627, those suspected of being Christians were made to trample on a *fumie* – a plaque bearing a picture of the Virgin and Child. There are still many of these plaques in Japanese museums, worn almost smooth by the pressure of countless feet. Still the number of Christians grew, and even more dreadful means of torture were employed to force missionaries, European and Japanese alike, into apostasy. The climax came with a revolt in Nagasaki in 1637–8. This started as a revolt against the imposition of high taxes, but many of the protesters carried banners bearing Christian symbols, and calling on Christ and the Virgin Mary. The result was a massacre in which thousands of Christians were put to death.

Japan closed its doors to the outside world, and remained in total isolation until the Meiji Restoration in 1865. Many Christians could not express their faith openly, but they preserved it, and transmitted it to their descendants for over two centuries. When the Europeans returned, they found people who still knew phrases in Latin and Portuguese, and who showed carefully preserved relics of the seventeenth-century martyrs.

Though Christianity is not a majority religion in Japan, it is still strong in the Nagasaki area, where the martyrs made their sacrifice.

AA.SS., Feb., 1, pp. 729–70; C. R. Boxer, *The Christian Century in Japan* (1951); O. Carey, *Christianity in Japan* (1976); *Butler*, Feb., pp. 57–63. N.C.E., 7, pp. 835–45 has a detailed account of the different persecutions and the names of the martyrs, together with a full bibliography. .

10. Scholastica (d. 547)   [*Commem.*]

Scholastica was the sister of *Benedict of Nursia, founder of the Benedictine Order. She founded a religious community for women which came under his direction at Plombariola, about five miles from Monte Cassino. She is the patron saint of Benedictine nuns. So much is ascertainable fact, but the only information about her life comes from the *Dialogues* of *Gregory the Great, and this is anecdotal rather than biographical.

We can assume that Scholastica also came from Nursia, that she was a very devout woman, and that she was much attached to her brother; but the only evidence of her learning comes from her name, and she and Benedict did not meet very often in adult life. Gregory tells us that once a year she would make a visit to Monte Cassino, and they would meet at a house near the monastery, which, as a woman, she could not enter. They would spend their time together in prayer and spiritual discussion. At their last meeting before her death, he was preparing to leave when she asked him to stay longer. Benedict quoted his Rule, which obliged him to return to the monastery. Scholastica prayed and a violent thunderstorm broke out, obliging him and his companions to stay the night. Benedict accused her of provoking the thunderstorm, and she replied that she had asked him to stay, and he had refused; then she asked God, and God granted her wish. She died three days later.

Gregory the Great, *Dialogues*, 2, chs 33—4; AA.SS., Feb., 2, pp. 390–412; O.D.S., · pp. 428–9; *Butler*, Feb., pp. 100–1.

14. Cyril (c.827–69) and Methodius (c.815–84)   [L.F.]

Methodius was the elder of these two brothers by twelve years, but Cyril is usually cited first because he died earlier. They were born in Thessalonika, a sea-port in eastern Greece. Cyril was a cleric and a scholar: he studied at Constantinople under Leo the Grammarian and

Photius, was highly regarded as a philosopher, and led a mission to the Ukraine. Methodius was for a time the governor of a Slav colony of the Eastern Empire in eastern Europe.

While the Western Church used only three languages, Hebrew, Greek and Latin, the Eastern Church had no inhibitions about translation into the vernacular. Both the brothers spoke the Slavonic language which then had no written form. Cyril developed an alphabet for it, inventing what was known as Glagolitic and later as Cyrillic script. He began the work of translating the Bible into Slavonic.

In 862, the brothers were sent to head a missionary delegation from Constantinople to Moravia (now part of the Czech Republic and extending into Slovakia). Moravia was disputed territory between the Eastern and Western Churches. The Christian duke of Moravia, Ratislav, sent to Constantinople for missionaries because he was trying to keep his territory clear of Frankish or German domination. Though the mission was successful, the missionaries were very much at the mercy of political and ecclesiastical forces beyond their control. They came into conflict with Western missionaries from Bavaria, and were in Venice on their way back to Byzantium in 867 when a theological dispute between East and West, the Photian schism, occurred. Pope Hadrian II sent for them, and they went to Rome, taking with them alleged relics of *St Clement. They were treated with great honour. Hadrian ordained Methodius, and had their Slavonic liturgy celebrated in churches in Rome. Cyril died in Rome, and was buried in the church of San Clemente, where there is a fresco commemorating the brothers. In 870, Methodius was consecrated archbishop of Moravia by Pope Hadrian: this action was in part a declaration that Moravia was part of the Western Church and not of the Eastern Church. Methodius still had to contend with the Bavarian bishops, and at one point he was arrested and brought before a synod at Regensburg. Hadrian's successor, Pope John VIII, secured his release, but forbade the use of the Slavonic liturgy for some years. This decision was reversed in 880. Methodius continued his brother's work in translating the Bible into Slavonic, and compiled a book of Byzantine ecclesiastical and civil law. He went to Constantinople in 882 to meet both the emperor and the patriarch, and to explain his work, which they approved. He died in what is now the Czech Republic two years later.

The feast of Cyril and Methodius is observed in both the Eastern and the Western Churches, and they are regarded as patrons of ecumenism.

F. Dvornik, (1931); A. F. N. Tachaios, *Cyril and Methodius of Thessalonika* (1989); F. Dvornik, *The Slavs, Their Early History and Civilisation* (1936); N.C.E., 4, pp. 379–81; P.B., 3, pp. 303–10, which includes an account from Slav sources.

Valentine, Martyr (?third century)   [Commem.]

St Valentine's Day is traditionally a day for lovers, but the little we know about Valentine makes no mention of lovers. The *Acta Sanctorum* records the Lives of two martyrs of this name, one a priest of Rome who was scourged and executed two miles outside the city on the Flaminian Way after a life of teaching and healing, and the other a bishop of Terni, some sixty miles north along the same road, who was imprisoned and beheaded in that city. The view that, though both Rome and Terni claimed him, the two Valentines were one and the same, is now generally accepted. His execution may have taken place under the Emperor Claudius II (268–70: not the emperor of Robert Graves' *I, Claudius*) in whose brief reign there was a renewal of persecution.

The association of St Valentine's Day with lovers may have come from the Roman festival of Lupercalia, when boys drew the names of girls in honour of the goddess Februara Juno. Christian holy days were often substituted for earlier festivals in this way. Chaucer suggested that birds mated on this day.

In *The Paston Letters*, written between 1420 and 1504, there is a letter from Elizabeth Drew to John Paston, her daughter's prospective husband, dating from February 1477. This notes: 'Upon Friday is St Valentine's Day, and every bird chooseth him a mate, and if it like you to come on Thursday at night . . . I trust to God that you shall speak to my husband, and I shall pray you that we bring the matter to a conclusion.' Her daughter wrote to John Paston as 'my right well beloved Valentine'.

In the 1955 edition of *Butler's Lives of the Saints*, the custom of regarding St Valentine's Day as a day for lovers was described as 'hardly more than a memory'. In the 2000 edition, Paul Burns notes its enthusiastic revival, though the connection with the martyr of Rome (or Terni) has become increasingly tenuous.

AA.SS., Feb., 2, pp. 752–63; H. Delehaye, *Les origines du culte des martyrs* (Brussels, 1933), pp. 270, 315–16; *The Paston Letters*: original letters (1787), ed. James Gairdner (1983); Delehaye, pp. 29, 30; *Butler*, Feb., pp. 148–50.

15. Sigfrid (d. ?1045)   *[Commem.]*

Two centuries after the death of *Anskar, his work in Scandinavia had been destroyed. The king of Norway, Olaf Tryggveson, was baptized a Christian while in exile in England, and when he returned to his own country, he asked King Aethelred to send him a missionary bishop. Sigfrid was sent in 995 with two assistants named John and Grimkel. Sigfrid was probably an Anglo-Saxon, and is generally thought to have been a monk of Glastonbury, though York has laid claim to him.

Olaf Tryggveson ruled in Norway only for five years: he was killed in battle in the year 1000. It seems that little was achieved in Norway, but Sigfrid found a missionary base in Sweden. He baptized the king of Sweden, consecrated bishops for east and west Gothland, and built a church at Växjö. Then, leaving his three nephews in charge of the established settlements, he pressed on into new territory. His nephews, Unaman, Sunamen and Vinaman, were captured by pagan tribes and beheaded. Sigfrid asked the king to spare the lives of the killers, and their sentence was commuted to a very large fine or blood-price. This Sigfrid refused to accept, even though he needed money for the cathedral he was building: he felt that his forgiveness must be total.

In art, Sigfrid is often shown carrying the heads of his three beloved nephews, though these are sometimes represented as three loaves of bread. He also worked in Denmark, and there are relics at Copenhagen and Roskilde. His ministry lasted for some forty-five years, and he is known as the Apostle of Sweden and Denmark. In old Swedish calendars, 15 February was traditionally marked by a cross and a hatchet – the cross representing Bishop Sigfrid, and the hatchet the death of his nephews.

Latin Lives in *AA.SS.*, Feb., 2, pp. 848–52. *Anal.Boll.*, 60 (1942), pp. 82–90 contains manuscript accounts now held in the British Museum and museums in Lund and Copenhagen. See also *P.B.*, 2, p. 645; *Butler*, Feb., pp. 157–8.

Thomas Bray (1658–1730)   [Commem.]

Thomas Bray, the son of a yeoman on the Welsh borders, was allowed to read in the splendid library of chained books owned by the vicar of Montgomery. He developed a passion for books. After studying at Oswestry Grammar School, he went as a poor scholar to All Souls, Oxford, probably acting as a servitor, waiting at table and running errands. He took his degree in 1678, but some years elapsed before he could afford the fee for his MA. He was made deacon in 1681 and priested in 1682. He acquired a patron in Sir Thomas Price of Park Hall, near Castle Bromwich, who made him his family chaplain, and in 1690 became vicar of the country parish of Sheldon.

The first volume of Bray's *Catechetical Lectures*, which eventually ran to four volumes, was published in 1696. It sold 3,000 copies, and made him £700 in royalties. More importantly, it attracted the attention of Henry Compton, bishop of London, who was responsible for the oversight of the American colonies, and was concerned about the situation in Maryland. The colony had been conceded to the Roman Catholic Lord Baltimore: the Crown took it back in 1691. The governor initiated a local Act creating 25 Anglican parishes, and providing for their maintenance with a tithe on the tobacco crop; but this Act required ratification by parliament in London. The Quakers, who were a very powerful force in the colony, opposed it, and when the governor died, no action was taken. Bray was appointed Commissary for Maryland, with the task of establishing the Church of England in this hotbed of sectarian rivalries.

In 1696, he went back to Oxford to acquire the degrees of BD and DD to give himself the necessary authority. He told the bishop of London that he must have books: theological libraries must be set up in Maryland, and public subscriptions raised to pay for them. Four other diocesans joined with London in promoting this scheme, with a joint statement: 'We look upon this design as one which will tend very much to *propagate Christian knowledge*'. The title of SPCK derives from this statement. Proposals for these 'parish libraries' were printed, and subscriptions poured in – one of 100 guineas from the Princess Anne, later Queen Anne. The capital city, renamed Annapolis in her honour, housed the Great Library for the province. Bray began to recruit missionaries, and to send them out with boxes of books. Sixteen clergy and 29 'libraries' were despatched in the first two years of the scheme.

In England, complaints were raised that the American missionaries were very well provided for, but that the home clergy lacked both books and learning. Bray revived the concept of rural deaneries, then almost obsolete, and proposed that each should have its own library. His detailed *Memorial on the Institution of Rural Deans*, which contained agendas for the first six meetings of the reconstituted deaneries, was instrumental in bringing the rural deaneries back into the organization of the Anglican parochial system.

Bray planned for SPCK to become an official body established by Royal Charter, but these plans were not successful. Instead, he set up a small society of four Anglican philanthropists to 'propagate the Gospel'. Its aims were to start free catechetical schools for poor planters, to provide libraries, to distribute funds for the maintenance of married clergy, and to give basic Christian education to young Indians and Negroes. Bray poured his energies and his own resources into the SPG scheme, even selling some of his rectory furniture to support it.

In December 1699, he at last sailed for Maryland with more boxes of books. He summoned the clergy for a Visitation, and gave them charges on preaching and pastoral care. He made extensive registers of local information, and asked them to do the same. Then, after three months, he sailed for England, expecting to return soon after.

He never went back to Maryland. It took him three years of lobbying to get the Act establishing the Church of England in the colony through parliament, and there was much more to be done from the English side. He tried to raise money for a permanent Commissary to Maryland, and later for four bishops in the American colonies, but there was no interest in official circles. SPG acquired a Royal Charter in 1700, and became a major missionary society. Thomas Bray went back to his rectory at Sheldon until 1708, when he became rector of St Botulph's, Aldgate. From this London base he was able to continue his work, training missionaries, compiling lists of books which the clergy should read, and administering contributions for his work in founding libraries. He died in 1730, and his Will made careful provisions for the preservation of his precious books and manuscripts.

Anon., *Publick Spirit, Illustrated in the Life and Designs of the Reverend Thomas Bray, D.D.* (1746, repr. 1808); Bernard C. Stein (1901); E. L. Pennington (Philadelphia, 1934); H. P. Thompson (1954); *Bridge Builders*, pp. 45–65; W. K. Lowther Clarke, *A History of the S.P.C.K.* (1959). Bray's Maryland journal and manuscripts are in Sion College, London.

17. Janani Luwum, Martyr (1922–1977)   [L.F.]

The development of an indigenous Church in Uganda has been achieved largely through the education of boys from rural backgrounds. Janani Luwum came from East Acholi, in the northern borders of Uganda with the Sudan. Like other village boys, he herded goats and sheep until his father, who became a Christian convert, managed to get him a place in Gulu High School. He went on to a teachers' training course pioneered by Bishop Usher Wilson of the Upper Nile – the only such course in Uganda held in the English language. After two years as a teacher and lay reader at Gulu, he was sent for two years to St Augustine's College, Canterbury, to train for the ministry. He was ordained in 1956, and went back to East Acholi as a priest, with twenty-four parishes to cover. Later, after a period as vice-principal of the theological college at Buluwasi, he was awarded a bursary for a second period of study in England, and passed the three-year ALCD course at the London College of Divinity in two years.

In 1969, he became bishop of Northern Uganda. By this time, he was as much at home in the international conferences of the Anglican Communion as he was in the Acholi villages, where he visited every parish. His warmth and sympathy, his broad grin, his understanding and his human concern became widely known. Wholly African and English-educated, he was a man of God who bridged two worlds.

In 1974, he was elected archbishop of Uganda, Burundi and Boga-Zaire, where *Apolo Kivebulaya had set up his mission station. He covered his archdiocese tirelessly, driving very fast, to the frequently voiced alarm of his clergy; but his position brought him into direct confrontation with the military dictator, Idi Amin. For a time, he managed to work with Amin, who was erratic and unstable, telephoning for advice in the middle of the night, or sending a car to the archbishop's office with a demand that he leave immediately for a consultation; but relations deteriorated. Amin suspected Christian leaders in Uganda of being in league with the state of Israel. Missionaries were banned from entering the country, and Christians began to disappear. Bodies were found floating on Lake Victoria, and there was a climate of fear and suspicion (see *Uganda Martyrs). Archbishop Janani spoke out fearlessly against the evils of the military dictatorship and went personally on many occasions to the headquarters of the security forces to enquire about missing Christians.

In March 1976, he was at the Anglican Consultative Council meeting in the Caribbean, where there was much concern at the risks he was taking in his own country. He went back to Uganda full of excitement about his plans for the centenary celebrations of the Church in Uganda; but in August, Makerere University was sacked in an outbreak of raping, looting and burning in which staff and students were killed by members of the security forces. Janani went there at once, to see for himself. The Christian leaders in Uganda met under his chairmanship, and sent President Amin a strongly worded memorandum, telling him that the whole world was outraged by the breakdown of law and order in Uganda.

On 5 February 1977, armed guards searched the archbishop's house for arms. He told them, 'There are no arms here. Our house is God's house. We pray for the president.' On 17 February, the president sent for him. The bishops and other clergy insisted on accompanying him. It was alleged that arms smuggled from China had been found near his family home, and there was some sort of a show trial in which he was accused of complicity in a plot to assassinate the president. Then the other clergy were dismissed one by one. Janani turned to another bishop and said, 'They are going to kill me. I am not afraid.' He was never seen again.

It was subsequently announced in the Press that he had died in a car crash; but the accompanying pictures were old ones: the two cars shown had been in garages in a crashed condition for weeks beforehand. There was a report from Tanzania that Amin was personally responsible for shooting him, though this was repeatedly denied. A memorial service was held in Nairobi, because it was too dangerous to hold one in Kampala. On 23 February, Amin ordered the massacre of the Langi and the Acholi tribes. This terrible period in Uganda's history ended in 1978, when invading forces from Tanzania overthrew the Amin government.

Archbishop Janani's statue is among those of the modern martyrs on the west front of Westminster Abbey.

Margaret Ford, *Janani: the making of a martyr* (1978, repr, 1979); Tom Tuma and Phares Mutibwa, eds, *A Century of Christianity in Uganda 1877–1977* (Kampala, 1978); J. F. Faubel, *African Holocaust* (2nd edn, 1965); George Ivan Smith, *Ghosts of Kampala: the rise and fall of Idi Amin* (1980); John Sentamu in Chandler, pp. 144–58.

23. Polycarp (*c.*69–*c.*160)   [L.F.]

Polycarp, bishop of Smyrna, is a link between the Apostles and the early Fathers of the Church. He was a disciple of *John the Evangelist, and in his old age he was able to repeat the words of St John (who himself lived to the end of the first century) to his own disciples. *Irenaeus, who went from Smyrna to missionize the Gauls, says, 'I myself saw him in my early years, for he lived so long.' He describes Polycarp as 'instructed by the apostles and conversant with many who had seen the Lord'.

Polycarp became bishop of Smyrna about 107. Irenaeus commends his gravity, his holy life and his pastoral care, and tells how he defended the Christian faith against two leading Gnostic heretics named Marcion and Valentinus, who taught the rejection of the physical world. Irenaeus was to attack the Gnostics himself in his *Contra Haereses*. When Polycarp was a very old man, he went to Rome to meet Anicetus, bishop of Rome. Differences were already developing between the Eastern Church and the Western Church, particularly over the date of Easter. The two conferred, but they could not agree, and finally decided to differ in charity. The problem has been with us ever since.

A letter from the church at Smyrna to other Christian churches, reproduced by the historian Eusebius, tells the story of Polycarp's martyrdom. It is not clear whether this took place in the reign of Antoninus Pius (138–61) or Marcus Aurelius (161–80). It was not a major persecution – simply one of the sporadic attacks on Christians which were stirred up by the mob from time to time. The people in the streets 'boiled with anger', but Polycarp preserved a firm and unshakeable manner, saying 'God's will be done'. He moved to a farm, outside Smyrna, but took no other steps to evade his pursuers. When they arrived, he spoke to them in 'a cheerful and gentle manner', had a meal set for them, said grace, and invited them to eat. They took him into the city, where the governor tried persuasion, urging him to 'respect his years', and telling him that it would be no great thing to show a little respect to Caesar. When Polycarp would not give way, threats followed, and then a trial, at which the old bishop said that he had served Christ for eighty-six years (presumably since infant baptism) and refused to deny his master. The mob demanded that he should be burned alive, but he was despatched by the sword, and his body was burned after his death.

'Later we took up his bones,' the letter concludes, 'more precious than stones of great price, more splendid than gold, and laid them where it seemed right . . . he was the twelfth to endure martyrdom in Smyrna, but he alone is specially remembered by all, so that even the heathen everywhere speak of him.'

Irenaeus, *Contra Haereses*, bk 3; Eusebius, *H.E.*, bk 4, chs 14 et seq.; *AA.SS.*, Jan., 2, pp. 671–707; text of contemporary documents in Lightfoot, pp. 165–211. H. Delehaye, *Les passions des martyrs et les genres littéraires* (1921), pp. 11–59; *Early Christian Fathers*, pp. 121–60; *N.C.E.*, 11, pp. 535–6; *Butler*, Feb., pp. 228–32.

27. George Herbert (1593–1633) [Commem.]

The Herbert family were Shropshire gentry, and the poet was born at Montgomery Castle, on the Shropshire borders. His elegant and pious mother, Magdalene Herbert, was widowed when he was very young, and he was still a child when she moved her family of nine children to London. She kept a large household, with her own chaplain, at Charing Cross. After Westminster School, George went to Trinity College, Cambridge, where he had a distinguished career. In 1620, he became University Orator – a post which involved welcoming the King and members of the royal family with a Latin oration, and conducting most of the University's business with the Court. His elder brother Edward became Lord Herbert of Cherbury in recognition of his services as ambassador to France. George, then more of a courtier than an academic, must have hoped for similar promotion; but his chances of a worldly career disappeared with the death of James I. He turned to the service of the Church with deep devotion. He pondered, 'How God's goodnesse strives with Man's refractoriness. Man would sit down at this world. God bids him sell it, and purchase a better.'

In 1624, he was made deacon, and like his Cambridge contemporary, *Nicholas Ferrar, whom he visited at Little Gidding, he was never priested. His circle of friends also included *John Donne, Isaac Walton and *Lancelot Andrewes. In 1626 he became a canon of Lincoln, and in 1629, at the age of thirty-six, he married Jane Danvers. Isaac Walton says that it was a love match – 'The eternal lover of mankind made them happy in each other's mutual and equal affection.' In the following year, he became rector of the rural parish of

Bemerton, near Salisbury. He was an exemplary parish priest, preaching simply and earnestly to his congregation, ordering worship according to the Bible and the Prayer Book, visiting the sick and caring for the poor. He ministered there for only three years before he died of consumption at the age of forty. When he was dying, he said, 'I am sorry I have nothing to present to God but sin and misery; but the first is pardoned, and a few hours shall put a period to the second.'

George Herbert's poems are undated. Many of them were collected and published after his death by Nicholas Ferrar, and copies exist in the distinctive Little Gidding hand. Some of them have become well-known hymns. 'Teach me, my God and King' includes the lines 'This is the famous stone/ Which turneth all to gold'. The scientists of Herbert's day were fascinated by alchemy, but he had come to the conviction that the service of God was the true secret of living, which made even 'drudgery divine'. 'Let all the world / In every corner sing' reflects his love of music, and his vision of the angels, the 'saints who toil below' and the 'blessed souls at rest' joining together in God's praise. We know that he played the lute and the viol, and that he would sometimes walk from Bemerton into Salisbury to play the cathedral organ. Among his best-loved poems, which suggest hours of meditation in his quiet country church, are 'Easter Wings' and 'Redemption'. Like John Donne, Herbert is rated a metaphysical poet, but he has none of Donne's artifice and complexity. In an age when the Church was beset by religious controversy and sectarianism, he expresses a deeply felt and perfectly balanced Anglicanism which is still an inspiration to the Church.

Isaac Walton (1678); T. S. Eliot (1962); A. M. Charles (1977). M. C. Schoenfeld (1991). Poems ed. W. H. Auden (1973) and other editions.

March

1. David of Menevia (?520–?589) [L.F.]

Little is known about the life of David, patron saint of Wales, apart from centuries of oral tradition and the biography of Rhugyfarch, son of Bishop Julien of St David's, dated about 1090. For many of the early Welsh saints, there are no contemporary written records. David is said to have been the son of a princely family, and to have been born at Henfynyw, near St Bride's Bay in Pembroke, about 520. David is often known in Wales as 'Dewi Sant'. His mother was Non or Nonna, commemorated as a holy woman in Cornwall and Brittany in the Middle Ages.

According to Rhugyfarch, David studied under St Paulinus of Wales, and founded, or became abbot of, the monastic community of Mynyw (Menevia), which was modelled on that of the Desert Fathers in the Thebaïd of Upper Egypt. The régime was a very ascetic one, with prolonged periods of silence and hard manual labour. The monks' diet consisted of bread, vegetables and salt, with water or a little milk. They kept vigil from Friday evening to dawn on Sunday with continuous prayer, except for an hour's sleep after Matins, which was said at midnight.

Rhugyfarch tells his readers that David made a number of missionary journeys, visiting the Holy Land and being consecrated archbishop by the patriarch of Jerusalem. Modern commentators are doubtful about these claims, but it is clear that David became a great and memorable abbot, and head of a national school of learning. He is mentioned in the eighth-century catalogue of the saints of Ireland, and in the Martyrology of Tallaght, which bears the date of his death, 1 March. More than fifty pre-Reformation churches in South Wales bore his dedication. His cult was approved by Pope Callistus II in 1120, and two pilgrimages to St David's were reckoned to be equal in merit to one pilgrimage to Rome.

Both William the Conqueror and Henry II visited his shrine.

In Wales, his name is sometimes spelled Dafydd, hence 'Taffy' as a generic term for Welshmen. The tradition of his fellow countrymen wearing leeks or daffodils on his feast day is an ancient one, but despite some ingenious suggestions, the explanation for it remains obscure.

The Life by Rhugyfarch is published as *Buched Dewi*, ed. D. S. Evans (Cardiff, 1959), and in A. Wade-Evans' translation as *The Life of St David* (1914, repr. 1923, 1927); *Men.E.W.*, pp. 92–3. For modern accounts, see E. Rhys (1927); S. M. Harris, *St David in the Liturgy* (Cardiff, 1927); J. Dixon (1948); D. Crowley (1954); *N.C.E.*, 4, p. 660; *O.D.S.*, pp. 127–8; *Butler*, Mar., pp. 1–2. See also *St Taffy's Day in Three Merry Cantos*, by C. L., a True Briton (1724). For Nonna, see *Men.E.W.*, p. 99.

2. Chad (d. 672)   [L.F.]

Chad was the brother of *Cedd (26 Oct.), and like him, educated at Lastingham and a disciple of *Aidan. He succeeded Chad as abbot of Lastingham. At this time, the Church in England was still heavily dependent on the Frankish Church, having few bishops and few monasteries. There were only two royal monasteries in Northumbria, Ripon and Lastingham. King Oswin sent *Wilfrid, abbot of Ripon, to Gaul to be consecrated bishop for his kingdom in Gaul; but when Wilfrid remained abroad for several years, Oswin tired of waiting for his return, and sent Chad to be consecrated at Canterbury. By the time Chad arrived, Archbishop Deusdedit had died, and had not yet been replaced, so he went on to Winchester, where he was consecrated by Bishop Wine and two other bishops. When Wilfrid returned, he claimed that Chad's consecration was irregular, and appealed to Deusdedit's successor, *Theodore of Tarsus, to uphold his claim. Theodore did so, and Chad, who had no desire to be a bishop, returned thankfully to Lastingham; but when King Wulfhere of Mercia asked for a bishop, he had to resume his episcopal status and go to Mercia.

His new diocese was a vast one, stretching across the Midlands to the east coast. Chad, like all the Celtic monks, was accustomed to go about on foot. Theodore insisted that he must ride, and when he refused, hoisted him bodily into the saddle. Theodore was an old man, but a very determined one, and Chad, after years of Celtic asceticism, was probably a featherweight. The incident became famous as typifying the move from the old, small-scale pastoral values to larger-scale administration.

King Wulfhere gave Chad land, and he founded a monastery at a place called At-Barwe, or 'At the Wood', in the province of Lindsey. *Bede, who is the main authority for his life, describes his holy life and his death, probably from the plague, in some detail.

Bede, *H.E.*, bk 3, ch. 28 and bk 4, ch. 3; Eddius Stephanus, ch. 14; C. E. Whiting, *St Chad* (1939); M. W. Greenslade, *St Chad of Lichfield and Birmingham* (1996); *D.N.B.*, 3, pp. 300–2; Mayr-Harting, pp. 88–9, 96–7; *O.D.S.*, pp. 94–5; *Butler, Mar.*, pp. 12–14.

7. Perpetua, Felicity and their Companions, Martyrs (d. 203) [L.F.]

In the persecutions of the Roman emperor Severus in Carthage, two young women were martyred with four men, Revocatus, Saturus, Saturninus, and Secundulus. Vivia Perpetua was twenty-two. She was a member of a well-known family in the city, and she had an infant son only a few months old. Felicity was a slave girl, married to Revocatus, and seven months pregnant. The first part of their joint story is told by Perpetua herself, probably by dictation, and the second part, the account of their martyrdom, comes from another Christian who was present at their execution.

Perpetua says that prison was a shock: she was appalled at 'the darkness and horror of the place; for till then I knew not what such sort of places were'. She was sore and battered from having been jostled by the crowd and ill-treated by the soldiers; but her chief concern was for her baby, and the deacons of the church managed to bribe the guards to let her nurse the child in 'a more commodius part of the prison'. 'My infant being brought to me almost famished, I gave it the breast,' and then she carefully handed the child over to her mother, and went back to her dark and terrible prison.

The male prisoners were scourged, and the two women beaten on the face. Felicity was eight months pregnant at the time, and she feared that she would not be martyred with the others, for under Roman law, a pregnant woman was not executed until after her delivery; but the birth came prematurely, probably because of the ill-treatment she had received. When she cried out in labour, one of the guards asked her how she would stand being thrown to the wild beasts if she could not stand the pangs of childbirth. She answered, 'It is I that suffer what I now suffer; but then there will be another in me that will suffer for me, because I shall suffer for him.' She was delivered of a daughter, and a Christian woman took the new-born baby to bring it up as her own child.

At this point, the story is taken up by the eye-witness. He says that 'on the day of their triumph', the five were taken to the amphitheatre. The occasion was in honour of Geta Caesar, son of the Emperor Severus. The women looked straight ahead, Felicity 'rejoicing to come from the midwife to the gladiator'; but the men shouted back at the crowd, affirming their faith. When they passed the balcony of the tribune Hilarius, they called to him, 'You judge us in this world, but God will judge you in the next.' The men were mauled by a leopard, a wild boar and a bear, and those who were not killed by the beasts were taken to the gate. The women were exposed to a wild cow, which tossed them. Perpetua got up, gathering her torn clothing about her, and tied up her hair, which was loose. Roman women only appeared with dishevelled hair when they were in mourning, and even in extremity, she was determined not to show fear or sorrow. Then she helped Felicity to her feet. 'They stood together, expecting another assault from the beasts, but the people crying out that it was enough, they were led to the gate.' A woman catechumen who saw them there said that Perpetua seemed to be in ecstasy, and unaware of what she had suffered. Then the fickle crowd changed its mind, and howled for them to be brought back to the arena. In full view of the blood-crazed crowd, they were despatched by the gladiators.

This exceptionally well-attested and valuable account of the martyrs may have been written by Tertullian, who was a Carthaginian and a contemporary. St Augustine and Bishop Victor of Vita also tell the story.

It was publicly read in the churches of North Africa in the fourth century. The names of Perpetua and Felicity are recorded in the earliest martyrologies, including the martyrology of Jerome. In 1907, an inscription in honour of the six martyrs was discovered by Father Delattre in the ruins of the Basilica Majorum at Carthage. When pieced together, it was found to record their names, and the fact that they died on the nones of March.

Tertullian, *Lib. de anima*, c.55. The best modern version is W. H. Shewing, *The Passion of Perpetua and Felicity* (1931), which contains both the Latin text and an English translation, with a good introduction. Augustine, Sermon 180; Victor of Vita, *Historia Wandelicae*, 1, 3; *Butler*, Mar., pp. 60–5.

8. Felix of Dunwich (d. 648)   *[Commem.]*

There are well over two hundred saints named Felix in the ancient martyrologies. This one was a Burgundian bishop. *Bede tells us that Sigbert, king of East Anglia, asked Honorius, archbishop of Canterbury, for a bishop, and Felix was sent to him. It is not clear how long he had been a bishop, or whether Sigbert, who had been an exile on the Continent, asked for him personally; but we know that Felix wanted to carry out missionary work in England. He went 'by his own desire', and was sent 'to preach the word of life to the Angles'. Sigbert designated him 'Apostle of the East Angles', and he carried out a mission in what are now the counties of Norfolk, Suffolk and Cambridgeshire. His episcopal seat was at Dunwich.

Bede says that 'like a good farmer, he reaped a rich harvest of believers'. He organized the Church in East Anglia on the lines of the Latin Church, and founded a monastery at Soham; Botulf (Botulph) of Ikanhoe, whose name is preserved in church dedications, founded another in 654. At the same time, Felix respected the Celtic tradition: he honoured *Aidan of Lindisfarne; and there was an eminent Irish ascetic named Fursa in his diocese, long remembered for his habit of sitting in the icy winds of an East Anglian winter, wearing a thin shirt, and sweating with the glory of his visions. Felix carried on his ministry for seventeen years, and 'ended his days in peace' in the monastery at Soham.

East Anglia stayed Christian until the Danish invasions of the early tenth century. Unfortunately, there was no chronicler to record its progress, and the details have long since been lost. Dunwich itself has disappeared into the sea as a result of coastal erosion, and Felix's mission is marked only by the preservation of his name in the town of Felixstowe. It has been suggested that Felixkirk in North Yorkshire also bears his name – in which case, he may have extended his mission across the Humber, or perhaps have visited Celtic monks in that area.

Bede, *H.E.*, bk 2, ch. 15; *AA.SS.*, Mar., pp. 779–81; P. Hunter Blair, *The World of Bede* (1970) pp. 107–9; Stenton, pp. 116–17, 125; *O.D.S.*, p. 173; *Butler*, Mar., p. 74.

Edward King (1829–1910)   [L.F.]

The two words which every writer uses about Bishop Edward King are 'gentle' and 'holy'. The son of a clergyman who became archdeacon of Rochester, he was a delicate child, educated at home until he went to Oxford. He was a High Churchman of strict and regular devotion. Because of his poor health, he was able only to take a pass degree, but he proceeded to Cuddesdon theological college, was ordained, and in 1858 became chaplain of the college. He became an excellent teacher and pastor, and devoted his life to his students until he became principal in 1863. He also became vicar of the small rural parish of Cuddesdon, which he organized to give his students pastoral experience. He ran the college with very few rules, but a great sense of warmth and community. Henry Scott Holland, who led the *Lux Mundi* group (see *F. D. Maurice) said that he 'could charm love out of a stone'.

He read widely – Plato, Aristotle and Dante as well as theological texts. There was astonishment in Oxford circles when Gladstone nominated him as Regius Professor of Pastoral Theology, because of his limited academic background; but he knew his subject, and the students flocked to hear him. Many came to him for confession and for spiritual direction.

In 1885, he became bishop of Lincoln. Lincoln was a Low Church diocese – 'soaked in the Methodist revival' as Owen Chadwick puts it; but Bishop King's sympathies were broad, and he said that he was glad to be going to John Wesley's diocese. He lived very simply, wearing shabby old clothes, travelling by train, and moving from the imposing bishop's palace to the Old Palace, which was smaller, dilapidated, and in the heart of Lincoln city. He improved training for his clergy, and was accessible to all who needed his help. When a prison chaplain was distressed by having to minister to a condemned man, he took on the responsibility himself, saying that it was a 'terrible privilege'. His great teacher was *Francis de Sales, another gentle man of God.

In 1880–90, Bishop King found himself on trial: the ultra-Protestant Church Association accused him of 'ritual acts contrary to the Prayer Book'. They complained that he took the eastward position at the Eucharist (facing Jerusalem) instead of celebrating from the north end of the altar, where the congregation could see what he was doing; he had lighted candles on the altar; he mixed water and wine in the chalice; he allowed the *Agnus Dei* to be sung; and he absolved and blessed the congregation with the sign of the Cross. For this list of 'offences', he was tried by the archbishop of Canterbury, A. F. Benson, and six Evangelical bishops. He protested that the court was weighted against him, but had to endure four years of anxiety and humiliation before a final decision was reached. Many churchmen came to his defence, and money was raised for his legal costs. The final verdict was that his practices were permissible except for the eastward position and the sign of the Cross. Many clergy continued to use both: the trial of Edward King virtually ended a series of litigious actions against 'ritualism', and gave Anglo-Catholics freedom to use their own symbols for worship. It has often been said that Edward King's simplicity and gentleness won his cause: a more combative defence might easily have lost it.

G. W. E. Russell (1912); B. W. Randolph and J. W. Townroe, *The Mind and Work of Bishop King* (1918); Lord Elton, *Edward King and Our Times* (1958); Owen Chadwick, Lincoln Minster pamphlet (1968); G. F. Wilgress in *Great Christians*, pp. 321–32; *Twentieth Century*, pp. 70–3. Works: *Spiritual Letters*, ed. B. W. Randolph (1910); *Sermons and Addresses* (1911); *The Love and Wisdom of God* (1918).

Geoffrey Studdert Kennedy (1883–1929)   *[Commem.]*

His friend *William Temple, then bishop of Manchester, described Studdert Kennedy as 'one of God's greatest gifts to our generation'. The generation was the one which saw great poverty in the industrial North during the late Victorian and Edwardian periods, endured the horrors of the First World War, and tried to make sense of the bitter disillusionment of the 1920s.

Geoffrey was the seventh son of the Rev. W. A. Studdert Kennedy, vicar of St Mary's, Quarry Hill, Leeds. He grew up in a large, affectionate family, familiar with the back streets of Leeds – the desperate struggle for survival, the dark alleys, the drunkenness and the violence. Trinity College, Dublin and Ripon Clergy College helped him to find his vocation. He enjoyed working in the small mission parishes as a student, and became a curate in Rugby in 1908, where the vicar criticized his sermons as 'too journalistic', but helped him to develop his gift for working with tramps, itinerant workers and poor families, and for open-air preaching. He combined an evangelical approach to mission with a deeply Catholic sense of ritual and worship. The Eucharist was as real to him when it was celebrated on an old packing-case as when it was celebrated on the most ancient and hallowed altar.

He was always vague, humble, unconventional, and warm-hearted: he lost things, he forgot things. He wore whatever clothes came to hand, and gave away his possessions and his money so freely that his housekeeper insisted on guarding both, and gave him only a few coins for his pocket. After some seven years in parish life, he volunteered to become a Chaplain to the Forces, and by the end of 1915, he was in France. He felt that his place was with the men who were suffering the horrors of trench warfare. He started where they were, 'twixt muck and a golden crown', and he gave them his own vision of a suffering God who was with them: the agony of Christ was always central to his faith. He wrote to his wife, 'I see Gethsemane. I always see it these days.'

'You can take it,' he wrote, 'that the best place for a padre . . . is where there is most danger . . . Living with the men, praying for them, if not with them.' He spent much time in the front line, talking, arguing, praying, and distributing comforts such as the cigarettes which earned him the nickname of 'Woodbine Willie'. He was often afraid, and understood the soldiers' fear. Danger gave him 'the wobbles inside'; but in August 1917 he was awarded the Military Cross for gallantry shown in fetching morphia for the wounded under heavy fire, and rescuing two men from shell-holes.

He was criticized and sometimes actively resented for his informality, his slangy sermons, and his complete disregard of the niceties of Army rank and social class. He had a habit of mounting a platform with a cigarette in one hand, saying, 'I know what you're all thinking: here comes a bloody parson' and then explaining earnestly that it was not 'soldierly' to swear. The troops respected the honesty and directness of his approach.

When he was demobilized in 1919, he was made a King's Chaplain. Requests for him to preach and speak flooded in. He went for a time to St Martin-in-the-Fields in London, where homeless and unemployed men found shelter. His vicar, Dick Shepherd, remembered him as 'an ugly little man with wonderful eyes, wearing an immense collar', and was struck by 'the Christ-likeness of the little Irishman'. Then he was given a City living as his base, St Edmund's, Lombard Street. By this time, he was working for the Industrial Christian Fellowship, which tried to make the Christian faith relevant to the needs of the modern industrial world in a period of unemployment and industrial unrest. He toured the United Kingdom, preaching and speaking at public meetings; he took retreats; he addressed conferences. He continued to follow a taxing schedule in spite of worsening health. After contracting influenza, he died on a mission in Liverpool on the night of 7–8 March 1929, at the age of forty-six.

J. Mozley, ed., *G. A. Studdert Kennedy, by his Friends* (1929); Alan Wilkinson, *The Church of England in the First Great War* (1978); Gerald Studdert Kennedy, *Dog-Collar Democracy* (1982); *Twentieth Century*, pp. 89–94; *Great Christians*, pp. 299–317; *D.N.B. Missing Persons Volume* (ed. C. S. Nicholls, 1993), pp. 647–8.

17. Patrick (d. *c*.400) [L.F.]

Very little is known about the origins of Patrick, patron of Ireland, except that he was Romano-British, and came from somewhere on or near the west coast of Britain. The Severn estuary and Dumbarton, at the western end of Hadrian's Wall, both claim him. He came of a family which owned a landed estate: his father was a deacon, and his grandfather a priest. Before he was sixteen, he was captured by Irish raiders, and taken to Armagh as a slave. Pagan Ireland was a land of blood-stained tribal wars and savagery, of spells, wizards and warlocks.

In the conditions of his captivity, when he tended animals on a Northern Irish hillside, he began to pray incessantly, by night and day. After six years, he made his escape, and eventually found his way back to England, where his family begged him to stay; but he could not forget his Irish experiences. He says in his *Confession* that he had a vision, and the conviction grew that he must return to Ireland as a missionary. He does not say where he trained for the priesthood, though suggestions have been made that he did so in Gaul – possibly at Lérins, the great monastery on the Mediterranean coast of Gaul, or Auxerre, where Bishop Germanus already had links with the English Church.

It is not clear when Patrick was consecrated bishop, but we know that he returned to Armagh with a small party of followers, and began to preach the Gospel. He set up a 'family' – that is, a group of clergy praying together – and a school for training clergy. He says that he baptised 'thousands', and ordained many Irish clergy. Recent academic studies of his life present him not as a great organizer of the Irish Church, but as a charismatic preacher who drew large crowds, established a local structure, and moved on to fresh work. The early Irish bishops did not have dioceses with territorial boundaries like bishops in Italy or Gaul.

The *Confession* and the *Letter of Coroticus* are generally acknowledged to be the authentic work of Patrick. They speak eloquently of his spiritual struggles, and the strength of his faith. He writes in Latin, lamenting his own lack of education. The *Confession* starts '*Ego, Patricius, peccator et rusticissimus*' – 'I Patrick, a sinner, and very unlearned'; but though his Latin has been criticized as less scholarly than that of his contemporaries in Rome, colloquial Latin would have been his first language, and he writes as he speaks. He knows the Psalms and the Scriptures, and gives a version of the Creed which is clearly based on that agreed at the Council of Nicaea. The *Lorica*, 'St Patrick's Breastplate', with its splendid invocation of the Trinity, best known as a hymn in the translation of Mrs C. F. Alexander, may have originated with him, with other verses added later. Many other works were subsequently attributed to him, as he became the most famous figure in the history of Christian mission in Ireland. Extravagant claims were made that many other Irish saints had worked with him, some of them born a century or more later; but the simplicity, humanity and implicit trust in God which he inspired in the Irish Church are unmistakable.

Only a few years after his death, *Columba was to take the Celtic monastic system to Iona, whence it spread to Scotland, and through *Aidan, to Northumbria. Many legends are told about Patrick. Some of these, like the legend that he banished the snakes from Ireland, suggest the kind of magical pretensions which he condemned in the pagan priests of Armagh. Possibly some of the true stories about his achievements should be credited to other people, for he was by no means the only Christian missionary in Ireland at the time; but when all the accretions are stripped away, there remains the figure of this man of blazing faith, with the Spirit seething within him, resolutely facing spiritual and physical dangers to bring Christianity to the people who once enslaved him.

L. Bieler, trans. and ed., *The Works of St Patrick* (1953); *Men.E.W.* pp. 120–1; R. P. C. Hanson, *The Life and Writings of the Historical St Patrick* (1983); E. A. Thompson, *Who was St Patrick?* (1985); D. Adam, *The Cry of the Deer* (1987); *O.D.S.*, pp. 379–81.

18. Cyril of Jerusalem (*c.*315–86) [*Commem.*]

Cyril was a boy in Jerusalem when *Helena arrived to see the excavation of the True Cross. He is reported to have been twelve years old when she reached the city in 327. Later, he told the story to his nephew Galatius of Caesarea, through whom it reached the ancient historians Sozomen and Socrates the Philosopher. Cyril was well educated by monks, and became a priest. In 350, he was consecrated bishop of Jerusalem.

It was Cyril's misfortune to live in a time of political and ecclesiastical turbulence. He was involved in conflict with the Arians, who alleged that his consecration was irregular. At the second Ecumenical Council of Constantinople in 381, he was declared 'the lawful bishop of the Mother of all the churches'; but his metropolitan, Acacius, bishop of Caesarea, was an Arian. He accused Cyril, among other acts of 'insubordination', of selling church property to feed the poor in a famine. Cyril was three times deposed by pro-Arian emperors, and forced into exile, and three times recalled. In all, he was bishop of Jerusalem for thirty-five years, and spent sixteen of them in exile.

Cyril steadfastly stood for the beliefs of the Nicene Creed, despite much hostility and misrepresentation. His *Catechetical Instructions* are a valuable source of material on Church instruction and ritual in the fourth century, and he is credited with the introduction of the Holy Week liturgy, which is still in use in both the Eastern and the Western Churches.

A. Fortescue, *The Greek Fathers* (1908); *Later Christian Fathers*, pp. 35–47; F. L. Cross, *St Cyril of Jerusalem's Lectures on the Christian Sacraments* (1951); N.C.E., 4, pp. 576–8; Works in N.P.N.F., 8.

19. Joseph of Nazareth Festival

Joseph is the husband of the *Virgin Mary, and the adoptive father of Jesus. *Matthew specifies his lineage – fourteen generations from Abraham to David, fourteen generations from David (Matthew 1:1–17), to fulfil the prophecy that the Messiah will be of the house of David. He is a just man: when he discovers that his bride is with child, he is unwilling to expose her to public disgrace, and plans to dismiss her quietly; but he learns in a dream that the child is of the Holy Spirit, and accepts the responsibility of caring for her and the baby (Matthew 1:18–24). He sets out with Mary for Bethlehem, is with her when the child is born (Luke 2:16), and escorts her for the presentation in the Temple (Luke 2:22–39). He takes them both to Egypt for two years to avoid Herod's massacre of the *Innocents (Matthew 2:13–15), and they live in Nazareth, 'their own city', going up to Jerusalem every year for the feast of the Passover at least until Jesus is twelve years old (Luke 2:41–2). We know that Joseph was a craftsman, a carpenter by trade (Matthew 13:55). Thereafter, he disappears from the Gospel narrative; and since Mary is commended to the care of the Beloved Disciple at the time of the Crucifixion, it can be assumed that she was then a widow.

The apocryphal *Protoevangelium* of James describes Joseph as an old man at the time of Jesus's birth, but he must have been sufficiently active to have made the journey to Egypt, and the repeated journeys of about fifty miles each way to Jerusalem, and sufficiently strong to protect his wife and child. In Matthew 13:55, there is mention of Jesus's brothers and sisters: some commentators have interpreted this as a reference to members of the wider family, who would today be designated as cousins, while others have speculated that Joseph was a widower with children of an earlier marriage at the time of his marriage to Mary. This is possible, since there was no tradition of celibacy in Jewish culture. The *History of Joseph the Carpenter*, dating from the fifth or sixth century, describes Joseph as being fearful of his approaching death, but being comforted by Mary and Jesus.

In mediaeval mystery plays, Joseph is sometimes treated as a comic figure, and it may have been in reaction against this bawdy interpretation that a devotion to him developed. His feast was celebrated at Winchester, Worcester and Ely before 1100, and by the sixteenth century, he was very highly regarded in Spain. *Teresa of Avila dedicated the mother house of her reformed Carmelites in his name, and *Ignatius of Loyola encouraged his cult in the Society of Jesus. He is the patron saint of fathers of families and of manual workers.

AA.SS., Mar., 3, pp. 4–25; F. L. Filas, *The Man nearest to Christ* (1947); H. Rondel, trans. and ed. D. Attwater (New York, 1956); N.C.E., 7, pp. 1106–12; O.D.S., pp. 268–9; O.C.B., p. 382.

20. Cuthbert (*c.*635–687)

Cuthbert came from the Scottish border country, probably the Lammermuir Hills, which in his time were part of the kingdom of Northumbria. He felt a call to the monastic life from an early age, and went to Melrose Abbey, on the banks of the River Tweed. In time, he became prior, and trained others. He did not stay within the monastery walls, but tramped the countryside, talking to ordinary people as he met them. Many had relapsed into superstitions and idolatry in an attempt to ward off the plague during an epidemic. He would leave the monastery for as much as a month at a time, visiting villages 'whose barbarity and squalor daunted other teachers' according to *Bede.

In 661, his abbot, Eata, took Cuthbert to Ripon, where *Wilfrid was already practising the Latin rites. They both seem to have understood that the days of the Celtic system were numbered. After the Synod of Whitby in 664, when the Latin system was enjoined on the Church in Northumbria, Abbot Eata, who had jurisdiction over Lindisfarne as well as Melrose, sent Cuthbert to Lindisfarne to bring the monastery into conformity with the Latin Church. Cuthbert seems to have taken the view that much of the argument was about externals, and not about the essentials of faith. He persuaded the monks to observe the Latin date of Easter, and to adopt the Latin tonsure, shaving the crowns of their heads instead of the front. He was a unifier, prepared to work to bring the two traditions together to strengthen the Church.

He kept his Celtic spirituality. The two life-styles were very different. Celtic monks fasted for long periods on nothing but bread and water, kept night vigils, and were quite capable of standing up to their necks in freezing water to subdue the rebellious flesh. They lived in poverty, despising material possessions. The new Roman monks who came into the province had very different values. They feasted and drank wine in noble houses, believing that this was the way to influence the influential; they lived in considerable comfort; and they amassed money for their monasteries, spending it on rich decorations for their churches: statues, vestments, embroideries, and vessels of gold and silver. There was a good deal of wealth in Northumbria: much of it was loot from conquest, and a battle-hardened warrior would try to save his soul by giving to the Church.

The Lives of Cuthbert tend to omit dates, but he is thought to have stayed at Lindisfarne for about twelve years. Then this out-going pastor felt called to a solitary life, and became a hermit. He chose the island of Farne – far out to sea from Lindisfarne. Bede says that there were evil spirits on the island, and Cuthbert defeated them; but he had to face his own internal spiritual struggles. The Lindisfarne monks built him a hut containing a cell and an oratory, on the Celtic pattern, surrounded by a high wall, so that he could see 'nothing but the heaven which he desired so ardently'. When they dug a well in the hut, clear water filled it. Cuthbert sowed wheat, but it would not grow. In the second year, he sowed barley, and obtained a good crop. He lived on barley bread and water.

He stayed on Farne for many years. People came to see him, and he built a small guest-house for visitors, but he remained in close communion with God, away from the world. Then *Archbishop Theodore held a great synod, and he was elected bishop of Lindisfarne. He left his beloved retreat in tears.

As a bishop, Cuthbert was patient, gentle and kindly to those in need of comfort. People found him 'afire with heavenly love', Bede says. After two years, he found that he had a mortal illness. He resigned willingly, and went back to Farne Island to die. There he endured storm and tempest and great physical pain; but the monks were with him when he died. He asked to be buried on the island, but they pleaded that they should be allowed to take his body back to Lindisfarne.

Cuthbert was a man of great sweetness and simplicity. His tomb was credited with many healing miracles in mediaeval times, and his memory is still held in much affection in Northumbria. His shrine in Durham cathedral is still a place of pilgrimage.

Bede, *H.E.*, bk 4, chs 27—32; C. Eyre (1858); J. Raine (1828); B. Colgrave, trans., *Two Lives of St Cuthbert* (1940); G. Bonner, D. Rollason and C. Stancliffe, eds, *St Cuthbert, His Cult and His Community* (1989); E. Power, 'St Cuthbert and St Wilfrid', in D. H. Farmer, ed., *Benedict's Disciples* (1980, repr. 1985); Mayr-Harting, pp. 161–3, 165–7, 240–1; *O.D.S.*, pp. 116–18.

21. Thomas Cranmer (1489–1556)   [L.F.]

Cranmer was a fellow of Jesus College, Cambridge and Reader in Divinity when the theological implications of Henry VIII's quarrel with the pope became a matter for academic discussion. He was a quiet scholar of forty, and in touch with the Continental reformers. In discussion with other divines, he suggested that the king might avoid conflict with the papacy by appealing to the universities of Christendom, so that the issue of his marriage might be settled by men learned in theology and canon law.

He found himself catapulted into prominence. Henry VIII appointed him a royal chaplain, and he was recruited to the team of theologians attempting to find a solution to the king's problems. He was sent on diplomatic missions: one to Rome, where the pope was hesitating over his verdict on the marriage question, and one to Charles V of Germany. This second journey brought him into close links with Lutheran divines, and he met and married Margaret, a niece of the theologian Andreas Osiander. He was summoned back to England to become archbishop of Canterbury, and consecrated in March 1532. He took the oath of allegiance to the pope – but added a formal declaration that he was not bound thereby to do anything against God's law, the king's realm or the law and prerogatives of England.

In matters of state, he obeyed the king's will. He was president of Convocation when Henry's marriage to Catherine of Aragon was declared null and void, and his marriage to Anne Boleyn declared valid. He conducted Anne Boleyn's coronation, and he stood as god-father to her daughter Elizabeth. Thereafter he presided over all the king's marital affairs in his frantic search for male heirs. He was the king's trusted servant, and the king was legally the supreme head of the English Church. To some extent, he was a restraining influence on his dangerous monarch. Though he pleaded in vain for the lives of *Thomas More, of *John Fisher, of Anne Boleyn and ultimately of Thomas Cromwell, he saved others.

Royal affairs were probably of much less concern to him than the work he was able to do in reforming the English Church. Henry VIII was not a Lutheran. Luther growled, 'Junker Henry means to be God, and do as he pleases' when Henry refused to subscribe to the Con-fession of Augsburg; but Cranmer was given the opportunity to initiate moderate reform in the English Church. Authoritative versions of the Creed, the Lord's Prayer and the Ten Commandments were issued in English, so that the people might understand them. The Great Bible, a combination of the translations of Miles Coverdale and *William Tyndale, was published. Cranmer's preface to the editions of 1540 and 1541 described it as 'the Word of God, the most precious jewel and most holy relic that remaineth on earth'. The first *Book of Common*

Prayer was compiled – basically a combination of Sarum Use (see *Osmund) and the reformed breviary of the Spanish Cardinal Quignon, but translated into clear and beautiful English which was for the most part Cranmer's own work.

In the six years of Edward VI's reign, Cranmer resisted the extreme Protestantism of Protector Northumberland; but when Mary Tudor, the Catholic daughter of Catherine of Aragon, was proclaimed queen on 19 July 1553, he knew that his life was in danger. He refused to escape. He had been archbishop for twenty-one years, and he believed in the moderate reform he had carried out. He was sent to the Tower of London, condemned and excommunicated in November, and deprived of his archbishopric in December.

In the following year, England was reconciled to Rome, and the bishops were dismissed from their posts, being replaced by Catholics. Mary married Philip of Spain, and the whole of the Protestant legal framework was swept away by parliament. In March 1554, Cranmer and his friends Hugh Latimer, bishop of Worcester, and Nicholas Ridley, bishop of London, were imprisoned in Oxford, and forced to take part in a lengthy disputation with Catholic divines: a sort of theological show trial. When Cranmer was questioned on whether Christ was actually present in the elements at the Eucharist, his reply was, 'His true body is truly present in them that truly believe him; but spiritually.' In January 1555, he was tried before a papal commission, and condemned as a heretic.

Cranmer was subjected to intense psychological pressure by Spanish priests who skilfully manipulated his state of mind between fear and hope. He was told that Queen Mary would have him recant: if he did not, there would be 'no Cranmer at all'. He began to sign statements which at first simply expressed his submission to the queen's authority, but which gradually carried him further into conflict with his conscience. The pressure was intensified. On 14 February 1554, he was taken into the cathedral at Christ Church, and ceremonially disgraded. He was stripped of his robes, and even his fingers and nails were scraped to remove the last vestiges of the chrism bestowed on him at his consecration. On 16 October 1555, Latimer and Ridley were burned at the stake. Cranmer's own ordeal continued with remorseless daily questioning designed to force him to a complete recantation. He signed the final statement on 19 March 1556, and with it his death-warrant. Two days later, he was taken to the doors of the church of St Mary the Virgin to recant in public before his execution. When it became clear that he was not recanting, but re-stating his belief in the Reformation, he was hurried away to the stake. There he thrust the hand which had signed the recantations into the flames without flinching before he died.

He left us a framework for a Church both Catholic and reformed, the devotional insights and the literary beauty of the Prayer Book, and the memory of his final act of courage.

John Strype, *Memorials of Thomas Cranmer* (3 vols, 1848–54); *Cantuar*, pp. 133–42; *Bridge Builders*, pp. 1–19; M. Johnson, ed., *Thomas Cranmer: Essays in Commemoration of the 500th Anniversary of his Death* (1990); P. Ayris and D. Selwyn, *Thomas Cranmer: Churchman and Scholar* (1998); D. MacCulloch, *Thomas Cranmer* (1996) has a full bibliography. Cranmer's Commonplace Books are in the British Museum.

24. Walter Hilton (d. ?1396)   *[Commem.]*

Hilton's great spiritual classic, *The Ladder of Perfection*, sometimes called *The Scale of Perfection*, was originally written for the guidance of an anchoress. He is one of the company of English fourteenth-century mystics, including also *Richard Rolle, *Julian of Norwich and the anonymous author of *The Cloud of Unknowing*, whose work has survived through the centuries for the guidance of Christians. *Margery Kempe read 'Hilton's book', and spoke of it to Julian when she visited Norwich.

Hilton was a Canon Regular of the Augustinian Order in the priory of St Peter at Thurgarten, near Southwell. The Order was a scholarly one, devoted to education, preaching and writing, and in particular to the exposition and translation of the Scriptures in the English tongue. It seems to have been at the front line in correcting some of the wilder assertions of the Lollards, who combined a justifiable attack on abuses in the Church with dubious scriptural interpretations probably arising from their lack of Latin. In 1388, the prior of Thurgarten was appointed to a commission which examined those accused of adhering to 'the unsound doctrines of Master Wyclif'. Chapter 18 in *The Ladder of Perfection* – 'Why humble people should respect others, and regard themselves as inferior to all' – may have been written with the Lollards in mind.

But Hilton was not primarily concerned with attacks on the Church: his aim was simply to provide a spiritual path which Christians might follow. He wrote in English: the book was later translated into Latin as *Scala Perfectionis*.

He begins by distinguishing between the active life and the contemplative life: one or other, as *Pope Gregory the Great laid down, is necessary to salvation. The active life consists in 'love and charity shown outwardly in good works, and performing the seven corporal and spiritual works of mercy for the benefit of our fellow-Christians'. This is 'the life suited to those who live in the world, and who enjoy wealth and ample goods'. They are advised to discipline their bodies by fasts and vigils; but the contemplative life is of a higher order: this is the way of 'perfect love and charity inwardly experienced through the spiritual virtues' – a life for 'those who for love of God forsake all worldly riches, honours and outward affairs, and devote themselves body and soul to the service of God in spiritual occupations'. For them, he draws up a ladder or scale by means of which they can ascend to God. They will pass through a 'glowing darkness' in which they know nothing and ask nothing, as they progress by grace towards 'Love uncreated', that is, God himself. It has been suggested that Hilton is also the author of *The Cloud of Unknowing*, but this is now thought unlikely.

Hilton may have left the Augustinian Order to become a Carthusian, adopting the Charterhouse monks' more ascetic and solitary way of life; but this is not certain, and he is thought to have died at Thurgarten.

The Ladder of Perfection is published in many editions, including a translation from the fourteenth-century English by Leo Sherley-Price (1957). There are manuscript copies in the British Museum and the Bodleian Library at Oxford. See also Evelyn Underhill (1923); *D.N.B.*, 9, pp. 886–7; *N.C.E.*, 6, pp. 1119–20; *Dict. Spir.*, 7, pt 1, cols 525–30.

Oscar Romero (1917–80)   [*Commem.*]

This quiet and unassuming priest was seen as a safe choice as archbishop of El Salvador, a country riven with political and social conflict. He came from a poor peasant family in a remote area, went to a seminary in San Miguel, and graduated at the Gregorian University in Rome. He was ordained in 1942, and became secretary to his diocese – an orthodox and somewhat conservative cleric with a devotion to Our Lady of Peace. He took no part in the upheavals in the Roman

Catholic Church which followed Vatican II. He became an auxiliary bishop in 1970, bishop of Santiago de Maria in 1974, and archbishop of El Salvador in 1977, standing for the eternal verities against the winds of change; but a belief in the eternal verities inevitably brought him into conflict with a repressive and corrupt military dictatorship.

He was moved to sharp protest as bishop of Santiago de Maria when military forces raided a hamlet in his diocese, killing five peasants. He wrote in anger and pain to the president, and started a newspaper, *El Apóstol*, which campaigned for justice for the masses suffering from poverty and destitution under an unjust régime. By the time he became archbishop, there was a concerted campaign against him.When he preached, government agents sat in the congregation with tape-recorders, and his statements were deliberately misinterpreted. When he put forward plans for public works and housing for the poor, he was accused of being a Marxist. Government-inspired allegations were made against him in the Press by 'the Salvadorean Catholic Association' and 'the Association of Catholic Women' – bodies which did not exist. He continued to make it plain that he was no revolutionary: he spoke only for Christian justice, without political affiliation. In May 1979, he went to Rome, where he had an audience with the pope and deposited seven dossiers containing information about the conditions in El Salvador.

In October 1979, there was a military coup which plunged El Salvador into further repression and chaos. The National Guard and the police terrorized the country. Priests were murdered: anyone thought to be a trouble-maker was liable to disappear without trace. Archbishop Romero preached on Christ's temptation in the wilderness, saying, 'Let them not keep killing those of us who are trying to achieve a more just sharing of the wealth and power of our country.' Though he knew that his life was in danger, he continued to speak out with courage against the oppressors.

He moved into a cancer hospital run by a religious Order to escape from the pressures of office. On 15 March 1980, he took the funeral of a murdered Christian Democrat. On 24 March, he celebrated a funeral Mass for the mother of a friend, praying that the sacraments of bread and wine might strengthen the congregation: 'that we may give our body and our blood to suffering and pain – like Christ, not for self, but to give concepts of justice and peace to our people'. As he prayed, a shot rang out, and he died at the altar for his beliefs. His killer was never caught.

Archbishop Romero is included among the twentieth-century martyrs whose statues stand on the west front of Westminster Abbey. His quiet resistance to evil caught the imagination of the world, though, tragically, the evils continue in his own troubled country.

James Brockman, *Romero: a Life* (New York, 1982); Jon Sobrino, *Archbishop Romero: memories and reflections* (New York, 1990); Philip Berryman in Chandler, pp. 159–181. *The Violence of Love: the pastoral wisdom of Archbishop Oscar Romero*, ed. James Brockman (San Francisco, 1988).

26. Harriet Monsell (1811–83)   *[Commem.]*

Harriet was the daughter of an Irish baronet. When she was eighteen, she married Charles Monsell, son of the archdeacon of Derry, who became his father's curate, and then a prebendary of Limerick. Her husband developed tuberculosis, which was then incurable, and in 1850, they travelled to southern Italy, where the climate was thought to be beneficial. He died in Naples. Harriet describes in her journal how she watched and waited in his final hours, and then found herself 'alone with God'. She went to stay with her sister and brother-in-law at Clewer, near Windsor, and the vicar of Clewer, the Revd T. T. Carter, helped her through her long period of grief.

She determined to devote the remainder of her life to Christian service, and began to help in his project for prostitutes and unmarried mothers in a 'House of Mercy'. *Dr Pusey's call for Anglican sisterhoods met her need. In 1851, with the consent of the Bishop of Oxford, Samuel Wilberforce, Harriet adopted a religious habit, and was formally clothed as a Sister of Mercy. During the following year, two other women came to join her, and in November 1852 they were professed as members of the Community of St John the Baptist in the presence of the bishop. Bishop Wilberforce was concerned that the new community should not move too close to Roman Catholic models for women's Orders. He expressed doubts about the introduction of private confession, a practice encouraged by Pusey and Newman, and at one point removed all the crucifixes from the house. At the same time, Father Carter, an enthusiastic Tractarian, encouraged Catholic practice in the community, but placed it under the direction of an all-male committee, holding that 'a woman cannot be recognized a responsible authority – this is not in accordance with Scripture and natural law'. It seems likely that only the fact that Harriet was the Hon. Mrs Monsell (her brother had succeeded as Lord Inchilquin) gave her the authority to become an effective superior.

As Mother Harriet, she became known as a wise counsellor. Her advice was simple and practical. 'Plans are God's, not yours,' she would say. 'Leave them to him, and let him gradually unfold what he would have you do.' Queen Victoria visited the community from Windsor, and thought her 'an excellent person', commenting with some surprise that the house was 'pretty, not gloomy'. The work of the Community at Clewer was rapidly extended. Sisters served in orphanages, schools, hospitals and missions, and foundations were made in India and the United States.

Mother Harriet retired as superior in 1875 because of ill-health, and spent the last eight years of her life in a cottage near the community house in Folkestone.

T. T. Carter, *Harriet Monsell: a memoir* (undated); anon., *The Founders of Clewer: a short account of the Rev. T. T. Carter and Harriet Monsell to celebrate the Centenary of the Community of St John the Baptist in 1952* (1952); Valerie Bonham, *A Joyous Service* (Windsor, 1989); *Victorian Church*, i, pp. 509–11; *Far Above Rubies*, pp. 161–74.

31. John Donne (1572–1631)   [*Commem.*]

Donne, who became the outstanding apologist of his generation for the Anglican Church, was born into a staunch Catholic family. His mother was a descendant of *Thomas More's sister. His uncle, Jasper Heywood, became superior of the English Jesuits, the first mission priests sent from Rome to re-convert Elizabethan England to the Roman Catholic faith; but as a student at Oxford, and later at Cambridge, John developed an independent and enquiring mind. In 1591, when he was nineteen or twenty years old, he moved to London to study law at Lincoln's Inn, and came in contact with the new thinking of his day. It was an intellectual liberation. Copernicus and Galileo had opened up the heavens, and produced a new cosmology. Columbus and Cortés and Raleigh had opened up the Americas. In this marvellous age of discovery, the old mediaeval certainties no longer held men's minds. He began to find his own way through the current complexities of religious belief, and his horizons broadened. He came to recognize the barbarity of religious persecution by Protestants and

Catholics alike, and could subscribe neither to Rome nor to Calvin's Geneva. He wrote:

> To adore or scorn an image, or protest
> May all be bad. Doubt wisely: in strange way
> To stand inquiring right is not to stray;
> To doubt or run wrong is.

He took his time in doubting wisely, and employed all his gifts of scholarship in working out how he could worship with integrity. During this period, he lived the life of any young Elizabethan lawyer of good family with a taste for scholarship and adventure. The imagery of his poems suggests that he also became familiar with the grimmer side of London life – with prisons and the surgeons' dissecting rooms.

For some fourteen years, he and his young wife lived in penury as a result of a marriage which roused the wrath of her uncle, his eminent patron. 'John Donne, Anne Donne, Un-done,' he lamented. He wrote poetry, and he read exhaustively, studying canon and civil law.

Donne has had his detractors, perhaps motivated by sectarian bitterness, who have accused him of place-seeking; but it was not until 1615, when he was forty-three years old, that he was finally prepared to accept the Anglican position. He was made deacon and ordained priest on the same day in January 1615 by the bishop of London.

His main concern was with theological scholarship – the laborious work of exegesis, of assiduous preparation, and of writing long and carefully scripted sermons. If his sixteenth-century prose, spiced with epigrams, alliteration and every other literary device of the age, is too elaborate for modern taste, it greatly appealed to his contemporaries. It is said that all London flocked to hear him preach; and his sermons have been published in ten volumes.

His teaching was essentially sacramental: he said that the sacraments 'exhibit and convey grace; and grace is such a light, such a torch, such a beacon, as where it is, it is easily seen'. He recognized the Eucharist as the central Christian act of worship, but could not support either the Roman Catholic view that the elements became literally the Body and Blood of Christ, nor the Protestant view that the service was merely a memorial. He refused to define the manner of Christ's presence in the sacrament, because God had not revealed the nature of the mystery in the Scriptures for the guidance of the Church.

In 1621, he became dean of St Paul's, a position of much honour.

He remained there for ten years, working assiduously in the ecclesiastical courts and on cathedral business. His preoccupation with death in his final years earned him the title of 'the gloomy Dean'. He died on 31 March 1631 after posing for a drawing of himself in a shroud, and his memorial in St Paul's cathedral is taken from this drawing.

Perhaps the best clue to the personality of this complex and enigmatic man, from his time as a carefree student and witty young man about town to his care-laden old age, comes from his poems. In the context of English Literature, they are usually divided into two categories: the 'love poems', assigned to his youth, and the 'divine poems', assigned to his period in Holy Orders; but the quality and consistency of his religious belief comes through in both. Donne is a metaphysical poet, always conscious of the invisible world beyond the senses. The best of the love poems give joyous expression to a love between a man and a woman which is deeply sacramental and has a cosmic significance. He was enough of a neo-Platonist to believe that human life was a microcosm of the mighty activity of God's greater creations, the stars and the planets. His consciousness of sin was strong, but the greatest Christians often have the strongest sense of sin; and he was not gloomy about death: he had looked death in the face, and had seen beyond it to the eternal purpose of the Creator.

W. M. Mueller, *John Donne: Preacher* (Princeton, 1962); Isaac Walton, *Lives* (1640); Sir Richard Baker, ed., *A Chronicle of the Kings of England*, p. 450; D.N.B., 5, pp. 1128–39; E. M. Simpson and G. R. Potter, *The Sermons of John Donne*, (10 vols, 1930–62); J. B. Leishman, *The Monarch of Wit: an Analytical and Comparative Study of the Poetry of John Donne* (1951); Milton A. Rugoff, *Donne's Imagery* (New York 1962); *John Donne, The Complete English Poems*, ed. A. J. Smith (1971); Itrat Husain, *The Dogmatic and Mystical Theology of John Donne* (1971); Peter Amadeus Fiori, ed., *Just So Much Honour: Essays commemorating the Four-Hundredth Anniversary of the Birth of John Donne* (1972); John Carey, *John Donne, Life, Mind and Art* (1981).

April

1. Frederick Denison Maurice (1805–72) [Commem.]

While Evangelicals and Tractarians clashed in the mid-nineteenth century, a different kind of movement led by Frederick Denison Maurice and his colleague Charles Kingsley began to make its mark. They were largely uninterested in the questions of doctrine which shook the ancient universities: their concern was with the world of their own generation. They were 'Christian Socialists' in the sense that they brought a new social emphasis to Christian living. They were essentially inclusive in their philosophy: they looked for unity between the churches and unity between rich and poor, and their means was the education of the working classes.

Maurice was the son of a Unitarian minister. After attending Cambridge as a Dissenter, he took up a literary career in London. Samuel Taylor Coleridge persuaded him to become an Anglican, and he went back to Cambridge to prepare for ordination. He returned to London as chaplain to Guy's Hospital and then to Lincoln's Inn. He and Charles Kingsley, who was vicar of a parish in Hampshire and the author of *The Water Babies*, supported the Chartist movement in 1848, and started a newspaper, *The Christian Socialist*. Their *Tracts for Priests and People* were widely distributed, and Maurice became President of the Society for Promoting Working Men's Associations. There were no public libraries before 1850, and cheap literature was almost inevitably anti-religious. In 1854, his commitment to the education of the working classes led to the foundation of the Working Men's College, and he became its first principal. In 1846, he was appointed a professor at King's College, London, teaching English Literature, Modern History and Theology, and he helped his sister and the other founders of Queen's College for Women, which opened in 1854.

Maurice was frequently criticized in the two ancient universities because his intellectual interests were broad rather than deep: but his task of bringing knowledge to people without educational advantages necessitated a broad approach. He also attracted hostility from extreme Anglo-Catholics and extreme Evangelicals because of his indifference to doctrinal issues. He was dismissed from his post at King's College in 1853 for not being sufficiently enthusiastic about the pains of hell. He said, 'I am obliged to believe in an abyss of love which is deeper than the abyss of death; I dare not lose faith in that love. I sink into death, eternal death, if I do.' To him, Christianity was not a set of intellectual propositions but a response to the living God. He continued to write, and in 1866 he was finally offered a Chair of Moral Theology by his own university, Cambridge, which he occupied until his death in 1872.

F. Maurice, ed., *The Life of Frederick Dennison Maurice chiefly told in his own Letters* (2 vols, 1884); A. R. Vidler, *F. D. Maurice and Company* (1960); Ian T. Ramsey, *On Being Sure in Religion* (Maurice Lectures at King's College, 1963). *Victorian Church*, I, pp. 346–63, 547–9. Maurice's writings include *The Kingdom of Christ* (1838); *What is Revelation?* (1859); *Theological Essays* (1853); *The Conscience* (Cambridge Lectures, 1868).

9. Dietrich Bonhoeffer (1906–45)   *[Commem.]*

Dietrich Bonhoeffer was born in Breslau in 1906, the son of an eminent psychiatrist. He studied in Tübingen and Berlin, where he was much influenced by the teaching of Karl Barth, and was ordained into the Lutheran Church. Like Barth, he believed that his Church must return to the principles of the Reformation, and that a transcendent God had revealed himself to the human race only through the life of Christ and the Scriptures. His teaching inevitably brought him into conflict with those who supported Nazism, with its semi-mystical appeal to Aryan dominance, Hegelian dialectic and near-paganism. When the Weimar Republic collapsed in 1933, and the Nazis took control, he opposed the persecution of the Jews, and was forced to leave Germany.

By this time, Bonhoeffer already had an international reputation as a Protestant theologian. He had lectured in Spain and in the United States, and from 1933 to 1935 he ministered to German congregations in London, and made clear his unequivocal opposition to the activities of Hitler's Third Reich. He undertook a major lecture tour in the

United States, and became well known in ecumenical circles as an interpreter of what was happening in Germany. He was working with C. F. Andrews, the author of *The Christ of the Indian Road*, on a projected visit to Gandhi when he received a call asking him to return to his own country to lead the work of a breakaway group of Lutheran theologians and their students. He thus became one of the leaders of the 'Confessing Church' which opposed the Nazi régime. Forbidden to preach in Germany by the Nazi authorities, in 1937 he published *The Cost of Discipleship*.

In 1939, when on a lecture tour in the United States, he caught one of the last ships returning to Germany before the outbreak of the Second World War – knowing that his life would be in danger, but prepared for martyrdom. In 1943 he was arrested and imprisoned. His *Letters and Papers from Prison* are an eloquent testimony both to his faith and to his sufferings.

In one letter he wrote to a friend that 'we must throw ourselves completely into the arms of God, taking seriously, not our own sufferings, but those of God in the world – watching with Christ in Gethsemane'.

He struggled with his own doubts and fears. In the poem 'Who am I?' he asks whether he is really a brave man prepared for martyrdom, or a lonely and frightened weakling. He thinks that at best there is something in him 'still like a beaten army / Fleeing in disorder from victory already achieved'. Only God knows who he is; and he clings to God in the face of desolation. This was his own Gethsemane.

Pastor Bonhoeffer was hanged at Flossenbürg concentration camp on 9 April 1945, only a month before it was liberated by the Allied Forces. On the west front of Westminster Abbey his statue is among those of the twentieth-century martyrs.

Audrey Constant, *The Last Days of Dietrich Bonhoeffer* (1983); Charles Marsh, *Reclaiming Dietrich Bonhoeffer* (1994); Ian Stockton with Hugh Searle, *Bonhoeffer Fifty Years On* (1994); Klemens von Kemperer in Chandler, pp. 81–101. *Twentieth Century*, pp. 100–1; Stephen Plant (2000), Works: *Sanctorum Communio* (1927); English translations: *Art and Being* (1931); *The Cost of Discipleship* (1948); *Ethics* (published posthumously, 1949); *Letters and Papers from Prison* (1953) contains a memoir by the editor, Eberhard Bethge.

10. **William of Ockham** (d. 1349) *[Commem.]*

The date of William's birth is not known. He is thought to have come from the village of Ockham (Occam in his day) in Surrey. He studied at Oxford, probably under Duns Scotus, and became a Franciscan friar. He took his BD at Oxford, and his DD at the Sorbonne in Paris. His field of study was the history and nature of logical thought, and the term 'Occam's razor' comes from his maxim that 'it is vain to do with more what can be done with less': that is, explanations should involve as few assumptions as possible.

William became involved in a controversy between the Franciscans and Pope John XXII over whether Christ and his disciples ever owned any property: Franciscans took a vow of absolute poverty, while the papacy was wealthy. The Dominicans accused him of errors and heresy, and he was called to Avignon to be examined by a papal commission. He was imprisoned for some time (probably four months rather than the four years which are sometimes quoted) and then fled to the protection of the Holy Roman Emperor, Ludwig of Bavaria. He stayed for a time in Padua, where he is thought to have influenced the political philosopher Marsiglio of Padua, who wrote against the temporal power of the papacy and bishops. He moved to a Franciscan house in Munich, where he wrote many works, including *De dogmatibus Papae Johannis XXII*, opposing the pope's views on the saints, and *Compendium errorum papae*, in which he accused the pope of seven heresies and seventy-seven errors. He argued that popes could be 'stupid, inexperienced, corrupted by wicked passions and desires, malicious, and in every way remote from the life and wisdom of the clergy'; and that papal governance had been set up by Christ not for the sake of popes, but for the sake of the people. His own Order supported him, and he died at Munich, unreconciled to the pope. He had planned a great work in ten treatises, but only two of these (on the authority of the pope and clergy, and on the authority of the emperor) were completed.

L. Wadding, ed., *Annales Minorum*, (Rome, 1736) vols 7, 8; E. A. Moody, *The Logic of William of Ockham* (1935); L. Baudry, *Guillaume d'Occam* (1939); C. Giaco (1945); A. S. Brett, *On the Power of Emperor and Pope* (1998); R. L. Poole, *Illustrations of the History of Mediaeval Thought* (1881), pp. 276–81; *D.N.B.*, 14, pp. 802–7. Works: *A Short Discourse on Tyrannical Government*, trans. J. Kilcullen, ed. A. S. McGrade (1992).

William Law (1686–1761)   [L.F.]

Law was a Fellow of Emmanuel College, Cambridge and a Classics specialist at the time when George of Hanover became king of England. The Hanoverian succession revived the 'non-juring' controversy, for while clerics and university teachers could conscientiously swear allegiance to the daughters of Charles II, some held that the crown must revert to 'the king over the water', rather than go to the Protestant descendants of the Electress of Hanover. William Law took this view, and was eventually forced to resign his fellowship.

He became private tutor to the family of Mr Edward Gibbon, father of the historian. He was ordained priest in 1728, and was said to be the 'much honoured friend and spiritual director of the whole family'. This would not have included the future author of *The Decline and Fall of the Roman Empire*, who was not born until 1737 and was only three years old when his father died. After the elder Gibbon's death, Law returned to his native village, King's Cliffe, Northamptonshire, as a member of a remarkable household. The other members were two elderly ladies, Edward Gibbon's sister and her friend Mrs Hutcheson. The three appear to have pooled their incomes, which amounted to some £3,000 a year, and to have spent only about £300 a year, devoting the rest to charity. They lived a very regular and devout life, summoning the servants for devotions three times a day.

Their charities were many: Law set up a home for fourteen destitute girls, and Mrs Hutcheson one for fourteen boys, besides caring for four deserving widows. These and other benefactions raised the wrath of the rector of the parish, who wrote to Law to complain that he and the two ladies were attracting 'idle vagrants, shiftless spongers and incorrigible rogues' to the village, and giving the lower orders ideas above their station.

This tranquil, structured life gave Law the freedom to read and to write. He spent most of every day in his study, meditating on the works of Jacob Böhme, *Francis de Sales, Fénelon and other mystical writers; and he followed his classic work, *A Serious Call to a Devout and Holy Life*, with a number of other works which showed a genuine spirituality in a very materialistic age. He inspired *Dr Johnson, a convinced Anglican, *John and *Charles Wesley and that other prominent Methodist, George Whitefield. It was later said, perhaps in jest, that he was the true founder of Methodism. His literary style was clear and lucid in an age when florid writing was still the fashion, and his comments on contemporary follies were often sharp and witty. Even the author of *The Decline and Fall of the Roman Empire*, himself a rationalist, said of Law that 'if he finds a spark of piety in his reader's mind, he will soon kindle it into a flame'.

A. W. Hopkinson, *About William Law* (1848); J. H. Overton, *William Law, Non-Juror and Mystic* (1881); *D.N.B.*, 11, pp. 677–81; *Bridge Builders*, pp. 24–44. Works: *Selected Writings of William Law*, ed. S. H. Hobhouse (1927); *A Serious Call to a Devout and Holy Life* (1728, now in several editions).

11. George Augustus Selwyn (1809–78)　　　　[*Commem.*]

Very few Anglican clergymen are offered a bishopric at the age of thirty-two; but George Augustus Selwyn had distinguished himself at Eton, where a fellow-student was *John Henry Newman, and at Cambridge. He became a Doctor of Divinity, was ordained in 1833, and served a curacy at Windsor. When this able and well-connected young man expressed an interest in distant New Zealand, which came under British jurisdiction in 1840, he was offered the bishopric. He left England on 26 December 1841, ten weeks after his consecration. He was a man of many skills and boundless energy. The journey was a long and hazardous one: by the time he arrived, he had learned Maori, and also learned to sail a ship.

His first task was to make a thorough visitation of the North and South Islands. He travelled over rough territory, meeting the Maoris, talking with them in their own language, and getting to know their problems. After that, he undertook a journey under sail to the Pacific Islands. It was due to his efforts and inspiration that *John Coleridge Patteson was consecrated as the first bishop of Melanesia. In 1854, he was back in England with plans for subdividing his diocese and developing synodical government. The English bishops were impressed with his plans: bishops were appointed for the North and South Islands respectively, and New Zealand had its first general synod in 1859.

As archbishop, he unhesitatingly championed the Maoris against greedy land companies which tried to buy up or annexe their land, and during the Maori War of 1855 he acted as a peace-maker between the two groups – a role which led him into considerable personal danger, since he was attacked by both sides. He is counted as one of the founders of modern New Zealand.

He was fifty-eight years old when he finally relinquished his arch-bishopric and returned to England. He became bishop of Lichfield, married, and had two sons. His son John subsequently became the second bishop of Melanesia, after Bishop Patteson's death at the hands of tribesmen. Selwyn College, Cambridge was founded from subscriptions raised in memory of Bishop John Selwyn, but is also a fitting memorial to his father's work.

Memoirs: H. W. Tucker, (2 vols., 1879) G. H. Curteis (1879); SPCK pamphlet (1918); *The Times*, 12 Apr. 1878; *D.N.B.*,17, pp. 1170-1; Charles E. Fox, *Lord of the Southern Isles: the story of the Anglican Mission in Melanesia, 1849–1949* (1958), pp. 1–11. Stock, ch. 28. *Letters on the Melanesian Mission* (1855).

16. Isabella Gilmore (1842–1925)   [*Commem.*]

Isabella was a younger sister of the Victorian artist, craftsman and writer William Morris. Since there were nine children in the family, and William saw little of his brothers and sisters in later life, his biographers say little or nothing about Isabella. She is said to have 'resembled William in her looks'. She married a naval officer, and when he died, she determined to become a hospital nurse. Her family was horrified, for despite the pioneer work of *Florence Nightingale and her companions, nursing was still not regarded as a suitable profession for a lady, and they thought that she had let them down socially. She worked at Guy's Hospital for a time, until Bishop Thorold of Rochester asked her to pioneer the work of deaconesses in his diocese. They planned the work together, and Isabella was made deaconess in 1887 at the age of 45.

Though somewhat earlier foundations for women's work had been in the form of religious communities (see *Elizabeth Ferard, *Harriet Monsell), the Rochester deaconesses set a different pattern with a status of its own, closer to that of a deacon. In 1908, Mrs Gilmore wrote a paper on 'Deaconesses, their Qualifications and Status' in which she stated: 'Those who are admitted . . . cannot be dispensed from it as from a vow, but they receive character which is life-long'. The deaconess should be 'a sort of mother to the parish', but much of the teaching work was in practice restricted to Sunday Schools and groups for women and girls. Charles Booth, author of the 17-volume *Life and Labour of the People in London*, commended the work of the deaconesses, but spoke of their 'helpful subordination' to the parish clergy.

Mrs Gilmore worked in the slums of South London, becoming head of the Rochester and Southwark Mission. She trained head deaconesses for at least seven other dioceses. The Lambeth Conference in 1920 resolved that 'the Order of Deaconesses is for women the one and only Order of Ministry which we can recommend that our branch of the Catholic Church should recognise and use'. At Mrs Gilmore's funeral in 1923, the archbishop of Canterbury, Dr Randall Davidson, attributed much of the revival of the Deaconess Order to her life and example. There is a plaque commemorating her work in Southwark Cathedral.

In 1930, the next Lambeth Conference effectively quashed any claims to independent status for deaconesses by resolving that they were not female deacons, but 'outside the historic Orders of the Ministry – supplementary and complementary to them'.

Jack Lindsey, *William Morris, His Life and Work* (1995) pp. 36–7; Cecilia Robinson's *The Ministry of Deaconesses* (1908) contains a long appendix written by her brother, a professor of Divinity, on 'Deaconesses in the Apostolic Constitutions'; Brian Heeney, *The Women's Movement in the Church of England, 1850–1930* (1971).

19. Alphege (c.953–1012) [L.F.]

During Dunstan's time as archbishop of Canterbury, there was a considerable revival of monastic life. Alphege joined a community at Deerhurst in Gloucester for some years, and then spent time as a hermit in Somerset, attracting a number of younger men as disciples and sending them to Dunstan's reformed monastery at Bath. Dunstan appointed him abbot of Bath, and in 984 he was consecrated bishop of Winchester, where he became celebrated for the holiness of his personal life and his generous almsgiving.

The Danes were pressing on the borders of Wessex, and carrying out extensive border raids. In 994, King Ethelred of Wessex sent Alphege to negotiate with their leaders, Sweyn and Anlaf. Sweyn was converted to Christianity, and though the Anglo-Saxons agreed to pay tribute to the Danes, he promised not to invade their territory again.

Alphege became archbishop of Canterbury in 1005: but though Sweyn kept his promise, there were new pagan Danish raiders, and

Ethelred was unable to contain them, even by the paying of Danegeld. In 1011 they overran much of southern England and besieged Canterbury. Alphege and a number of local magnates were imprisoned, and most were released on payment of a large ransom; but the ransom demanded for the archbishop was the huge sum of £3,000. Alphege refused to meet this demand, and forbade his people to raise the money. The Danes were outraged by this defiance, and at a drunken feast, they attacked him with blows from the huge bones of an ox, and finally killed him with an axe.

Alphege became a hero to the Anglo-Saxons. When Canute, who was a Christian, became king in 1017, he initiated a policy of reconciliation between Saxons and Danes. Alphege's remains were taken from St Paul's cathedral in London to Canterbury cathedral, where the monks venerated his shrine morning and evening.

After the Norman Conquest, *Lanfranc was less respectful of Anglo-Saxon traditions, and proposed to remove Alphege from the new Calendar; but he consulted *Anselm, then abbot of Bec, and that man of principle replied that Alphege was a martyr for justice, just as John the Baptist was a martyr for truth. Lanfranc accepted this judgement, and a monk of Canterbury named Osbern was commissioned to write a life and an office for Alphege.

In his last sermon before his own martyrdom, *Thomas Becket described Alphege as Canterbury's first martyr, and shortly before his death he commended himself to God and St Alphege.

AA.SS., Apr., 2, pp. 627–41; Osbern, *Vita S. Elphegi*, in H. Wharton, ed., *Anglia Sacra*, 2, (1691), pp. 122–47; Florence of Worcester, *Chronicles*, trans. T. Forrester, 1854, 1, pp. 165–6; Eadmer, *Life of St Anselm*, ed. R. W. Southern (1963); O.D.S., pp. 17–18; D.N.B., 1, pp. 150–2.

21. Anselm (1033–1109)   [L.F.]

Anselm was born at Aosta in northern Italy, the son of a Lombardian nobleman. He spent several years visiting monasteries and other centres of learning in France and Normandy, and was attracted to Bec-Hellouin by the teaching of *Lanfranc. He remained at Bec for thirty-four years, and achieved an international reputation as a scholar. His meditations and prayers became widely known, and in 1077–8 he wrote his *Monologion* and *Proslogion*, metaphysical works on the nature of being which included some fine poetry.

Anselm became abbot of Bec when Herluin died in 1078; and when Lanfranc died ten years later, he was considered the obvious candidate to succeed him as archbishop of Canterbury. William Rufus kept the archbishopric vacant for four years, largely because he wanted the very large revenues accruing from it, only giving way to pressure from the clergy in 1093, when he thought he was dying; but Anselm did not want the post: he protested that he was a monk and a scholar: he had no knowledge of or interest in statecraft or politics, and was quite unfitted for the appointment. He was installed as archbishop, still loudly protesting, and almost immediately came into conflict with the king. William Rufus was a violent man with a furious temper, while Anselm had no capacity for negotiation or compromise.

Their main differences came over the question of lay investiture. Archbishops and bishops had a double loyalty: as feudal overlords, they owed fealty and homage to the Crown for their estates and revenues; but in matters spiritual, they owed allegiance to the pope. Feudal monarchs (not only in England) claimed the right of appointment to ecclesiastical offices, and were apt to appoint their own kin or their major supporters, sometimes with scant regard to their suitability.

Anselm did not have the authority to hold a council of bishops or to consecrate new bishops until he had received the *pallium*, his symbol of office (see *Agnes) from the pope. He supported Pope Urban II, whom he had already acknowledged in his capacity as abbot of Bec. William Rufus supported an anti-pope. Relations between the infuriated monarch and the unbending archbishop deteriorated to such an extent that the king secretly sent a mission to Pope Urban II offering to acknowledge his position in return for the deposition of Anselm – thus humiliating his archbishop. The pope sent a papal legate to England to investigate the situation. The king acknowledged Urban, expecting Anselm to be deposed, but the legate then refused to depose Anselm – thus humiliating the king. In the next two years, Anselm made several requests to be allowed to go to Rome, but was refused permission. William Rufus had a fresh cause for fury when he demanded a levy of troops from his archbishop to undertake a war against the Welsh, and Anselm sent him raw and untrained men. Anselm went to Rome in November 1097 without leave from the king. There he was treated with great honour, and received his *pallium*; but he was unable to return to England, and remained in exile until the death of William Rufus in 1099. He spent part of his time in Italy, waiting for Pope Urban to excommunicate Rufus; but the pope never quite came to the point of doing so. Then he moved to France to stay with his old friend, Hugh, archbishop of Lyons. While he was in exile, he wrote his great treatise on the Incarnation, *Cur Deus Homo?*

He returned to England in 1100. Henry I, the new king, demanded homage. Anselm refused curtly. In 1103, he went into exile again over the issue. In 1105, Pope Paschal II excommunicated the bishops of Winchester, Hereford and Salisbury, who had done homage to Henry I, and Anselm threatened to excommunicate the king. A settlement was eventually negotiated by Bishop Ivo of Chartres, the friend and confidant of Henry's sister, Countess Adela of Blois. Like his predecessor, Pope Paschal was not willing, in the last resort, to sacrifice the support of a powerful Norman king for a principle: thereafter, the Church invested a bishop or archbishop with the staff and ring of office, but the king continued to make the appointments.

Anselm died only two years after his return to England. Of his nineteen years in office, seventeen had been spent in conflict with the Crown, and seven of these in exile. He was widely criticized among the clergy for his long absences, but he held more firmly to papal privilege than either Urban II or Paschal II.

The two major ecclesiastical decisions made during Anselm's time at Canterbury concerned the primacy of Canterbury over York and the celibacy of the clergy, but neither achieved a lasting settlement. After his death, Thurstan of York and his canons were to raise again the issue of the independence of the northern province, and to secure a temporary victory; while Henry I continued to issue licences to married clergy on payment of a fee (or fine) which went to the royal coffers.

Anselm's reputation owes more to his scholarship than to his politics. He was described by the compiler of the *Oxford Dictionary of Saints* as 'the most important Christian writer between Augustine and Aquinas'.

Contemporary Life by Eadmer, trans. and ed. R. W. Southern (1962); *AA.SS.*, Apr., 2, pp. 865–953; R. W. Southern (1991). Works, ed. F. S. Schmitt (7 vols, 1938–70). For an alternative view to Eadmer's of the controversy over the primacy, see Hugh the Chanter's *History of the Church of York, 1066–1127*, trans. and ed. C. Johnson, rev. M. Brett, C. N. L. Brooke, M. Winterbottom (1990).

23. George (d. *c*.303)   Festival

St George's fame spread throughout Christendom, and he is venerated as a saint in the Anglican, Roman Catholic, Eastern Orthodox and Coptic traditions. He is the patron of England, and also a patron of Venice, Genoa, Portugal, Aragon, Lithuania and Georgia. He is one of the Fourteen Holy Helpers in a fourteenth-century cult which spread from the Rhine Valley across Germany to Hungary and Sweden. He even occurs in Islamic tradition, where he is linked with Elias and named as El Khadar, the Living One. Yet very little is known about him apart from the fact of his martyrdom, which probably occurred in the persecutions of Diocletian.

He did not, as far as we know, slay a dragon and rescue a maiden. There are various suggested explanations for this story, but it does not appear to have been known until the eleventh century. One explanation is that it developed as a result of a misinterpretation by the Crusaders of an image in Constantinople, showing the emperor Constantine destroying the devil in the form of a serpent. Another is that the Greek legend of Perseus, who slew the Gorgon to save the virgin Andromeda, became confused with George's tradition.

In the fourth century, Eusebius of Caesarea mentioned the heroic exploits of a knight who is probably George, but did not give his name. Pope Gelasius, who died in 496, cited George in a decree as one among those 'whose names are greatly reverenced by men, but whose acts are known only to God'.

He is thought to have died as a martyr at Lydda, now Lod, in Israel. A monastery was dedicated in his name in Jerusalem in the fifth century, and his tomb at Lydda was visited by pilgrims from about the same time. There is a tradition that he came from Cappadocia in Asia Minor, but the Bollandist Father Delehaye takes the view that his legend became confused with that of George of Cappadocia, an opponent of *St Athanasius. Another tradition is that his mother was a Cappadocian. *Jerome included his name in the *Hieronymianum*.

George's martyrdom was known in England in Anglo-Saxon times: it occurs in the *Martyrology* of *Bede, and in the *Felire* or martyrology of the Ulster monk Oengus or Angus the Culdee, who died *c*.864. Oengus refers to him as 'George, a sun of victories with thirty great thousand', though it is not clear whether the thirty thousand were converts or companions in martyrdom.

The Crusaders brought back a new devotion to St George: the *Gesta Francorum* records that at the siege of Antioch in the First Crusade, a vision of St George and St Demetrius assisted the Crusaders in the defeat of the Saracens, and he became the patron saint of soldiers. In the Third Crusade, Richard I placed himself and his army under St George's special protection. We do not know whether Henry V actually invoked him before the battle of Agincourt as in Shakespeare's celebrated speech; but it is recorded fact that in 1415, after the battle, Archbishop Chichele of Canterbury raised George's commemoration to a major feast. Edward III may have originated the cry of 'St George for England!' when he adopted him as the patron saint of the Order of the Garter. By this time, George had become an honorary Englishman: in a comparatively late version of the legend, he is represented as having come to England via Ireland. The name of 'St George's Channel' for the Irish Sea is said to come from this version.

The popularity of St George, who has figured in many mystery plays, folk festivals and even pantomime, seems to come from the theme of the triumph of good over evil – he is often associated with St Michael, who is credited with defeating the Great Dragon (Revelation 20:2). He also came to represent the ideal of Christian chivalry in an age of war. His name was deleted from the revised Universal Roman Calendar in 1969, but he still has the status of a national saint. The Coptic Church celebrates his feast on 18 April.

The dramatic possibilities of the story of George and the dragon have inspired many artists, notably Ucello, whose painting hangs in the Sainsbury Wing of the National Gallery in London; Raphael, in the National Gallery of Art in Washington D.C.; Mantegna, in the Louvre; and Rubens, in the Prado.

The Acts of St George, written by Pasicrates and reproduced in *AA.SS.*, Apr., 3, pp. 100–63, inspired Jacobus de Voragine (*Golden Legend*, 1, pp. 238–42). They are comparatively late, and highly suspect, since the writer claims to have been a witness of the events he describes. For sounder evidence, see H. Delehaye, *Les legendes grecques des saints militaires* (Brussels, 1909), pp. 145–96; G. J. Marcus, *Saint George of England* (1939); I. H. Elder, *George of Lydda* (1949); N.C.E., 6, pp. 354–5.

24. Mellitus (d. 624) [*Commem.*]

The second band of missionaries sent to England in 601 by *Gregory the Great to support *Augustine and his party was headed by Mellitus, who was an Italian abbot. It was to Mellitus that Gregory sent his celebrated letter instructing the missionaries not to destroy the Saxon temples, but to dispose of the pagan statues and use the temples as churches; and similarly not to ignore their feast days, but to replace them with Christian feasts.

Augustine consecrated Mellitus as bishop of the East Saxons, who were ruled by Sabert. Their area stretched as far south as London, and London, which was then wholly north of the Thames, became the bishop's seat. Ethelbert of Kent, who was the overlord of the East Saxons and Sabert's uncle, had built the first church there, dedicated to St Paul. As bishop of London, Mellitus went to Rome in 610 to take part in a synod convened by Pope Boniface IV.

Sabert became a Christian, but when he died, Mellitus came into conflict with his three sons, who demanded Holy Communion, 'the white bread', but refused to be baptized. Mellitus told them sternly that as long as they rejected the water of life, they were unfit to receive the Bread of Life. They retorted, 'We refuse to enter that font and see no need for it, but we want to be strengthened with the bread.' When Mellitus would not give way, they drove him into exile. He stayed in Gaul for a time, and then returned to Canterbury, where *Archbishop Laurence had converted King Eadbald. He succeeded Laurence as archbishop in 619.

*Bede tells us that Mellitus became cripped with gout, but that 'his sound and ardent mind overcame his troublesome infirmity'. When the city of Canterbury caught fire, and water could not save the wooden houses, he had himself carried, infirm as he was, into the path of the 'leaping and darting' flames near the church of the Four Crowned Martyrs. He prayed. The wind changed; and 'the fires burned out and died'.

Mellitus died on 24 April 624, and was buried near Augustine in the abbey church at Canterbury.

Bede, bk 1, chs 29—30, bk 2, chs 3—8; *AA.SS.*, Apr., 3, pp. 280–3; Mayr-Harting, pp. 336–8; *N.C.E.*, 9, pp. 336–8.

25. Mark the Evangelist (first century)   Festival

Mark is the name of the author of the second Gospel. John Mark accompanied *Paul and *Barnabas to Cyprus, and left them in circumstances which caused a rift between them (Acts 15:37-9). Mark was with Paul in Rome (Colossians 4:10), and *Peter writes of his presence there in his first Epistle. Traditionally, John Mark is identified as the young man who fled, leaving his garment in the hands of his pursuers, after Christ was arrested (Mark 14:51-2). Do all this references apply to the same person? Mark was a very common name in both Roman and Greek society, but there are two references in the Acts of the Apostles to 'John, whose other name was Mark' (Acts, 12:12 and 25) and one to 'John who was called Mark' (Acts 15:37), so biblical scholars have generally concluded that they are one and the same.

We learn very little directly from the Gospel about the author; but we do know that he was fluent in Greek, and so probably a Hellenic Jew: the Jews of Palestine had a less firm grasp of the Greek language. Barnabas was a Greek-speaking Cypriot from Salamis, and John Mark was his cousin (Colossians 4:10) – which may explain why he defended him against Paul. This strengthens the possibility that the Mark of the Gospel is John Mark, who worked with both Paul in Cyprus and Peter in Rome.

Eusebius of Caesarea says that Mark left Rome after the death of Peter and Paul, taking Christianity to Egypt and becoming the first bishop of Alexandria.

Content analysis of the Gospels suggests that Mark's Gospel was the first of the four to be written. Matthew and Luke both draw on it, as well as on another source or sources, and John's Gospel is known to be the last of the four to be written. It is generally accepted that the Gospel according to Mark was written either in Rome about the year 65, when Peter and Paul were martyred, or in Alexandria some five years later. It is the shortest of the Gospels, focussed on the events leading to the Crucifixion and the Resurrection. It remains the basic account of the events which shaped the Christian faith.

Mark has been venerated as a martyr since at least the fourth century, and his shrine at Alexandria became a place of pilgrimage. In the early ninth century, two merchants took his relics to Venice to save them from the Turks, and they remain under the high altar in the great basilica of St Mark's. He became the patron of Venice. His emblem, the winged lion (based on Ezekiel 1:5-12 and Revelation 4:7-8), was adopted as the symbol of the Venetian Republic. It can still be seen on the pillars by the landing-stage close to the Doge's palace.

Mark appears in the work of many famous artists, such as Bellini, Titian and Tintoretto, and in the Ravenna Mosaics. As one of the Four Evangelists, he is usually shown holding a book and a pen.

B. H. Lightfoot, *The Gospel Message of St Mark* (1950), pp. 514–57; H. B. Swete (1920), ed. V. Taylor (1952); C. E. B. Cranfield (1959); J. Schmid (1959); N. R. Telford, *The Interpretation of St Mark* (1985); M. D. Hooker, *The Gospel According to Mark* (1991); P. J. Achtermeier, in *The Anchor Bible Dictionary*, 4, (1992); N.C.E., 9, pp. 231–2; O.C.B., pp. 492–6.

27. Christina Rossetti (1830–94)   [Commem.]

The Rossettis were a distinguished, turbulent and gifted family of Italian refugees to England. Christina's own life has been described as 'submerged': she lived it wholly within the family circle, and what we know about her inner turmoil and her spiritual struggles comes almost entirely from her poetry, which is of an unusually personal nature.

Her father, Gabriele Rossetti, was an Italian revolutionary who had to leave Naples in 1821, when the Bourbons were restored. He supported his family by giving Italian lessons, and became Professor of Italian at King's College, London.

The Rossetti household was talented and creative, but there were many tensions and contradictions arising from the conflict between a colourful and passionate Neapolitan heritage and the constraints of Victorian middle-class London. Professor Rossetti was a Dante scholar, a radical and an agnostic. It was his half-English wife, Francesca, who saw to it that the children were brought up as members of the Church of England. The boys, Dante Gabriel and William, later became free-thinkers like their father, but the girls, Maria and Christina, were attracted to the Oxford Movement in the early 1840s, and went with their mother to Christ Church, Albany Street, one of the first parish churches to offer the ritual and colourful ceremonial of Anglo-Catholic practice.

There were many visitors to the Rossetti household – artists, poets, writers, revolutionaries and politicians. Christina's elder brother Dante Gabriel became a leading member of the Pre-Raphaelite Brotherhood. This fellowship of young artists, including William Morris, Edward

Burne-Jones and Holman Hunt, was a male coterie, but Christina was always on its fringes. Dante Gabriel painted her many times over, most notably as the Virgin Mary in a painting undertaken in 1848–9, now in the Tate Gallery in London.

Like many English girls of her class and time, Christina was said to be 'delicate', though it is not clear whether she had any identifiable ailment. She may have been anaemic; she may have been neurotic. She saw her brothers go out into an exciting wider world. Her sister became a nun, while her own life was bounded by the family and domestic chores. The contrast between her quiet, well-chaperoned spinster life and the intense and passionate nature of her love poetry has intrigued many commentators. Whatever the details of her experience (and there has been much speculation about two possible suitors), the emotions involved were unmistakably real. She kept the details to herself.

Christina's faith was never a crutch: it was the unifying force which kept the contradictory elements in her character under control. She lived under great emotional strain, frequently depressed, and writing of herself as 'a poor dove that must not coo' and 'an eagle that must not soar'. She and her elderly mother nursed Dante Gabriel through his last few years until his death in 1882. He was a difficult patient – partially blind, and see-sawing from mania to suicidal depression under the influence of drugs.

Christina was a regular communicant. The Christmas carol 'In the bleak midwinter' and 'Up-hill' ('Does the road wind up-hill all the way?') are her best-known religious poems. In her last years, she wrote four small religious texts for SPCK which testify to the depth of her continuing religious experience and her love of the Anglican Church. In her old age, she regularly attended Christ Church, Woburn Square. She died on 29 December 1894.

Over 300 books and articles were published about Christina Rossetti between 1900 and 1932. Three biographies were published at the time of the centenary celebrations in 1930, by Mary F. Sanders, Dorothy Stuart, and Eleanor W. Thomas. There are more recent biographies by Marya Zaturenska (1949), Margaret Sawtell (1955), Georgina Battiscombe (1981), D. A. Kent (1991) and Jan Marsh (1994) among others. Edward Shillito in *Great Christians*, pp. 467–80. See also *Letters*, ed. Antony H. Harrison (Charlotteville, Virginia, 4 vols, 1997–9). Christina Rossetti's SPCK pamphlets are *Seek and Find* (1879), *Called to be Saints* (1880), *Time Flies* (1885), *The Face of the Deep* (1892).

Peter Chanel, Martyr (1808–41)   *[Commem.]*

The farm on which Pierre Louis-Marie Chanel grew up was former Church land, seized at the time of the French Revolution. He determined to devote his life to the service of the Church in reparation. After studying at a seminary in Belley, he was ordained in 1827. He was eager to go to the mission field, but he served some years as a parish priest at Crozer, near Geneva, and then taught at Belley, before this became possible. He had joined the Society of Mary or Marists, who were mission priests, and at last in 1836 he was given a missionary appointment, 'to preach the Gospel in the islands of the South Pacific Ocean'. The vagueness of this remit suggests that his superiors had very little idea of what the mission would entail. Peter's preparation was negligible. He and an assistant landed on the island of Futuna, struggled with the language, and began to preach and teach; but the traders had arrived before them, and the island was suffering from the worst excesses of colonialism. Some of the traders cheated and stole, and abused the Polynesian women. The presence of French and British gunboats, patrolling offshore to protect the traders, increased the local resentment against the Europeans, and the missionaries bore the brunt of it. In 1841, when one of the king's sons wanted to be baptized, the king was so appalled that he ordered all the missionaries to be killed.

Peter said, 'It does not matter whether I am killed. The religion has taken root on the island, and it will not be destroyed by my death, since it comes not from men but from God.' He was clubbed to death.

Only a year later, following the death of the king, the whole island became Christian. Peter Chanel was canonized by the Roman Catholic Church in 1854, and is recognized as the protomartyr of Oceania and of the Marists.

W. J. Symes (1964); P. Graystone (1994); *Butler*, Apr., pp. 195–7. Writings: *Les écrits de Saint Pierre Chanel*, ed. C. Rozier (1960).

29. Catherine of Siena (d. 1380)   [L.F.]

Raymond of Capua, who was Catherine's confessor for many years, and later the Superior-General of the Dominican Order, tells her story in the idiom of fourteenth-century Tuscany, complete with miracles and marvels. Modern readers may find fuller explanation in the circumstances of her life. She was the daughter of Giacomo Benincasa, a prosperous dyer, and his wife Lapa: their twenty-third child, one of twins. The family lived in Siena in the Street of the Dyers, almost opposite the church of San Domenico, where she could daily see the Dominican friars coming and going.

She was a child with a very strong pictorial imagination. A story is told of how, when they were children, she and her brother Stefano saw a glorious sunset behind San Domenico; but while pragmatic Stefano saw only the sun setting, Catherine saw Christ in glory. Wandering through her father's dyeing sheds, she would have seen the glowing colours of the early Italian Renaissance – the golds and scarlets and vivid blues and greens which Duccio, another Sienese, was painting in her own lifetime. Unable to read or write, she saw heavenly pictures.

She was attracted to the Dominican Order, and must have known some of the friars, for her foster-brother Tommaso della Fonte joined them. She and her small friends practised Dominican-style prayers and penances. She grew up resisting her mother's attempts to make her behave as a conventional daughter, praying, fasting and scourging herself, lamenting her sins and falling into trances. Her deep sense of guilt may have come from the fact that her twin had died. It is not uncommon for a surviving twin to feel responsibility for the death of the one who died, and self-mutilation and anorexia are ways in which young women often express distress. Catherine was determined not to marry, and she told her family that she was the bride of Christ. Long and vociferous family altercations were finally stopped by her father, who said very sensibly, 'She is to be left free and in peace to serve her Bridegroom, and continally pray for us. We could never get a bridegroom of mightier kindred.'

Catherine had a dream: she saw the Christ-child with a vine growing out of his heart. The vine bore a heavy crop of grapes, and big white dogs with black spots çame to bear bunches to the little dogs which could not reach them. The dream expressed her desire to join the Dominicans: the friars wore black and white habits, and were often called *Domini canes*, the dogs of the Lord; but she could not become a Dominican, because it was a male Order. Then she had another dream, in which she saw St Dominic holding out a religious habit to her: not the Dominican habit, but the habit of the *Mantellate*, the women tertiaries who worked with the sick and poor of the city. She was only seventeen or eighteen. Though the *Mantellate* usually accepted only older women, most of them widows, she was finally allowed to join them in response to her pleading and obvious distress.

Her problems did not cease. She was still a deeply unhappy and disturbed girl, and even the *Mantellate* became impatient at her constant tears, her violent sweats and her trances. Her psychological crisis came on Shrove Tuesday 1367. She was troubled by sexual excitement, and by the sights and sounds of carnival in the streets before the austerities of Lent. She had a vision, known as the Spiritual Espousal, in which she was married to Christ by the Blessed Virgin, with St Paul, St John the Evangelist and St Dominic as witnesses. Her troth was pledged with a gold ring which she could feel on her finger for the rest of her life.

Thereafter she was at peace, and her life changed completely. The Lord commanded her to go out and serve the poor, and she obeyed. She took food to poor families, nursed lepers (some of them very ungrateful), and nursed in the hospital when the plague came to Siena in 1374. She made regular visits to prisons, and accompanied at least one condemned man to the scaffold. Then she received another blessing: at some time in her twenties, she learned to read, teaching herself from an ABC. She read her way through the Scriptures, the Divine Office and the works of the Early Fathers. She became a scholarly and wise woman to whom many went for counsel, including leading citizens of Siena and Dominican friars. A circle of friends and disciples joined her, calling themselves the *Caterinati*, and her reputation spread to other Italian cities.

Some four hundred of Catherine's letters survive, many of them concerned to bring peace among warring factions in the Italian states. Among them are six letters to the pope, Gregory XI, who was in exile in Avignon. Catherine told him of the laxity and corruption in the Church in Italy, urging him to return to Rome. She visited him in Avignon, but was unable to persuade him to return to the Holy See, though his successor did so.

She went back to Siena to write her *Dialogue*, which the *Caterinati* simply called 'The Book'. This treatise is her synthesis of Christian belief and doctrine, the result of her unceasing search for truth. Though commentators have attempted to trace the influence of *Augustine of Hippo and *Thomas Aquinas on her thinking, it is very much her own work. She would have heard of both from the Dominicans, but it seems unlikely that she read their works.

Catherine died at the age of thirty-three. The Benincasa house in the Street of the Dyers may still be seen in Siena.

The most important primary materials for Catherine's Life are the *Leggenda Major* of Raymond di Capua; the *Supplementum* and the *Leggenda Minor* of Thomas Caffarini; and the documents for her canonization in 1461, together with her letters. The letters present many difficulties of transcription and dating. Lives: Raymond di Capua (trans. G. Lamb, 1960); E. G. Gardner (1950); A. Levasti, *My Servant Catherine* (trans. D. M. White, 1954); J. Jorgensen (trans. I. Lund, 1938); A. Curtayne (1929, 2nd ed. 1935). Works: *The Dialogue*, trans. and intro. Suzanne Noltke (1980). *Saint Catherine of Siena as seen in her Letters*, trans. and ed. V. D. Scudder (1905).

30. Mary Ramabai (1858–1922)   [*Commem.*]

This Indian scholar is often known as Pandita Mary Ramabai. 'Pandita' is the female form of 'Pandit', a term of respect. She was the daughter of a Brahmin family. Her father, Anant Shastri, was a Sanskrit scholar who established an ashram; but he had to sell his land to pay his debts, and the family had to move from village to village, reading the Sanskrit Scriptures aloud to the villagers. People were usually generous to these wandering scholars, but there was a great famine in South India in 1876–7: Ramabai's father, mother and sister all died of starvation, and only she and her brother survived. In 1878, they reached Calcutta, and came in contact with Christian missionaries, who helped them. They joined Brahmo Samaj, a reformist group drawing on Christian theological insights.

Ramabai, who had been well educated by her father, was asked to lecture to women's groups on their duties according to Hindu law and the sacred books of Hinduism. She found this increasingly difficult, because of the low status accorded to women in Hinduism. They were forbidden to read the Vedas, and were taught that they could only reach liberation from the endless cycle of reincarnation by total subservience to their husbands. She began to work for the education of women, opposing the caste system and child marriage. She lectured in the University of Calcutta on female emancipation, and it was there that she was first called 'Pandita'.

Ramabai married in 1870 and had a child in the following year; but her husband died of cholera. For the rest of her life, she wore the white sari and the short hair of an Indian widow. She and the little girl

Monorama went to Poona, where the climate was healthier for the child, and Ramabai lectured on social questions. It was in Poona that she came in contact with the Community of St Mary the Virgin, the Wantage Sisters, and through their interest and support that she went to England. She and Mono had a six-berth cabin to themselves all the way, because none of the other passengers on the ship would share with 'natives'.

Through the teaching of the Wantage Sisters, Ramabai was baptized and confirmed into the Church of England. She was sent to Cheltenham Ladies' College, where she learned English, natural science, mathematics and Greek, and in return she taught Sanskrit at Cheltenham College to boys preparing to enter the Indian Civil Service. Then she went to Philadelphia, where her cousin was the first Indian woman to receive a medical degree, and found support for the work she felt called to do in India. She wrote *The High Caste Indian Woman*, which had a considerable success. An interdenominational committee supported by the Episcopalians, Baptists and Methodists set up a Ramabai Association, and some sixty branches developed, raising money for her work. In 1889, she was back in Bombay, and founded a school for child widows, later accepting temple prostitutes and unwanted wives and daughters, whose needs were equally great. In the same year, she became the first woman to address the Indian National Congress.

Ramabai prayed and studied the Bible, but would not ally herself with any particular Christian group: she became impatient of sectarian issues, wanting to concentrate on taking the basic Christian message to Indians. She decided that she must translate the Bible for her own people, since only very poor translations were available. She learned Hebrew (she was already proficient in Greek), and she spent the last fifteen years of her life translating the Old and New Testaments into simple and accurate Marathi. During these years, she continued to manage her school, and set up several other institutions: a boys' school, homes for the aged, a teachers' training school. Culturally, she remained an Indian, and the extreme simplicity of her life-style has been compared to that of Mahatma Gandhi.

She died in April 1922 at the age of sixty-four, renowned as a pioneer in Indian social work and women's emancipation, one of the first women leaders in Indian public life.

Helen S. Dyer (1923); Nicol MacNicol (Calcutta, 1926); Jennie Chapel (1938);

P. Sen Gupta (1970); *Far Above Rubies*, pp. 45–68; *Twentieth Century*, pp. 80–5. *Letters and Correspondence of Pandita Ramabai*, ed. A. B. Shah (Bombay, 1977). Writing: *The High Caste Indian Woman* (Madras, 1975).

May

1. Philip and James, Apostles Festival

These two apostles share a feast day, and are usually cited together.
The New Testament is the only source of information about them, and
both may be confused with others of the same name: Philip the Apostle
is not Philip the Deacon, who baptized the eunuch of the queen (or
kandake) of Ethiopia, and James the Apostle, son of Alphaeus, has to
be distinguished from *James the Great, son of Zebedee, brother of
*John.

Philip came from Bethsaida, like *Andrew and *Peter. He was the
third apostle to be called, after these brothers. He found Nathanael
(*Bartholomew) and brought him to Christ (John 1:43-8). He was at
the feeding of the five thousand, and when Jesus asked how the crowd
was to be fed, he saw the problem in practical terms, and answered
that six months' wages would not be enough. It was Andrew who
found the boy with five loaves and two small fishes (John 6:5-9).
When a group of Greeks (practising Jews, because they had come 'to
worship at the festival') wanted to see Jesus, they approached Philip.
He told Andrew, and the two of them went together to tell Jesus (John
12:20-2). At the Last Supper, Philip said, 'Lord, show us the Father,
and we will be satisfied.' Jesus's first response is mildly reproachful:
'Have I been all this time with you, Philip, and you do not know me?
Anyone who has seen me has seen the Father'; but he goes on to
describe the nature of the relationship between himself and God the
Father in a passage of great theological importance (John 14:8-11).
Philip is mentioned by the writers of the synoptic Gospels among the
other apostles (Matthew 10:3; Mark 3:18; Luke 6:14), but only John
deals with him as an individual.

From these few references we can deduce that he had an enquiring
nature, and that he was probably a Greek (his name is Greek, and the
Greeks approached him rather than Andrew). While he is slower to

make leaps of faith than Peter or John, his attempts to understand lead to major expositions of Jesus's message. There is a tradition that Philip preached the gospel in Phrygia (on the eastern coast of the Sea of Marmora) and that he died and was buried at Hieropolis.

Matthew 10:2–3 lists James the son of Alphaeus and James the son of Zebedee separately as members of the twelve apostles. James the son of Zebedee is known as *James the Great. Mark 15.40 mentions 'James the Less', or the younger, and he has been identified with James 'the brother of the Lord' (Matthew 13:55), with the James who was 'an acknowledged pillar of the Church in Jerusalem' (Galatians 2:9–12), and with the author of the Letter of James. References to the brothers and sisters of Jesus may refer to an earlier marriage by Joseph, so that they were in fact step-brothers and step-sisters. The identification of 'James, the brother of the Lord' with the administrator of the church in Jerusalem is supported by a reference in Paul's Letter to the Galatians, written about the years 57–8, in which he mentions seeing Peter and 'James the Lord's brother' on a visit to Jerusalem three years earlier (Galatians 1:19). James is sometimes called 'the first bishop of Jerusalem', and he evidently stood next in authority to Peter. In Acts 12:17, when Peter comes out of prison, he tells Rhoda and others who eventually open the door to inform 'James and the believers' that he is free; in Acts 15:14–21, James sums up after a discussion among the disciples about the status of the Gentiles, and makes a policy statement; in Acts 21:18–19, Paul reports to James on his journey with Timothy; in Galatians 2:9, Paul mentions 'those respected pillars of our society, James, Cephas [Peter] and John'; and in Galatians 2:12 we are told that Peter has been taking his meals with Gentile Christians, and James disapproves. All these references suggest a man capable of holding authority, orthodox and somewhat inflexible compared to the innovative Peter.

The Letter of James seems to come from such a person: it is a pastoral letter to all the churches consisting of moral exhortations relating to trials, temptations, having respect for the poor and doing good works. It is written in reasonable Greek, but it contains many hebraic phrases, and the style of argument is semitic. If it was not written by James himself (and it has been dated to about the years 49 or 57, when Paul's Letter to the Galatians says that James was still in Jerusalem) it was clearly written very much in his tradition. It may have been written by James, and then edited or re-phrased by another hand after his death.

Many theological debates on the respective importance of faith and works (not least those generated by Martin Luther) hang on the apparent differences in doctrine between Paul and James. The two must have met only rarely – Paul was not in sympathy with the church in Jerusalem, and indeed was fairly bitter about it (2 Corinthians 11:22–33). The consequence is that they use key words in different contexts: when Paul talks of 'faith', he means a total commitment to God which must inevitably produce good works, while James uses 'faith' to mean mere assent to doctrine. When Paul speaks of 'works' he means ritual acts, like circumcision, while James means works of charity. Paul writes an individual letter to particular churches in the light of their circumstances: James sends an encyclical to all the churches. Paul travelled all over the eastern Mediterranean, while James stayed in Jerusalem. Their experience was very different; but the apparent doctrinal differences seem to be largely a matter of semantics.

James 'the Less' stayed in Jerusalem, and is said to have been beaten to death by order of the Sanhedrin. An ancient inscription on the church of Santi Apostoli in Rome records that it was originally dedicated to Philip and James, the joint dedication distinguishing them from Philip the Deacon and James the Great respectively.

AA.SS., May, 1, pp. 7–34 (Philip); W. Patrick, *James, the Lord's Brother* (1906); R. P. Bedford, *St James the Less: a study in Christian iconography* (1911); O.D.S., pp. 251 and 397–8; N.C.E., 11, p. 269 and 7, pp. 885–6; *Butler*, May, pp. 17–19.

2. Athanasius (295–373)   [L.F.]

Athanasius was born and died in Alexandria. As a junior deacon, he accompanied the patriarch of Alexandria to the Council of Nicaea in 325, when the Nicene Creed was first drafted, and the issues relating to the nature of Christ were debated. Arius (born c.250) was a priest of Alexandria, and a major subject of contention was his belief that Christ was not co-existent with God the Father, but a creation of God the Father.

The Council of Nicaea did not settle this argument. Arianism gained in strength in the Eastern Church, though it was rejected in Rome. Constantine himself was baptized on his death-bed in Byzantium by an Arian bishop. Athanasius became patriarch of Alexandria by popular acclaim when he was still in his thirties, and found himself in the centre of controversy. Alexandria was under the jurisdiction of the Eastern Church, then dominated by Arians, and Athanasius held to the decision of Nicaea that the Father and the Son were consubstantial and co-eternal.

The popular acclaim which had lifted Athanasius to the patriarchate did not last. He was not a diplomatic character, and the issues at stake were not matters on which he could compromise. Alexandria was a city given to riots and intrigue, and he made enemies. Eusebius of Nicomedia was set up as a rival patriarch. Athanasius appealed to Rome, which cannot have made him popular with the Eastern bishops. At the Council of Sardica in 346, the Eastern and Western bishops refused to talk to one another; but after pressure from Pope Julius I, Athanasius was reinstated.

In Byzantium, the emperors continued to oppose him. Constantius, son of Constantine, was an Arian. In 356, he sent an armed guard to capture Athanasius. They surrounded a church where he was holding a night vigil, and though he escaped, his followers were hunted down for some eighteen months, and many of them imprisoned. Athanasius fled to the Thebaïd in Upper Egypt. In the time of the emperor Julian the Apostate, orders were issued that he was to be captured dead or alive, and under Valens, Julian's successor, he was exiled.

In all, Athanasius was only able to hold office as patriarch in peace for some ten years, between 346 and 356. He was said to be an excellent administrator who appointed good bishops and upheld the monastic virtues. He was a friend of Pachomius, abbot and founder of communal monasticism in the Thebaïd, and he wrote a life of *Antony, who visited Alexandria in 355, and preached against the Arians; but the circumstances of his life were such that he was continually plunged into controversy. He is chiefly celebrated for his defence of the orthodox view of the nature of the Trinity, now enshrined in what has become known as the Athanasian Creed.

AA.SS., May, 1, pp. 1186–1258; G. Bardy (1914); F. L. Cross (1947); J. H. Leroux (1956); A. Petterson (1995); *Butler*, May, pp. 8–11.

4. English Saints and Martyrs of the Reformation Era   [L.F.]

In the sixteenth and seventeenth centuries, a great company of English men and women died for their faith – not in witness against paganism, but in witness against different religious allegiances: Protestants killed Catholics, and Catholics killed Protestants.

The great gulf which developed between Catholic and Protestant was not about the fundamentals of belief: it was about ecclesiastical politics in the first instance, and then increasingly about national politics, culture, family and group loyalties, custom and temperament. Henry VIII's execution of those he regarded as his political opponents, including *Thomas More, *John Fisher and the abbots of Colchester, Reading and Glastonbury, was compounded by the sack of the monasteries and the virtual end of monastic life in England for three centuries. The extreme Protestantism of the reign of Edward VI followed – to be replaced by the equally extreme Catholicism of Mary Tudor, when many churchmen died by fire, including *Thomas Cranmer, *Hugh Latimer and *Nicholas Ridley.

The Elizabethan Settlement of 1559 created a broad national Church. Clergy were required to take the oath of allegiance to the Crown; the laity were only required to attend a Sunday service, but no enquiry was made into personal beliefs: outward conformity was all that was necessary. It was a papal bull of Pope Pius V, issued under pressure from Catholic Spain, which made new martyrs. This charged Elizabeth I with heresy, formally deposed her from the throne of England, and excommunicated her. All who continued to obey her laws were to be excommunicated. In the following year, an Act of the English parliament declared it to be high treason to affirm that Elizabeth was not, or ought not to be, queen; or that she was a heretic, schismatic, tyrant, infidel or usurper of the crown. The English Mission, spearheaded by the Jesuits, followed. The martyrs of that period, like Edmund Campion and Alexander Briant, insisted that their only aim was religious conversion, and that they had no political motives; but despite their undoubted heroism, they seem to have been totally ignorant of a political situation in which Elizabeth was defending her throne against Philip of Spain and Mary of Scotland, and the Spanish Armada was threatening English coasts.

Catholics hoped for toleration under James I, Mary's son; but the Gunpowder Plot of 1605 (regretted by many Catholics) led inevitably to a fresh wave of repressive measures and more deaths. The Civil War and the death of *Charles I brought a new wave of extreme Protestantism, in which politics and religion were again inextricably mixed; but after the Restoration, the Church of England survived as a bridge Church, both Catholic and Protestant, based on the Bible and the sacraments, allowing a wide range of forms of worship and belief within the scope of the 1662 Prayer Book, which has been supplemented but never replaced.

In a time of growing ecumenism, Catholics, Anglicans and members of the Free Churches have found it increasingly appropriate to honour all those who died for faith and conscience, irrespective of their allegiance. The British Council of Churches stated in 1970 that 'the martyr tradition is one which all have shared and from which all may draw strength, even across ecumenical boundaries'.

8. Julian of Norwich (1342–?1413) [L.F.]

We do not know the baptismal name of this fourteenth-century visionary. She took the name 'Julian' from St Julian's church in Norwich, a Norman foundation given to the nuns of Carrow by King Stephen in 1146. She must have been a member of the community, a Benedictine nun who was at some stage in her life accorded the right to live as an anchoress. This did not imply being sealed off from the world: the 'cell' was usually of two or three rooms, with three windows: one which looked into the church, where she might see Christ's body made and receive the sacrament of Holy Communion; one to the parlour where people might come to consult her privately, and one to the outside world. There she lived a life of constant prayer. The world was full of barbarity, suffering and sickness: she upheld it with her prayers, and though she did not go out, the world came to her.

Julian says that she was 'a simple creature, unlettered', but her writing is admirably direct and concise. She records her visions in considerable detail. On 8 May 1373, when she was 'thirty and a half', she had been ill and in pain for nearly a week, and her life was despaired of. She prayed that she might see Christ's Passion, and her prayer was granted in fifteen visions between four o'clock and nine o'clock in the morning. She was awake at the time. In the first vision, she saw 'the red blood trickle down from under the Garland, hot and freshly and right plenteously, as it were in the time of the Passion, when the red Garland was pressed on his blessed head who was both God and Man'; and she saw our Lady, 'a simple maid and a meek, young of age and little waxen above a child'. In the second, God showed her 'a little thing, the quality of an hazel-nut, in the palm of my hand' and when she asked what it was, she was told, 'It is all that is made.' She feared that it might have 'fallen to nought for littleness', but she was told that 'it lasteth and ever shall, for God loveth it'. She was 'greatly moved in charity to mine even-Christians' – that is, to her fellow-Christians.

As the visions develop, she sees God in a point, 'by which sight I see that he is in all things', and she comes to understand that 'prayer oneth the soul to God'. And in the end, she is told, there is 'a marvellous high mystery hid in God: all shall be well and all shall be well and all manner of thing shall be well'.

Julian does not set out to teach or to argue: she simply reports. She has nothing to say about the techniques of prayer, or treading the *via negativa*, like other fourteenth-century mystics such as Walter Hilton and *Richard Rolle: she simply opens her soul to God. On the night after her visions, she had a dream of devils and temptations, but she rejected it sturdily, knowing that it was only a dream; and on the next night, she had her sixteenth and final vision, 'a delectable sight and a restful shewing'; and she replied, 'Lord, blessed mayest thou be, for it is thus: it is well.' After that, she recovered her health.

Julian's book *The Revelations of Divine Love* has became a classic in the literature of Christian mysticism. The church of St Julian still stands in Norwich, and there is a Julian shrine.

The Sloane ms. of *The Revelations of Divine Love* is the British Museum. There are several translations, including one by Grace Warrack (1901, repr. 1949) with a good commentary, and *The Shewings of Julian of Norwich*, ed. Georgia R. Crampton, Western Michigan University, Ann Arbor, 1994. See also Michael Ramsey, *Be Still and Know* (1982) ch. 9, pp. 92–105; many references in Evelyn Underhill, *Mysticism* (1911, repr. 1994).

14. Matthias the Apostle   Festival

After the death of Judas, *Peter stood up in front of about a hundred and twenty disciples, and proposed the election of another apostle to take his place, 'one of the men who have accompanied us throughout the time that the Lord Jesus went in and out with us' (Acts 1:15–26). Two names were put forward, those of Joseph Barsabbas and Matthias. They drew lots, and Matthias was elected.

After that, we have only tradition to draw on. Matthias is said to have preached in Judaea. The Greeks claimed that he held a mission in Cappadocia. He has been linked with Ethiopia, and an apocryphal

Gospel, now lost, was attributed to him. Some legends say that he was crucified, and others that he was martyred by being beheaded. He is sometimes shown in art with an axe or a halberd, which supports the latter contention. His relics were claimed by Jerusalem, and *Helena, mother of Constantine, is said to have sent them back to Rome.

In some mediaeval representations of the apostles, Matthias is replaced as one of the Twelve by *Paul.

AA.SS., Feb., 3, pp. 431–54; *N.C.E.*, 9, p. 503; *Butler*, May, p. 7.

16. Caroline Chisholm (1808–77)   [*Commem.*]

At the age of twenty-two, Caroline Jones, from an Evangelical family in Northamptonshire, married Captain Archibald Chisholm, a Roman Catholic officer in the service of the East India Company. She accompanied him to Madras, where she was appalled at the Company's lack of care for the wives and children of its British troops. The girls in particular led a dismal life in bleak barracks, and she founded a school where they could acquire a basic education, and also learn useful skills like book-keeping, child care or simple nursing.

In 1838, the Chisholms, with their two infant sons, went to spend a leave in Australia. They found that under the convict system there were ten times as many men in New South Wales as women. Women went out to join their husbands on release, and girls also emigrated in the hope of marriage. They undertook the long journey in dreadful conditions, and there was a high mortality rate from disease. Those who survived the journey arrived with no idea where to go for help, and many of the girls drifted into brothels. It was a problem which *Elizabeth Fry had tried to tackle in the previous century, but her barracks stood empty and infested with rats. Caroline induced the Governor to open it again, slept there herself, and dealt with the rats. She managed it as a shelter, and escorted parties through the bush, sometimes riding at the head of a convoy with a child on each side of her saddle. Her husband returned to India to complete his tour, but retired on pension in 1840 to continue the work with her in New South Wales. The Anglican bishop was dubious at first because they were Roman Catholics, but he found Mrs Chisholm 'a ladylike person and very prepossessing and interesting', and authorized the clergy to co-operate with them. Contributions and offers of help began to flow in.

In seven years, with no official authority, Caroline settled some 11,000 people, reunited 600 familes, and brought about many marriages. In 1846, she and her husband went to London to establish a connecting link between emigration policy in England and immigration policy in Australia. He was always her loyal supporter, though she bore the brunt of the campaign. She besieged the Home Office, the Colonial Office and the emigration authorities, and gave evidence before Select Committees of the House of Lords, pleading for a system which would give colonists advice before they left England, decent ships to travel in, and jobs and shelter when they arrived. She raised public support for a Family Colonisation Loan Society Committee to enable free colonists to pay the cost of their passage in retrospect by instalments. *Lord Shaftesbury became the chairman, and Charles Dickens publicized the issues, publishing many letters and emigrants' histories in *Household Words*. (In *David Copperfield*, the Peggotys and Mr Micawber finally emigrate to Australia, and Mr Micawber, rather improbably, becomes a magistrate.) She also wrote a number of pamphlets, including 'The ABC of Colonisation' and 'Emigration and Transportation Relatively Considered'. Improvements came quickly. New ships were built, and the first was named the *Caroline Chisholm*. In her own day, Caroline was as famous in London as *Florence Nightingale.

In Australia, the situation was changing. The transportation of convicts was being discontinued, and the Gold Rush of 1851 led to a demand for free emigrants to replace the men who had left their employment for the excitement of Ballarat. The Chisholms returned to Australia – Archibald Chisholm to establish branches of the Loan Society, and Caroline to continue her work with the women. When they finally returned to England in 1866, Caroline was voted a civil list pension in recognition of her work.

M. Kiddle (Melbourne, 1850); Eneas Mackenzie, *A Memoir of Caroline Chisholm* (1852); *The Emigrant's Guide to Australia, with a memoir of Mrs Chisholm* (1853); M. Hoban, *51 Pieces of Wedding Cake* (Victoria, Australia, 1973); *The Illustrated London News*, 17 April 1852; *Far Above Rubies*, pp. 92–115.

19. Dunstan (c.909–88) [L.F.]

In the early part of the ninth century, there were monastic houses for women in Wessex, at Wilton, Shaftesbury and Winchester, but apart from the somewhat unsuccessful monastery founded by *Alfred the Great at Athelney for Gallic monks, there appear to have been no monastic houses for men. Edward the Elder founded the New Minster at Winchester, but this was a house of clerks, not a monastery. Dunstan has the distinction of bringing monastic life for men back to England, and thereby strengthening both religion and learning.

He was a nobleman of Wessex, related to the royal family by marriage – a link which was to lead him to high office when he had the royal favour; but the kings of Wessex in this period died young, and the royal favour was not always with him. He was brought to court during Athelstan's reign by his uncle, Athelm, archbishop of Canterbury. When Edmund (939–46) became king, he and Dunstan were close companions. Edmund appointed him abbot of Glastonbury, giving him land and promising him whatever he needed to establish a monastery.

Dunstan spent fifteen years at Glastonbury, and developed the first organized monastic community for men for several generations. Edmund and his successor Edred (946–55) supported him, and when the monastery was established, part of the royal treasure was kept there. In 955, Dunstan offended the new king, Edwy or Eadwig (955–9), by rebuking him for his behaviour at his coronation feast. He was driven into exile and went to Ghent. In a period of some two years in Continental monasteries, he learned much about the Benedictine way of life and the standards of scholarship which it promoted – though it appears that he did not go to Cluny, then the centre of the Benedictine way of life, and some Benedictines have considered his monastic system not entirely orthodox.

Edwy's successor, Edgar, brought Dunstan back. Dunstan was appointed bishop of Worcester in the same year, bishop of London in 959 and archbishop of Canterbury in 960. He became the leader of a remarkable triumvirate with bishops Oswald and Aethelwold. Dunstan himself revived monastic life at Malmesbury, Bath, Athelney, Muchelney and Westminster. Oswald, the nephew of Archbishop Odo of Canterbury, had trained as a monk at Fleury in France. He became bishop of Worcester in Dunstan's place when he went to London, and archbishop of York in 972, reviving the monastery at Westbury-on-Trym. Aethelwold was a monk of Glastonbury who became abbot of Abingdon about 955 and refounded the monastery there before becoming bishop of Winchester in 963.

Dunstan was responsible for devising the ceremony for Edgar's coronation at Bath Abbey in 973, when he was crowned and recognized as overlord by the other rulers in Britain. The liturgical framework has remained very much the same ever since.

W. Stubbs, *Memorials of St Dunstan* (Rolls Series no. 63, 1874) contains all the early Lives; *Men.E.W.*, pp. 215–16; see also N. Ramsey et al., *St Dunstan, His Life, Times and Cults* (1992); *Cantuar*, pp. 32–7; *Butler*, May, pp. 100–2; Stenton, pp. 446–71.

20. Alcuin (*c.*735–804)   [L.F.]

Alcuin was one of the great founders of mediaeval scholarship. He was born at or near York between 730 and 735, and joined the Minster school founded by Archbishop Egbert of York, who had been a pupil of *Bede's.

He became Egbert's favourite pupil, stayed at York to teach and help in the founding of the Minster Library, and in 778 became head of the school, a post he held for fourteen years.

Teaching was on the lines prescribed by *St Augustine: Christian doctrine, the works of the early Fathers, Church history and the Bible formed the foundation, but the classical studies of grammar, rhetoric, apologetics, mathematics, music and astronomy were also taught. The aim was not to find fresh knowledge, but to conserve and order the great teaching of the past so that it could be transmitted to new generations. Alcuin was not a monk, and never a priest, though he later took deacon's Orders. He was pre-eminently a teacher.

During his time at York he wrote a series of text books on Latin, stressing accuracy rather than polished composition: accuracy was necessary for the taking of oaths and other legal formulae. He was also a considerable poet, an encyclopaedic reader and a prolific letter writer.

In 781, Charlemagne asked him to head a new school which he had founded at Aachen, and after some misgivings, Alcuin agreed. He did not entirely desert York, for he returned there in 789 and for most of the three years from 790 to 793; but for the fourteen years from 782 to 796 his chief work was done in the Frankish empire, which offered a much greater scope and more intellectual stimulus. Charlemagne assembled a company of the most intelligent and cultured men in Europe, and lived with them on close personal terms. Alcuin became his chief religious adviser, his adviser on all matters concerned with England and the English, and his friend. His own academic interests broadened: he developed the study of philosophy and abstract logic; he revived the study of the works of Boethius (*c.*480–524), who linked classical philosophy to the first developments in scholastic theology; he wrote theological treatises on heresies; he wrote new commentaries on the offices of the Church. He learned from his brighter pupils, and often their new work was developed in collaboration with him.

Charlemagne issued decrees that schools should be set up in every diocese and monastery in his kingdom to teach on the lines established at the palace school. In a very basic and necessary reform, handwriting was standardized, and books were copied in very large numbers for the new schools.

In 796, Alcuin retired to Tours. He remained there as abbot until his death in 804, turning the monastery into a distinguished centre of learning. He was able to devote himself to a stricter form of monastic life, and to receive visits from many old friends, some of whom were carrying on his work. He continued to study, writing a major work on the Trinity and revising the Latin text of the Bible before his death in 804.

Men.E.W., p. 219; Eleanor S. Duckett, *Alcuin, Friend of Charlemagne* (1951); D. Bullough, *The Age of Charlemagne* (1965); S. Allott, *Alcuin of York, his Life and Letters* (1974). *D.N.B.*, 1, pp. 279–80.; Levison, pp. 153–73; Stenton, pp. 188–91. Works in *P.L.*, vols 100, 101.

21. Helena (*c.*250–330)   *[Commem.]*

Helena was the mother of the Roman emperor Constantine the Great. The twelfth-century chronicler Geoffrey of Monmouth endowed her with a royal and British background, as the daughter of King Coel of Essex (Old King Cole), and Evelyn Waugh's *Helena* is, as the author says in his introduction, fiction based on this premise; but in fact her origin was more humble. Bishop Eusebius of Caesarea, who was Constantine's contemporary and friend, records that she was born in Drepanum, in Asia Minor, the daughter of an innkeeper. In or about the year 270, she married the Roman general Constantius Chlorus. She seems to have travelled on some of his campaigns, for Constantine, their only child, was born in 274 at a military base on the Danube; but when Constantius became involved in imperial affairs in Rome (which had their dangers), she returned to Drepanum, and Constantine was brought up there.

Constantine succeeded his father as Roman emperor in 306, and had Helena brought to Rome, paying her great honour. About 312, Helena became a Christian. We know that Constantine raised the Chi Rho sign on his standard before the battle of the Milvian Bridge in that year, but at this stage in his life he was not himself a committed Christian. It is not clear whether his action was a tribute to his mother's faith, or whether she became a Christian after the battle, perhaps in thanksgiving for his victory; but there is no doubt about her whole-hearted conversion. She began to live very simply, spending much time in prayer and works of charity. She knew the churches of Rome and their needs. Though he was not baptized until shortly before his own death in 337, Constantine made many munificent gifts to the churches, recorded in the *Liber Pontificum*. He was responsible for the building of the first church of St Peter on Vatican hill, for the Council of Nicaea, and for many other acts which made Christianity central to the life of the Roman Empire. Helena was his constant guide and adviser in all this activity, often the only person in whom he could place complete trust.

In 327, Constantine sent Helena on a pilgrimage to Jerusalem. He had written to the bishop of Jerusalem, asking him to destroy the temple of Venus on Mount Calvary, and to search for the remains of the True Cross. Three hundred years had passed since the Crucifixion, but the spot had been marked by Christians from the earliest times (see *Justin). Helena went in state with her court, carrying full imperial authority, making gifts to churches, holding discussions with bishops, priests, and scholars, visiting monasteries, releasing prisoners and ordering people to be brought back from exile. It was an arduous mission of peace and humane action.

The story that she was personally present when the Cross was discovered is recorded by the fourth-century historians Socrates and Sozomen from the report of *Cyril of Jerusalem, who was in the city and twelve years old at the time. Helena is said to have taken three nails from the Cross, and to have sent them to Constantine, who put one on his helmet and two on his horse's bit and bridle. She had a basilica built on the Mount of Olives, and a first church on the site of the Nativity in Bethlehem. Constantine was to build a larger one after her death.

Helena was nearly eighty years old. She became ill in the Holy Land, but managed to reach Constantine and his court in Nicomedia. He was with her when she died.

Helena had her detractors. Two anti-Christian writers, Zosimus and Orosius, spread the story that she was a prostitute, and that she was only Constantius' mistress, not his wife. This may be why *Bede refers to her as a concubine; but the honour paid to her by Constantine, who had her declared Augusta, Empress, and struck coins bearing her image, was clearly intended to give the lie to such slanders.

The story of the finding of the True Cross was re-told many times in mediaeval poetry and song. The Anglo-Saxon poet Cynewolf described it as 'the tree of glory', graced with 'gold and gems, with fairest precious stones'. If the facts were less poetic, the story remains a memorial to a remarkable pilgrimage, and the woman who carried it out on her son's behalf.

Eusebius, *H.E.*, book 3, and *Life of Constantine*; Socrates, *H.E.*, 1, 17; Sozomen, *H.E.*, 2, 1; Theodoret, *H.E.*, Book 1 – all in *N.P.N.F.*; *AA.SS.*, Aug., 3, pp. 548–654; Geoffrey of Monmouth, *History of the Kings of Britain*, trans. Lewis Thomas, Penguin Classics (1968), pp. 132, 233; *Anal.Boll.*, 57 (1940), pp. 199–205; Cynewulf, *Elena*, ed. P. O. E. Gradon (1958), *O.D.S.*, p. 225; Evelyn Waugh, *Helena* (1950, repr. 1963).

23. Petroc (sixth century)   [*Commem.*]

The name of Petroc or Pedrog is celebrated in Devon and Cornwall. The place where his monastery was situated became known as Padristowe and later Padstow. Little Petherick and Trebetheric are also named after him. Many churches in the area have dedications in his honour, and he is well known in Cornish folklore.

The legends say that he was the son of a Welsh chieftain, or even 'King of the Cumbrians' in his own right; that he had miraculous adventures in India; that he tamed a monster, and healed a dragon which came to him with a splinter in its eye; but there are several mediaeval accounts of his life which corroborate each other in essential detail. They appear to be drawn from earlier accounts now lost, and from even earlier oral traditions.

The mediaeval Life from the abbey of St Méen in Brittany, which appears to be based on an earlier Life written at Bodmin Priory, says that Pedroc studied in Ireland for some twenty years, and this is confirmed by the Latin Life of Abbot Kevin of Glendalough, which was one of the great Irish monastic schools. Petroc and his companions took a ship for England to establish a new settlement. They sailed into the estuary of the River Camel, and settled at a place named Llanwethinoc, after an earlier monk named Wethinoc. There Petroc spent his time in prayer and deeds of charity, healing many sick people. The 'Gotha Life', a fourteenth-century account based on accounts from Bodmin and St Méen which came to light in 1937, describes how he established a second community at Little Petherick, where he built a chapel and a mill. He lived a most austere life in his community for thirty years, and then made a pilgrimage to Rome and Jerusalem.

Nicholas Roscarrock's *Lives of the Saints of Devon and Cornwall* tells a story which seems to have the ring of authenticity. Petroc returned from his pilgrimage and was greatly admired by his monks, who listened spellbound to his accounts of his travels. The monastery was being battered by storms and, inspired, as he thought, by the Holy Spirit, Petroc told them that the storms would cease on the following day; but the storms did not abate, and he came to the conclusion that he had been arrogant in expecting the Holy Spirit to give him the power of prophecy, so he went all the way back to Jerusalem as a penance. It was on this second journey, reputed to have taken seven years, that he reached the 'East Ocean' – probably not India, as the legends say, but possibly the Gulf of Aqaba, some two hundred miles to the south of Jerusalem.

By this time, he must have been a very old man. After his return, he withdrew to a remote place on Bodmin Moor, intending to live as a hermit; but again some of the brothers came to join him. When he knew that his life was coming to an end, he went to make a last visit to the communities at Little Petherick and Lanwithenoc. He became seriously ill when he was travelling from one to the other, and died in the house of a man named Rovel. The present farmhouse of Treravel is thought to mark the spot.

Petroc's feast is listed in the Bosworth Psalter, the Missal of Robert of Jumièges, early West Country calendars and the Sarum calendar. His shrine was a place of pilgrimage in the eleventh century. Roger of Howden, a reliable chronicler of the period, describes how a canon of Bodmin Priory took the relics from Bodmin to the abbey of St Méen in Brittany. The prior of Bodmin appealed to King Henry II, who ordered that they should be returned. They were ceremonially brought back and re-interred in a splendid ivory reliquary of Sicilian workmanship, the gift of Count Walter of Coutances, who was the Keeper of the Great Seal. The king and all his court prostrated themselves in front of it.

In the fifteenth century, William Worcestre noted that he had seen the reliquary and greatly admired it. Three centuries later, it was discovered, empty, in a room above the south porch of Bodmin parish church. It remained there until 1970, and is now in the British Museum.

AA.SS., June, 1, pp. 391–4, contains the Life by John of Tynmouth; *N.L.A.*, 2, pp. 317–20; William Worcestre, pp. 87, 103, 113; Roscarrock, pp. 101–4, 164–5; G. H. Doble, *St Petrock*, Cornish Saints Series 11 (3rd edn, 1938); P. Grosjean, 'Vie et miracles de S Petroc', *Anal.Boll.*, 74 (1956), pp. 131–88; R. H. Pinder-Wilson and C. N. L. Brooke, 'The Reliquary of St Petroc and the Ivories of Norman Sicily,' *Archaeologia*, 104 (1973), pp. 261–306; *Men.E.W.*, pp. 254–5; *D.N.B.*, 15, pp. 651–2; *O.D.S.*, pp. 395–6.

24. John and Charles Wesley (1703–91 and 1707–88)   [L.F.]

John Wesley was the fifteenth of the nineteen children born to the Revd Samuel Wesley, rector of Epworth, Lincs., and his remarkable wife Susannah. Nine of the children died in infancy. Charles was John's younger brother by four years. Their upbringing was pious and regularly ordered. Mrs Wesley led her children in a rigorous life of prayer and Bible reading. Though the family lived in fairly straitened circumstances, both John and Charles went to the Charterhouse School, and then to Christ Church, Oxford, chiefly as a result of their father's diligence in finding patrons.

John maintained his religious practices at Oxford, and lived the life of a poor scholar. When he became a Fellow of Lincoln College, he gave away most of his income to charity. In 1729, Charles, who had joined him at Oxford, formed 'The Holy Club' of like-minded young men, and John became a member. The group became known as 'the new methodists' because of their strict attention to method in both prayer and study. By 1736, both the brothers had been ordained, and they sailed for the American colonies with Governor Oglethorpe, the new governor of Georgia. On the way out, they shared the ship with a group of Moravians, German Lutherans whose doctrines were strongly influenced by the teaching of John Hus, the fourteenth-century Bohemian reformer. They relied entirely on the Bible for inspiration, and had a zeal which John found lacking in the Anglican Church – then cold, formal, often lax in observance, and remote from the ordinary people.

Though the mission to Georgia was not a success, John Wesley returned to England on fire with the Spirit. He attended Moravian meetings in London, and it was at one of these meetings on 24 May 1738 that he had an overwhelming conversion experience. Many Methodists date their movement from that day. He began to preach in the open air, and crowds of people came to hear him – labourers, miners and the inhabitants of the growing city slums. He offered hope to people who lived in squalor and despair, their lives dislocated by agricultural change and the first phase of ruthless industrial development. In 1739, he founded the first Methodist chapel in Bristol, and bought the ruined Foundery in Moorfields, London, as a base for his work in the capital. The results of his preaching were astonishing: he was to tour England for more than half a century addressing huge crowds. He preached a social gospel to the poor, and sometimes ten, twenty or even thirty thousand people would gather to hear him, waiting patiently for hours for him to appear. His style was dry, precise and plain, but their reactions were extreme. Many wept. Some went into 'paroxysms' (possibly epileptic fits), and there were alarmist reports of the 'enthusiasm' he aroused from Cornwall to Northumbria. Perhaps the Age of Reason was suppressing its emotions: Wesley's sermons called them forth.

Anglican churches refused him their pulpits, and then closed their doors against him. He and his supporters were often abused, and roughly handled. He was accused of rabble-rousing and of causing insanity. When he tried to visit prisoners and lunatics, he was refused admission, and he commented in his diary that he was forbidden to visit Newgate for fear of making the inmates wicked, and Bedlam for fear of making them mad. He still regarded himself as being in Anglican Orders. Charles, who was his loyal lieutenant and carried out some evangelistic tours of his own, was even more anxious not to break the link with the Church in which they had been ordained. The Wesleyans separated from the Moravians in 1745, and from George Whitefield's Calvinistic Methodists (who were a great success in the American colonies) soon after. Though John Wesley sent out lay preachers, it was not until 1784 that he finally broke with Anglican tradition by ordaining missionaries for America and Scotland – to the distress of his brother. After that date, the Methodist Conference became the central organization for Wesleyan Methodists.

John Wesley is said to have travelled 26,000 miles and preached 40,000 sermons. He travelled England by horseback as long as he could, and in his later years used a chaise which was fitted with a shelf for his books and papers. His literary output was prodigious. His *Journal*, which contains a detailed record of his spiritual experiences and his travels, like his *Letters* and his *Sermons* has been published many times. Both John and Charles Wesley were hymn writers. Charles Wesley wrote over 5,000 hymns, including 'Jesu, lover of my soul', 'Love divine, all loves excelling', and 'Hark, the herald angels sing'.

The formal separation between Anglicanism and Methodism did not come until 1791, three years after Charles Wesley died, and in the year of John Wesley's death at the age of eighty-eight.

Wesley's *Journals* originally ran to 32 volumes (Bristol, 1771–4). They have been re-published several times in abridged form. Lives by John Whitehead (1793–6); Robert Southey (2 vols, 1820); J. H. Rigg, *The Living Wesley* (1905); C. E. Vulliamy (1931); W. L. Doughty (1935); J. F. K. Rowe (1987); Geoffrey W. Milburn, *The Travelling Preacher* (1987). *Letters of John Wesley*, ed. John Telford (1931); B. M. Jarvoe and K. E. Rowe, *John and Charles Wesley: a bibliography* (American Theological Library, New Jersey, 1987). Separate works on Charles Wesley: F. L. Wiseman (1932); John Telford (1938); Frank Colquhoun (1947).

25. Bede (c.672–735)   [L.F.]

When he was seven years old, Bede's family sent him to the monastery near Wearmouth, where *Benedict Biscop was abbot, and later Coelfrith. Bede acknowledges his debt to these two great abbots, who had brought much Latin learning into the Northumbrian monasteries. Both visited Rome, travelling through France and Italy, and learning much on the way. Benedict Biscop brought back many books and paintings, and Continental craftsmen to beautify the churches and chapels. Coelfrith, with the help of scribes, made three copies of the Latin Bible, and Bede may well have been one of the scribes.

He was probably not more than nine or ten when he moved to Jarrow. The two monasteries were twin foundations following a modified version of the Benedictine Rule. Bede stayed at Jarrow for the rest of his long and productive life. He once went to Lindisfarne and once to York, but he seems to have had no desire for further travel or for promotion. He became a deacon in his nineteenth year, and a priest in his thirtieth. He wrote in his old age: 'I have spent all the remainder of my life in this monastery, and devoted myself entirely to the study of the Scriptures. And while I have observed the regular discipline and sung the choir offices daily in church, my chief delight has always been in study, teaching and writing.'

His scholarship was based on the Latin Bible, though his own native tongue was Old English. Trained in the Latin rite after the controversies of the Synod of Whitby had died down, he praises the Celtic bishops such as Columba and Aidan for their holiness of life, but he is severe about their obduracy in refusing to keep the Latin date of Easter.

At the end of his monumental *History of the People of England*, which historians regard as the single most valuable source for Anglo-Saxon history, Bede sets down a list of his own works. In addition to the History he wrote Lives of the saints and abbots, hymns, homilies, biblical commentaries, a martyrology and many letters. Shortly before his death, when the *History* was completed, he was working on a translation of St John's Gospel into Anglo-Saxon.

Bede's death fitted his tranquil and scholarly life: his disciple *Cuthbert, who was to become abbot of Jarrow later, wrote a moving account of how Bede longed 'to see Christ my king in all his beauty', and died singing the *Gloria*. *Boniface said of his death, 'The candle of the Church, lit by the Holy Spirit, is extinguished.'

For subsequent generations, Bede set a standard of dedication, scholarship, devotion to accuracy and clarity of expression which few monastic chroniclers could equal. The twelfth-century chronicler William of Malmesbury, who wrote very much in Bede's tradition, spoke of him as 'marvellously learned, and not at all proud'. He is often referred to as 'the Venerable Bede', meaning 'worthy of respect' rather than 'old in years'.

Men.E.W., pp. 234–5; P. Hunter Blair, *The World of Bede* (1970); B. Ward, *The Venerable Bede* (1990); D. P. Kirby, *Bede's Historia Ecclesiastica Gentis Anglorum: its contemporary setting*, Jarrow Lecture (1992); Mayr-Harting, pp. 40–50, 205–19; N.C.E., 2, p. 217; O.D.S., pp. 43–4; *Butler*, May, pp. 130–3. A Greek copy and Latin copy of the Acts of the Apostles in Bede's own hand are in the Bodleian Library at Oxford, and there is a manuscript of his *Historia Ecclesiastica* in St Petersburg. Bede's Works in Latin are in *P.L.*, vols 90–5. There are many modern translations of the *Historia Ecclesiastica*. The Penguin Classics edition (1990) includes translations of Bede's Letter to Egbert and Cuthbert's Letter on Bede's death.

Aldhelm (639–700)   *[Commem.]*

Aldhelm was the first abbot of Malmesbury, and towards the end of his life became the first bishop of Sherborne. He was related to the kings of Wessex, and educated at Malmesbury and Canterbury. He is thought to have brought the monastery at Malmesbury under Benedictine rule, and he made other monastic foundations, at Frome in Somerset and Bradford-on-Avon.

He is chiefly known as a prolific writer, and has been claimed as the only southern cleric of his day comparable to Bede. He wrote in both Anglo-Saxon and Latin, though only his Latin works survive. His poems greatly inspired *Alfred, who sang them to the accompaniment of the harp. His best-known work is *On Virginity*, which gives examples of the lives of virgin saints. Unfortunately this was a work of piety rather than of accuracy, and has been responsible for many of the legends about the lives of women saints which have subsequently proved to be unsubstantiated. Aldhelm gained his reputation as a writer and a pastor, not as an historian.

In 696, the Wessex diocese was divided, and he became bishop of Sherborne. Bede mentions Aldhelm in his *Ecclesiastical History*, saying that he administered his diocese with great energy, and commending him for his treatise on the correct date for the observance of Easter. He says that he was 'a man of wide learning, with a polished style, and . . . extremely well-read both in biblical and general literature'.

Aldhelm was venerated as a saint before the Norman Conquest, and though, like many other Anglo-Saxon saints, he was removed from the Calendar by Lanfranc's commission, which substituted Norman saints, Bishop Osmund of Salisbury, William's nominee and possibly his nephew, had him restored. Osmund, himself a scholar, had a great respect for Aldhelm, wrote his Life, and assisted in the enshrining of his relics at Malmesbury.

Bede, *H.E.*, bk 5, ch. 18; William of Malmesbury, *Gesta Pontificum* (R.S. 52), bk 5, pp. 330–443; *Men.E.W.*, pp. 231–2; Stenton, pp. 151–90; Mayr-Harting, pp. 192–204, 205–19; *O.D.S.*, pp. 13–14; *Butler*, May p. 138. *Prose Works*, ed. M. Lapidge and M. Herren (1979); *Poetic Works* (1985), ed. M. Lapidge and J. L. Rosier (1989).

26. Augustine of Canterbury (d. 604)   [L.F.]

The idea for a mission to convert the English originated with *Pope Gregory the Great. The opportunity for a mission arose when King Ethelbert of Kent, who was the *bretwalda* or overlord of the southern English kingdoms, married Bertha, a Christian princess from the kingdom of the Franks. Her family had made it a condition of the marriage that she and her household, which would have included priests, should be free to practise their own religion. They worshipped in an old church from the days of Roman Britain, St Martin's in Canterbury.

Gregory was impatient with the failure of the French bishops to follow up this lead, and determined on a mission from Rome. He chose Augustine, who was the prior of his own monastery of St Andrew's on the Coelian Hill, to lead a party of thirty or forty monks. Bede says that 'they were appalled at the idea of going to a fierce and pagan nation, of whose very language they were ignorant'. The party left by sea for Marseilles in 596, but when they reached the Frankish territories, their hearts failed them, and Augustine went back to Rome to ask the pope to recall them. Gregory sent him back, and they reached England in 597.

Whether the story of his early interest in the possibility of an English mission is true or not, Gregory planned the mission very carefully. Augustine was given a well-worked-out plan for the conversion of the Anglo-Saxon kingdoms. It seems that Gregory was very well briefed on the the state of Britain when it had been a province of the Roman empire a hundred and fifty years earlier. There was a network of Roman roads, and despite the depredations of the earlier Germanic invaders, former Romano-British cities were still centres of population. There were even churches still standing; but Gregory and his advisers appear not to have understood that England at the end of the fifth century was not settled or predictable: it was a land of small unstable kingdoms, frequent wars and shifting boundaries. The plan provided for two archbishops, one in London and one in York, each to superintend twelve dioceses with their own bishops. Augustine was to find it impossible to implement. The gap between the plans made in Rome and the reality with which he had to grapple was very wide.

Though none of the party could speak English, they had no difficulty in finding interpreters when they reached the French coast: there was a good deal of trade across the English Channel, most of it centring on

London and the Kentish ports. Pope Gregory wrote to Ethelbert himself, and sent him gifts.

Augustine and his party were told to land on the Isle of Thanet, and to go to a meeting-place in the open air, because Ethelbert was afraid of the magical arts, which were most powerful in closed rooms. They approached the king and his party 'carrying a silver cross as their standard, and the likeness of our Saviour painted on a board'. Ethelbert received them courteously, and gave them a house in Canterbury. He explained that Christian ideas were new to him, and he could not abandon the age-old beliefs of his people without much thought; but he gave them permission to preach, and promised to consider the matter himself. He and his nobles were baptized four years later, in 601.

Augustine reported to Pope Gregory somewhat optimistically that 'the English had accepted the faith of Christ', but he must have seen from the outset that Gregory's plan could not be implemented in his lifetime. Kent was only one kingdom in a corner of England. It did not include London, which was then only on the north side of the Thames, and in the hands of the East Saxons. Augustine therefore made Canterbury his base in the southern province. A number of Romano-British churches were repaired, and the monastery of St Peter and St Paul was founded. Seven years elapsed before negotiations with the East Saxons made it possible for *Mellitus to be consecrated bishop of London. *Paulinus went to York in 625, but had to abandon the mission; and *Birinus went on a separate papal mission to Dorchester in 635.

Augustine failed to come to terms with the 'British bishops', as *Bede calls them – the Celtic bishops of northern England and Wales. It was to be more than half a century before the developing quarrel between the Latin monks and the Celtic monks was settled at Whitby.

Augustine died on May 28 604. At his death, the Latin Church was established in the territories of the South Saxons and the East Saxons, but Pope Gregory's ambitious plans for the whole of England were a long way from fulfilment. Augustine worked slowly and cautiously, advancing into areas where his monks were welcome, but not courting martyrdom; but a beginning was made which would eventually bring England into the mainstream of Christian experience in Europe.

AA.SS., Aug., 6, pp. 213–460; contemporary Life by Possidius in *The Western Fathers*; Bede, *H.E.*, bk 1, chs 23—34; bk 2, chs 2—3; E. Gilson (New York, 1960); G. L. Bonner (Philadelphia, 1964) Mary Clark (2000); Mayr-Harting, pp.

61–77, 265–73; *Cantuar*, pp. 2–15; *N.C.E.*, 1, pp. 1041–57; N. Brooks, *The Early History of the Church at Canterbury* (1985).

John Calvin (1509–64)   *[Commem.]*

Calvin has been called 'a second-generation reformer'. Born in 1509, he was only eleven years old when *Luther went to the Diet of Worms, and thirteen when Zurich accepted the reformed doctrines of Zwingli. The son of a prosperous bourgeois family in Noyon, France, he received the tonsure and was installed in a local benefice at the age of twelve; but his studies in Paris, Orleans and Bourges, first in Classics and then in law, soon brought him within the orbit of the Protestant doctrines which were gaining ground in Catholic France. At some stage he had a conversion experience, and began to study the Scriptures in depth in Erasmus's translation.

Active repression of the reformers began in France in 1533. Calvin had to leave France, and went to Basle, where in 1536 he published the first edition of his *Christianae Religionis Instituto*, or 'Institutes of the Christian Religion'. This work was based on a framework of the Catechism, and dealt with Law, Faith, Sacraments, Grace and Liberty. Calvin was a trained lawyer, and he took his stand on the Scriptures as God's law. His doctrine of predestination was uncompromising: only God's elect could hope for eternal life: 'God adopts some to hope of life, and sentences others to eternal death.' He laid it down that there were only two sacraments in place of the traditional seven: baptism and the Holy Supper: the first a sign of acceptance by the congregation, the second a memorial in which the bread and wine remained bread and wine.

Successive editions of this massive work, which has been compared to the *Summa Theologica* of Thomas Aquinas, absorbed much of Calvin's intellectual energy for many years. Revision increased it to three times its original length, and greatly extended its scope. The final Latin edition was published in 1559, and the first English edition in 1561.

Calvin spent about a year in Basle from 1535 to 1536, then decided to go to Strasbourg. On the way, he stopped at Geneva, and encountered the reformer Guillaume Farel. The city had a population of some 10,000, and was virtually self-governing within the Swiss Confederation. The Catholic bishop had been expelled, and on 21

May 1536, the Council of Two Hundred, its debating body, had agreed by a show of hands to 'promise before God that we should live in future according to his holy evangelical laws and by the Word of God, and that we should abandon all masses and other ceremonies and papal abuses and everything which is added to them'.

Three months later, Calvin arrived. Apart from a period from 1538 to 1541 when they were driven out by their opponents, he and Farel were to work there together for the rest of his life. Geneva was to be his model evangelical community, an example to the rest of the world.

The laws devised by Calvin were much less rigorously observed in the rural areas of the canton; but within this small city, magistrates and elders of the church together enforced a stringent moral and social code. There were fines for non-attendance at church; denying God was punished by three days' imprisonment on bread and water in the first instance, and a whipping for further offences; all festivals were abolished except for Sunday, the Lord's Day; Christmas was to be celebrated on the Sunday following 25 December; swearing, the singing of bawdy or promiscuous songs, and provocative dances were all proscribed.

This régime often aroused strong opposition. Shortly before his death, Calvin noted that he had been taunted, howled down and even shot at by people who opposed their measures – 'Just imagine how that frightened a poor scholar as timid as I am'; but his work developed an immense reputation in Protestant Europe. His influence has been traced on the Scottish Presbyterians led by John Knox, the English Puritans of the seventeenth century, the Dutch Reformed Church which later dominated colonial South Africa, and many other movements.

Calvin died in Geneva on 26 or 27 May 1564. By that time, popular admiration for him was so great that his friends and supporters feared that the evangelicals would be accused of starting a cult. He was buried very quickly, as he had asked, in a common cemetery without a tombstone, so that no superstition should follow his passing.

G. E. Duffield (1966); T. H. L. Parker (1975) contains a good bibliography; W. G. Naphy (Manchester, 1994); D. C. Steinmetz (1995). Works: Calvin Translation Society, Edinburgh (47 vols, 1845 ff.); selections ed. G. R. Potter and M. Greengrass (1983).

Philip Neri (1515–95) *[Commem.]*

Philip was born in Florence only seventeen years after the execution of the Dominican friar Savonarola for heresy and schism. He was educated by the Dominicans, who showed him Savonarola's portrait, his cell and his Bible. Though Philip was a much gentler personality, his firm refusal to join one of the established religious Orders or to take any part in the organizational life of the Church came from a similar belief that it needed to be cleansed of corruption in order to get back to the values of its Founder.

At the age of sixteen or seventeen, Philip was sent to stay with an uncle in San Germano, about half-way between Rome and Naples. The uncle was a merchant, and it was intended that Philip should enter his business; but he visited Monte Cassino, and learned about the Benedictine heritage, and then went to spend some time alone in a mountain chapel before going to Rome. There he lived a religious life in great simplicity. He lived on bread, olives and a little wine; he studied the mighty works of *Thomas Aquinas; and he spent his nights in prayer in one of the seven great churches of the city. After a time he sold most of his books in order to concentrate on prayer, and went to the catacombs, where he could pray with the martyrs of the early Christian era. In Rome, he met both *Ignatius Loyola and *Francis Xavier; but the near-military discipline of the Jesuits and the work of missions was not for him. During the day, he would sometimes wander the streets of Rome, talking to young people employed in the city. Though he was shy, he had a gift for friendship, and he induced some of them to join him in helping patients in the city hospitals, and to visit churches with him. In 1548, he founded a confraternity to look after pilgrims to Rome and care for the convalescent. In 1551, he was ordained priest, and found a corner for himself in San Girolamo, a college of secular priests who received their board and lodging, but no stipend.

San Girolamo suited him ideally. He began to hear confessions, and because he was really interested in the people who came to him, and treated them kindly, many came to him for spiritual guidance. His informal confraternity acquired a very minimal framework: they would gather together to read a book, usually a passage of Scripture or the work of one of the mystics. There would be a time of prayer, and then they would go to visit a church or to listen to religious music. Those who came to join him came from all classes of Roman society –

rich and poor, learned and unlearned. They were all told to beg for the poor, and to work with the sick.

This was the start of the Oratory. At first the movement aroused great suspicion among the Roman clergy, including Pope Paul IV. Philip was accused of ambition, pride and (worse) 'introducing novelties'. For a week or two, he was suspended from his priestly ministry, and there was talk of closing the Oratory down; but Charles Borromeo, the enlightened archbishop of Milan, interceded on his behalf. He continued to suffer from gossip, suspicion and envy until Gregory XIII became pope in 1572. Gregory was a reforming pope – he also approved *Teresa of Avila's Carmelite reforms. He gave Philip a church of his own, and 8,000 crowns to assist in its renovation and extension. Other people provided donations, large and small, and a cardinal found the confraternity a derelict convent to live in. Recruits came in large numbers – sometimes too many to be accepted. Other houses were set up in Bologna and Naples, and by the time Philip died in 1595, there were seven houses in Italy. There were very few rules: the spirit was more important than the letter.

The centre of Philip's ministry was the confessional: he spent forty-five years in all in the spiritual direction of individuals – a very different approach from that of the Dominicans, with their unrelenting intellectualism, or the Jesuits, who baptized people in their thousands. People loved Philip for his evident holiness, his gentleness with sinners, his informality, and the sheer joyousness of his faith.

The Oratorian movement has now spread to many countries. Among many celebrated Oratorians is *John Henry Newman.

J. H. Newman, 'The Mission of St Philip Neri' in *Sermons Preached on Various Occasions* (1904, repr. 1968); M. Trevor, *Apostle of Rome* (1966); L. Bouyer, *St Philip Neri: a Portrait* (Eng. trans. 1995); P. Turks, *Philip Neri, the Fire of Joy* (Eng. trans. 1995); *Butler*, May, pp. 144–7.

28. Lanfranc (1005–89)   [Commem.]

Lanfranc was not a Norman, but an Italian, from Pavia. He was educated in Italy and then in Paris. He gained a reputation as a scholar and a teacher in Burgundy and Normandy, and in 1042 he entered the monastery of Bec-Hellouin, then a new foundation. Within three years he was prior of Bec. He was a brilliant administrator, with a gift for clear and lucid thought and an unrivalled knowledge of canon and civil law. He wrote commentaries on the Letters of Paul, a text called *A Monastic Constitution* and a treatise on the nature of Holy Communion. In 1063, Duke William of Normandy made him abbot of his own new foundation at Caen, and four years after the Norman conquest of England, with the pope's approval, William asked him to become archbishop of Canterbury.

Nothing would have taken him to the alien and conquered territories of the English except his devotion to William. He yielded to royal pressure, and proceeded to Normanize the Anglo-Saxon Church. Though the Church in England had its own culture, based on the work of *Dunstan, Ethelwold and Oswald about a century earlier, Lanfranc regarded it as backward and unsophisticated. Normans were placed in bishoprics and cathedral posts. Monasteries were given new Norman abbots and priors.

Lanfranc held three General Councils, in 1072, 1075 and 1076. Through these bodies he virtually reorganized the Church in England, giving bishops new responsibilities, requiring them to hold synods twice a year in their own dioceses, drawing up new diocesan boundaries, and moving the bishop's seat in some cases from depopulated areas to new towns. New dioceses were formed, with cathedrals at Norwich, Rochester, Durham and Coventry. Measures to promote the celibacy of the clergy (many of the secular Anglo-Saxon clergy were married), and to put down superstitious practices, were promulgated. Monastic life was revitalized and new monasteries set up. With William's help, Lanfranc set up courts of ecclesiastical jurisdiction.

One of his most controversial measures was his cavalier treatment of the Anglo-Saxon saints and their cults. A clerical commission was sent round England to change church dedications, substituting the names of saints from the Roman calendar for much-loved Anglo-Saxon ones. *Alphege was only saved from oblivion by the intervention of *Anselm of Bec, and *Dunstan by Oswald of Winchester.

After his death, Lanfranc was venerated as a saint in Pavia, his birthplace, in Bayeux and in Bec; but perhaps it is understandable that a cult never developed at Canterbury.

P.L., 150, pp. 19–58; *Men.E.W.*, pp. 229–30; A. J. MacDonald (2nd edn, 1944); M. T. Gibson, *Lanfranc of Bec* (1978); H. Clover and M. T. Gibson, *The Letters of Lanfranc* (1979); Stenton, pp. 658–79; *N.C.E.*, 8, pp. 361–2; *Butler*, May, pp. 160–1.

30. Joan of Arc (1412–31)   [Commem.]

The story of Jeanne d'Arc has been told so many times, and with such
a variety of emphases, that it is difficult to make an assessment of her
life. The soundest evidence of who she was and what she was like
comes from the transcript of her trial, which is available in English
translation.

The Hundred Years' War, which in fact lasted from 1340 to 1450,
was a conflict between the English and French royal houses for the
territory of France. After the battle of Agincourt in 1415, negotiations
led to the Treaty of Troyes of 1420. Under the terms of the treaty,
Henry V of England was recognized as the heir of Charles VI of
France, and married his daughter Katharine, while the 'so-called
Dauphin' of France was declared illegitimate. This is the final happy
scene in Shakespeare's *Henry V*; but the peace lasted only two years.
Henry V and Charles VI both died in 1422. The English proclaimed
the infant Henry VI 'King of France and of England,' while the French
proclaimed the Dauphin 'Charles VII'; but Henry VI was too young to
be crowned, and the Dauphin, legitimate or not, could not be
crowned, because the English held Rheims, where French coronations
took place. The battles dragged on, and there was a prophecy in
France that 'The Kingdom of Fleur-de-Lys' would be saved by a
pucelle, a young virgin.

In 1426, when she was fourteen, Jeanne had repeated visions in
which *St Margaret of Antioch and *St Catherine of Alexandria told
her that she must save France. There were statues of these saints in the
church of Domrémy, her birthplace. She was sponsored by two noblemen, and taken to see the Dauphin. In order to test her, the Dauphin
placed one of his courtiers on the throne, and stood among the other
courtiers; but Jeanne recognized him at once. She went up to him and
said, 'I tell you in the name of God that you are the lawful heir of
France and the son of the King!' She is also said to have handed him a
secret, never divulged, which attested to the authenticity of her
mission. Theologians examined her for a period of three weeks, but
could not shake her convictions, and they advised the Dauphin to
follow her lead.

This gave the Dauphin new heart. She went into battle with him,
wearing white armour and the fleur-de-lys on her hat, and carrying the
banner of the Knights Templar as a sign that she would rally all

Christendom for a new Crusade. In June 1429, she was wounded at Orléans, but the city was liberated. Rheims surrendered to the Dauphin a month later, and there was a hasty coronation on the following day. In September, the Dauphin's forces marched on Paris, and succeeded in driving the English out of the district of Saint-Denys so that the King could be enthroned in the abbey. In May 1430, on a small expedition, Jeanne was taken prisoner by the Burgundians, who were allies of the English, at Rheims. They handed her over to the English for 10,000 gold livres.

She was tried by the ecclesiastical court of the bishop of Beauvais, Pierre de Cauchon. She refused to testify to her origins or her age, but made an impressive and spirited defence of her position without any kind of legal support. The judges managed to trip her up on her use of ecclesiastical terms, since she was no theologian, but they could not shake her manifestly honest conviction that she was sent by God to free France from the English. Charles VII seems to have made little attempt to save her. She was maltreated in prison, accused almost hysterically of witchcraft, heresy and unnatural behaviour (in that she wore men's clothes), and finally condemned and handed over to the secular arm – that is, the English authorities – for execution. At one point, intimidated by the strength of the forces ranged against her, she made a partial recantation; but she then withdrew it, and faced her death bravely. On 30 May 1431, she was burned at the stake in Rouen market-place.

This terrible story rouses many emotions. She is a national heroine and a patron saint of France. Many devout French people believe that she was, as she claimed, directly inspired by God, and she is the second patron of France. George Bernard Shaw's *St Joan* makes her a sensible, sturdy country girl resisting ecclesiastical tyranny and English aggression. Orléanists in France have long maintained that the story of the *pucelle* was deliberately fostered; that Jeanne was an illegitimate daughter of the Duke of Orléans, half-sister to the Dauphin, and brought into prominence in what was primarily a brilliant publicity coup, to fulfil the prophecy about a *pucelle* who would save France. The Roman Catholic Church long delayed her canonization. It was not proclaimed until 1920, and she is recognized as a virgin, but not a martyr.

Whatever the truth of the matter, we are left with the story of a brave and pious girl who did what she thought was her duty, and died for it.

G. Goyau (Paris, 1920); V. Sackville-West (1936); R. Pernoud (1954, Eng. trans. 1961); M. Warner (1980); G. B. Shaw, *St Joan* (1923); P. Tisset and Y. Lanhers, *Procès de Jeanne d'Arc* (Société de l'Histoire de France, 3 vols, Paris, 1960–71); J. P. Barrett, *The Trial of Joan of Arc* (1931); M. D. Darnac, *The True Story of the Maid of Orléans*, trans. Peter de Polnay (1969).

Josephine Butler (1828–1906)   [L.F.]

Josephine Butler was the wife of the Revd George Butler. They were Gladstonian Liberals – deeply religious, and quite unconventional. He was a teacher, the son of a headmaster of Harrow School, and in Holy Orders. In 1865, after some years at Oxford and in Cheltenham, he was appointed principal of Liverpool College, and they moved north with their four children.

They found Liverpool very different from Oxford and Cheltenham – a sprawling port with mass poverty, many immigrants and a very mixed population. While George Butler was absorbed in the school, where he introduced many progressive innovations, Josephine turned to charitable work, taking sick and malnourished prostitutes from the docks into her own home. At one time, five of them were dying at once. With her husband's full support, she became involved in the controversy over the Contagious Diseases Acts of 1866.

These Acts, passed very quietly, set up a Continental-type system for the regulation of prostitutes, with regular medical inspections to prevent the spread of venereal disease. A special corps of plain-clothes police was to keep a list of licensed prostitutes, and was given the power to arrest any woman whom they had 'good cause to believe a prostitute'. 'Good cause' was left undefined, and there was a risk that girls could be harassed, threatened or falsely accused. At this time, the age of consent was twelve, and no social stigma attached to the men who paid for sex with young girls.

The Acts codified the Victorian double standard, and Josephine Butler saw this as a clear case of the contravention of human rights. She invoked Magna Carta, Habeas Corpus, Blackstone, the Bill of Rights and Alexis de Tocqueville in her book *The Constitution Violated* (1872). She pointed out that in law, an accused person was presumed innocent until proved guilty, but women arrested under the Acts had no right of appeal. It was unjust that, in an act involving two people, one should be punished. She drew a clear distinction between sin, which was the business of the Church, and crime, which was the business of the state; and between moral and legal issues. She maintained that there were other solutions to the problem of venereal disease – but they involved giving women rights which they were being denied: education, employment, the right to vote.

On the last day of December 1867, the campaign, which was supported by *Florence Nightingale and the Society of Friends, but not by most of the clergy, reached the Press. The public reaction was one of shock and horror. The subject was unmentionable, and 'good women' were not supposed to know about such things: 'Have these ladies no better occupation?' thundered one newspaper, commenting that they indulged in 'a hobby too nasty to mention'. Mrs Butler replied that the Acts involved a gross violation of women's dignity. There were measures the state might legitimately take to reduce prostitution. It might stop procuring and solicitation, stop the public flaunting of vice; but any measures must apply equally to both sexes. 'I have seen girls bought and sold just as young girls were at the time of the slave trade.'

She gave evidence to a Royal Commission which produced a report floundering in inconsistencies. She led a deputation to the Home Office bearing a petition signed by a quarter of a million women, and found the Home Secretary (A. H. Bruce) 'sullenly defiant'. She toured England, addressing meetings of both men and women – not without some personal risk.

Gradually, the Abolitionists, as they called themselves, secured support. By 1876, there were resolutions in their favour from the General Assembly of the Free Church of Scotland, 700 Wesleyan ministers in conference, and 1,500 Anglican clergy, including the dean of Carlisle (but no bishops). In 1883, the compulsory examination of suspected prostitutes was condemned in a private member's motion in the House of Commons. Josephine and her supporters had been keeping vigils and praying continuously. The special police were disbanded, and three years later, the Contagious Diseases Acts were repealed.

By that time, her husband had moved to a canonry at Winchester, and the Butlers had eight happy years in the cathedral close before he died; but Josephine's work continued. She had founded an international movement which spread into many countries. In her sixteen years of widowhood, she travelled widely in Europe. She went to Rome to see Pope Leo XIII, who issued an encyclical against legalized brothels in 1895. She supported *Catherine Booth in Geneva, where the authorities complained that the Salvation Army was emptying the brothels. She attacked the white slave trade in Belgium, and campaigned for the closure of Army brothels in India.

Josephine Butler was a woman of strong religious faith, and one biographer, Moberley Bell, calls her a mystic. She wrote a life of *Catherine of Siena, for whom she had a special devotion. In the discussions on extending the list of saints before the approval of the ASB Calendar in 1978, objections were made in Synod that the new list contained hardly any women. According to Richard Symonds, after some spirited debates, Josephine Butler 'scraped into the ASB as the only British post-Reformation woman' to the acompaniment of 'some grumbling'. She was saved by one vote in the House of Bishops, chiefly 'in recognition of the contribution made to the Church by parsons' wives'. She is now accorded a Lesser Festival, and assured of more whole-hearted support.

W. T. Stead (1887); M. Fawcett and E. M. Turner (1927); A. S. G. Butler (1954). E. Moberley Bell (1962); *Great Christians*, pp. 81–93; *Far Above Rubies*, pp. 2–3, 251. Works include *Women's Work and Women's Culture* (1869); *The Constitution Violated* (1872); *Catherine of Siena* (1879); *Personal Recollections of a Great Crusade* (1896).

Apolo Kivebulaya (d. 1933)   *[Commem.]*

Apolo came from a Ugandan village about forty miles north of Lake Victoria. There is no evidence on the date of his birth, but he was a boy when *Bishop James Hannington was murdered in 1885, and the *Uganda Martyrs were executed in the following year. He was picked up by a gang of Moslem soldiers, and forced to join them for a time, but he escaped, and in the confusion following the rebellion of 1888, he joined a group of Christians on the move through the bush. He had met a celebrated Scottish missionary-engineer, Alexander Murdoch Mackay, known as 'Mackay of the Great Lake'. He was much impressed by Mackay, and read the Gospel according to Matthew, which Mackay had translated into Luganda, the language of southern Uganda. When life became normal again, Apolo returned to his village, and was thinking of asking for baptism when the chief directed him to lead a party building a road into the country of the Toro, to the west of Uganda. It was a land of dense forests leading to the

Mountains of the Moon (now in the Congo). Whilst on this expedition, Apolo formed a determination to take the Christian message to the people of the forests. He went back to his village, was baptized, and set out with the blessing of the Church.

He had probably made some advance contacts on his road-building expedition. The chief of the Toro was friendly, listened to his message, and was baptized. Apolo was able to influence him to free slaves, put down witchcraft, and stop the opium trade among his people. The Toro turned to peaceful ways, and ceased to raid the cattle of the neighbouring tribes. Then the chief provided guides to lead Apolo round Mount Ruwenzori and into the forests. He reached Boga, a small tribal settlement, where he ran into disaster: the witch-doctors plotted against him, and he was beaten and left for dead; but his apparent resurrection the next morning was greeted with considerable respect. When it became known that he was the man who had stopped the Toro from raiding the Mboga cattle, the respect increased. He converted the chief, built a small thatched church, and set to work. Missionaries came to see him, and in 1903 he was ordained. He organized a school, trained teachers and catechists and went out into the forests to contact the pygmy people. He translated the Gospel according to Mark (which is possibly easier to translate than Matthew) into the pygmy language, taught, baptized, and brought English missionaries to meet them.

In all, Apolo worked in Boga and the surrounding area for thirty years. When he died, his work was taken over by the Church Missionary Society, which sent out missionaries to build on his achievements. Boga became a powerful Anglican centre, part of the diocese of Uganda, Burundi and Boga-Zaire. When *Archbishop Janani Luwum made a visitation to Boga in the mid 1970s, the road was still not easy to negotiate, and the rivers were flooded. He led his party across the water, purple shirt flapping and silver cross swinging, to the settlement where Apolo Kivebulaya had set up the Church of Christ in the forests of the Congo.

Margaret Sinker, *Into the Great Forest: the story of Apolo Kivebulaya* (1950); Margaret Ford, *Janani: the making of a martyr* (1978).

June

1. Justin (c.100–65) [L.F.]

Justin, who is usually known as Justin Martyr, was a Greek, born in Samaria. He received a classical Greek education, and became a philosopher, searching for 'the vision of God' in the schools of philosophy at Ephesus and Alexandria. He rejected in turn the beliefs of the Stoics, the Peripatetics, and the Pythagoreans, and for a time accepted Platonic idealism. Then one day, about the year 135, while walking on the sea shore near Ephesus, he met a 'respectable old man of meek and venerable mien' who told him about Christianity. He writes: 'My spirit was immediately set on fire, and an affection for the Prophets and for those who are friends of Christ took hold of me.' This was the truth he had been seeking.

Justin taught Christian apologetics in the philosophy school at Ephesus, debating with Jews, Gnostics, and those who held the classical beliefs of Greece and Rome. About the year 150, he went to Rome, where he founded his own school of philosophy, and wrote his major works.

While most of the early Fathers of the Church wrote to edify Christian communities, Justin wrote to defend the Church against attack by the many other belief systems current in the second century.

An ascetic and austere personality, he lived for intellectual debate, and was frequently involved in public controversy. His chief opponent was Crescens the Cynic, whom he derided as 'the lover not of wisdom but of false opinions'. *Jerome says that Crescens was involved in Justin's arrest in the persecutions of the reign of Marcus Aurelius, about the year 165. The record of the judicial proceedings survives. Justin stated his beliefs, refused to sacrifice to the Roman gods, and accepted martyrdom. He was beheaded with six other Christians.

In his two *Apologies* and his *Dialogue with Trypho*, Justin sees

Platonism and Christianity as different but compatible revelations from God. He argues that God sent the prophets to prepare the Jews for the coming of Christ, and the Greek philosophers, such as Socrates and Plato, to prepare the Graeco-Roman world to receive him. The *Logos* fulfilled both traditions – Light of Light, like the flame passed from one torch to another. The Incarnation is not a break with history, but the fulfilment of history. *Augustine of Hippo and *Thomas Aquinas were profoundly influenced by Justin's writings.

Justin also provides an insight into the life and doctrines of the Church only a century after the Crucifixion, when Christians were highly suspect in Roman society, and often called 'atheists' because they refused to attend public worship of the gods. They were accused of practising incest, cannibalism and black magic. Justin made Judaism and Christianity, which the Romans still regarded as marginal beliefs developed in a remote and backward province of the Empire, intellectually comprehensible to Roman philosophers. He insisted that Christians were good citizens, trading honourably, paying their taxes and living peaceably. He had visited both Bethlehem and Calvary: so many Christian pilgrims had already venerated both holy places that the Romans had built temples there to deter them – though, as Jerome was to comment later, this marked the sites out more clearly. He taught that baptism is a new birth, and the Eucharist is participation in the life of Christ himself. He described both rites carefully to distinguish them from the rites of less reputable groups. Justin's devotion to truth makes him an excellent and reliable witness to the faith of the early Church under attack.

Eusebius, *H.E.*, bk 4, chs 6 and 16—18; Jerome, *Lives of Illustrious Men*, ch. 23; M. J. Lagrange (1914); C. C. Martindale (1923); E. Goodenough (1930); L. W. Barnard (1967). See also A. L. Williams, *Justin Martyr: The Dialogue with Trypho* (New York, 1930); T. B. Falls, *The Writing of Saint Justin Martyr* (New York, 1948); Henry Chadwick, 'Justin Martyr's Defence of Christians,' *Bulletin of the John Ryland's Library* 47 (1965), pp. 275–97; Justin's first Apology is in *Early Christian Fathers*, pp. 225–89.

3. The Martyrs of Uganda (1886 and 1971-9)   [Commem.]

After Stanley's much publicized discovery of the Scottish missionary David Livingstone at Ujiji in 1871, many Christian missions were sent out from Europe to Central Africa. Mtesa, the *kabaka* or king of the

Baganda, in southern Uganda, allowed the missionaries to work in his territory; but when he died in 1884, he was succeeded by his son Mwanga, who was only eighteen years old and of limited intelligence. Though he had attended mission school, he could neither read nor write. When he became *kabaka*, counsellors told him that the foreigners would 'eat the country' and take it over for themselves. In the 'scramble for Africa', both British and German traders were coming to the area. The witch-doctors, whose power was threatened by the missionaries, persuaded Mwanga that the tribal ancestors were angry at their coming. His personality began to deteriorate. He smoked hemp, he drank alcohol excessively, and his behaviour became irrational. He was angry when he saw the missionaries teaching the young men to read and write, and roused to irrational fury when they told Christian boys not to give way to his demands for homosexual practices. (It is said that he had learned these practices from Arab traders. They were not common among the Baganda.) He developed murderous outbursts of rage in which he would seize a boy and ask, 'Do you read?' meaning, 'Are you a Christian?'

In 1885, the newly appointed Anglican bishop *James Hannington and his companions were seized and murdered on Mwanga's orders. In November, the master of the pages, Joseph Mkasa, who was a Catholic catechist, was beheaded; and in the following May, an order for mass execution was issued. Guards were posted round the palace to prevent anyone escaping, witch-doctors were sent for, and the drums beat to summon the executioners. All the pages were commanded to appear before the *kabaka*, and those who were Christians were ordered to stand out. They were asked if they would abandon their faith. When they refused, the order was given to put them to death.

They were marched to the *matámbiro*, or place of ritual sacrifice, at Namugongo, sixteen miles from Kampala, and made to construct a huge pyre. After a week of harsh imprisonment, they were brought out on Ascension Day, 3 June 1886. They were stripped of their clothes, bound, and each wrapped in a mat of reeds. Before he was placed on the pyre, one of the martyrs, Bruno Serúnkuma, said to his brother, 'A well which has many sources never runs dry. When we are gone, others will come after us.'

When they were stacked on the pyre, it was set alight, and the martyrs were burned alive to the sound of the ritual chants of the executioners. One executioner said afterwards that they went on praying until they died. The two magnificent shrines erected at Namugongo in their memory have become centres of great devotion. They list respectively the names of twenty-four Anglican and Free Church martyrs, and twenty-two Catholic martyrs.

In 1888 Mwanga decided to arrest all the religious leaders, Christian and Muslim, and to throw them to the crocodiles, but there was a rebellion. Mwanga left the country, and eventually, in 1890, a British administration was set up. By that time, there were ten thousand Christians in Buganda, converted by the example of the martyrs.

The days of savagery were not over: after Uganda achieved independence, the military dictatorship of Idi Amin from 1971 to 1978 was responsible for the death of many Christians who spoke out against a corrupt and blood-stained régime. Amin was convinced that many clergy were agents of the US Central Intelligence Agency, and repeated pressure from the United Nations, the Western powers and other central African states had no lasting effect. After the death of *Archbishop Janani Luwum in February 1977, he assured the remaining bishops that he was not anti-Christian – and four days later banned all religious groups. Among the Christian victims of Amin's régime were many clergy, university teachers and judges. Again the Church in Uganda survived. In a country stricken by poverty, AIDS and the threat of war on its borders, the example of the martyrs has meant much to devout Christian communities.

J. P. Thoonen, *Black Martyrs* (1941); A. E. Howell, *The Fires of Namugongo* (1948); J. F. Faupel, *African Holocaust* (1962); D. Wooding and R. Barnett, *Uganda Holocaust* (1980); J. J. Jorgensen, *Uganda: A Modern History* (1981); S. Decalo, *Psychoses of Power: African Personal Dictatorships* (1989); Giles Foden's fictionalized account of the atrocities of the Amin régime, *The Last King of Scotland* (1998), is said to be factually based.

5. Boniface (Wynfrith) (c.675–754) [L.F.]

Boniface is known as 'the Apostle of Germany'. Though the Rhineland and Bavaria had become Christian before his time, he organized the systematic evangelization of the great central plains of Germany, and also reformed the Frankish Church.

He was a Devon man, probably born at Crediton. He went to school at a monastery near Exeter, and then to the abbey of Nursling in the Winchester diocese, where he became director of studies. He is said to have written the first Latin grammar known to have been compiled in

England, and to have been an inspiring lecturer. His lectures were so much appreciated that copies of notes were made, and circulated to other monasteries. He was ordained to the priesthood at the age of thirty, and wrote many sermons and instructions based on the Bible. In 716, refusing preferment in England, he went to work among the war-like tribes of Friesland (now in the Netherlands), but had to withdraw when the local chief became hostile, declaring that he was 'not prepared to go to heaven with a handful.of beggars'. He worked for a time in the more settled regions of Bavaria and Hesse, then went back to the Low Countries to help Bishop Willibrord of Utrecht. Willibrord wanted Boniface to be his successor, but Boniface obtained a general commission to work in Germany from Pope Gregory II, and went back to his missionary work.

His methods of challenging tribal beliefs in the old Norse gods were direct and sometimes confrontational. A story is told of how he chopped down an oak tree on Mount Gudenberg, the source of much local superstition, with an axe. Crowds came to watch him, expecting the Norse gods to strike him down; but his first few blows sent the tree crashing to the ground. This was accounted a miracle, and many conversions followed.

His missionary work was so successful that he was consecrated a regionary bishop. He wrote a famous letter to the English monasteries, asking for their prayers and help in the mission to 'those who are of one blood and bone with you'. They sent him money, books, vestments and relics. Parties of monks and nuns, many of them from noble houses, went out to join him. He established a number of monasteries which were to become celebrated as centres of faith and learning. In 732, he became archbishop, with the power to consecrate bishops in the territories beyond the Rhine.

In 741, Charles Martel, the ruler of the Franks, who had given him protection for his work in Germany, asked him to regenerate the Frankish Church. Bishoprics were being bought and sold, given to unsuitable clergy or even laymen, or left vacant. The clergy were poorly taught, and often unfit for office. Between 741 and 747, Boniface presided over five reforming synods, in which many abuses were remedied, and the monasteries brought back to the Benedictine Rule.

Boniface was a great missionary preacher, an outstanding administrator, and a learned and holy man. Many of his letters are still available to readers. They show how he dealt with a variety of human problems, with wisdom and gentleness. When he was eighty, he resigned all his great offices and went back to evangelize the Friesians. He led a mission into a hostile area, and was quietly reading in his tent in preparation for a confirmation when his party was suddenly attacked by tribesmen. He would not allow others to defend him, and was one of the first to fall. After his death, his body was taken back to the monastery at Fulda, where it still lies. The monastery preserves the book with which he is said to have warded off the first blows. It is dented with sword-cuts, and the cover is stained with what is thought to be his blood.

Soon after Boniface's death, Archbishop Cuthbert of Canterbury wrote, 'We in England lovingly count him as one of the best and greatest teachers of the true faith', and a Church synod agreed that his feast should be celebrated equally with that of *Augustine of Canterbury; but his reputation, like that of many Anglo-Saxon saints, was devalued after the Norman Conquest, and he is much better known in Germany and the Netherlands than in his own country.

There are edited versions of early Lives in *N.L.A.*, 1, pp. 122–30. A better edition is that of W. Levison, *Vitae sancti Bonifacii epis. Moguntini* (Eng. trans. 1916). See also *Men.E.W.*, pp. 255–8; G. F. Browne, *Boniface of Crediton* (1910); G. Kurth, (1902; Eng. trans. 1935); G. W. Greenaway (1955); T. Reuter (ed.) *The Greatest Englishman* (1980); C. Dawson, *The Making of Europe* (1946), p. 166. Boniface's letters have been edited by M. Tangl in *Monumenta Germanicae Historica, Scriptores: Epistolae Selectae.* Some of these letters are trans. in C. H. Talbot, *Anglo-Saxon Missionaries in Germany* (1954). Works of Boniface are in many translations.

6. Ini Kopuria (d. 1945)   [Commem.]

The Melanesian Mission started in the 1850s with the ministry of *John Coleridge Patteson, and was strengthened by his martyrdom and that of his companions. Thereafter, it developed steadily. Ini Kopuria was a mission school boy – baptized 'Ini' after a Christian king of Dorset. He became a police officer in Guadalcanal until 1924, when he had a serious illness. He spent months in meditation, and had a vision of Jesus calling him to a new way of life. With the approval of Bishop Seward of Melanesia, he became an evangelist, taking the gospel to remote villages and islands. As others came to join him, he formed them into the Melanesian Brotherhood, which was established in 1935.

Ini prepared a Rule for the Brotherhood. Men made a five-year commitment to service, though many stayed much longer. During the period of their vow, they were not to marry, not to receive pay, and to promise to obey his direction. The bishop was the Father of the Brotherhood. They were organized in 'households' of eight, and worked in pairs. Their dress was a black loincloth and a white singlet, and they went bare-headed and bare-footed. Ini himself made a life-long vow, and donated his land on the Guadalcanal coast to the Brotherhood. The numbers grew to 1,500, and it became one of the largest religious communities in the Anglican Communion. There was also an Order of Companions, men and women in groups of eight, who renewed their baptismal vows, met weekly to pray for the Brotherhood and the village, and undertook works of charity, such as visiting the sick.

The movement was not without its critics. Some English missionaries thought that Ini was 'conceited'. Though he respected the authority of the bishop, he may not have taken kindly to those who assumed that they were his superiors by virtue of their colour and education. Perhaps he thought that he understood his own people better than the missionaries did. Dr Charles Fox, who wrote a journal of the Melanesian Mission, described Ini's dedication and his joyous attitude to his work, adding that he was 'the most reverent Melanesian I have ever met, and that was saying a lot'. He describes Ini as a man of very strong personality, short, thick-set, curly-haired and very dark in colour, 'always merry and very wise'. Ini was a gifted and very effective evangelist with his own people, and the Brothers loved him. He took deacon's Orders, but never became a priest, though a few of the Brothers did so.

Then came the entry of Japan into the Second World War. From 1942, the islands became a battle zone, with the American forces on the ground, and the Japanese at sea and in the air. The Melanesian way of life disintegrated, and when the Japanese invaded, the Brotherhood ceased to function. The Japanese burned the mission centre, and shot some of the brothers. Others took to the bush. Ini got away, and Dr Fox tells us very little of what happened to him – only that he was dispensed from his vows, and that he went 'into a far country'; but when the Japanese were driven out of the islands, he returned, and prepared to rebuild the work of the Brotherhood. He died in June 1945, before this could be achieved, and before the final defeat of Japan; but there were others to build on his work and honour his memory.

Charles E. Fox, *Missionary Journal of the Melanesian Mission* (1946), and *Lord of the Southern Isles: the Anglican Mission in Melanesia 1849–1949* (1958), pp. 193–5. (The latter includes the Rule of the Melanesian Brotherhood on pp. 268–72).

8. Thomas Ken (1637–1711) [L.F.]

After his mother's early death, Thomas was brought up largely by his half-sister, Anne, who was the wife of Isaac Walton, author of *The Compleat Angler*. Since the Waltons spent much of their lives in stately homes or the houses of eminent clergy, Thomas grew up with wide social contacts. He went to Winchester and then to Hart Hall, Oxford, became chaplain to the bishop of Winchester, and after holding several livings became a prebendary of Winchester cathedral. In 1679, he was appointed chaplain to the Princess Mary, daughter of Charles II.

Mary had married her cousin William of Orange two years earlier, and though she was a devout Anglican, William's tendencies were Calvinistic. He was a morose and authoritarian prince, and Thomas Ken soon incurred his wrath: when one of William's courtiers seduced one of Mary's maids of honour, Ken gave pastoral advice to them both and married them without asking William's permission. Ken had to leave for the Netherlands, but he returned to London to become a royal chaplain to Charles II. Again, he stood by his principles in the face of possible royal fury: when Charles went to Winchester accompanied by Nell Gwynn, he was asked to vacate his house for Mistress Gwynn's occupation. He refused: but Charles was not a man to hold grudges. Only a year or two later, he cheerfully agreed to the appointment of 'little Ken, who refused Nelly a lodging' as bishop of Bath.

Charles II died in February 1685, and was succeeded by his brother James, who immediately alarmed the Anglicans by hearing Mass in Whitehall with open doors, receiving the papal nuncio in state, and dismissing senior army officers and academics, replacing them with Roman Catholic appointees. In April 1687, eighteen months after he had prorogued parliament, he attempted to obtain the support of the Dissenters by an Order in Council repealing the Test Acts, which imposed civil disabilities on Roman Catholics and Dissenters alike, and simultaneously repealing *Habeas Corpus*. In May 1688 he issued a second declaration of intent, and required that it should be read in every church and chapel in the land. The issue was not religious toleration, but the exercise of an unconstitutional royal prerogative. The archbishop of Canterbury and seven bishops, including Thomas Ken, protested. They were promptly arrested and sent to the Tower of London. They were charged with seditious libel and arraigned in court; and the courts promptly acquitted them. By the end of that year, William of Orange had been sent for, and James was a refugee in France.

Thomas Ken had on a number of occasions stood by his conscience against powerful opposition, but now came the greatest test of all. He and the other bishops had opposed James II when they thought that the king's actions were unlawful; but James had been crowned, and they had sworn allegiance to him at his coronation. They could not conscientiously swear allegiance to William III in his place. They debated whether William might be proclaimed regent on a legal fiction that James was incapacitated from holding office. William tried to get a clause inserted into the Act of Settlement which exempted the bishops from having to take another oath; but parliament, now exercising its functions again, refused to consider either possibility. The Act of Settlement was passed on 23 February 1689, and the clergy were required to take the oath of allegiance to the new king by 1 August.

The archbishop of Canterbury, Thomas Ken, seven other English bishops, four hundred English clergy and nearly all the bishops and clergy in Scotland refused to take the oath, and despite great public controversy, they were all formally deprived of their offices. The 'Non-Juring Schism' deprived the Church of England of many of its best clergy, and the effects were felt for many years after.

Thomas Ken retired to Longleat, the home of his friend Lord Weymouth, and never held office again, though he lived for a further twenty-two years. He is remembered for his keen conscience, his piety and two hymns which he composed: 'Awake my soul, and with the sun' and 'Glory to thee, my God, this night'.

W. T. Bowles (2 vols, 1830; E. H. Plumptre (2 vols, 1878); H. A. L. Rice (1958); E. Marston, *Thomas Ken and Isaac Walton* (1908). See also *The History of King James's Commission containing the Proceedings against . . . the Seven Bishops* (1711); J. H. Overton, *The Non-Jurors* (1902); J. W. C. Wand, *The High Church Schism* (1951); *Bridge Builders*, pp. 23–34.

9. Ephrem of Syria (c.306–73)   *[Commem.]*

Ephrem (Ephraim or Efrem) was celebrated in his own lifetime as one of the great Fathers of the Eastern Church, but his writings were not translated into Latin until the 1730s, and have been slow to reach a Western readership. The Church in Syria, both Eastern Orthodox and Roman Catholic, calls him 'the Harp of the Holy Ghost', and his homilies and poems are still in use in the Orthodox liturgy. In 1920, Pope Benedict XV declared him a Doctor of the Church, the only Syrian Father to receive this honour.

He was born in Nisibia, in Mesopotamia. There are differing accounts of his family background, but at the age of eighteen he was baptized and came under the tutelage of Bishop James of Nisibia. He is said to have accompanied the bishop to the Council of Nicaea in 325. He became head of the cathedral school, and worked there through several sieges by the Persians, until the emperor Jovian ceded the city to the Persian Empire in 350. The Christians abandoned the city, and Ephrem retired to a cave in a cliff near Edessa, where he lived a very austere life – a small, bald, shrivelled man who ate only a little barley bread and a few vegetables.

He was not a hermit: many people came to him, and he frequently preached to crowds in the city of Edessa. Much of his teaching concerned the errors of Gnosticism, a semi-occult belief system which was strong in that area of the Middle East. He noticed that the Gnostics taught by setting their beliefs to popular tunes, and he copied them – writing his own words to be sung to the same tunes, and training the women to sing them in church. This is thought to be the origin of organized hymn-singing as a regular part of Christian worship.

Ephrem was quite elderly when he was made a deacon, and it is not clear whether he was ever ordained priest. About the year 370, he undertook a journey to Caesarea in order to meet its bishop. Both *Basil of Caesarea and his brother *Gregory of Nyssa were much impressed with him, and Basil described him as 'one who is conversant with all that is true'. The meeting is recorded in both Basil's and Gregory's writings.

In the winter of 372–3, there was a famine in and around Edessa. Some wealthy magnates had full granaries, but they refused to open them to the starving people, because they said that nobody could be trusted with the distribution of corn. Then Ephrem offered to oversee the distribution. So great was the public respect for him that the offer was accepted. He administered very large quantities of grain and other supplies, handled large amounts of money, and organized a relief service for the sick poor, to the general approval. When his work was complete, he went back to his cave, and died only a month later.

Ephrem was a very prolific writer. His Bible commentaries include nearly all the Old Testament and much of the New Testament, the latter from the only version then current in Syria, called the *Diatesseron*. Only an Armenian translation remains of this version. He also wrote the Nisibian Hymns, seventy-two of which have survived, and the canticles for the seasons which the Syrian Orthodox Church still uses. He meditated on the great mysteries of the Christian faith, particularly on the Last Supper, Christ's sufferings and the Crucifixion, marvelling that the God who 'spread all over the earth the veil of the skies, who poised the earth over the waters and sent down the blazing lighting-flash' should be beaten and killed by 'infamous wretches'. On the Eucharist, he wrote, 'The Lord himself became true altar, priest, and bread and chalice of salvation. He alone sufficeth . . . Altar he is, and lamb, victim and sacrificer, priest as well as food.'

*Jerome mentions him in a list of the great Christian writers:

Ephraem, deacon of the Church of Edessa, composed many works in Syriac, and became so distinguished that his writings are repeated publicly in some churches after the reading of the Scriptures. I once read in Greek a volume by him, 'On the Holy Spirit', which someone had translated from the Syriac, and recognized, even in translation, the incisive power of lofty genius.

Jerome, *Lives of Illustrious Men*, ch. 116 in *N.P.N.F.*, 2nd series, 3, p. 382. Lives by C. Emerau (1919); G. Ricciotti (1925); A. Vööbus (1958). See also *D.T.C.*, 5, pt 1, 188–93. Works in 6 vols, ed. J. S. Assemani (1732–46) with a translation in Latin, are now said to be incomplete and inexact. Much new work is available in the *Corpus Scriptorum Ecclesiasticorum Orientalum* (1903–), listed in the *Encyclopaedia of the Early Church*, 1, 276–7. *Selected Metrical Hymns and Homilies of Ephraim Syrus*, trans. and ed. H. Burgess (1853); *Selection from the Hymns and Homilies of Ephraim the Syrian*, ed. J. Gwynn (1979); *The Harp of the Spirit: Eighteen Poems of St Ephrem*, ed. M. Roncaglia, trans. S. Brock (1983).

Columba (c.521–97)　　　[L.F.]

Columba was born in County Donegal, and descended from two of the royal houses of Ireland. He studied under the bards, who made poetic records of Irish history and literature, and his name is associated with two of the famous monastic schools of the period. He is known as one of the Twelve Apostles of Erin. After he was ordained priest, his family gave him a fort at Daire Calgaich (now Daire, Derry or Londonderry) where he founded his first monastery.

Columba spent fifteen years preaching and founding monasteries in Ireland, including the monastery at Kells. Following a war between his clan and the followers of King Diarmid, when three thousand men were killed in battle, he had to leave Ireland. In 561, he and twelve kinsmen set sail in a wicker coracle covered with hide, and landed on the island now known as Iona, which lies off the coast of Mull, at Pentecost. Columba is said to have mourned over his exile, choosing a place for his cell where he could no longer see the coast of Ireland.

For two years, he taught the people of the nearby area of the Scottish mainland, who were of Irish descent and had some knowledge of Christianity, before going on to evangelize the Picts of the north. He was a giant of a man, with a voice 'so loud that it could be heard a mile off' according to his chief biographer, Adomnán. He and his party went to the castle of King Brude at Inverness. The king had given orders that they were not to be admitted, but when Columba raised a great arm and made the sign of the Cross, bolts were hastily withdrawn, and gates opened. Brude listened to him, confirmed his possession of Iona, and gave him leave to evangelize the Scots. He undertook missions to Ardnamurchan, Skye, Kintyre, Loch Ness and Lochaber. He was later credited with having evangelized Aberdeenshire and the whole of Pictland, but this may have been the work of his followers.

Columba never lost touch with Ireland, and returned several times, but he made his headquarters at Iona, where many people came to him for spiritual counsel or healing. He demanded extreme austerity of his followers, and practised it himself, but Adomnán describes him as mellowing in his later years, living in love and peace with his monks and with the natural world. He had a great love of learning, and when his great physical strength left him, he spent much time in transcribing manuscripts and writing poetry. It is said that he transcribed three hundred copies of the Gospels. In one long narrative poem, he deals with the whole epic of the Scriptures – the nature of God, the Creation, the Fall, the Last Judgement, hell and paradise. He died lying before the altar in his beloved church.

Adomnán, born some thirty years after Columba's death, was his kinsman, and became abbot of Iona. He writes of Columba that 'he was of an excellent nature, polished in speech, holy in deed, great in counsel'. He praises his fasting and his vigils, his labours for the monasteries of Scotland, and says that 'in the midst of all his toils, he appeared loving unto all, serene and holy, rejoicing in the joy of the Holy Spirit in his inmost heart'.

The Celtic Church in Ireland, Scotland and Northumbria followed Columba's liturgical traditions until the Synod of Whitby in 664, when Wilfrid was instrumental in securing the acceptance of the Roman tradition brought to southern England by *Augustine. *Bede says that the monks of Iona were 'distinguished for their purity of life, their love of God, and their loyalty to the monastic rule', and notes that they 'held on to their own manner of keeping Easter' for many years. The monastic rule drawn up by Columba was used by many monasteries in Western Europe until it was superseded by the milder rule of the Benedictines.

AA.SS., June, 2, pp. 179–283. Adomnán's Life is the most valuable source on Columba, and this is available in several editions, including translations by A. O. Anderson and M. O. Anderson (1961, repr. 1990); and R. Sharpe (1995), which has a good commentary. See also Bede, H.E., bk 3, chs 4 and 25; bk 5, ch. 9; D.N.B., 4, pp. 865–9; K. Hughes, *Early Christian Ireland* (1972) and *Early Christianity in Pictland* (Jarrow Lecture, 1970); N. Chadwick, *The Age of the Saints in the Early Celtic Church* (1961); Máire Herbert, *Iona, Kells and Derry* (Oxford, 1988); L.S.S., pp. 46–174. For Columba's poems, see the *Irish Liber Hymnorum* (1898), 1, pp. 62–89; 2, pp. 23–8 and 140–57.

11. Barnabas the Apostle   Festival

Barnabas was a Levite from Cyprus. His first name was Joseph, but the apostles surnamed him Barnabas, which meant 'son of encouragement' (Acts 4:36). He was not one of the original twelve, but he is referred to as an apostle in the New Testament because of his special commission to spread the gospel beyond Jerusalem.

He was a generous and trusting man. When the Christians in Jerusalem decided to have all things in common, he sold his land and contributed the money. He trusted *Paul when all the other disciples were 'in dread of him' (Acts 9:26–7). The disciples sent him to instruct a group of Christians in Antioch, and he and Paul worked together there for a year (Acts 11:22–6). When they heard that there was a famine in Jerusalem, they collected money and went back with funds to provide relief to the Christian community. There they met *John Mark, and the three set sail for a mission in Barnabas' homeland of Cyprus. They landed at Salamis in the north-east, confronted the false prophet bar-Jesus at Paphos, and preached all over the island. Then John Mark left them to go back to Jerusalem, and Barnabas and Paul continued their mission in the cities of Asia Minor (Acts 13:2–52).

It is evident that Barnabas was the leader on this great joint mission. He was trusted in Jerusalem, while Paul, who had been involved in the stoning of *Stephen, was not. At Lystra, the people thought that they were Greek gods: Barnabas was assumed to be Jupiter, and Paul to be Mercury (this suggests that Barnabas was the elder of the two). When they denied that they were gods, the crowd turned against them, and they nearly suffered the same fate as Stephen: a Jewish mob tried to stone them, and Paul was wounded. They completed their journey in Derbe, and then retraced their steps, appointing elders for the churches, and telling how God had 'thrown open the gates of faith to the Gentiles' (Acts 14).

They had planned a second major missionary journey together, but they were divided over the issue of whether it was necessary for Gentile converts to be instructed in the Mosaic law, and for the males to be circumcised. Barnabas, like *Peter, was concerned not to separate the faith from its Jewish roots. Paul wanted to free it from the trammels of Jewish ritual observance. They also differed sharply over John Mark, who had deserted them after their mission in Cyprus. Barnabas, still trusting, wanted to take him with them; Paul refused. Finally, Barnabas undertook a mission with John Mark, while Paul took Silas as a companion, and travelled in a different direction (Acts 15:36–41).

There is no more about Barnabas in the Acts of the Apostles. It seems that they overcame their differences, for Paul makes it clear in his first Letter to the Corinthians that Barnabas was still alive and carrying out his missionary activities. He demands to know why he and Barnabas are the only two who have to work for their living (1 Corinthians 9:5–6). This letter was written in the year 56 or 57; but when he was a prisoner in Rome a few years later, Paul asked John Mark to go to him, and it seems likely that by then, Barnabas was dead. There is a tradition that he went back to Cyprus, and was martyred by stoning in Salamis.

There are many paintings of Barnabas in the city of Venice, including a splendid one showing him robed as a bishop above the high altar in the church which bears his name.

The Acts of Barnabas, an apocryphal work, gives a full account up to and including his death and burial, but it probably dates from the fifth century, and was not written by John Mark, as claimed in *AA.SS.*, June, 2, pp. 415–54. W. Axon, in the *Journal of Theological Studies*, April 1902, pp. 441–51, makes reference to a work called *The Gospel of Barnabas* which was once known in Islamic scholarship. O.C.B., pp. 74–5.

14. Richard Baxter (1615–91)　　　　　　*[Commem.]*

When he became a Presbyterian divine, Baxter frequently lamented the deficiencies of his education. He says that when he left school, he was 'destitute of all mathematical and physical science, ignorant of Hebrew, a mere smatterer in Greek, and possessed of as much Latin as enabled him to use it in after-life with reckless facility'. He did not go to Oxford or Cambridge, though he could have done so, since his family, minor gentry in Shropshire, were Anglicans. He immersed himself in the great library at Ludlow Castle, reading the works of *Aquinas, Duns Scotus, *William of Ockham and many other theologians. He was weakly and consumptive, frequently coughing and spitting blood. Perhaps because he thought he would not live long, he became grave and serious. In his reading, he came to question many Anglican practices: he approved of episcopacy, and thought kneeling in prayer lawful, but he came to the conclusion that the wearing of a surplice was unlawful, and the liturgy was confused. Above all, he was appalled at the low standards of the parish clergy of his area – ill-educated men, some of whom led dissolute and immoral lives – and the lack of Church discipline.

He was ordained, and became headmaster of a small school in Dudley for a time before becoming assistant to a parish priest in Bridgnorth. He began to be drawn to the Dissenters, and in March 1640, he was called to minister to a dissenting congregation in Kidderminster. He was a chaplain in Cromwell's New Model Army for a time, though he refused to justify either side in the Civil War. Poor health forced him to retire to Kidderminster, where 'in the time of his languishing, when God took him off from public employment', he turned to writing his voluminous works. He wrote over one hundred separate works, and his *Practical Works*, collected and published in 1868, occupy twenty-three volumes.

Richard Baxter became well known and respected through his writings, as a man of piety who scrupulously kept his own conscience. He stood for the nation and the people's rights, but he opposed the execution of Charles I, and preached before parliament in favour of the Restoration. Charles II appointed him a King's Chaplain, and he was offered the bishopric of Hereford, but refused it. In the public reaction against dissent, this led to his arrest and trial before Judge Jeffreys, who wanted to have him 'whipped through London at the cart tail'. He was fined, and imprisoned for eighteen months. He married late and happily, returned to his writing, and survived to the age of seventy-six.

F. J. Powicke (1924); *D.N.B.*, 1, pp. 1349–59. Works: *Reliquae Baxterianae*, ed. Matthew Sylvester (1696, published in one volume by Edmund Calamy, 1702); *Aphorisms of Justification* (1649); *The Saints' Everlasting Rest* (1650).

15. Evelyn Underhill (1875–1941)   [*Commem.*]

Evelyn was born in Wolverhampton, the daughter of a barrister, and took her degree in History, Philosophy and Social Science at King's College for Women in London. Underhill was her family name, which she kept after her marriage to the barrister Hubert Stuart Moore in 1907. She had been brought up as an Anglican, but though she was deeply committed to religious study, she hesitated for some years to make a commitment to a particular form of worship. She published a major book, *Mysticism*, in 1911 which brought her into contact with the Catholic theologian and biblical scholar Baron Friedrich von Hügel who lived in London. Though the book became a classic, it did not represent her mature thought: she was to deepen her knowledge and understanding of the subject later. She was strongly attracted to the Roman Catholic Church, and von Hügel became her spiritual director, but after a long period of scholarly investigation, she returned to the Church of England in which she had been confirmed as a girl. She wrote to the abbot of Downside in 1931, 'I solidly believe in the Catholic status of the Church of England as to Orders and sacraments. It seems to be a respectable suburb of the City of God – but all the same, part of Greater London.'

Evelyn Underhill's thinking was greatly influenced by von Hügel, and also by her study of the works of Teresa of Avila. One of her best-known works, *The House of the Soul*, reprinted many times, is a development from Teresa's *The Interior Castle*. She also carried out detailed and scholarly work on a number of mystics: the author of *The Cloud of Unknowing*; *Richard Rolle; John Ruysbroeck or Ruusbroec, a thirteenth-century monk in the Low countries, Jacopo da Todi, a fourteenth-century Franciscan 'Spiritual'; and Boehme. She travelled every year on the Continent either with her husband or with her friend and collaborator Lucy Menzies, visiting religious centres and shrines. Her journals from these tours were edited by Lucy Menzies as *Shrines and Cities of France and Italy* (1949). She was also deeply interested in the traditions of the Eastern Orthodox Church, studying Greek Orthodox tradition and becoming a member of the Fellowship of St Alban and St Sergius.

Evelyn Underhill became a scholar of great distinction on the subjects of mysticism and spirituality, and something more: from about 1925, she was in great demand as a spiritual director and a retreat conductor at a time when women were debarred from taking Orders in the Anglican Church. She taught that the spiritual life and the practical life went together, 'like bread and butter', and that 'all worship must start with adoration, which reveals to us the insignificance of the "luggage" of life over which we make most fuss'. She was gentle in her handling of other people's religious problems, saying that she 'hated pushing souls about'. She died on 15 June 1941. An obituary in the *Times Literary Supplement* commented that 'she never ceased teaching, and she never ceased learning'.

A collection of papers, *The Fruits of the Spirit*, ed. Lucy Menzies, contains a personal memoir. Biographies by Margaret B. Cropper (1958); C. R. J. Armstrong (1975); Dana Greene (New York, 1990); Grace Brame (New York, 1990). *Far Above Rubies*, pp. 139–57. *Letters of Evelyn Underhill*, ed. Charles Williams (1943). Works: *Mysticism* (1911); *Worship* (1936); *The House of the Soul* (1919); *Ruysbroeck* (1915); *Jacopone da Todi* (1919); *Concerning the Inner Life* (1936). *Twentieth Century*, pp. 160–3.

16. Richard of Chichester (1197–1253)   [L.F.]

Richard de Wych was born at Droitwich, the son of a yeoman farmer. He worked on his father's farm for several years before going to study at Oxford, Paris and Bologna. He spent seven years in Bologna studying canon law, and returned as a renowned scholar to become chancellor of the University of Oxford. His former tutor, *Edmund of Abingdon, became archbishop of Canterbury, and made Richard his chancellor. Richard stayed with Edmund during his exile, and was with him when he died.

After Edmund's death, he decided to become a priest, and studied with the Dominicans. He served in parishes at Charing and Deal, and was elected bishop of Chichester in 1244, but King Henry III and part of the cathedral chapter refused to accept him. Pope Innocent IV supported him, and consecrated him at Lyons. It was not until the pope had threatened king and cathedral clergy with excommunication that he was installed, and his property (by then damaged and despoiled) was returned to him.

Richard restored Church discipline, which was at a low ebb in the diocese. He ensured that the faithful received the sacrament without payment, and that Mass was said in a dignified manner. He insisted on the celibacy of the clergy and the wearing of clerical dress. A man of great devotion, he is the author of the prayer still in frequent use:

Thanks be to thee, my Lord Jesus Christ, for all the pains and insults which thou hast borne for me. May I know thee more clearly, love thee more dearly, and thus follow thee more nearly, day by day.

Contemporary Life by Richard Beeching in *AA.SS.*, Apr., 1, pp. 282–318. This is abridged in *N.L.A.*, 2, pp. 318–28. C. M. Duncan-Jones (1953); R. C. Stevens (1962); *N.C.E.*, 12, p. 478; *O.D.S.*, p. 416.

Joseph Butler (1692–1762)   *[Commem.]*

When Joseph Butler was offered the archbishopric of Canterbury, he declined, saying that it was 'too late to support a failing Church'. The life of the Anglican Church was at a low ebb in the first half of the eighteenth century – suffering from the attacks of rationalist science and the strength of the dissenting Protestant sects. He came of a non-conforming family, and his father, a prosperous draper, intended him to enter the Presbyterian ministry. Non-Conformists were barred from Oxford and Cambridge, and he studied at a dissenting academy in Gloucester; but he decided to conform to the Church of England, and went to Oriel College, Oxford in about 1714, to study Divinity. His tutor became bishop of Salisbury and, impressed by Butler's powerful intellectual grasp and his ability as a preacher, furthered his career. Butler became clerk of the closet to George II's very able queen, Caroline of Brunswick, who worked closely with Robert Walpole, England's first 'prime minister'. He refused many offers of promotion, but became bishop of Bristol in 1738, and dean of St Paul's in 1740. His calm, well-ordered sermons, based on reason and authority, suited the spirit of the age, and were widely influential.

Butler met *John Wesley, but, like many churchmen of his day, was alarmed at the 'enthusiasm' which Wesley's sermons were producing in the crowds which flocked to his meetings. He had a horror of 'claims to extraordinary revelations and gifts of the Holy Spirit'. He was probably right to refuse to go to Canterbury: he was a scholar, not an administrator; but in 1750, he accepted the bishopric of Durham, where the prince-bishop still had a considerable freedom of action. Horace Walpole said that he 'wafted to his see on a cloud of metaphysics, and remained absorbed in it'. He took no part in politics, and devoted himself to the study of natural theology and ethical principles.

Butler's most celebrated work was *The Analogy of Religion: natural and revealed*, rated the greatest theological work of his time. It might be described as the ecclesiastical counterpart to John Locke's *Of Civil Government*, employing the same clarity and vigour on the subject of God's power and authority over his creation. He was sometimes accused of 'Romish practices', chiefly because he studied the lives of the saints; but his work was so highly regarded by William Ewart Gladstone that in his later years, the former Liberal prime minister undertook the editing of his complete works.

Thomas Bartlett (1839); Ian Ramsay (1969); *D.N.B.*, pp. 519–25. *Complete Works*, ed. W. E. Gladstone (2 vols., 1896); *Some Remains of Bishop Butler*, ed. E. Steere (1858).

17. Samuel Barnett (1844–1913) and Henrietta Barnett (1851–1936)   [Commem.]

Samuel Barnett was the elder son of a wealthy manufacturer. He went to Oxford, reading Law and Modern History, taught for two years, and then visited the United States, 'which knocked all the toryism out of me'.

He returned to England to prepare for ordination, and in 1867 became a curate in London at St Mary's, Bryanston Square. He soon became involved in the work of the Charity Organisation Society in the parish, administered by Octavia Hill. He married Henrietta Rowland, who was one of Miss Hill's assistants, and shared his enthusiasm for work with the poor. They were to work together for more than forty years.

In 1873, they went to the parish of St Jude's, Whitechapel. The bishop told Samuel Barnett that it was 'the worst in the diocese, inhabited mainly by a criminal population', but they devoted their lives to educational work and relieving poverty. Samuel was a Poor Law Guardian for twenty-nine years, and chairman of the Board of Guardians for twelve. He promoted reading and discussion groups and art classes, and was one of the founders of the Whitechapel Art Gallery. He campaigned for improved housing for the poor in a movement which culminated in the Artisans' Dwelling Act of 1875. He became an advocate of university settlements, and was one of the founders of Toynbee Hall in 1884, designed as a bridge between the university-educated and the working classes, and a protest against class distinction.

Henrietta worked with him on all these enterprises, and was the initiator in some others, such as the Country Holiday Fund, which gave children from the slums of London a chance to breathe fresh air and come to terms with the world of nature. She became the first nominated woman Poor Law Guardian, and was active in setting up the London Pupil Teachers' Association in 1884. She was involved in the Hampstead Garden Suburb Trust, and several of Octavia Hill's housing and planning enterprises. After Samuel's death in 1913, she devoted much of her time to education, and the Henrietta Barnett School at Golders Green is named after her. Barnett House, Oxford, now the headquarters of the University's department of Social and Administrative Studies, commemorates them both. Henrietta became a DBE in 1924, and lived on until 1936.

Henrietta Barnett, *Canon Barnett: his life, work and friends* (2 vols, 1918). *D.N.B.*, *1912-21*, pp. 31-2 (Samuel) and *D.N.B.*, *1931-40*, pp. 44-5 (Henrietta).

18. Bernard Mizeki (?1860–1896)   *[Commem.]*

Nobody is sure when Bernard Mizeki was born. He was probably fourteen or fifteen when he joined a group of young Africans who had offended the paramount chief of Imbahane in Mozambique, and travelled with them to Cape Town. There he found work in a butchery, and went to a night school which was taken over in 1885 by the Mission Priests of St John the Evangelist, the Cowley Fathers. Father Frederick Pullen, who directed the SSJE in Cape Town, became his spiritual director, and he was fortunate in his teacher, Baroness von Blomberg, who spent much time tutoring an unlikely pupil. Bernard could not understand why two and two made four, or the difference between a noun and a pronoun; but when it came to religious studies, his responses were different from those of the other students. When they were asked, 'Who made the world – the mountains and valleys and trees?' some laughed and said, 'The English government – that's why we have to pay taxes'; but Bernard said, 'God cares for me . . . This is something I haven't known. I ought to do something for God, working for him and serving him.'

When the Cowley Fathers started a boarding house, he was one of seven chosen for baptism. He became the cleaner for the house, living on very little so that he could concentrate on his studies. He was still shy, anxious and slow, but Baroness von Blomberg continued to help him, and saw him develop into an intelligent and strong young man, calm, cheerful and ready for any kind of Christian service. He had an unexpected gift for languages: he spoke English, High Dutch, Portuguese and several African languages, and a priest at the Mission tutored him in French, Latin and Greek. In 1891, after a period at Zonnebloem College, where black, white and coloured students were taught together, he volunteered for Mashonaland.

He went with Bishop Knight Bruce, the first bishop of Mashonaland, who had already visited the area and reported on it. Lobengula, king of the Matabele, dominated Mashonaland, and he had given a mining concession to the British South Africa Company, one of Cecil Rhodes' enterprises. That meant industrial development and in 1891, the bishop returned with six catechists to found missions in the area. Bernard, now an *Umfundisi* or teacher, was one of them, and earned the bishop's special commendation on a difficult journey through unknown territory. Bishop Knight Bruce left Bernard to found a mission for a Mashona tribe on Mount Mahopo, near Marandellas in what is now Zimbabwe. Mangwende, the chief, was friendly, and he and Bernard spent many hours under the stars discussing the one great God.

Bernard built a mission hut, said his daily Offices, learned the Shona language, and taught both adults and children. The Mashona loved music, and he led them in singing in his splendid deep voice. Until he had helpers, he hunted, fetched his own water and made a vegetable garden to grow his own food. He made long journeys into the surrounding area preaching the gospel, and after a time he made a Christian marriage to one of the chief's many grand-daughters.

Then in 1893 came the Matabele rising, which spread to the Mashona. White settlers and their African workers were massacred, and Christian missionaries shared their fate. Mangwende's sons, who hated Bernard's influence over their father and wanted to take power, stirred up the *ngangas* (witch-doctors), who accused Bernard of sorcery. Bernard had been warned to leave the area; but the bishop had told him to 'stay at Mangwende's', and the bishop was out of the country, so he stayed at his post. On 18 June 1896, three of Mangwende's disaffected sons went to his hut by night and attacked him with a spear in front of his young, pregnant wife. He dragged himself as far as a nearby river, but while his wife and another woman went to fetch food, he disappeared. Some local people accounted this a miracle, while others assumed that the killers returned, murdered him, and disposed of his body.

Bernard's shrine at Theydon, near Marandellas, is a place of annual pilgrimage, and Bernard Mizeki College honours his name.

Jean C. Farrant, *Mashonaland Martyr: Bernard Mizeki and the Pioneer Church*, 1966; J. P. R. Wallace, *Matabele Mission: the correspondence of J. and E. Moffat, Livingstone and Others* (1945); Stafford Glass, *The Matabele War*, ch. 4, ch. 5, pp. 41–59.

19. Sundar Singh (1889–1929) [*Commem.*]

Among the many peoples of India, the Sikhs hold a special place – a small sect holding a reformed and purified form of Hinduism, with a five-hundred-year-old tradition of religious fervour and military exploits. All the men bear the family name of Singh, which means a lion. Sundar was the youngest child of a wealthy Sikh landowner in the state of Patiala. He was sent to an American Presbyterian school, but rejected Bible teaching, because his people had their own sacred books, the *Bhagavad Gita* and the *Adi Granth*. Sundar became the leader of a group of boys who tore pages out of the Bible and burned them as a protest against Christian teaching. Even the name of Christ raised his anger and resentment, and he turned to the study of the *Gita* and the *Granth* to find God. He was sixteen when he picked up the Bible and read the words, 'Come unto me, and I will give you rest.' He had found the answer he was seeking; but the prospect of becoming a Christian, of facing the incomprehension and hostility of his family, was so appalling that he contemplated suicide.

His father pleaded with him, reminding him of his high position and his responsibilities to his family. An uncle offered him all his own wealth if he would remain a Sikh. The villagers became angry: the shops refused to serve the American Presbyterian mission, and it had to close. His family sent Sundar to the American Presbyterian school in Ludhiana to continue his studies, perhaps thinking that he was going through an adolescent phase, and that further contact with Christians would disillusion him; but when he returned home, he cut off the long tuft of hair which every orthodox Sikh cherishes. It was a symbolic act which drastically separated him from the Sikh community. His father disowned him, and he left home with nothing more than the clothes he wore and his fare to Patiala.

On the way, he stopped at Ropur to visit an Indian pastor and his wife, and became violently ill. They called a physician, who said that he had been poisoned. Evidently the shame to a proud family was such that his relatives had not intended him to reach Patiala alive. Even after he completed his journey, members of his family came to the American Mission to plead with him to return home, and on at least one occasion an attempt was made to capture him by violence. The American missionaries sent him to a small station near Simla where he could be at peace, read his Bible and pray. On 3 September 1905, he was baptized by an Anglican priest, the Revd J. Redman. Just over a month later, he gave away all his possessions, adopted the saffron robe of an Indian Sádhu or holy man, and set out barefoot to make Christ known to the mountain peoples of the Punjab and Afghanistan.

Holy men were generally welcomed and respected in Indian communities, but when he declared that he was a Christian, he was often driven out, hungry, to sleep in a cave or a jungle clearing. In 1907, he worked in the Leper Asylum at Sabathu, and in a plague camp in

Lahore, with an American missionary. In 1908, he went alone into Tibet. When he returned, his friends advised him to undertake a period of study, and he spent two years at St John's College, Lahore, where he passed his theology examinations without difficulty. He was recommended for deacon's Orders by the Diocesan Mission Council, and given a licence to preach; but after much prayer, he decided that the life of an Anglican mission priest was not for him: he must have the freedom to cross religious boundaries, to speak directly to Hindus and Buddhists. He returned the licence, and the bishop accepted it with understanding. He went into the jungle to fast and pray for enlightenment. He was gone so long that his death was reported, and a memorial service was held in Simla; but he returned to continue his lonely ministry. He narrowly avoided death from frostbite in the mountains, from drowning in rivers, from sleeping next to a cobra, and from a black panther in the jungle. He was imprisoned and tortured in Nepal, condemned to death and thrown into a well in Tibet, and often attacked or driven out by hostile villagers; yet he also received much kindness and help on his journeys, sometimes from the most unexpected people. He called them 'angels'.

He sought no disciples, holding that every man must listen to his own distinct call from God; but when he returned to Ludhiana and other mission centres, an arresting figure with his dark beard, saffron robe and turban, he would address conferences and talk to groups of Christians, many of whom would visit him for personal advice. He was invited to Ceylon (now Sri Lanka), Burma, Singapore, China and Japan, and visited all these countries, preaching his message. In 1929, suffering from the strain of his constant missionary journeys, and in poor health, he went back to his beloved Tibet. He never returned, and was reported missing, presumed murdered.

R. J. Parker (Mrs Arthur Parker), *Sādhu Sundar Singh: called of God* (1920). *Twentieth Century*, pp. 146–50.

22. Alban, Martyr (?c.254)   [L.F.]

Alban has the distinction of being the protomartyr of Britain: his is the earliest recorded case of an execution on a charge of being a Christian during the Roman occupation. He sheltered a Christian confessor who was being hunted by the imperial forces, and was greatly impressed by the confessor's faith, his vigils and his prayers. He asked to receive instruction, and became a Christian himself. When the imperial soldiers came to search his house, he wore the confessor's long cloak and allowed himself to be arrested in his place, thus giving his guest time to escape. At his trial, he declared himself to be a Christian, and refused to sacrifice to the Roman gods. After being flogged, he was taken outside the city and beheaded with a companion.

Legends and miracles have been added to the basic story over the centuries, and the place, the date, and the identity of Alban's companion have been much debated. He must have been a Roman citizen, because only Roman citizens were given the dignity of being beheaded. There were crueller deaths for conquered peoples. If he had been a Roman soldier, he would have been executed in the military barracks without publicity. Alban seems to have been a prominent citizen of Verulamium. He had a house large enough to shelter the fugitive, and he was sufficiently educated to ask for instruction. Thousands of people are said to have followed him to his place of execution, leaving 'Caesar' (the military commander) unattended. Executions were common events in Roman Britain, so this suggests that he was well known, that it was a show trial and a show execution, to deter others from Christian allegiance.

Our accounts of Alban's martyrdom come from two monks: Gildas, writing from an island in the Bristol Channel in the sixth century, and *Bede, writing from Jarrow in Northumbria in the eighth century. Neither could have had knowledge of local traditions about Alban, but there is sufficient similarity between the two accounts to support the contention that there was an earlier text, now lost, which both had read. Partial and largely unreadable manuscripts discovered by Professor Meyer of Göttingen, now preserved in Paris and Turin, appear to come from this source.

Bede gives the fuller account, and he is precise about the place and the day and month of Alban's death: it occurred 'on the twenty-second day of June near the city of Verulamium, which the English now call Verlamcestir or Vaeclingacaestir'. The ruins of Verulamium lie just outside the present city of St Albans, and the topography closely matches Bede's account of how he went to his death: across a river, up a gently sloping hill covered with flowers (as it would be in June) about five hundred paces on the other side. The abbey and the city of St Albans developed on the site of Alban's martyrdom in the Anglo-Saxon period, and his tomb is thought to have been on the hill where the abbey now stands.

Bede tells us that the martyrdom occurred during the persecutions of Diocletian, which lasted for ten years; but Diocletian's savage attack on the Christians lasted only two years (303–5), and was largely confined to Italy and the Eastern Empire. Alban's death probably took place in an earlier persecution, either that of Septimus Severus (*c.*209) or that of Decius (*c.*254). Lengthy scholastic debate has failed to decide between the two possibilities, but recent excavations of the abbey site make the latter date the more likely.

Who was 'Amphibalus', Alban's companion in martyrdom? Some accounts suggest that he was the confessor Alban sheltered, who was subsequently caught and executed. Some suggest that he was an executioner who is said to have refused to strike the fatal blow, and who was also put to death. An intriguing theory is that the name derived from a word for Alban's cloak or surcoat: that some mediaeval transcriber mistakenly wrote '*cum amphibalo,*' and this was subsequently misinterpreted by the imaginative but often unreliable twelfth-century chronicler Geoffrey of Monmouth. The shrine of St Amphibalus in St Albans abbey commemorates Alban's Christian confessor, whatever his actual name.

The story of Alban the Martyr was carried to the Continent by Bishop Germanus of Auxerre, who visited his tomb in 429. Constantius of Lyons wrote the *Vita S. Germani* about 480, and repeated the story, thus spreading spread Alban's fame through Gaul and the Rhineland, and as far as Denmark. The St Albans Psalter (*c.*1119–23) contains several pictures of his execution, and similar scenes can be found on mediaeval stained glass windows.

Gildas, *De Excidio Brittaniae* chs 10—11; Bede, *H.E.*, bk 1, chs 7, 17—21; Matthew Paris, *Gesta Abbatum S Albani*, 1, pp. 12–18, 94, and *Chronica Majora*, 2, pp. 306–8; Geoffrey of Monmouth, *History of the Kings of Britain*, 5, p. 5. T. D. Hardy, *Catalogue of Materials, History of Great Britain and Ireland* (R.S. 26), 1, pp. 3–30, lists and comments on eighty-six manuscript Lives of Alban. The full account of the finding of the Turin and Paris documents is in the *Abhandlungen der Königlichen Gesellschaft der Wissenschaften zu Göttingen*, Phil. Hist. Klasse, N. F. VIII, 1 (1904), pp. 3–81. A more accessible version is that of W. Levison, 'St Alban and St Albans', *Antiquity* 15 (1941), pp. 337–59. R. M. Wilson in *The Lost Literature of Mediaeval England* (1952), pp. 92–3, considers the possibility of a lost (and even earlier) Life of St Alban 'written in the English or British language'. See also John Morris, 'The Date of Saint Alban', *Hertfordshire Archaeology* 1 (1968), pp. 1–7; Charles Thomas, *Christianity in Roman Britain* (1981), pp. 48–50; O. Pächt, C. R. Dodwell, and F. Wormald, eds, *The St Albans Psalter* (1960).

23. Etheldreda (d. 679)   [L.F.]

Etheldreda (otherwise known as Aethelthryth or Audry) was one of the four daughters of King Anna of East Anglia, all of whom entered the religious life. When she was young, a marriage was arranged for her with a prince of the Fen country, named Tonbert. According to Bede, Tonbert died 'shortly after the wedding', the marriage was unconsummated. He had given Etheldreda the island of Ely, then surrounded by swamps and marshes, as a wedding gift, and she retired there to lead a life of prayer and chastity; but five years later another marriage was arranged for her to Egfrid, son of King Oswy, who was only fifteen. This marriage was also unconsummated, but when Egfrid grew older and became a king, he demanded that she should live with him as his wife.

Etheldreda claimed that she had dedicated her virginity to God, and appealed to *Wilfrid, who was then Bishop of York, to support her claim. Wilfrid's decision was that she should be allowed to enter the religious life. Egfrid, who had tried to bribe Wilfrid, had his revenge by inducing *Theodore, archbishop of Canterbury, to divide the York diocese, leaving Wilfrid only with the small diocese of Hexham.

Etheldreda went to a religious house at Coldingham, where the abbess was her aunt, and after a year there, returned to Ely. Wilfrid installed her as abbess, and she founded a double monastery, for both men and women, over which she ruled for the rest of her life. It is thought that she adopted the Rule of St Benedict. She is reputed to have lived with great austerity, eating sparely, wearing the rough woollen clothing of the poor, and praying with great devotion, often through the night after Matins, which was sung at midnight. She asked to be buried in a simple wooden coffin.

The magnificent shrine of St Etheldreda at Ely became a place of pilgrimage in the mediaeval period. In 1144 it was stripped of its gold and jewels by Nigel, Bishop of Ely, to pay a fine imposed by King Stephen for his support of the Empress Matilda. It disappeared in the Reformation, but there is still a shrine in Ely cathedral, and incidents from Etheldreda's life are carved round the great Lantern Tower which looks out over the fens. Until the sixteenth century, there was a fair in Ely on her feast day, and cheap jewellery and other goods sold there were called 'tawdry', a corruption of St Audrey.

A very unsympathetic account of her life in the *Dictionary of National Biography* takes the view that Egfrid 'had a natural desire for wifely companionship' and that 'the wronged husband's consent was extorted' by Wilfrid; but since Etheldreda was a mere pawn in political marriages, like many noblewomen of her time, other commentators have respected her decision and endorsed Wilfrid's judgement.

Bede, *H.E.*, bk 4, chs 19—20; *Men.E.W.*, p. 285; E. O. Blake, ed., *Liber Eliensis* (1962); *N.L.A.*, 1, pp. 424-9; *D.N.B.*, 6, pp. 883-4; *D.C.B.*, 2, pp. 220-2.

24. The Birth of John the Baptist   Festival

Though the Beheading of John the Baptist is celebrated as a Lesser Festival on 29 August, his main feast has long been the one which celebrates his birth. *Augustine of Hippo explained the reason for this in a sermon: John 'met' the Christ-child before either of them was born, on the day of the Visitation, when the *Blessed Virgin Mary visited her cousin Elizabeth. 'This day of the nativity is handed down to us, and is this day celebrated,' writes Augustine. 'We have received this by tradition from our forefathers, and we transmit it to our descendants to be celebrated with like devotion.'

Augustine refers to the words of John the Baptist reported in the Fourth Gospel: 'He must increase, while I must decrease' (John 1:30 in older versions). The *New Revised Standard Version* translation, 'After me comes a man who ranks ahead of me, because he was before me', does not convey this meaning, as the Latin text does. Augustine finds the date appropriate because, as he points out, after the birthday of John the days grow shorter, while after the birthday of Christ the days grow longer.

The events surrounding John's birth are set out in chapter 1 of the Gospel according to Luke. His father was a priest named Zechariah, and his mother Elizabeth was also of priestly descent. They were both 'upright and devout, blamelessly observing all the commandments and ordinances of the Lord'. They were childless, and elderly. They lived 'in a Judaean town in the hill country', and from time to time, Zechariah had to go away from home to undertake priestly duties for his division. While Zechariah was at the altar offering incense, he had a vision in which an angel appeared, standing by the altar. The angel told him not to be afraid, and assured him that Elizabeth would bear him a son, who was to be called John. It was predicted that 'even before his birth he will be filled with the Holy Spirit, and he will turn many of the people of Israel to the Lord their God.' Zechariah pointed out that he was an old man, and Elizabeth was 'getting on in years'. The angel told him that because he had doubted, he would lose the power of speech until after the child was born. Meanwhile, a crowd had gathered outside the Temple, wondering why he had delayed so long. He was unable to speak to them, and they realized that he had had a vision.

Zechariah finished his term of duty, and went home. Some time later, Elizabeth conceived, and she remained in seclusion for five months, thanking God for her pregnancy, because among her people barrenness was a great reproach. In the sixth month of her pregnancy she received a visit from Mary, who may have been her kinswoman. When she heard Mary's salutation, the child in her womb 'leapt for joy', and she said, 'Blessed are you among all women, and blessed is the fruit of your womb.' The Visitation of the Blessed Virgin Mary to Elizabeth is celebrated as a feast on 31 May.

The two women stayed together for three months, and when Elizabeth's child was nearly due, Mary went back to her own home in Nazareth. Elizabeth bore her son, and all her relatives and neighbours were delighted. Zechariah remained unable to speak until the eighth day, when there was an argument about the child's name. The relatives wanted him to be called Zechariah after his father, but Elizabeth insisted that his name was John. They protested that John was not a family name, but Zechariah sent for a writing tablet, and wrote, 'His name is John.' Immediately he was able to speak again. The neighbours were deeply impressed and awe-struck, and everybody in the uplands of Judaea heard the story, and wondered what the child would become.

We are told no more of John's life until Luke 3, when, after living a life of solitary meditation in the wilderness, he begins his ministry in about the year 27, very much in the style of the Old Testament prophets. He comes quoting Isaiah: 'Prepare the way of the Lord, make his paths straight. Every valley shall be filled, every mountain and hill laid low' (Isaiah 40:3–4). He preaches repentance in preparation for the coming of the Messiah and baptizes in the river Jordan. He tells the man with two shirts to give one away, the man with food to share it with him who has none, and the soldiers to be content with their pay, not to indulge in bullying and blackmail. Jesus of Nazareth comes to him for his Baptism at the start of his ministry (Luke 3: 21).

John's death occurs because of his denunciation of Herod Antipas, the ruler of Galilee, for an incestuous marriage with Herodias, his niece and his brother's wife. Through the machinations of her mother, Salome, daughter of Herodias, exacts a promise from Herod that she may have the head of John the Baptist; and John is executed in prison without trial (Matthew 14:3–12; Mark 6:14–29).

As the precursor of Christ, John the Baptist has always been held in great reverence in both the Eastern and Western Churches.

Augustine, Sermon 292, *Natalis Johannis Bapt.*; D. Buzy, *The Life of St John the Baptist* (1947), has a good bibliography. See also W. Wink, *John the Baptist in the Gospel Tradition* (1968); Carl R. Kazmierski, *John the Baptist: Prophet and Evangelist* (Collegeville, Minnesota, 1996); *D.A.C.L.*, 7, cols 2167–84.

27. Cyril of Alexandria (376–444)   [Commem.]

Cyril, patriarch (or archbishop) of Alexandria from 412 to his death in 444, was a controversial figure in his own time, and remains one today. He was a champion of orthodoxy who defended the doctrine of the person of Christ as formulated at the Council of Nicaea in 325, but he refused to consider any doctrine which could not be found in the work of the early Fathers of the Church, thereby denying the possibility of continuous revelation. *Athanasius, *Basil of Caesarea and *Gregory Nazianzen were his authorities. Cyril is commemorated in the Syrian and Maronite Mass as 'a tower of strength and interpreter of the Word of God made flesh'; but he was also rigid in his interpretation of the faith, and a somewhat unscrupulous ecclesiastical tactician.

In Cyril's lifetime, there was a strong rivalry between the patriarchs of Alexandria and Constantinople, and he was involved in the deposition of two Constantinople patriarchs. The first, the deposition of *John Chrysostom, occurred when Theophilus, Cyril's uncle, was patriarch of Alexandria. Theophilus, with Cyril's assistance, succeeded in driving him into a long and painful exile. The second, that of Nestorius, occurred after Cyril had succeeded his uncle as patriarch. This did involve issues of doctrine, but they might perhaps have been resolved peaceably if Cyril had been prepared to engage in prayerful theological debate.

Nestorius became patriarch of Constantinople in 428. He came from the school of theology at Antioch, which taught that Christ's two natures, human and divine, were united only in the sense that the Godhead inhabited a human body. The divine spirit of the Logos had always existed (John 1:1–5), and therefore the Virgin Mary was *Christotokos*, Christ-bearing, but not *Theotokos*, God-bearing. Cyril argued that this doctrine undermined the significance of the Incarnation, and the honour due to the Mother of God. The issue was referred to Rome, where Pope Celestine I deposed Nestorius and threatened him and his followers with excommunication if they did not retract. Nestorius, many miles from Rome, refused to retract, or to accept his deposition. Cyril then convened a Council at Ephesus to condemn him and his doctrines. Nestorius refused to appear before the Council, and was hastily condemned in his absence – before the arrival at the Council of either the papal legates or that of the archbishop of Antioch and forty-one bishops who were prepared to support him. The result was schism. The Nestorian Church, which was large and well organized, split from Rome, and went on to carry out much missionary work in India and China before it was finally overwhelmed by the Mongol invasions in the fourteenth century.

The historian Socrates says that, like his uncle, Cyril accumulated power and wealth, and went beyond the limit of his episcopal functions. The Jews were driven out of Alexandria. A schismatic group called the Novationists had their churches shut, their sacred vessels confiscated, and their bishop stripped of all his property. A celebrated woman philosopher, Hypatia, who advised the Imperial prefect and was a neo-Platonist, was brutally murdered in the street by Cyril's supporters.

Alexandria was a city of much violence and intrigue, where many contradictory religious and philosophical beliefs existed. Cyril is respected for safeguarding the purity of Christian doctrine; but the manner in which he did so has long been open to criticism.

Socrates, *H.E.*, bk 7, ch. 7. See also *D.T.C.*, 3, pt 2, pp. 2475–527, 'Cyrille d'Alexandrie', and 5, pt 1, pp. 137–63, 'Ephèse, Concile d''; *N.C.E.*, 4, pp. 571–6; W. Burghardt, *The Image of God in Man According to Cyril of Alexandria* (1957); *Orientalis ecclesiae decus*, encyclical letter of Pope Pius XII (1944); *Later Christian Fathers*, pp. 252–68. Cyril's Works are in the *Patrologia Graeca*, ed. J. P. Migne (112 vols, Paris, 1857–66), vols 67–77.

28. Irenaeus of Lyons (c.125–202)   [L.F.]

In the second century, traders from the ports of the eastern Mediterranean made regular voyages to Marseilles, and up the Rhône

valley to the city of Lugdonum, which is now Lyons. This explains
how Irenaeus, who was a Greek, probably from Smyrna, came to be
bishop of that city, where a small Christian community developed.

Irenaeus had been a disciple of *Polycarp, bishop of Smyrna, who
was himself a disciple of *John the Evangelist, so he carried a living
tradition from the apostle himself. He recalled how Polycarp had told
his flock of having listened to John and others who had known Jesus
Christ during his earthly ministry. 'These things being told to me by
the mercy of God, I listened to them attentively, noting them down not
on paper but in my heart.' Irenaeus was well versed in the Scriptures
and in Greek philosophy, and studied in Rome under *Justin Martyr.
He was one of the early missionaries sent to Gaul, where he was
attached to the first Bishop of Lyons, Pothinus. In 177, he was sent
back to Rome on an important mission, and thus missed the terrible
persecution of the Martyrs of Lyons, in which Pothinus and many
others died in the arena, torn to pieces by wild beasts. When he
returned to Gaul, it was as a bishop, with the task of re-building the
Christian community.

The rest of his life was spent in his diocese in peaceful circumstances.
We are told that he habitually spoke the language of Gaul rather than
Latin or his native Greek, which suggests that he was a good pastor,
with a sympathy for his people; he sponsored missions along the
Rhône valley, where five priests were martyred in another outbreak of
persecution some years after his death; and he devoted himself to his
writings, which have become celebrated as a defence of Christianity
against the Gnostics.

Gnosticism is very difficult to define, because it took many forms. It
was a mixture of Greek philosophy and Eastern beliefs which existed
in Palestine in Christ's day (the Gnostics claimed him as one of their
teachers) and was widespread in Gaul during Irenaeus' episcopate. It
operated through secrecy, initiation rites and occult practices. Irenaeus,
determined to 'strip the fox', as he put it, published a treatise in five
books, *Adversus Haereses*, setting out the basic tenets of Gnosticism.
Gnostics believed that the world was created and ruled by angels,
while God remained aloof from it. Irenaeus contrasted this belief
system with Christianity, in which 'God's splendour is the source of
life, those who see him share his life . . . God sustains the universe in
being. . . . The Father is above all, and he is the head of Christ, but the
Word is through all things, and he is himself the head of the Church,
while the Spirit is in us all.' From the time when *Adversus Haereses*

was published, Gnosticism declined, and the treatise has remained a powerful example of early Christian apologetics.

Irenaeus probably died about the year 202. Later it was thought that he had been martyred, but this belief probably arose because of his association with the Martyrs of Lyons. His feast has long been observed in the Eastern Orthodox Church, but was not adopted by the Roman Catholic Church until 1922.

The shrines of Irenaeus and the Martyrs of Lyons were desecrated in the sixteenth century, and destroyed during the French Revolution.

Eusebius, *H.E.*, bk 5, ch. 20; F. R. M. Hitchcock, *Irenaeus of Lugdunum* (1914); *D.T.C.*, 7, pp. 2394–533 (an entry of nearly 150 columns); Ruinart, *Acta Martyrum Sincera* (Paris, 1859), pp. 117–19, classifies Irenaeus as a martyr. For the arguments for and against the martyrdom of St Irenaeus, see Delehaye in the *Hieronymianum*, pp. 341–2. Eng. trans. of *Adversus Haereses: Against Heresies*, ed. F. R. M. Hitchock (1898) and in *Early Christian Fathers*, pp. 343–97. See also John Lawson, *The Biblical Theology of St Irenaeus* (1948).

29. Peter and Paul, Apostles   Festival

In the Vatican Museum, there is a bronze medal showing the heads of the apostles Peter and Paul. It dates from the early part of the second century, and may have been based on an oral tradition of what they looked like, on sketches, or even on living memory. Peter is sturdy and big-boned, with a full beard. Paul is thin and hollow-eyed and bald. They are much as they have subsequently been painted by artists through the centuries. In the catacombs of Rome, near the church of St Sebastian, there is a room, discovered in 1910, dated to about the year 250. The walls are covered with Greek and Latin inscriptions dating from that time, and many of them refer to the two apostles: 'Paul and Peter, make intercession for Victor', 'Peter and Paul, do not forget Antonius Bassus', and others of the same kind. Clearly their names were bracketed together from the earliest days of the Christian era, which is why they have traditionally shared a feast day; and yet they were very different. Peter was a Galilean fisherman who followed Christ during his earthly ministry. Paul was a city man from Tarsus, now in southern Turkey, an intellectual converted after Christ's death and Resurrection.

We know a good deal about Peter's background from the Gospels.

He was the brother of *Andrew, their father was John or Jonah, and they worked on the Lake of Galilee as commercial fishermen with *James and *John, the sons of Zebedee. He was married and lived at Capernaum with his wife and her mother, whom Christ cured of a fever. His name was Symeon in Aramaic and Simon in Greek. Christ told him at their first meeting that he should be called *Képa'*, which meant a rock in Aramaic, and translated as *Cephas* or *Petros* in Greek. When Christ asked the disciples, 'Who do you say that I am?' Peter replied, 'You are the Messiah, the Son of the living God'; and Christ answered him with, 'You are Peter, the Rock; and on this rock I will build my church, and the gates of Hades shall never prevail against it' (Matthew 16:17–18). Peter was courageous and impulsive: he tried to walk on the water of the lake to reach his master; on the occasion of the Transfiguration, he wanted to make tents on the mountain for Christ, Moses and Elijah; and he was determined to keep faith with Christ, even if all the others deserted him. The story of his triple denial of Christ on the night before the Crucifixion is told by all four Evangelists; John tells in detail the story of how Christ forgave him after the Resurrection, with the triple question, 'Simon, son of Jonah, do you love me?' and the three-fold injunction, 'Feed my lambs', 'Feed my sheep' (John 21:15–17).

On the day of Pentecost, Peter was the first of the apostles to address the crowds in the power of the Spirit, telling them to repent and be baptized. He performed the first healing miracle, telling the lame man at the Temple gate, 'I have no silver or gold, but what I have I give you. In the name of Jesus Christ, stand up and walk!' (Acts 3:6). He faced the Sanhedrin with John, and the elders and scribes were astonished at the boldness of his testimony, considering that he was an untrained layman. It was Peter who had the revelation – which must have gone against all his instincts as a good Jew – that the faith was not only for Jews, but must be spread to the Gentiles; and he baptized the centurion Cornelius and his household. He began to undertake missions, carrying out a healing ministry in Galilee, Lydda, Sharon and Joppa. Paul tells us that his wife usually accompanied him (1 Corinthians 9:5). When King Herod Agrippa killed *James the Less, who was administering the church in Jerusalem, Peter was thrown into prison. He must have been thought an important prisoner, because he was heavily chained and guarded; but on the night before his trial he was rescued, by an angel according to Acts 12: 1–11.

It is recorded that he 'left and went to another place'. From this time on, he is not mentioned in the Acts of the Apostles, except in connection with the Council in Jerusalem in the year 49 or 50, when he and Paul clashed angrily on the status of the Gentile converts. Paul accused Peter of being half-hearted. Subsequently, Paul mentions that Peter was in Corinth, and there is an ancient tradition that he founded the church in Antioch.

The tradition that Peter ministered in Rome has been long debated. Most commentators now accept that he did not rule the church in Rome for twenty-five years, as once claimed, but that he was martyred there in the reign of Nero (54–68), probably in the gardens of the Imperial palace, where so many executions took place. Tradition, supported by third-century historians, says that at his own wish he was crucified upside down. Twentieth-century excavations on Vatican Hill have established beyond reasonable doubt that his tomb lies beneath the great basilica of St Peter, but so far it has not been conclusively proved that the relics discovered in the 1960s are his.

Paul (then Saul), was a Roman citizen, which suggests that his family was wealthy, and that they collaborated with the Roman authorities. He was well educated, and had studied under the great rabbinical teacher Gamaliel in Jerusalem. He was a Pharisee, taught the meticulous observance of the Judaic law; and he worked for the Temple authorities. When Stephen was stoned, he guarded the coats of the official witnesses who supervised his execution, and approved of the killing (Acts 7:58). He harried the Church, and sent men and women to prison. Then he asked the high priest to send him to Damascus, to continue the persecutions there. On the way, he had an overwhelming experience. The Conversion of Paul is of such great importance to the Church that it is kept as a separate feast, on 28 January. 'In the end,' he tells the people of Corinth, 'he appeared even to me, as to someone untimely born . . . I had persecuted the church of God . . . however, but by the grace of God, I am what I am, and his grace towards me had not been given to me in vain' (1 Corinthians 15:8–10). The Christians of Damascus took him in, blind and confused, baptized him, and helped him to escape from the fury of the city's synagogue. In Jerusalem, he was less welcome. The Greek Christians wanted to kill him, because they thought he was a spy.

Paul was always an outsider. He never held any authority in the church in Jerusalem. *Barnabas, another outsider because he was a Cypriot, spoke for him and accompanied him on his missionary journeys. Their first visit outside Palestine was to Cyprus, where tradition has it that Paul was flogged at the pillars which still stand half a mile out of Paphos. He took the gospel round the Eastern Mediterranean in three great missionary journeys between the years 46 and 57, establishing churches, writing them letters of advice and guidance, and re-visiting them to give them new inspiration. It was difficult and very dangerous work. He told the Corinthians that he had done as much as any of the brethren. 'Are they Hebrews? So am I. Israelites? So am I. Abraham's descendants? So am I,' and he catalogued his sufferings – the cold and hunger and lack of sleep, the shipwrecks, the floggings, and the mob violence (2 Corinthians 11:22–9).

Paul has been accused of taking the simple faith of Galilean fishermen and over-elaborating it. This view does not stand up to a reading of his Letters. The faith was far from simple. It needed a scholar and a theologian to explain it first to the Jews and then to the Graeco-Roman world. Paul was uniquely placed to do both. He takes the great events of the Incarnation, the Crucifixion, the Resurrection and the coming of the Holy Spirit, and explains them as the central drama of world history.

Paul was in Rome and under house arrest for two years. Though he was released, he was detained again, and then executed at Tre Fontane probably in the year 65. As a Roman citizen, he would have been beheaded rather than suffering crucifixion. He was buried where the basilica of St Paul's Without the Walls now stands. There is no evidence for the belief that he and Peter died on the same day, but the devotion shown in Rome to their joint memory from the earliest Christian times suggests that, despite their differences, their ministries were regarded as complementary, and they were regarded as the joint consolidators of Christ's Church.

There is an enormous literature on Peter and Paul, and none of it is a substitute for reading the Acts of the Apostles and Paul's Letters to the Churches, particularly those to Christians in Rome and Corinth. *The New Catholic Encyclopaedia* has lengthy entries, well illustrated. See also O. Karrer, *Peter and the Church* (1963); D. W. O'Connor, *Peter in Rome: the Literary, Liturgical and Archaeological Evidence* (1969); W. J. Conybeare and J. S. Howson, *Life of St Paul* (2 vols, 1951); G. Ogg, *The Chronology of St Paul* (1966); F. Prat, *The Theology of St Paul* (Eng. trans., 2 vols, 1927–34); J. B. Phillips, *Letters to Young Churches* (1947); J. Murphy O'Connor, *St Paul: a Critical Study* (1996). For the excavations, see E. Kirschbaum, *The Tombs of St Peter and St Paul* (1959); A. A. de Marco, *The Tomb of St Peter* (1964); J. Smith and A. S. Barnes, *St Peter in Rome* (1975).

July

1. Henry Venn the Elder (1725–97), John Venn (1758–1813) and Henry Venn the Younger (1796–1873) [Commem.]

The three Venns, father, son and grandson, were part of a remarkable clerical dynasty. Henry Venn the Elder was the fourth in a line of clergy fathers and sons. He was a curate at Clapham parish church when his son John was born, and went on to become rector of Huddersfield, where he was a celebrated Evangelical preacher. A Cambridge man, he welcomed undergraduates to his parish, and greatly influenced *Charles Simeon in his formative period. He spent his last years in the rectory at Clapham, during his son John's incumbency.

John Venn also went to Cambridge, and, as rector of Clapham, was a leading member of the Clapham Sect, an influential association of Evangelical social reformers. The French historian Élie Halévy describes the Clapham Sect as 'a species of Anglican Methodism'. Most of them had experience in the world of commerce, and some, like *William Wilberforce, who fought against the slave trade, and the two prison reformers, Fowell Buxton and William Whitbread, were members of parliament. Their circle also included the governor of the Bank of England, members of the House of Lords, and Hannah More, the 'Somerset blue-stocking', who was both a playwright and a writer on religious topics. They were known as 'the Saints', and they combined a rigorous examination of their own conduct with a care for the poor and oppressed.

The influence of this group on nineteenth-century English social reform was very great. In the years 1795–1808 they played a considerable part in British political life, and were responsible for promoting a variety of good causes, both in parliament and through voluntary associations. John Venn joined Wilberforce in his battle against the slave trade, finally abolished in 1807. He was a founder of the Church Missionary Society in 1797, and of the interdenominational British and Foreign Bible Society, established in 1804.

Henry Venn the younger was John's son, born in the rectory at Clapham, and known as 'Grandpa's boy'. After some years as a university lecturer at Cambridge, he went in 1834 to St John's, Holloway, in north London. In 1846, he was appointed as a prebendary of St Paul's cathedral, and became secretary of the CMS, a post he held for thirty-two years through the period of major expansion in foreign missions. His policy was to encourage missionaries to concentrate on preaching, and on the exposition of the Bible. Unlike many of his contemporaries, he saw that it was important for them to learn to communicate in the languages of the people they were going to serve rather than relying on interpreters, and he promoted translations of the Bible. He was ahead of his time in his belief that missionaries were pioneers, and that mission stations should work towards indigenous leadership.

D.N.B., 20, pp. 208–9, deals with all three Venns. Stock, ch. 25 (John Venn) and chs 25 to end (Henry Venn); Life of John Venn by W. Knight (1880); Wilbert Shenk, *Henry Venn, Missionary and Statesman* (1983). See also Lives of William Wilberforce (30 July).

3. Thomas the Apostle   Festival

There is some doubt over Doubting Thomas's feast day. The traditional date is 21 December, still kept by the Syrian and Malabar Churches, but the Greek Orthodox Church celebrates the feast on October 6. The revised Universal Roman Calendar has moved it to 3 July, while the Anglican Calendar cautiously specifies '3 July or 21 December'.

The Fourth Gospel calls Thomas *Didymus*, or 'the twin', and he emerges clearly in all the Gospels as a devoted disciple, but an arch-doubter. He is prepared to go with Christ wherever he is going, and to die with him (John 11:16), but he asks how they are to know the way (John 14:5–6), eliciting the response, 'I am the way, and the truth, and the life.' At the Resurrection appearance in the upper room, he wants to see the print of the nails and the wound in Christ's side, and he is allowed to put his hand into the wounds. Again the incident leads to greater understanding among the apostles, for his response is, 'My Lord and my God' (John 20:24–8).

The tradition that Thomas was the first missionary in India is strong and persistent. When the Portuguese reached south India in the 1520s, they found existing Christian communities there and they were shown his tomb at Mylapore. The place is now called San Tomé. The Mar Thoma Church of South India claims him as its founder. Many apocryphal accounts of his travels – *The Acts of Thomas, The Apocalypse of Thomas, the Gospel of Thomas* and others – circulated in the early Church, some of them from Gnostic or Manichaean groups.

Mediaeval theologians debated whether Thomas was to be blamed for his lack of faith or praised for having provided proof of the Resurrection for sceptics. *Pope Gregory the Great resolved the matter by pointing to the words of Christ which followed in the incident in the upper room: 'But blessed are those who have not seen, and have come to believe.'

G. F. Medlycott, *India and the Apostle Thomas* (1905); J. N. Farquhar, 'The Apostle Thomas in North India', *Bulletin of John Ryland's Library*, 10 (1926), pp. 86–111 and 'The Apostle Thomas in South India', 11 (1927), pp. 20–50; *N.C.E.*, 14, p. 101; *O.D.S.*, pp. 458–9.

6. John Fisher (1469–1535)   [Commem.]

Fisher was one of the new men of the early Tudor period: a draper's son from Beverley in Yorkshire who went to Cambridge at the age of eighteen, became a priest, and rose to become vice-chancellor of the university. His patron was Lady Margaret Beaufort, the mother of Henry VII. Lady Margaret, a very wealthy woman, founded Christ's College and St John's College, and instituted Lady Margaret Chairs of Divinity at both Oxford and Cambridge. When Fisher went to Cambridge, the University Library contained no more than three hundred books, and no Latin or Greek was taught. He built up the library, revived the ancient languages, and encouraged the new Humanist scholarship of his day. In 1504, he was appointed chancellor of the university, a post he held until his death in 1535.

Henry VIII appointed Fisher as bishop of Rochester, and though he had no desire to leave the university, he proved to be a good and conscientious pastor. Later he was offered more wealthy sees, but he refused them. He lived very austerely, eating little, sleeping only four hours a night, and keeping a skull on his desk to remind him of mortality. His studies continued: he learned Greek when he was forty-eight years old, and Hebrew at fifty-one. He preached against the worldliness and corruption of the Church, but wished to see it reformed from within. He wrote a massive four-volume work against Lutheranism, arguing that it was essential to preserve the unity of Christendom in the Western world.

When Henry VIII sought to have his marriage to Catherine of Aragon nullified, Fisher was one of the Queen's counsellors. He argued her case before a papal court at Blackfriars in 1529, and proved to be her most able champion. Though earlier popes had proved more accommodating to royal dynastic ambition, allowing decrees of nullity on what were often very flimsy grounds, Pope Clement VII refused: Catherine was the daughter of the Catholic monarchs of Spain, Ferdinand and Isabella, and she had borne Henry a succession of sons, all of whom had died. Henry determined to make himself supreme governor of the Church, and Fisher opposed him by powerful speeches in Convocation. Inevitably he attracted the king's fury. He was three times imprisoned, an attempt was made to poison him, and a gunshot shattered his library window.

Fisher was not totally inflexible, and he would have bent to the king's will if it had been possible in conscience. He proposed the addition of the words 'so far as the law of Christ allows' to the oath of allegiance required by the Act of Supremacy of 1534, and this quieted many consciences; but the Act of Succession required more: assent to the statement that the king's marriage to Catherine of Aragon had not been valid, recognition of the legitimacy of the issue of his marriage to Anne Boleyn, and the repudiation of the authority of 'any foreign authority, prince or potentate', including the pope. Fisher could not subscribe to this oath: he was arrested on a charge of treason, and conveyed to the Tower of London.

Pope Paul III fuelled the king's anger by sending Fisher a cardinal's hat: the king swore that he should not have a head to set it on. By this time, Fisher was so emaciated and so weak from repeated confinement that one visitor said that his frail body could scarcely bear the weight of his clothes. He was condemned to death on 17 June 1535, and roused five days later to be told that he would be executed that day. He was so weak that he had to be taken to Tower Hill in a chair; but he walked up the hill and mounted the scaffold unassisted, pardoned the executioner, and turned to address the crowd. He told them in a clear voice that he was dying for Christ's Holy Catholic Church, and asked them to pray that he might make a good death. Then he recited the *Te Deum* and Psalm 11, *In te, Domine, speravi*. He accepted the blind-fold, and knelt calmly for his execution.

His head was impaled on London Bridge for fourteen days, and then replaced by that of his friend and fellow-martyr, Thomas More. Their feasts are celebrated on the same day. If John Fisher's death has attracted less attention than More's this is probably because of the extreme simplicity and austerity of his life. His character had no quirks, and his life little drama until its final courageous chapter.

The Letters and Papers, Foreign and Domestic, of the Reign of Henry VIII, published by the Public Record Office, provide very full primary materials for the Life of St John Fisher. An important biography written some time after 1567 is published in *Anal.Boll.*, 10, pp. 119–365, and 12, pp. 97–287, and there is a version ed. Philip Hughes (1935) in modern English, with a commentary. See also Lives by T. Bridgett (3rd edn, 1902); E. A. Benians (1935); N. M. Wilby (1929); E. E. Reynolds (1955); M. Macklem (1967); L. Surtz (1967); and R. L. Smith, *John Fisher and Thomas More* (1933). *Bishop Fisher's English Works*, pt 1, ed. J. E. B. Mayor (1876), pt 2, ed. R. Bayne (1915), are published by the Early English Text Society. See also *A Spiritual Consolation and other Treatises*, ed. D. O'Connor (1935).

Thomas More (1478–1535)   *[Commem.]*

Thomas went to Oxford at the age of fourteen. His father, Sir John More, who was a barrister, disapproved of both his enthusiasm for Greek and the company he kept, for the boy was attracted by the new Humanist ideas which were coming from the Low Countries. Sir John recalled his son to London, and set him to studying law, in the hope that this would have a sobering influence; but though Thomas obeyed, and became a lecturer in law, he encountered Humanists in London, too. Dean Colet of St Paul's was his spiritual adviser, Thomas Linacre his tutor in Greek; and in London, he met Erasmus, the monk whose merciless satires on the Church were spiced with the wit of classical Greek scholarship.

More's father insisted that he should follow a secular career, but he was deeply attracted to monastic life. He wore a hair shirt, used a log for a pillow, restricted his sleep, and attended the Charterhouse daily, taking part in the spiritual exercises of the Carthusians. He married because his father expected him to do so, and when his wife Jane died after four years of marriage and four children, he married Alice Middleton within a month, to give the children a mother and his household a competent housekeeper. His home became a centre of hospitality and brilliant conversation: Linacre, Colet, and *John Fisher were frequent visitors, and Erasmus came to stay – too frequently for Alice's wishes. The household met daily for prayers, and at meals the children read passages from the Scriptures. There was a chapel in the house, and More acted as server at the daily Mass.

He was an excellent lawyer. By 1510, he was a reader of Lincoln's Inn and under-sheriff of London. The new king, Henry VIII, gave him a knighthood, and enjoyed his company. His life was so full that he had little time for study and writing until chance gave him an unexpected opportunity to escape his daily preoccupations. Cardinal Wolsey sent him to the Netherlands as a member of a trade delegation. Negotiations went slowly, and for six months he lived in the house of a Humanist friend, Peter Gillies, who was town clerk of Antwerp. There he wrote the second part of *Utopia*, which deals with an imaginary country. The first part of *Utopia*, written after his return to England, is sharp social criticism of Henry VIII's kingdom: the cruel and unjust state of the criminal law, the evils of the enclosure movement which dispossessed the agricultural poor and drove them to crime; but Part II is perhaps best described as early science fiction. 'Utopia' means 'no place'. The book is full of learned puns and paradoxes. Not surprisingly, his imaginary country is in many respects like a monastic community: there is no money, no private property, and no privacy. People live communally, and share the manual labour without distinction of class; but the influence of Humanism leads him to some surprising speculations. In Utopia, divorce is possible (once, though repeated adultery is punishable by death); euthanasia is allowed; and there are women priests. He is very careful not to let the reader know whether he is being serious or not, but the book was immediately hailed as a major contribution to Humanist thought.

In many ways, More was a very conservative Catholic. He wrote against Protestantism, particularly against *William Tyndale: he was strongly opposed to the free circulation of the Bible in the vernacular. He wrote *Utopia* in Latin so that it should not lead the unlearned astray; and he administered the letter of the law, though with as much humanity as he could. He became a counsel, a judge, and in 1529 Henry VIII's chancellor.

Perhaps Henry VIII, who was not unlearned himself, hoped that a Humanist chancellor who had written about divorce would take his side in his battle with the papacy; but like Bishop Fisher, More believed that the unity of the Church must be preserved at all costs. Reform must come from within, not by schism. He was a very cautious man. He explained the legal issues clearly and impartially to parliament, but refused to give his own opinion. When he was pressed, he resigned. He had been lord chancellor for less than three years.

He had never cared about piling up wealth, though he had had many opportunities to do so. Now his household was reduced to poverty. He refused to attend the king's marriage to Anne Boleyn, and lived very quietly, hoping that his silence would be enough to save him. When he was called to Lambeth to take the oath following the Act of Succession, he refused to take the oath, but would not say why, believing that he could not be tried for treason if he said nothing treasonable; but he was committed to the Tower of London.

More spent fifteen months in the Tower. His serenity and his endurance, despite his anguish at what his stand on a matter of conscience was doing to his family, is eloquently recorded in the biography by his daughter Margaret's husband, William Roper. It was not that he would not help them: he could not, even when his wife Alice had to sell her clothes to buy food. He was tried in Westminster Hall on 1 July 1535. He told the jury: 'Ye must understand that, in things touching conscience, every true and good subject is more bound to have respect to his said conscience and to his soul than to any other thing in the world beside.' Though he still refused to say why he would not take the oath, he was convicted on false evidence, and condemned to death. Then at last he spoke, and characteristically said that he would pray for his judges in the hope that 'we may yet hereafter in heaven merrily all meet together in everlasting salvation'.

He was taken to Tower Hill four days later. He wore his best clothes, spoke with friends on the way to the scaffold, and asked for the prayers of the people, saying that he was 'the king's good servant – but God's first'. Then he comforted the executioner, and bound his own eyes before placing his head on the block.

Thomas More lived and died in the spirit of his own prayer:

Give me, good Lord, a longing to be with thee: not for the avoiding of the calamities of this wicked world, nor of the pains of hell neither, nor so much for attaining the joys of heaven . . . as even for a very love of thee.

More has been the subject of many biographies, and the play and film *A Man for All Seasons* brought his story before a new public. There are famous portraits, including several by Holbein.

William Roper's *The Mirror of Vertue in Worldly Greatness, or the Life of Sir Thomas More* was probably first published in London during the reign of Mary Tudor. There is an edition ed. E. V. Hitchcock (1935). Other early Lives include one by Thomas Stapleton in *Tres Thomae* (1588), trans. P. E. Hallett, ed. E. E. Reynolds (1966). Among modern biographies the standard work is that by R. W. Chambers (1935): see review in *Anal.Boll.*, 54 (1936), p. 245. For more recent biographies, see C. Hollis (1961); David Knowles (1970); J. A. Guy (1980); Antony Kenny (1983); Richard Maines (1984); Frank Barlow (1986); Louis Martz (1990). Thomas More is claimed as a Franciscan tertiary: see *F.B.S.*, pp. 453–6. There is an account of the trial by E. E. Reynolds (1953). More's correspondence has been edited by E. F. Rogers (Princeton, 1947). *Utopia* is available in many editions. A University of Yale edition of the complete works commenced in 1963. *The Likeness of Thomas More*, a survey by Stanley Morison and Nicolas Barker (1965), provides a detailed study of portraits and engravings over three centuries.

11. Benedict of Nursia (*c*.480–550) [L.F.]

Monasticism came to Europe from Egypt and Palestine, where it was well established by the time of *Antony (d. 356). Benedict, who was born near Naples and studied in Rome, encountered it through the Byzantine tradition, which was much discussed in theological circles at that time. He became a hermit at Subiaco, near Rome, and others came to join him. He moved to Monte Cassino, and learned from the works of John Cassian and *Basil the Great; but while the main Eastern tradition was one of very loose association between hermits who generally met only for worship and an occasional meal, Benedict developed a more close-knit model of community life, similar to the model which Basil instituted at Pontus and elsewhere in Cappadocia.

Benedict was not a priest, and originally had no intention of founding a religious Order; but he developed a system based on liturgical prayer, the reading of sacred texts and manual work which became a pattern for monastic houses all over Europe, much commended for its moderation, flexibility and stability. Benedictine monasteries became great centres of learning, of hospitality, of agriculture and of healing.

The Benedictine Rule was the basis of virtually all monastic life until the twelfth century, when *Bernard of Clairvaux developed the reformed variant, the Cistercian Rule. In the thirteenth century, Orders of friars, Franciscans, Augustinians and Dominicans, introduced new patterns of religious practice.

Benedict died at Monte Cassino on 21 March, but in both the Revised Roman Calendar and the Anglican Calendar, his feast day is celebrated on 11 July, to keep this important festival clear of Easter. He is known as 'the patron of Europe'. His work is chiefly known through the *Dialogues* of *Pope Gregory the Great (d. 604). His original monastery at Monte Cassino was destroyed by Lombard invaders about 577, but was rebuilt, and has since continued to be a centre of world-wide influence.

AA.SS., March, 3, pp. 274–357; Gregory the Great, *Dialogues*, bk 2, in *P.L.*, 77, pp. 149–430; Christopher Butler, *Benedictine Monasticism* (1924); David Knowles, *The Monastic Order in England, 940–1216* (1939, repr. 1966). J. M. McCann (1937); T. Fry (1980); *N.C.E.*, 2, pp. 271–3; D. H. Farmer, ed., *Benedict's Disciples* (1980). The oldest existing copy of the Benedictine Rule is in the Bodleian Library at Oxford (Hatton 48). The Rule has been translated by J. M. McCann (1951) and by D. Parry (1980).

14. John Keble (1792–1868)   [L.F.]

John Keble's famous 'Assize Sermon' of 14 July 1833 is usually taken as the starting-point of the Oxford (Tractarian) movement. He and *John Henry Newman were friends and colleagues, both Fellows of Oriel College, Oxford. Keble, the son of the vicar of Fairford, Gloucestershire, had been ordained in 1815, and served in small parishes while retaining his Oxford fellowship. From 1826, when his father became ill, he spent much of his time back at Fairford, ministering to his father's parishioners. He had refused the archdeaconry of Barbados and a valuable living at Paignton in order to fulfil his obligations at home.

In addition to parish work, he wrote poetry: in 1827 the publication of his collection of poems, *The Christian Year*, won him acclaim, and in 1831 he was elected Oxford Professor of Poetry. This was an honour, but one which carried few responsibilities and only limited emoluments. Unlike Newman or *Edward Pusey, Keble had no taste for public life or controversy. He lived an intense inner life which found outward expression in his poetry and in a parish ministry. He continued to help his father until the older man's death in 1835. After that, he married a young woman who was already part of his family circle: the sister of his brother's wife. In 1836, he accepted the living of Hurley, near Winchester, where he had served a curacy for a year after his ordination; and he remained at Hurley for thirty years, content to be a good parish priest, taking daily services, preparing young people for confirmation, faithfully visiting his parishioners, and writing biblical commentaries.

John Keble was a High Churchman of the old school, much attached to the memory of *Charles I, and largely aloof from the anguished theological debate of his own day. Though he spoke in the Assize Sermon of the danger that the Apostolical Church might be 'forsaken, degraded, nay, trampled on and despoiled, by the State and the people of England', he recommended prayer, resignation to God and 'the daily and hourly duties of piety, purity and justice' rather than a public campaign to defend the Apostolic Succession and restore ritual in worship.

Keble's most popular hymn is 'New every morning', in which the lines 'The daily round, the common task / Should furnish all we ought to ask' express his deeply held conviction about the importance of everyday living. In the curiously elliptical 'There is a book who runs may read', he writes:

> Two worlds are ours: 'tis only sin
> Forbids us to descry
> The mystic Heav'n and earth within
> Plain as the sea and sky.

For him, the mystic heaven was always plain, and he asked for nothing more. After his death in 1868, a subscription was raised to build a college in Oxford 'in strict fidelity to the Church of England'. The splendours of Keble College are perhaps more of a memorial to the architectural and artistic tastes of the Tractarians than to the shy and unambitious man for whom it is named.

S. T. Coleridge, *A Memoir of John Keble* (1869); K. Ingram (1939); Georgina Battiscombe (1963); B. W. Martin (1976); *Victorian Church*, 1, pp. 66–79; D.N.B., 10, pp. 1179–83. *Selections from the Writings of John Keble, M.A.* (1890).

15. Swithun (d. 862)   [L.F.]

Swithun was born in Wessex, ordained at Winchester, and chosen by King Egbert of Wessex to be his court chaplain. Egbert fought a series of battles against the Mercians, captured London, and styled himself *Rex Merciorum* for a time. One of Swithun's responsibilities was to educate Egbert's heir, Ethelwulf, who became under-king of Kent, and then king of Wessex in 839. Ethelwulf, in gratitude, nominated Swithun bishop of Winchester. He held his appointment for the final ten years of his life, during which time he built a number of churches, and was renowned for his charity.

Swithun died on 2 July 862, a day on which the weather appears to have been unremarkable. He was buried, at his own request, in the cemetery, just outside the west door of the Old Minster. His feast day marks the translation of his bones to Winchester cathedral on 15 July 964. Apparently there was heavy rain all day, hence the superstition that if there is rain on St Swithun's day, it will rain for forty days after.

His shrine was a popular place of pilgrimage in mediaeval times, but was demolished at the Reformation. It was restored in 1962.

AA.SS., Jul., 1, pp. 294–9. Life by Goscelin, ed. E. P. Sauvage, in *Anal.Boll.*, 7 (1868), pp. 373–80; Old English Life in W. W. Skeat, ed., *Aelfric's Lives of the Saints*, E.E.T.S. (1881), pp. 440–71. *O.D.S.*, pp. 445–6.

Bonaventure (c.1218–74)   [Commem.]

Bonaventure was born near Orvieto in northern Italy. In 1243, he joined the Friars Minor (Franciscans). He studied and later taught at the Sorbonne in Paris, where he was a contemporary of the great Dominican, *Thomas Aquinas; but while Thomist thought was strictly rational and practical, Bonaventure developed a mystical theology based on the thought of Pseudo-Dionysius, *Augustine of Hippo and *John of Damascus. He saw the natural world as 'the footprint of God', and drew from it illumination on the nature of eternal truth. His best-known work is *The Journey of the Mind to God*.

In 1257, while still under forty, he became minister-general of the Franciscan Order, and brought a much-needed influence for spiritual devotion and scholarship to a somewhat disorganized movement. Some thirty years after the death of its founder, the Franciscan movement was split by dissension. The *Zelanti* or Spirituals were inclined to excessive asceticism and visions, while other friars were not keeping to their vow of poverty. Bonaventure worked for unity and moderation.

Gentle and courteous, he is known as 'the second founder of the Franciscan movement' because he reinstituted the original Rule, curbing the excesses and correcting abuses. The Franciscans were not known for their learning, but he insisted on the need for study, for books and for libraries to house them, and encouraged Franciscan study and teaching in the universities. He was a simple and unassuming prior. When Pope Gregory X nominated him as cardinal-bishop of Albano, commanding him not to refuse the honour, he was found to be washing dishes in a friary near Florence. It is said that he kept the papal messengers waiting until the dishes were dried.

When he became a cardinal, he resigned the generalate of the Franciscan Order, and took a leading part in the movement to re-unite the Eastern and Western Churches which culminated in the Council of Lyons. He preached reconciliation, and the movement was temporarily successful, though the Eastern Orthodox Church subsequently withdrew from the agreement.

Bonaventure died at Lyons in 1274. He was declared a Doctor of the Church in 1588, and is frequently referred to as 'the Seraphic Doctor'. (Thomas Aquinas is 'the Angelic Doctor'.)

AA.SS., July, 3, pp. 811–60; E. H. Gilson, *The Philosophy of St Bonaventure* (1928); *N.C.E.*, 2, pp. 658–64; *O.D.S.*, pp. 58–9; Works: ed. E. Cousins (1978).

16. Osmund (d. 1099)   [*Commem.*]

In 1078, William the Conqueror nominated Osmund as bishop of Salisbury, and he was consecrated by *Archbishop Lanfranc. Osmund had come to England after the Norman Conquest, and had acted as William's chancellor for the previous two years. According to a fifteenth-century document, he was William's nephew, the son of his half-sister Isabella and Henry, Count of Séez. In addition to his episcopal functions, he continued to be involved in affairs of state: he was one of the royal commissioners appointed for the Domesday Survey, and responsible for the surveys in much of the Midlands and the North of England.

Like all Lanfranc's bishops, Osmund was erudite and energetic. He took charge of the building work at Old Sarum, where a cathedral was being erected, and ensured the foundation and endowment of a cathedral chapter. The canons were bound to residence, which was the procedure in Normandy, but an innovation in England. The liturgical use at Salisbury was somewhat haphazard, a mass of old service books which were not clearly ordered. Osmund drew up regulations for the celebration of Mass and the other sacraments on a uniform basis throughout his diocese, and within a century these revised Offices 'according to the use of the Distinguished and Noble Church of Sarum' were in use in most of the dioceses of England and Wales. They continued to be used until the middle of the sixteenth century, when they were replaced for Roman Catholics by the revised offices of Pope Pius V. After the re-establishment of the Roman Catholic hierarchy in England in 1850, there was some discussion of re-introducing the Sarum Use, and though this did not happen, the Mass and Offices of the Dominicans still closely resemble it.

Osmund was a scholar, and he built up a large and well-stocked library at Salisbury. He spent much time there, studying manuscripts and copying and binding books himself. Unlike Lanfranc and most of the Norman bishops, he had some knowledge of Anglo-Saxon religious traditions, and a particular devotion to the memory of *Aldhelm, bishop of Sherborne. He is credited with preventing the abolition of Aldhelm's feast day when the new Calendar was drawn up, and with having written a life of Aldhelm, though the manuscript has not survived. He assisted in the enshrining of Aldhelm's relics at Malmesbury in 1078.

Osmund's cathedral at Salisbury was completed and consecrated in 1092. Five days after the consecration, it was struck by lightning and badly damaged. This event was probably regarded in the area as a sign of divine disapproval, but Osmund had the cathedral repaired, and the worship at Sarum, with its chapter of residentiary canons and its revised pattern of services, became a model for others to follow.

William of Malmesbury says that Osmund had very high standards of personal morality. He was severe with his penitents, but equally severe on himself. He lived quietly, and was neither ambitious nor avaricious, as so many other prelates were. He died at Salisbury on the night of 3–4 December 1099, and was buried in his cathedral. Though his shrine was destroyed in Henry VIII's reign, there is a slab from his tomb in one of the bays of the cathedral nave, inscribed with the date MXCIX.

The main details of Osmund's life come from William of Malmesbury, *Gesta Pontificum* (R.S. 52), pp. 98, 424, 428, and *Gesta Regum* (R.S. 90), pp. 372, 375; and from Eadmer, *Historia Novella*, pp. 72, 82. See also W. H. Rich-Jones, ed., *The Register of St Osmund*, (2 vols, 1883–4); A. R. Malden, ed., *The Canonisation of Saint Osmund from the ms. records in the muniment room of Salisbury Cathedral*, (Wilts. Record Society, 1901); W. H. Frere, ed., *Antiphonale Sarisburiense*, (2 vols 1896 and 1901); W. H. R. Jones, *Vetus Registrum Sarisberiense, alias dictum S. Osmundii episcopi*, (2 vols 1883–4); William Worcestre, *Itineraries*, ed. J. H. Harvey (1969), pp. 53, 89, 157; *D.N.B.*, 14, pp. 1207–9; *Men.E.W.*, pp. 583–4; W. J. Torrance, *St Osmund of Salisbury* (1920, repr. 1941).

18. Elizabeth Ferard (d. 1883)   [*Commem.*]

In August 1855, the bishop of London, A. C. Tait, visited Kaiserswerth, the Lutheran deaconess institution on the Rhine where *Florence Nightingale had stayed four years earlier to learn about nurse training. At his suggestion, Elizabeth Ferard, a young woman who was seeking an opportunity of serving the Church, went there in the following year. The Kaiserswerth system, established by Pastor Fliedner in 1836, consisted of 'Protestant Sisters of Charity' who worked in poor parishes. They lived in community, but unlike nuns did not make vows and were not liturgically commissioned. The Tractarian movement (see *Pusey) had resulted in the formation of the first religious communities for women in the Church of England on models very similar to those of the Roman Catholic Church, but the bishop and Miss Ferard were looking for a Protestant model. Later, in her Journal, she writes of her anxiety to avoid 'the stumbling block of Romanism'.

When she returned to England, she began to make plans for a deaconess community in London. In 1861, she settled with two associates in a house in the very poor Somers Town district of King's Cross. The house was formally constituted as the North London Deaconess Institution on St Andrew's Day 1861, and the community as the Community of St Andrew. In July 1862, Elizabeth Ferard became the first deaconess licensed in the Church of England.

There was much discussion of biblical precedents for this new role for women. The word *diakonos* is used in the Greek New Testament to describe the work of the seven Hellenists (Jews from outside Palestine) who were appointed to care for their widows in the daily distribution of food (see *Stephen). The only occasion on which the word was applied to a woman is in *St Paul's mention of Phoebe in Romans 16:1. In the Authorized Version of the Bible *diakonos* is translated here as 'a servant of the Church', though the word 'deacon' is used for men. Many clergy in the 1860s were resistant to the idea of a formal ecclesiastical status for deaconesses, citing St Paul's strictures on the women of Corinth (1 Corinthians 14) who were firmly told to be silent in church. The supporters of the movement claimed that they were reviving a practice from the early Christian period, but the *Church Times* commented rather acidly that 'we copied the Lutheran Deaconess from Kaiserswerth, and then spent vast erudition on identifying her with the Deaconess of the Primitive Church'.

The Community of St Andrew made no controversial claims to ecclesiastical status. They claimed only to serve, and as their numbers increased, the opportunities for service were many. They were overwhelmed by requests from parishes, from schools, from hospitals. They taught in the schools, cared for children, organized sewing parties and Bible classes for mothers, ran soup kitchens, nursed the sick, and took dying people into the Community house. They had a very high view of their vocation. Elizabeth Ferard wrote:

> To them is committed the care of the sick, the poor, the education of young children, and generally the help of the needy of whatever kind. And also it is their office to be helpers, either directly or indirectly, to the ministers of the Church. They must therefore have the qualities which the Apostle requires from deacons [Acts 6:3]. They must first be of good report, and second, be full of faith and good works.

They were 'the servants of the Lord Jesus, and servants of the needy for Christ's sake'. In 1871, she drew up the House Rules, which laid down an exacting pattern of daily prayer and service. They were to assist the parish clergy 'in all womanly modesty and submission'. It was not until the time of *Isabella Gilmore that some deaconesses in other foundations began to claim to be in Holy Orders, like male deacons.

In 1873, much of Somers Town was demolished to make way for the railway network leading into King's Cross and St Pancras stations, and the Community moved to Tavistock Crescent, Notting Hill. Deaconess Ferard resigned on the grounds of ill-health in that same year, and moved to Redhill, where she managed a small children's home at her own expense until her death.

Elizabeth Ferard's Journal (which includes her statement 'On the Deaconess Office in General') and other documents are in the CSA archives; Cecilia Robinson, *The Ministry of Deaconesses* (1908); Brian Heeney, *The Women's Movement in the Church of England, 1830–1850* (1988).

19. Gregory of Nyssa (d. *c.*395) and Macrina the Younger (d. 379)   [L.F.]

Gregory and Macrina were brother and sister to *Basil of Caesarea. Macrina is called 'the Younger' because her paternal grandmother, Macrina the Elder, is also included in the Orthodox and Roman Catholic Calendars.

Young Macrina was the eldest daughter, and possibly the eldest child, of Basil the Elder and his wife Emmelia. The year of her birth is variously given as 327, 329 or 330. She shared with her mother and grandmother the upbringing and education of the younger children, as many elder daughters did in the days of large families. Like her grandmother, she was scholarly, and she became a devout and learned Christian.

Basil was either a year older or a year younger than Macrina. He met *Gregory of Nazianzus while studying in Athens, and Macrina is said to have been betrothed to Gregory's brother, who died before they could marry. When Basil completed his studies, he and Macrina held long discussions on whether to make vows of celibacy, and they both did so. In 370, Basil became bishop of Caesarea. When he came home full of his new responsibilities, Macrina 'reproved him for vainglory' – or put him in his place, as sisters are apt to do to self-important brothers.

Gregory (later of Nyssa) was Macrina's youngest brother, and much closer to her. He followed Basil in studying at Athens, married and became a teacher of rhetoric. It is not known whether his wife died, or became a nun, but after some time, he became a monk. In 371 he was made bishop of Nyssa. He is named with Basil of Caesarea and *Gregory Nazianzen as a Doctor of the Eastern Church, and the three are known as the Three Cappadocian Fathers, champions of orthodoxy in a period when the basic tenets of Christianity were under attack from Arianism and the many other unorthodox beliefs which flourished in Asia Minor. Gregory of Nyssa is thought to have been the most philosophical and speculative of the three. His writings against

Arianism, his treatises on the Song of Songs and his Life of Moses indicate a subtle intellect and an intuitive grasp of religious truth.

Macrina became a consecrated virgin, and then a nun in the religious community founded by her mother on the banks of the river Iris, near Pontus. In 379, Gregory visited her on his way back to Nyssa from Antioch. He had not seen his sister, whom he calls 'the Teacher', for eight years. Basil had recently died, and he wanted to discuss the Church's teaching on life after death. He found Macrina very ill, and near death herself, breathing with great difficulty. She was evidently a skilled spiritual counsellor. He compares her to a chariot driver who gives his horses their head, and then reins them in when they have finished galloping. She let him express all his grief and anger and doubt over their brother's death, and then, 'like a skilful driver', she reasoned with him and cured his distress, expounding the hope of the Resurrection. He speaks of her in tones of deep affection and respect. His account of their discussions, *On the Soul and Resurrection*, is also known as the *Macriniae*.

The suggestion of some commentators that these were really Gregory's ideas, and that he put them in the mouth of his sister as a literary device, is really not tenable. Women in the fourth-century Church of Asia Minor had opportunities for theological study which were later denied to women in Italy and southern Europe. Macrina had taught Gregory when he was a child, and he went back to a beloved elder sister for counsel in their joint bereavement.

Macrina died soon afterwards, and Gregory wrote her biography. This and the *Macriniae* were not known at all in the West until the eleventh century, when they were finally translated into Latin.

Gregory of Nyssa: *AA.SS.*, Mar., 2, pp. 4–10; *N.C.E.*, 6, pp. 794–6. Works ed. W. Jaeger (1921–60). The *Vitae Sanctae Macriniae* is in *AA.SS.*, July, 4, pp. 589–604, and in W. Callahan, ed., *St Gregory of Nyssa: Ascetical Works* (1967), pp. 159–91; entitled *On the Soul and the Resurrection* in N.P.N.F., 5, pp. 428–68; *Later Christian Fathers*, pp. 129–65. *The Life of St Macrina*, trans. and ed. W. K. Lowther Clarke (1916). For a new translation and commentary, see Joan M. Petersen, *Handmaids of the Lord* (Cistercian Publications, Kalamazoo, Michigan, 1996), pp. 41–86. Modern Life of Macrina by P. Maraval (1977).

20. **Margaret of Antioch** (?early fourth century)   [*Commem.*]

Early Christian martyrs in the Middle East are understandably difficult to document: later Saracen invasions destroyed tombs and written records, and centuries of oral tradition often produced some bizarre variations on the original story.

Margaret is said to have been the daughter of a priest of some local religion, named Aedisius. When she became a Christian, her family turned her out, and she became a shepherdess. Olybius, the governor of Antioch, tried to seduce her, and then offered to marry her, but she was determined to remain a virgin. She declared her faith, and remained firm against temptation, bribery and torture. According to one account, she was swallowed by a dragon, which then burst open, releasing her (a story which sounds like a version of Jonah and the whale). She was finally beheaded, probably in the persecutions of Diocletian.

This is one of many such stories about virgin saints. The male persecutor was often said to be a governor, a consul or even an emperor because this added to the impact of the story. However, the detail about Margaret's background sounds specific, and the theological school at Antioch had a rather better reputation in the matter of saints than that at Alexandria. It is typical of these early stories from countries where women had a very low social status that female saints are given a feminine reason for martyrdom – refusal to marry – while male saints are assumed to face martyrdom for their religious convictions.

Margaret's story did not reach the West until the ninth century, when she was mentioned in the martyrology of Rabanus Maurus. The Crusaders brought a devotion to her back from Antioch, and she became very popular in England and Western Europe during the Middle Ages. According to the Sarum Breviary, she promised that those who invoked her on their death-bed would have her protection; that those who dedicated churches in her name, or burned candles or lamps in her honour, would obtain the good things they prayed for, and that women who prayed to her during childbirth would have a safe delivery and a healthy child. She was, in short, a thoroughly useful saint. In the Rhineland she was named as one of the Fourteen Holy Helpers, and in England over two hundred churches were dedicated to her. She appears in many mediaeval paintings, and on stained glass windows.

Behind the legends, there may be the record of a real young woman – or more than one young woman – of Antioch who died for Christ many centuries ago.

AA.SS., July, 5, pp. 22–4; H. Delehaye, *Légendes hagiographiques*, Brussels, 1927, pp. 222–34; *Golden Legend*, 1, pp. 368–70; O.D.S., pp. 318–19.

Bartolomé de las Casas (1474–1566)   [*Commem.*]

Bartolomé was born in Seville, the city from which Christopher Columbus sailed to the Indies in 1492, and where the populace lined the banks of the Guadalquivir to greet him on his return. His father, a nobleman of the city, sailed with Columbus on his second expedition, and developed profitable interests in Hispaniola (now divided between Haiti and the Dominican Republic). He brought back a present for Bartolomé: a young Indian boy slave; but Queen Isabella of Spain, who had commissioned Columbus, decreed that slavery was forbidden in Spain, and the boy was sent back to Hispaniola.

Bartolomé shared the Spanish dream of the wealth of the Indies. In 1502, when he was twenty-eight, he sailed to Hispaniola, hoping to make his fortune; but, perhaps because of his boyhood experience, he developed an instinctive sympathy for the Indian poor and oppressed, who were treated with great callousness and brutality by the settlers. When four Dominican friars arrived in 1610, he sought ordination, joined their Order, and devoted his life to campaigning for the Indians. He tells the story himself in his *History of the Indies*. Though he is reticent about his own ministry, his anger and distress come through very strongly.

The Indians were quiet and inoffensive people. 'They are of a clean, unspoiled and vivacious intellect', he wrote, 'very capable, and receptive to every good doctrine . . . these people have scarce more strength and courage than children of ten years old.' They made good converts to Christianity; but they were being forced to hard labour with whips and cudgels, and dying in their thousands. When Spanish troops ran amok and cut down two thousand on a single day without provocation, he protested vehemently to the commander, and lodged complaints with the authorities; but he encountered only hostility and incomprehension. He told them that slavery was forbidden by Spanish law: they ignored him. Slavery was profitable, and Spain was many days distant by sail.

Bartolomé carried his protests to Spain. In all, he made the hazardous journey across the Atlantic seven times in each direction. There was a lively debate in Spain about the treatment of the Indians, but many powerful churchmen were shareholders in the new colonial enterprises, and slow to support him. He appealed to the King's Council without result. The Holy Roman Emperor Charles V, who was married to the daughter of Ferdinand and Isabella of Spain, took no great interest in the source of Spain's wealth. Bartolomé made representations to bishops and archbishops, and to the aristocracy, telling them that the land in the Indies was fertile, the resources were vast, and the people gentle and co-operative: the colonies needed honest and frugal settlers, not the murderous and dissolute freebooters who were killing off the Indians like cattle. He calculated that the settlers of New Spain killed some two million people in ten years, 'so that scarce two thousand are left in the vast Expanse of it'. He warned his fellow-countrymen that 'God will visit his wrath and ire on Spain for her share . . . in the blood-stained riches obtained by theft and usurpation accompanied by such slaughter and annihilation.'

In 1519, Bartolomé was consecrated bishop of Chiapa, on the north-eastern coast of Mexico. This removed him from the desolation of Hispaniola, and he continued to preach and write powerfully against the lust for gold and the cruelties of Spanish conquest. In 1543, he became bishop of Mexico. His passion for peace and justice for the Indians was prodding consciences in Spain, if not among the settlers. Eventually he retired, and lived in the Dominican house at Valladolid in Spain, continuing his campaign:

> I leave, in the Indies, Jesus Christ, our God, scourged and afflicted and buffeted and crucified, not once, but millions of times, on the part of all the Spaniards who ruin and destroy these people . . . depriving them of life before their time, so that they die without faith and without the sacraments.

He died at the age of ninety-two. The Istituto de Las Casas in Lima, Peru, commemorates his name and continues his work.

Gustavo Gutiérrez, *Fray Bartolomé de las Casas: su tiempo y su apostólado* (1878), trans. A. McNutt (New York, 1909). Works: *Historia de las Indias*, trans. as *In Defense of Indians* by S. Poole (Northern Illinois, 1974). Bartolomé de las Casas' *En busca de los pobres de JésuCristo* (In search of the poor of Jesus Christ), ed. Gustavo Gutiérrez, was re-published in Lima in 1992.

22. Mary Magdalene   Festival

Mary was a woman from Magdala. The Gospel according to Luke describes her as one of a group of women who had been 'cured of infirmities and evil spirits', and who followed Jesus on his mission from town to town and village to village. She is said to be one from whom 'seven demons had gone out' (Luke 8:1–2): demonic possession was the usual explanation at that time for a variety of conditions which would now be diagnosed as forms of mental illness or epilepsy.

All four Evangelists record that she was one of the women who stood near the Cross, *John specifying that she stood with *Mary the mother of Jesus and her sister Mary the wife of Clopas or Cleopas (John 19:25). She was present when Joseph of Arimathea asked Pilate for the body at dusk, and placed it in his own tomb; and when he rolled the stone against the door, she sat outside with 'the other Mary', opposite the grave (Mark 15:40, 47 in the longer ending).

The Jewish Sabbath began at dusk on Friday, and nothing further could be done until dawn on Sunday. Then Mary came to the tomb early, and Mark says that she brought oils to anoint the body (16:1–2). After that, the chronology is a little confused: in Mark's brief narrative, she sees Christ and goes to tell the disciples, who do not believe her (16:9–10). Matthew says that Mary Magdalene and the 'other Mary' were together, and describes an earthquake and an angel who rolls away the stone. The angel tells them that Jesus is risen, and bids them tell the disciples. On the way, Jesus himself appears to them, tells them not to be afraid, and gives them a similar message (Matthew 28:1–10). Luke says that the group of women who had followed Christ prepared spices and perfumes, and took them to the tomb. He describes the encounter with the angel, but does not say that they met Christ himself (Luke 23:55—24: 1). Considering that the disciples were in a state of great emotional tension, and that they got the story at second hand from the women, the accounts are sufficiently congruent; but as often occurs, it is John, writing later, who pulls the story into focus. He says that Mary Magdalene went to the tomb 'while it was still dark'. She saw that the stone had been moved, and ran to tell the disciples, 'They have taken the Lord out of the tomb, and we do not know where they have laid him' (which suggests that there were other women with her). After Peter and the other disciple have seen the empty tomb, she stays alone by the tomb, weeping. It is then that she encounters a man who she thinks at first is the gardener. He says 'Mary' and she recognizes him (John 20:1–18).

Because Mary Magdalene is said to have been the first person to see the risen Christ, and went to tell the disciples, she was known in the Middle Ages as 'the apostle to the apostles'. The Gospel according to John has a fuller account than the other Gospels (and one which seems to come from Mary herself). An Eastern tradition says that she subsequently went to Ephesus with Christ's mother and John the apostle, who had been charged to care for her.

There are now thought to be no grounds for identifying Mary Magdalene with Mary the sister of Lazarus and Martha. Mary or Miriam was a very common name. The persistent tradition that she was a woman who had repented of an unchaste life, elaborated by *Gregory the Great and expressed in many mediaeval paintings and stained glass windows, has no basis in the Gospels.

AA.SS., July 5, 188–225; O.C.B., p. 499; H. M. Garth, *St Mary Magdalene in Mediaeval Literature*; N.C.E., 9, pp. 387–9.

23. Bridget of Sweden (1302/3–1373)   [*Commem.*]

Until the coming of Lutheranism in the sixteenth century, Sweden was a Catholic kingdom. Bridget's father was a member of the king's council, a judge, and a benefactor to many churches. His brother was the prior of the Dominican Order, and later became a bishop. Bridget is said to have had mystical revelations from the age of ten. She was married to a young Christian knight, Ulf Gudmarsson, at the age of fourteen, and they had four sons and four daughters. Together, they managed their extensive estates, carried out good works, and encouraged learning, bringing the first printing press to Sweden. In 1330, Ulf was appointed a judge, and later he became a member of the Privy Council.

After the birth of their eighth child, Cecilia, Ulf and Bridget went on a pilgrimage to Santiago de Compostela in northern Spain. The journey was over two thousand miles in each direction. Some time later, Ulf entered the religious life in the Cistercian monastery at Alvastra (now Alvesta, near Växjo in southern Sweden), where he died in 1344.

Bridget was forty-two years old when Ulf died. She settled estates and property on her children, gave much to the poor, and moved to a small building close to the monastery of Alvastra, living a simple and penitential life centred on the Eucharist. King Magnus II was impressed by her piety, and in 1346 she persuaded him to endow a double monastery in the castle at Vadstena on Lake Vattern, for sixty nuns and twenty-five monks. The rule was modelled on that of the Benedictine double monastery of Fontrevault in France.

It was at this time that Bridget wrote the first of her denunciatory letters to Pope Clement VI about the state of the Church, and resolved that she must go to Rome to seek papal approval for her monastery. She never returned to Sweden. The Church was in a scandalous state of abuse and neglect, and Rome was a desolate city of ruins. The papal court was in exile at Avignon, but Bridget did not go there to meet the pope. She had been commanded to await the papal return to Rome, and she did so. It took more than seventeen years, during which time she wrote to successive popes exhorting, prophesying, and declaiming, telling them of the lamentable state of the Church and the nations, and reminding them of their responsibilities. This was a dark period in the history of Rome. Bridget experienced all the agonies of the doom threatening a faithless Church and its faithless people. Her 'Thus saith the Lord' was the voice of the Old Testament prophets.

Bridget was not the strapping Swede of popular imagining. She was little, and very modest. *Margery Kempe spoke to her maid in Rome: 'the maiden said that her lady saint Bridget was kind and meek to every creature, and had a laughing face'. She lived austerely, and knelt in prayer so much that 'her knees became hard as those of a camel'. When she grew old, she rode on a white mule which became a familiar sight in the city. In spite of her modest demeanour and poor clothes, some people called her the *principessa*, and greatly respected her compassion and charitable work for the poorest people of the city. Others thought she was a witch and a heretic, and one woman emptied a bucket over her from an upstairs window as she walked along the street.

When Pope Urban V, a Frenchman, finally brought the papal court back to Rome in 1367, Bridget rejoiced, but he did not stay long. She rode out to see him on her white mule, prophesying that if he returned to Avignon 'the Holy Spirit (would) cool in him and leave him'. He left Rome in June 1370, and died before the end of the same year.

Bridget had made two of the three great pilgrimages, to Rome and to

Santiago de Compostela. In 1371, she set out on the third, to Jerusalem. She continued to receive revelations, foretelling the destruction of Cyprus and the ruin of the Eastern Empire. In 1373, she returned to Rome, and died there. She left eight books of revelations; but because she wrote in Swedish, and never mastered the art of Latin composition, it is difficult to disentangle her thought from that of over-zealous transcribers and translators. She has been venerated for the quality of a holy life rather than for her obscure and often doom-laden prophecies.

AA.SS., Oct., 4, pp. 368–560. Modern Lives in English by H. Redpath (1947); J. Jorgensen (Eng. trans. I. Lund, 1954). The Life by A. Andersson (1980) corrects a number of common errors in shorter accounts. See also the detailed and scholarly *Studies in St Birgitta and the Brigittine Order*, ed. J. Hogg (2 vols, 1980); E. Graf, *Revelations: Saint Birgitta of Sweden* (1972); D.H.G.E., 10, 718–28; *Dict. Spir.*, 1, cols 1943–58; D.T.C., 10, pp. 719–31; N.C.E., 2, p. 799; *The Book of Margery Kempe*, modernized and ed. W. Butler-Bowdon (1954), pp. 51, 61, 122–3.

25. James the Great (d. 44)   Festival

James and John, sons of Zebedee, were called *Boanerges* or 'sons of thunder' by the Evangelists, indicating their fervent and impetuous temperaments. This James, apostle and martyr, is known as James the Great. *James the Apostle, son of Alphaeus, whose feast day is on 1 May, is known as 'St James the Less' to distinguish the two.

The sons of Zebedee were called by Christ as they mended their fishing nets by the sea of Galilee (Matthew 4:21–2). James was with Jesus at the Transfiguration (Matthew 17:1) and in the Garden of Gethsemane before the Crucifixion (Mark 14:33). He is thought to have been the leader of the disciples after *Peter's imprisonment in Jerusalem, for when Peter escaped, he told the maid Rhoda and others, 'Tell this to James and to the believers' (Acts 12.17). *Paul was also taken to James after his conversion (Acts 21.18). James died before the other apostles, being killed with a sword-thrust on the orders of Herod Agrippa (Acts 12.2).

In mediaeval Spain, the cult of St James (Santiago) as a warrior saint, invoked to defend the country against the Moors and the power of Islam, was very powerful. The three great mediaeval pilgrimages were those to Rome, to Jerusalem and to Santiago de Compostela, his reputed burial-place. Many stories of miracles circulated, and kings, princes and popes went to Compostela to do him honour. The pilgrim's hat and scallop-shell became his emblems.

The pilgrim routes across Europe, even from as far as Russia and Scandinavia, were well trodden for centuries, and hostels and hospices developed along the way. Some of these are still in use as modern pilgrims make their way to Compostela. Many still come on foot, and carry the traditional staff and scallop-shell, others by more modern means of travel. On St James's Day, 25 July, there is a great High Mass in the cathedral. The bust of James, which is said to contain his relics, is ceremonially processed, and the great smoking *botufumeiro* or censer swings perilously over the heads of the packed congregation.

There is documentary evidence in a ninth-century martyrology that James's relics were translated from Jerusalem to Spain, and the Empress Matilda is said to have given his hand to Reading Abbey in the twelfth century; but there is no firm evidence that James was buried at Compostela, or that he went to Spain during his lifetime.

AA.SS., July, 6, pp. 5–124; J. C. Stone, *The Cult of Santiago* (1927); *O.D.S.*, pp. 250–1; *N.C.E.*, 7, p. 806.

26. Anne and Joachim　　　　　　　　　　　　　　　[L.F.]

These are the traditional names of the parents of the *Virgin Mary. They are not mentioned in the New Testament, but early Christians naturally speculated about the infancy of the Blessed Virgin. It was reasonable to think that her parents had been specially chosen to give life to this child who would be exalted above all women.

The names Anne and Joachim are recorded in the *Protoevangelium Jacobi*, or Gospel of James, written about 170–80. This is the most famous of the apocryphal writings relating to the New Testament. The story is the familiar biblical one of a married couple who remain childless, and long for a child. Joachim and Anne separated to express their sorrow: he went into the desert to fast and pray, while she stayed in their home, weeping and beseeching God. They had similar (or identical) visions, in which an angel appeared and said that they would have a wonderful child. Anne waited at the gate of the city for Joachim's return, and when she saw him approach, she ran and embraced him, saying, 'Now I know that the Lord has wondrously heard my prayers. I was a widow, and am a widow no longer. I who was once barren have conceived in my womb.' There is a celebrated painting by Albrecht Dürer showing this meeting at the Golden Gate of Jerusalem.

The story bears a strong resemblance to that of the birth of Samuel (1 Samuel 1), whose mother's name was Hannah; but there are some different features. Anne and Joachim's sorrow drives them apart, instead of drawing them closer; unusually in a narrative from a patriarchal society, it is the husband, not the wife, who is said to be sterile; and the child over whom they rejoice is a girl, not a first-born son.

Many early Christian writers praised St Anne, including *Gregory of Nyssa in the fourth century and *John of Damascus in the seventh. In the fifth century, the emperor Justinian built a church in her honour in Constantinople. Her cult was known in some areas of England before the Norman Conquest, but acquired much greater devotion when the Crusaders brought back news of her veneration in the Eastern Empire. She appears on the columns of St Mark's basilica in Venice, and in many religious paintings, including Leonardo da Vinci's *The Virgin with St Anne and John the Baptist* and Giotto's cycle in the Arena chapel at Padua. There is stained glass showing the marriage of Anne and Joachim at Great Malvern Priory, Hereford and Worcester.

AA.SS., Mar., 3, pp. 77–80 (Joachim) and July, 6, pp. 233–97 (Anne). *O.D.S.*, pp. 22–3, 253–4; *N.C.E.*, 1, pp. 558–9.

27. Brooke Foss Westcott (1825–1901) [Commem.]

Westcott was one of a remarkable group of young Cambridge scholars. Several of his contemporaries became bishops or professors, and when he became a tutor, he had both J. B. Lightfoot, a future bishop of Durham, and E. W. Benson, a future archbishop of Canterbury, among his students. In 1851, Westcott took Holy Orders, and in the following year he became a master at Harrow School. Teaching presented some difficulties: he was said 'not to understand the ordinary boy', and he had a weak voice, which meant that he had problems keeping order in class. However, he had much to offer to boys with intellectual promise, who respected his learning. He stayed at Harrow for eighteen years, during which time he wrote some of his greatest commentaries on the Bible, and initiated a revival of biblical study. In 1870, he returned to Cambridge as Regius Professor of

Divinity. He took a leading part in raising the standard of divinity studies in the university, drafting new regulations for the degrees of BD and DD, and organizing programmes of lectures. He promoted the work of the Cambridge Mission to Delhi, and worked to develop better training both for missionaries and for parish clergy. He became examining chaplain to Archbishop Benson, and Gladstone secured for him a canonry at Westminster.

Westcott refused all offers of promotion until 1890, when he was offered the bishopric of Durham after the death of his former student, Lightfoot. He was sixty-five years old, and of a retiring, donnish temperament; but he came to the conclusion that it was his duty to face 'some of the gravest problems of national and social life', and entered on a new phase in his ministry. He opposed the build-up of armaments in the major Western powers, worked for international arbitration as an alternative to war, and became involved in labour relations. Long before the foundation of the Industrial Christian Fellowship, he held conferences with employers and trade union leaders, and investigated the effects of unemployment. When there was a massive strike in the Durham coalfields, he called representatives of both sides together, and secured a settlement. In 1894, he addressed thousands at the traditional Miners' Gala, and spoke with great eloquence. Auckland Castle, where he lived with his wife and his large family (seven sons and three daughters) became a centre for the whole diocese. He made a practice of inviting six or eight ordinands to live there for a year at a time, and they were known as 'sons of the house'.

In the Durham diocese, Westcott is remembered as the bishop who started a tradition of social concern for the mining communities in times of economic distress. His biblical commentaries have served generations of theological students, and the clergy training school in Cambridge which he helped to shape was re-named Westcott House in his memory.

B. F. Westcott's *Life and Letters*, ed. A. Westcott (son), (2 vols, 1903); Lives by Joseph Clayton (1906); H. Scott Holland (1910); Arthur G. B. West (1936). *D.N.B.*, *1901–11*, pp. 635–41; *Great Christians*, pp. 593–604. Works: *A General History of the Canon of the New Testament during the First Four Centuries* (1855); *An Introduction to the Study of the Gospels* (1860); *The Bible in the Church* (1864).

29. Mary, Martha and Lazarus [L.F.]

These two sisters and their brother are well known to us from the Gospels. They lived in Bethany, to the south-east of Jerusalem. *Luke tells the story of how Martha invited Jesus to her home, and how she worked in the house while Mary sat at his feet and listened to his words. When she asked Jesus to tell her sister to come and help her, he told her that Mary had chosen the better part. Martha was 'worried and distracted by her many tasks', but only one thing was necessary: to listen to the word of God. It was a gentle rebuke, but a real one (Luke 10:38–42). This story does not occur in the Gospel according to *Matthew, *Mark or *John. As is often the case, Luke is the Gospel writer who picks up the human nuances of a situation.

Both Martha and Mary appear in John's story of the raising of Lazarus (John 11:1–44). The sisters send a message to Jesus, saying, 'Lord, he whom you love is ill', but he delays for two days before telling his disciples, 'Our friend Lazarus has fallen asleep', and proposing that they should go to Bethany. It takes them another two days to reach Bethany: Lazarus has been dead for four days. People have come to condole with the sisters on his death, and Mary stays at home, while Martha comes out, active as ever, to tell Jesus that she thinks her brother would have lived if he had come sooner; but she adds that she believes that God will do whatever Jesus asks. This leap of faith evokes the tremendous response, 'I am the resurrection and the life.' He asks if she believes this, and she makes another leap of faith: 'I believe that you are the Messiah, the son of God, the one coming into the world.'

Jesus and the disciples are still outside the village, near the tomb of Lazarus. Martha runs to tell Mary that they are coming, and Mary goes out quickly, still weeping, and followed by the mourners. She falls at Jesus's feet, saying, 'Lord, if you had been here, my brother would not have died.' Jesus is greatly moved. He sighs heavily, and weeps for their sorrow. He tells them to move the stone, and practical Martha objects that since the body has been there for four days in a hot climate, it will be decaying. Then, summoning tremendous energy, Jesus gives a great cry, 'Lazarus, come out'; and Lazarus comes out, still wrapped in his grave-clothes. When Caiaphas the high priest is told, the series of events which will lead to the Crucifixion is set in train.

Six days before the Passover, Jesus returns to Bethany on his way to

Jerusalem. There is a supper in the house of Lazarus to do him honour. Lazarus sits with Jesus, Martha serves supper, and Mary comes in with a jar of very costly ointment, and anoints Jesus's feet, so that the whole house is filled with the fragrance. Judas Iscariot, who acts as treasurer for the group, objects that this is a waste of money which might have been given to the poor, but Christ replies sombrely that Mary should be left alone: she is preparing him for his burial (John 12:1–7).

This extraordinarily vivid little story ends with the chief priests deciding to do away with Lazarus as well as Jesus; but Lazarus and his sisters do not appear in the Acts of the Apostles, and we have only legends to suggest what may have happened to them afterwards. The pseudo-Clementine writings say that Lazarus followed *St Peter (29 June) into Syria. There is a Byzantine story that the three were placed in a leaky boat off the coast near Jaffa, and that they all sailed to Cyprus, where Lazarus became bishop of Kition (Larnaca), and ruled his diocese for thirty years.

A more ambitious 'leaky boat' story originated in France in the eleventh century: the boat was not merely leaky, but oarless and rudderless. The three were said to have sailed to Marseilles, where Lazarus became bishop and was martyred in the time of the emperor Domitian (81–96) on the site of the Saint-Lazare prison. He was then buried in a cave, over which the abbey of St Victor was subsequently built. There is some confusion in the Gallic traditions between Lazarus of Bethany and the fictitious Lazarus in Christ's parable of Dives and Lazarus (Luke 16:20), who was 'full of sores'. It was the latter, not the former, who gave his name to the *lazarettos* of Europe. This led to the erroneous association of Lazarus of Bethany with the Saint-Lazare prison of Marseilles. The military Order of Knights-Hospitaller of St Lazarus of Jerusalem took its name from the fictitious Lazarus, not the historical one; and the more recent Order of Lazarus, founded by *Vincent de Paul (27 Sept.), took its name from the Paris church associated with the nearby *lazare*.

More reliable is the evidence of a Spanish lady named Etheria or Egeria, who visited the Holy Land about the year 390. She wrote of a procession on the Saturday of Passion Week to the place where Lazarus was raised from the dead. She was much impressed by the great crowds that attended. At Milan, Passion Sunday was called Domenica de Lazaro, and *Augustine records that the Gospel of the restoring of life to Lazarus was read at the night office before the dawn of Palm Sunday.

D.A.C.L., 8, cols 2009–86; *N.C.E.*, 8, p. 584; H. Thurston in the Irish quarterly *Studies* 23 (1934), 110–23; G. Morin, 'St Lazare et St Maximin', *Mémoire de la Soc. des Antiquaires de France* 56 (Paris, 1897), pp. 27–51.

30. William Wilberforce (1759–1833) [L.F.]

The Wilberforce family were highly respected merchants of Hull, where William's grandfather was twice Lord Mayor. William stood for parliament in 1780, at the age of twenty-one. He was never a minister of the Crown, but he became the moral voice of the House of Commons. He joined the Evangelical movement, and was a leading member of the Clapham sect (see *John Venn). He gave away a quarter of his income annually, and joined a number of the organizations for promoting good causes or abolishing abuses which were a feature of late eighteenth-century English life. His greatest contribution was to the movement to abolish slavery and the slave trade.

The transportation of slaves from East and West Africa to the Americas had been started by the Portuguese and the Dutch, but by the 1780s British traders had the largest share of the trade, and were transporting 25,000 slaves a year, mostly to the West Indies. They were chained, often ill-treated, and crammed into ships. In 1787, Sir William Dolben told the House of Commons that he had seen them 'packed between the decks like books on shelves'. Many died on the way. The Society of Friends opposed this cruel trade unequivocally. *Richard Baxter wrote in his *Christian Dictionary* that 'slave-pirates are the common enemies of mankind'. *John Wesley wrote a pamphlet against 'the infamous traffic in slavery' in 1774, and writers of the standing of John Locke, Adam Smith, Daniel Defoe and Alexander Pope had all condemned it; but the plantation owners had strong lobbies in parliament.

The Committee for the Abolition of the Slave Trade was set up in 1787, and Wilberforce was its parliamentary leader. He undertook the task with high seriousness, carrying out a thorough investigation. He chaired public meetings, wrote pamphlets and gave his findings to the House of Commons. The opposition hardened. He was told that the slave-owners were doing the slaves a favour by rescuing them from 'the gross and impenetrable gloom of barbarism'; that the pleasant voyage from Africa was often the happiest time of their lives; that the future of British colonialism depended on the slave trade; and that, if he continued his campaign, there would be a rebellion in the West Indies, and all the white settlers would be massacred.

In the House of Commons, every parliamentary device was used to defeat him. Bills went into committee, and never emerged. Others went untabled at the end of a parliamentary session, and so lapsed. There was a 'Great Debate' in 1792 in which the House grudgingly agreed to a motion that 'the slave trade ought to be *gradually* abolished', but that led to no action.

Pitt, Charles James Fox and Edmund Burke all made powerful speeches supporting Wilberforce; but when England went to war with revolutionary France, liberty, equality and fraternity could not be invoked, and the Abolitionists were accused of being Jacobins and traitors. When the worst of the Revolution was over and the war ended, Wilberforce returned to the attack, annually proposing a motion for a Bill against the slave trade. Annually, the Commons voted him down. At last, in 1807, a Bill became law. Slavery still existed, but the profitable slave trade had been stopped in England and the colonies.

Wilberforce turned his attention to the international scene. One of the terms of the Treaty of Vienna in 1815 obliged France to liberate slaves in the remaining French colonies over a five-year period. Wilberforce worked incessantly, assiduously attending the House of Commons and sitting on committees, making speeches, interviewing and answering an enormous correspondence. He continued to collect evidence of cruelty and moral degradation, and to follow up individual cases. He and his colleagues incurred the full anger of the sugar-planters, who blamed them for riots and insurrections.

The abolition of slavery was finally carried by a reformed House of Commons in 1833. Wilberforce died in the same year, and on 31 July 1834 his work was completed when 800,000 slaves in the British colonies were freed.

Wilberforce worked for many Anglican causes. The British and Foreign Bible Society was largely his creation. He was involved in the setting up of the Church Missionary Society and the London Missionary Society, and a leader in the movement for stricter Sunday observance; but it is for his patient, persistent work for the Anti-Slavery Movement that he is chiefly honoured.

Lives by Robert and Samuel Wilberforce (5 vols, 1838); R. Coupland (1923); M. Hennell (1947); Oliver Warner (1962); *D.N.B.*, 21, pp. 208–17. Stock, ch. 5. *The Private Papers of William Wilberforce*, ed. Anna Maria Wilberforce (1837).

31. Ignatius of Loyola (1491–1556)   *[Commem.]*

Ignatius (properly Iñigo Lopéz de Recalde) was one of eleven children of a Basque nobleman. At thirteen, he became a page in the court of Ferdinand and Isabella of Spain, and then entered on a military career. He was a seasoned soldier, thirty years old, when he was wounded by a French cannon ball at the siege of Pamplona in 1521. It shattered the bones of one leg. The leg was set, but set badly: it had to be broken and re-set. Even then, it was substantially shorter than the other leg. Efforts were made to stretch it. Ignatius suffered excruciating pain for months when he could neither stand nor walk.

During this period, he realized that his military career was over. He asked for books to pass the time, specifying tales of chivalry and armed exploits; but all that could be found was a life of Christ and a book on the legends of the saints. These brought about his conversion. When he was able to walk again, he went to live alone for a year of prayer and penance near the abbey of Monserrat. It was at this time that he wrote the first draft of his *Spiritual Exercises*. In 1523, he undertook a pilgrimage to Jerusalem, begging his way. His intention was to convert the Saracens, but the Franciscans, who guarded the holy places and had seen some of their own friars martyred in similar endeavours, managed to dissuade him from attempting this exercise alone. He returned to Spain, and was imprisoned for a time as a suspected heretic.

He realized that he would have to study. He went to the University of Paris, studied Latin, philosophy and theology, and graduated as Master of Arts in 1528. By that time he had collected six disciples, including a fellow-Basque, *Francis Xavier. They set out for the Holy Land, but when they reached Venice, war had been declared on the Turks. They decided that their first aim would still be foreign mission, but that they would also engage in works of charity and teaching the uneducated, particularly young people. In 1540, their organization, called the Society of Jesus, was given papal approval. It had a military-style discipline, demanding total and unhesitating obedience and a readiness to face martyrdom. Ignatius spent the rest of his life in Rome, organizing and directing the Order, and fashioning it into a powerful weapon. Francis Xavier went to the Far East to found missions, and another Jesuit, Peter Canisius, organized the Counter-Reformation in Germany. By the time Ignatius died on 31 July 1556, there were over one thousand Jesuits working in Europe alone. The 'English Mission', sent by Pope Gregory III in 1579, resulted in the deaths of some brave men like Edmund Campion and Alexander Briant, whose total obedience to papal orders did not allow them to question his anathema on Queen Elizabeth I and the rightness of attempting to put Philip II of Spain on the English throne.

The teaching which Ignatius instilled into his Order was born of his own experience: military discipline, non-attachment, stoicism. He taught his followers that they must not desire health rather than sickness, wealth rather than poverty, or fame rather than disgrace: they must desire only what would bring them closer to God. He set up a tradition of spiritual guidance and direction which was to become influential in many countries.

His *Spiritual Exercises* are widely used by many Christians, though what is now termed 'the Ignatian method' includes some modifications and developments.

AA.SS., Jul., 7, pp. 409–864; Modern Lives by C. Hollis (1931); J. Brodrick (1956); V. Larranaga (1956); F. Wulf, ed., *Ignatius of Loyola, his Personality and Spiritual Heritage* (1977). Works: *Constitution*, trans. and ed. G. N. Gauss (1970); *Letters*, trans. D. F. O'Leary (1914); *Spiritual Exercises*, trans. and ed. T. Corbishley (1963), trans. and ed. H. Backhouse (1989). *Monumenta Ignatiana* (Rome, 1964).

August

4. Jean-Baptiste Vianney (1786–1859)   *[Commem.]*

The priest who became famous as 'the Curé d'Ars' was only three years old when the French Revolution broke out. He had to make his First Communion secretly at the age of thirteen; but by the time he was twenty, there was a resurgence of Catholicism. In the upheavals of the Napoleonic period, many people looked back nostalgically to the certainties of the *ancien régime*.

Jean's father was a peasant farmer in Dordilly, near Lyons. The boy had very little education – no more than a few years at the village school – but in 1806 he was able to enter a seminary. He found his studies very difficult, especially Latin. The bishop of Lyons called him 'the most unlearned seminarian in Lyons', but added that he was also the most devout. He finally became a priest in 1815, and after a two-year curacy, was sent to the remote village of Ars-en-Doubes, which had only 250 inhabitants. There he made war on the devil.

He attacked the village taverns, and drove at least one out of business by steering his flock away from it. He forbade swearing, and would use the forbidden words in the pulpit, so that the villagers knew exactly what it was that they must not say. He demanded that the women should dress modestly, and he forbade dancing. Over the chapel of St John Baptist, he had painted the words, 'His head was the price of a dance'; and he preached hell-fire from the pulpit.

There were unexplained noises and voices in his clergy-house, and he suffered physical violence. His bed was burned, and objects were moved and damaged, apparently by poltergeists. Given the violent anti-clericalism of the period, it is possible that his attackers were all too human; and he was clearly in a very nervous state. He lived largely on potatoes, kept long, sleepless vigils, and punished himself for the sins of his people. At the same time, he did much good work in the area. The Bishop of Belley trusted him, and sent him on missions. He sent two village girls to a convent for training, and then put them in charge of a school for girls which grew into La Providence, a shelter for homeless children, taking sixty at one time.

He began to acquire a reputation for healing. Modestly, he told people that the cures were not his work, but that of a virgin martyr, St Philomena, to whom he had a special devotion. The pilgrims came in increasing numbers. Lyons railway station had to open a special booking office for Ars. Some came to pray, some came to be healed, and many came for spiritual direction. Father Vianney would spend up to sixteen hours a day in the confessional box, listening to their sins. He was a good listener. As he grew older, he mellowed, and gave much wise and kindly advice. The crowds knelt to receive his blessing, and some tore pieces from his cassock as holy relics.

He stayed at Ars for the rest of his life. Three times he left to become a monk, and three times he returned, because his vocation was in Ars. The bishop made him an honorary canon. He was created a Knight of the Imperial Order of the Légion d'Honneur, but he did not want honours. For more than thirty years, this spare, tired man laboured in his tiny parish, and drew the world to him. By 1858–9, he was serving over a thousand pilgrims a week. If the devotion he aroused was excessive, that was other people's doing. He did not welcome it, and he was not impressed by it. He left an enduring image of the simple, devout priest who was faithful to his calling in an increasingly secular society.

M. Trochu, *The Insight of the Curé d'Ars*, ed. and trans. V. F. Martlet (1969); D. Pézeril (Eng. trans. 1961); F. J. Sheed, *The Secret of the Curé d'Ars* (1929); L.C. Sheppard, *Curé d'Ars: Portrait of a Parish Priest* (1958); O.D.S., pp. 477–8; *Butler*, Aug., pp. 28–33.

5. Oswald of Northumbria (c.605–42)   [L.F.]

'The most Christian King of Northumbria' is *Bede's description of Oswald. He was the second son of King Aethelfrith of Bernicia. When he was a child, Northumbria was divided into two kingdoms, Deira, which roughly covered the present area of Yorkshire, and Bernicia, covering Northumberland and Durham as far as the ill-defined and changing Scottish borders. In 616, when Oswald was about ten years old, Bernicia was overwhelmed by the forces of Edwin of Deira, and Aethelfrith was killed in battle. Oswald and his brother Oswy had to go into exile, and lived for some eighteen years on Iona. Oswald was taught by the monks, and much influenced by their way of life, receiving baptism.

In 633, Edwin was killed in a battle against Penda of Mercia and his ally Cadwalla of Wales. For a year, the north of England was ravaged by Cadwalla, a heathen who, Bede says, 'acted not as a victorious king, but as a savage tyrant, ravaging them with ghastly slaughter'. Then Oswald returned, to do battle for Deira and Bernicia. The two sides confronted each other near Hexham. On the night before the battle, Oswald set up a wooden cross, holding it in place himself while the soldiers firmed the earth around it, and prayed for victory in Christ's name.

After his victory, the two kingdoms were united, and he ruled them for eight years. One of Oswald's first acts was to send to Iona for a monk to re-introduce the Christian faith into his territories. After a false start, *Aidan was sent to him, and the two worked together in friendship and trust. The king 'always listened readily and humbly to Aidan's advice', and understood that Aidan could not always live in royal palaces: he needed the silence and serenity of Lindisfarne; but they seem often to have travelled together when Aidan was preaching and teaching in the countryside. Aidan, coming from a monastery of Irish monks, was not fluent in English, and Oswald, who 'had obtained perfect command of the Irish tongue during his long exile', often interpreted for him.

Oswald was a merciful and generous king. He 'never failed to provide for the sick and needy, and to give them alms and aid'. He died in battle against his old enemy Penda of Mercia on 5 August 642. Bede says that he was thirty-eight years old. After his death, the place where he fell became a place of pilgrimage, and many healing miracles were reported there. Few kings of England can have earned a comparable reputation for both valour in battle and sanctity in living.

AA.SS., Aug, 1, pp. 83–103; Bede, H.E., bk 3, chs 1—3, 6, 9, 10; N.C.E., 10, p. 810; D.N.B., 14, pp. 1215–17; Stenton, pp. 81–3, 118.

7. John Mason Neale (1818–66)   [Commem.]

J. M. Neale was brought up in his mother's strict Evangelical household in Chiswick. When he went to Trinity College, Cambridge, he

immediately responded to the liturgical and ceremonial revival of the
Tractarian movement (see *Pusey, *Newman). He developed a passion
for Byzantine art and the Eastern Orthodox liturgies, and helped to
found a journal, *The Ecclesiologist*. He was regarded as a coming man
in High Church circles. When he was ordained priest in 1842, he
was immediately offered the benefice of Crawley, Sussex at the age of
twenty-four.

After only a few weeks, he resigned the living on the grounds of ill-
health. He spent several winters in Cornwall or Madeira to avoid the
rigours of the English winter; but it seems likely that the villagers of
Crawley did not take kindly to High Church practices – or that he
realized that parish work was not his forte. He married, and had
children. He embarked on his monumental *History of the Holy
Eastern Church*, of which he completed four volumes, the fifth being
completed by a colleague after his death. In 1846, he was offered the
wardenship of Sackville College, East Grinstead, an almshouse for
thirty 'poor and aged householders'. The income was small, but he had
private means. He restored the buildings, cared for the old people,
took services for them in the chapel, and devoted himself to study.

Even in this backwater, the angry public reaction against the High
Church innovations reached him. A self-appointed inquisitor, a layman from another parish in another diocese, insisted on inspecting his
chapel, and was shocked to find a copy of the Vulgate Bible (used by
Roman Catholics) and a Roman breviary in his stall. Neale explained
to his patron, Earl de la Warr, and the bishop of Chichester that these
were his personal possessions, and for his own devotions: in services
for his elderly congregation, he used the Authorized Version of the
Bible and the *Book of Common Prayer*. Earl de la Warr was satisfied,
but the bishop made a visitation and was horrified to find 'unspiritual
adjuncts of worship' in the chapel. He accused Neale of 'debasing the
minds of these poor people with his spiritual haberdashery' and
banned him from officiating in any church in the diocese apart from
his own chapel. This ban was to operate for sixteen years.

Neale published the first two volumes of his *History* in 1847. They
were very well received, and he had many letters of approval. The
Morning Chronicle asked him to write three articles a week on Church
affairs, and he continued to contribute these for some years. He had a
remarkable facility for languages: he learned Slavonic Russian, and
translated the first volumes of the *History* for the Czar, who was
delighted and sent him £100. He was invited to preach and lecture in

many dioceses other than Chichester, was frequently asked to conduct retreats, and exercised a pastoral ministry as a confessor. He helped to found an Anglican sisterhood, the Society of St Margaret, at Westminster Hospital, and was associated with his sister Elizabeth in founding the Community of the Holy Cross.

He also translated many ancient and mediaeval hymns from Latin into English. Among those still to be found in Anglican hymn books are such favourites as 'Brightest and best of the sons of the morning', 'The royal banners forward go', 'From Greenland's icy mountains', 'Holy, holy, holy', and 'Jerusalem the golden'. His own compositions included 'O happy band of pilgrims', and 'Art thou weary, art thou languid'.

Memoir by E. A. Towle (1906); *Bridge Builders*, pp. 130–57; *D.N.B.*, 14, pp. 143–6; Works: *Selections from the Writings of John Mason Neale*, ed. H. Lawson (1910); *A History of the Holy Eastern Church* (1834).

8. Dominic (1170–1221) [L.F.]

The founder of the Order of Preachers, otherwise known as Black Friars or Dominicans, was born in Calaruega in Castile, where his father was the warden of the city. He became an Augustinian friar, and a canon of Osma cathedral. He was prior of the community when, in 1203, he accompanied Bishop Diego de Azevado of Osma to Denmark to arrange a royal marriage. They passed through Languedoc in southern France, and came in contact with the Cathars, who had been branded as heretics. A mission by *Bernard of Clairvaux had been unsuccessful, and in the following year, Bishop Diego and Prior Dominic were asked to carry out a new preaching mission. The bishop had to return to his diocese, and most of the work of the mission devolved on Dominic.

The Catharist movement, sometimes called Albigensian, because it centred on the city of Albi, was basically Manichaean in its beliefs. These ideas had originally come from Persia, and had been transmitted to Europe by the Bogomils, a sect in the Balkans. They believed that good and evil were equal but opposing forces; that the material world was evil; that Christ was an angel; that only the elect would be saved; and that procreation was a sin. The inner circle consisted of the *Perfecti*, who led a life more austere than that of the most rigorous monastic orders. These peaceful if misguided people were subjected to a savage military crusade, led by Simon de Montfort, following the murder of the papal legate, Peter of Castelnau, by a servant of the Cathar count of Toulouse in 1208. The fall of Toulouse in 1214 was accompanied by much slaughter. The *Perfecti* were driven to their final refuge in the castle of Count Raymond of Toulouse, besieged, and finally massacred.

Dominic was a close friend of Simon de Montfort, operating from his fortresses, and Simon funded the preachers, who were vowed to poverty; but it is likely that Dominic did not approve of the killing. He reproved Fulk, bishop of Toulouse, who rode armed into battle, by saying 'Arm yourself with prayer, not a sword. Wear humility, not fine clothes!' and he frequently said that he would have nothing to do with warfare. His task was to organize a small band of special preachers, well trained in the faith, to give religious instruction.

This developed into a powerful intellectual arm of the Catholic Church. Dominic proved to be a talented organizer. An Institute of Preachers was set up, and though the fourth Lateran Council decided against the creation of new religious Orders, the pope, Innocent III, gave it his personal approval. In 1217, the Friars Preachers were given separate status as an Order. Dominic refused a bishopric. He set up houses for the Order in Madrid, Paris, Milan and many other European cities. The movement spread – to Denmark, Poland and Germany, to Palestine and Morocco, and in England to London and Oxford. It was a mendicant Order, based on simplicity of life and rigorous study.

Dominic travelled indefatigably, ate little, slept little, and prayed unceasingly. He died in Treviso, on a journey to Italy, 'in Brother Moneta's bed, because he had none of his own; in Brother Montana's habit, because he had no other to replace the one he had worn so long'. He did not spare himself – and he did not spare his potential converts. When the Dominicans were put in charge of the Inquisition, he said, 'It is better to be the hammer than the anvil'; and it is as the Hammer of God that he is remembered.

E. C. Lehner, trans. and ed., *Saint Dominic: Biographical Documents* (1964); B. Jarrett (1924); P. Mandonnet (1937, Eng. trans. 1944); M. H. Vicaire, *Histoire de Saint Dominique* (2 vols, 1957, Eng. trans. 1964); O.D.S., pp. 133–5; *Butler*, Aug., pp. 55–66.

9. Mary Sumner (1828–1921) [L.F.]

Mary Heywood was only eighteen when in 1847 she met George Sumner, the youngest son of the bishop of Winchester, in Rome during her 'coming out winter'. He returned to England to be ordained, and they married in 1848. Their very happy marriage was to last sixty-one years. Two daughters and a son followed fairly rapidly, and Mary's experience of motherhood led her to the conclusion that 'mothers had one of the greatest and most important professions in the world'.

She began to hold meetings for the women of her husband's parish in the rectory: she was nervous at first, but she found the women eager to listen to her, and she designed a prayer card for them; but it was not until she was fifty-seven years old, George Sumner was an archdeacon, and her own children were all married and independent that she was encouraged to found a wider movement. In the 1880s, there was a growing national concern about child life. The birth rate was dropping rapidly, and fifteen out of every hundred children died before their first birthday – often from enteritis caused by faulty rearing practices. At the Church Congress in Portsmouth in 1885, the bishop of Newcastle introduced Mary to a mass meeting for women. She spoke of starting a Mothers' Union to 'raise the Home life of our Nation'. The MU was to be her 'youngest child'.

She started with a diocesan organization. Two years of intense activity, travelling, addressing meetings, drafting rules and leaflets, and answering a rapidly mounting correspondence, led to a diocesan conference in 1887. By that time there were fifty-seven branches, and eleven more were planned. 'The training of children is a profession,' she told the delegates at Winchester. 'It needs faith, love, patience, method, self-control and some knowledge of the principles of character-training.' The membership card stressed the importance of the two sacraments of Baptism and Holy Communion. Though the Mothers' Union never insisted that members should be confirmed, it was a condition of membership that the children should be baptized.

The movement grew very rapidly, The *Mothers' Union Journal* was launched in 1888, and by the end of the following year the circulation was over 46,000. By 1892 there were twenty-eight diocesan organizations, 1,550 branches, and a membership of over 60,000. Three years later, when her husband was bishop of Guildford, a central organization was set up, with a council of diocesan presidents. Mary Sumner became the central president, and in 1897, Queen Victoria became the movement's patron. Before the end of the century, the movement had spread world-wide: first to the British Empire – Australia, New Zealand, Canada, India – then to the West Indies, Japan and South America. In 1908, when Mary Sumner was nearly eighty, she addressed 8,000 women in the Albert Hall in her clear, musical voice. She was still full of energy and interest, and faith in her mission.

Bishop Sumner died in 1909, shortly after their diamond wedding. Mary continued to teach the duties and responsibilities of mother-hood, and the indissolubility of marriage.

In June 1917, after years of cramped accommodation in the base-ment of Church House, the central headquarters of the Mothers' Union was established in Westminster. In 1925 it moved to its present premises as Mary Sumner House. At a celebration in St Paul's cathedral, the bishop of London called Mary Sumner 'the mother of the Mothers' Union'.

Her work in raising the dignity of mothers and stressing the values of family life was of great social and religious value in the late Victorian context, and her successors have worked hard to keep it relevant to a changing society.

Mary Sumner: her life and work (1921) includes a *Memoir* by Mary Porter, and *A Short History of the Mothers' Union* by Mary Woodward, both based on a manu-script by Lady Horatia Erskine. This includes a list of Mary Sumner's many pamphlets and articles on p. 102.

10. Laurence (d. 258)   [L.F.]

Laurence was one of the seven deacons of Rome in the time of Pope Sixtus II (257–8). The deacons seem to have had much the same responsibilities as those allotted to the first seven deacons by the apostles in Jerusalem (see Acts 6). Laurence was responsible for caring for Church property, and for distributing alms to the poor.

The Emperor Valerian instituted a persecution against the Christians, and Pope Sixtus was one of the first to suffer martyrdom. When he was arrested, he told Laurence, who had worked with him closely, that he would soon follow him to death. Laurence was arrested and executed four days later.

So much is history, but the story of Laurence was embroidered out of all recognition. The *Acts of St Laurence* introduced elaborate myths and miracles which were later picked up and repeated by such authorities as *Ambrose and *Augustine. One of the more memorable stories, perhaps with some foundation of truth, is that Laurence was ordered by the prefect of Rome to provide an inventory of all the Church's sacred vessels and other treasures. He sold them, and gave the money to the poor people of Rome. When the prefect returned for the treasures, he found all the blind, lame, lepers and beggars of the city assembled before him, and Laurence said, 'These are my treasures.' This led to his execution.

We can say with some certainty that Laurence did not die on a grid-iron, though many mediaeval paintings and stained glass windows were to show him with this instrument of torture as a way of distinguishing him from other saints. As a Roman citizen, he would have been executed with a sword-thrust, as Pope Sixtus was. Laurence's relics are mentioned in a letter from Pope Vitalian to King Oswy of Northumberland, reproduced by Bede.

P.L., 16, pp. 84–5; AA.SS., Aug., 2, pp. 485–532; Bede, H.E., bk 3, ch. 29; Butler, Aug., pp. 79–82; O.D.S., pp. 288–9.

11. Clare of Assisi (1194–1253)   [L.F.]

In 1209, *Francis of Assisi founded the Order of Friars Minor. Three years later he went back to Assisi to preach at the church of San Giorgio, and Clare, then eighteen years old, came forward to join the movement. She was a member of the wealthy and powerful Offreduccio family, and her male relatives were pressing her to marry, but the conviction grew in her that she was called, like Francis, to abandon the world and serve God. Francis and the friars escorted her to the city's Benedictine nunnery.

The men of her family, her uncles and brothers, were outraged. To them, unmarried girls were primarily pawns in the marriage market, useful for the consolidation of large estates and financial interests, and the men of the family had the right to dispose of them as they saw fit. They went in a body to the nunnery to fetch Clare home, violating the enclosure and pursuing her into the church. Clare clung frantically to the altar, and they tried to drag her away from it, pulling off the altar cloths and frontals. Then she broke away, and took off her head-covering. When they saw her shaven head, they understood that they had lost her.

By 1215, Clare had a small community, some of them women from other noble families. Her widowed mother, her aunt and two of her sisters came to join her. The nuns settled in a small house near the church of San Damiano, and Francis appointed Clare as abbess. She tried to lay down her office after three years, but he insisted that she should continue. She had promised obedience to Francis; but soon after, his guidance was removed, and she had to act alone. The Vatican was much exercised by the possibilities of scandal in religious Orders which included women, and ordered Francis and his friars to keep away from Clare and her nuns. This ruling posed great difficulties for the nuns. They were strictly enclosed, as all women in convents were, and they depended on the friars not only for confession and the sacraments, but for all their contacts with the outside world, and doing heavy work. They were vowed to poverty, so they had no servants. Attempts were made to impose the Benedictine Rule on the nuns, as it was considered the only 'safe' Rule for women. For a time, Benedictine clergy were sent into the convent to hear confessions and celebrate Mass; but Clare remained firm to her own conception of what her Order should be. At different times, five different constitutions were imposed on her, but she clung to her ideal of a religious Order for women who were allowed to go outside the convent walls, to beg and minister to the poor as the Franciscans did.

Clare's nuns became known as the Poor Ladies of St Clare, then the Poor Clares for short. Clare herself did not go outside the convent, but she waited for her sisters to return, kissing their feet and serving them. She was always ready to do the humblest tasks, waiting at table, nursing the sick, ringing the bell for chapel services, and lighting the first candle in the morning, before the others were awake. Her movement became strengthened in 1236, when Agnes, the daughter of King Ottokar of Bohemia, was allowed to found and enter a convent in Prague on the pattern of San Damiano. Clare sent five nuns from Assisi, and wrote affectionate and helpful letters of advice to Agnes. Four of these letters survive.

It was not until 1253, shortly before Clare's death, that the Rule as she envisaged it was finally confirmed by Pope Innocent III. She was the first foundress to be allowed to draw up her own Rule. The pope visited her at San Damiano, gave her absolution, and commented, 'Would to God I had as little need of it.' Her contemporary biographer, thought to be Thomas of Celano, calls her 'the silver dove'; but she was a dove with great powers of endurance.

AA.SS., Aug., 2, pp. 754–67. Eng. trans. of Thomas of Celano's Life by Paschal Robinson (1910, revised edn 1953). See also E. Gilliat Smith (1914); M. Fassbinder (1934); L. Wadding (Rome, 1635); Ingrid Peterson (1993); *O.D.S.*, pp. 109–10; *Butler*, Aug., pp. 83–9.

John Henry Newman (1801–90)   *[Commem.]*

With the exception of *St Augustine, no Christian writer has given us a more detailed and agonizing honest account of his religious journey than John Henry Newman. In *Apologia Pro Vita Sua*, he tells his readers that he was brought up in the Calvinist tradition. His father was of Dutch extraction, and his mother from a French Huguenot family. He was an imaginative child, and he evidently found Calvinism bleak. He was fascinated by the Arabian Nights, and wished that it might all be true, and he enjoyed the romantic novels of Sir Walter Scott. When he was old enough to think seriously about religion, he was much impressed by *William Law's *A Serious Call to a Devout and Holy Life*; but High Church practices had no attraction for him, and he believed, as he had been taught, that the pope was anti-Christ.

After he was elected a Fellow of Oriel College, he took private pupils, and joined the Evangelical wing of the Church of England. He was ordained in 1824, becoming curate of St Clement's. He made friends with *John Keble, with *Edward Pusey and with the vicar of the University church of St Mary the Virgin, Edward Hawkins. In 1828, still only twenty-seven, he followed Hawkins as vicar of St Mary's.

In 1830, he parted from the Evangelical movement, being 'turned out of the secretaryship of the Church Missionary Society'. He made a trip to the Continent with a friend, Hurrell Froude, visiting Sicily, Naples and Rome for the first time. He was overwhelmed by the glory and majesty of Rome, though not by Roman Catholicism, which he found 'idolatrous'. In July 1833, he heard Keble's Assize Sermon, and found himself at home in the Oxford Movement as an Anglo-Catholic. It was he who had the inspiration – 'out of my own head', he writes – for the series of *Tracts for the Times* which gave the group the name of Tractarians. His sermons at St Mary's, defending the Apostolic

Succession and the *Book of Common Prayer*, packed the great church.

Newman was always a furiously hard worker. He worked standing up at a desk, usually for at least nine hours a day, and wrote until his fingers ached. He was engaged on a major work on the Early Fathers of the Church, but he also wrote a series of books defending the Anglo-Catholic position. It was in 1839, while he was working on the Monophysite heresy, that he began to question whether the Roman Catholic view of authority, which 'gave him a stomach-ache', might after all be true.

His search was long, slow and painful. By 1831, he says, 'I was on my death-bed as regards my membership of the Anglican Church.' He withdrew from the university, and went to live at nearby Littlemore with a group of young men with similar theological problems. They spent their lives in seclusion, in study, prayer and fasting, and were dubbed 'the Littlemore monastery'. By 1844, Newman's research on the Early Fathers had convinced him that the Roman Catholic Church was right about authority, and the Church of England was wrong.

At the time, his conversion was a great blow to the Church of England. Both Gladstone and Disraeli were among the many people who wrote to dissuade him; but he resigned his living, and was received into the Roman Catholic Church by a visiting Passionist Father, Dominic Barbieri. He left Oxford in 1846, and went to Rome, where he was ordained as a priest and given the degree of Doctor of Divinity. At the end of 1847, he returned to England with a commission: to establish a community of Oratorian Fathers on the lines of the Order founded by *St Philip Neri. The first, which subsequently became known as 'the little Oratory', was founded in Birmingham, and was followed by what is now the Brompton Oratory.

In 1850, the Catholic hierarchy, abolished in the reign of Henry VIII, was restored to England. The Anglicans, particularly the Anglo-Catholics, who were most threatened, opposed it, and it became known as 'the Papal Aggression'. Newman was to spend nearly half of his very long life as a Roman Catholic, and more than half of that time was spent in comparative obscurity, in writing. There were moves to make him a bishop, but they came to nothing. He had a distaste for controversy, but controversy followed him. He gave a series of lectures in the University of Dublin which became *The Idea of a University*, a book which has inspired many generations of university scholars since his day; and he practised a devout and faithful ministry. He was seventy-eight when he was finally created a cardinal, and nearly ninety when he died.

For Newman, only certainties would do: the Anglican compromise was not an option for him. So he fought again in his own brilliant and sensitive mind the battles which had bitterly divided Europe in the sixteenth century.

J. Moody (1946); C. S. Dessain (1966); T. R. Wright (1985); Ian Ker (1988); Ian Ker and A. G. Hill, *Newman After One Hundred Years* (1990); Avery Dulles, SJ, (2000). Works: ed. W. P. Ward (20 vols, 1912, abridged 1927); *Letters and Diaries*, ed. C. S. Dessain (31 vols, 1978); complete index to Works, Joseph Rickaby (1977); *Apologia Pro Vita Sua*, ed. Maisie Ward (1976).

13. Jeremy Taylor (1613–67) [L.F.]

The author of *Holy Living* and *Holy Dying* was the son of a Cambridge barber. He won a scholarship from the Perse school to the university, and his academic career was so outstanding that he graduated and was ordained before he reached his twenty-first birthday. A High Churchman, he attracted the notice of *Archbishop Laud while preaching for a friend at St Paul's, and was sent to Oxford as a Fellow of All Souls in 1636. He became a chaplain to the archbishop, and also chaplain to *Charles I, who made him a Doctor of Divinity by royal mandate.

Taylor was a convinced Anglican, with no inclination to Roman Catholicism. On the anniversary of the Gunpowder Plot in 1638, he preached a famous 'gunpowder sermon'. During the Civil War, he acted as chaplain to the royalist troops, and was taken prisoner three times by Cromwell's men. He retired to Llanfihangel, near Aberystwyth, with his second wife and three children. Cromwell seems to have tolerated him, but was doubtless pleased to get rid of him when he was offered the living of Ballinderry, near Lisburn in Northern Ireland, personally giving him a pass and protection for his family.

After the Restoration in 1660, Charles II made Taylor bishop of Down and Connor. This appointment precipitated him into bitter conflict. Though he was basically tolerant, and had written, in *A Discourse on the Liberty of Prophesying* (1848), of 'the unreasonableness of prescribing other men's faith and the iniquity of persecuting different opinions', he could not come to terms with either side in the religious divisions of Ireland. The Roman Catholic community regarded him as a Protestant; and his relations with Presbyterians and Anabaptists were even worse. He called them 'intolerable persons' and 'Scotch spiders', and regarded them as 'criminally disobedient' because they would not recognize his episcopal authority. He had thirty-two benefices declared vacant because the ministers had not been episcopally ordained. From 1661, he became administrator of the Dromore diocese in County Down, where the cathedral was in ruins. The restoration of the cathedral was chiefly his work, and close to his heart. He became ill after visiting a fever patient at Lisburn, and his last injunction was 'Bury me at Dromore.'

Jeremy Taylor was a prolific writer. His devotional work reflects deep scholarship and an intense prayer life. The circumstances of his life forced him to spend his last nine years in controversy, but since his own day, his writings, and his maintenance of the middle way in Anglican doctrine, have been a source of inspiration to many Christians.

H. E. Bonney (1815); Edmund Gosse (1903); Hugh R. Williamson (1952); Richard Tatlock, ed., *The Wisdom of Jeremy Taylor* (1954); D.N.B., 19, pp. 422–9. Works: ed. Reginald Heber (15 vols, 1832), revised by Page Eden (10 vols, 1847–52). Extracts from *Holy Living* (1650) and *Holy Dying* (1652) are to be found in many anthologies.

Florence Nightingale (1820–1910)   [*Commem.*]

It was not until the publication of Cecil Woodham-Smith's biography of Florence Nightingale in 1950 that the public image of 'the lady with a lamp' was replaced by the even more heroic figure of a nursing administrator of formidable will and intellect. Florence Nightingale reorganized the filthy and squalid military hospital at Scutari during the Crimean War in the face of military incompetence and medical obstructionism, and became a major social reformer. She had very little training in nursing. At Scutari, she found cholera, dysentery, and more men dying from neglect and filth than died in battle. She worked twenty hours a day, not only dressing wounds and assisting at amputations, but training and directing her nurses, supervising Turkish workmen, purchasing medical stores, coping with administrative chaos. When she came back to England, her health shattered, it was to find that England's first war correspondent, William Howard Russell of *The Times*, had made her a household name.

When she was young, Florence had wanted to offer her life to the Church of England, but could find no way of doing so. 'The Church of England,' she wrote, 'has for men bishoprics, archbishoprics, and a little work. For women, she has – what? I have no taste for theological discourses. I would have given her my head, my hand, my heart . . . she did not know what to do with them. She told me to go back and do crochet in my mother's dressing-room.'

She studied nursing briefly with the Catholic Sisters of Charity in Paris, and with Pastor Fliedner and the Lutheran deaconesses in Kaiserswerth. Then she found her own vocation in the Crimea. When she returned to England in 1856, she refused all publicity. She never made a public appearance, attended a public function, or made a public statement. She was very ill, and was thought to be dying. She lived for more than another fifty years as an invalid. Whether she was genuinely ill, or whether this was the only way in which she could secure the necessary privacy from her family to do her work is not clear; but it gave her the freedom to write a mass of memoranda, minutes and directives on hospital and nursing matters. As a woman, she could not take part in political life, but the politicians came to her. She wrote endless memoranda to Sidney Herbert, the War Minister, interviewed all the witnesses for the Royal Commission on the Health of the Army, provided facts and figures for Queen Victoria and Prince Albert, and devoted many years to 'the Indian sanitary question'. She worked for decades as an adviser to the War Office, and also advised the Union government in the American civil war, and both sides in the Franco-Prussian War. She was visited by foreign heads of state, by Cabinet ministers, and by fellow-reformers such as Edwin Chadwick and *Lord Shaftesbury. She extended her interests to civilian hospitals, scrutinized hospital plans, and saw the Nightingale School for nurses opened at St Thomas's Hospital in London in 1860, and a school for midwives in the following year. She knew every nurse personally, and saw many of them become matrons of well-known hospitals. She wrote *Notes on Hospitals*, the celebrated book which begins with the statement that the first duty of a hospital is to do the patient no harm. The answer to the high mortality rate in hospitals was not self-sacrifice, she argued: it was ventilation, cleanliness, and adequate drainage. *Notes on Nursing* was published in 1859. She dismissed the medical profession's requirement that nurses should be 'devoted and obedient' with: 'This definition might do just as well for a porter. It might even do for a horse. It would not do for a policeman.' She campaigned for better hospital statistics, sending out circulars of enquiry, drafting forms, and classifying diseases. She extended her interests to workhouse nursing, and then to district nursing.

She wanted nothing for herself. She refused a grace and favour apartment in Kensington Palace, and asked to be buried quietly in the family grave at East Wellow, not in Westminster Abbey. She may have had 'no taste for theological discourse', but she is known to have read the mystics: *Teresa of Avila, *John of the Cross, *Julian of Norwich and Angela of Foligno were her guides. 'Where shall I find God?' she wrote, 'In myself. That is the true mystical direction.'

C. Woodham-Smith (1950); M. Baly, *Florence Nightingale and the Nursing Legacy* (1986); *Far Above Rubies*, pp. 237–45; M. Vicinus and B. Neergaard, *Ever Yours, Florence Nightingale: Selected Letters* (1990). Works: *Notes on Hospitals* (1859); *Suggestions for Thought in the Search for Truth among Artisans* (1860, abridged version ed. M. Poovey, 1992); *Notes on Nursing; what it is, and what it is not* (1868); *Life or Death in India* (1874); *On Trained Nursing for the Sick Poor* (1876).

Octavia Hill (1838–1912)   [Commem.]

Caroline Hill, daughter of the sanitary reformer Dr Southwood Smith, was left with five young daughters after her husband's bankruptcy was followed by what was then called 'incurable insanity'. She and her daughters had to work to keep themselves out of poverty. They were fortunate in their friends. They came into contact with the Christian Socialists, and *F. D. Maurice was a great inspiration to them. Octavia Hill said later, 'It was Mr Maurice who showed me a life in the Creeds, the services and the Bible; who interpreted for me much that was dark and puzzling in life.' The artist John Ruskin gave her a series of commissions in glass painting. He suggested that she might enter a religious community, but she was a worker, not a contemplative. She found her métier at the age of twenty-seven when he asked her to manage three run-down houses.

She never called the properties 'slums'; but landlords did not bother about repairs to such properties because tenants often wrecked them, and rents were difficult to collect. Octavia introduced a new principle:

the reciprocal duties of landlord and tenant, and so started a new kind of housing management. The properties were repaired – broken windows mended, passages and stairs whitewashed, water supplies and wash-houses improved. In return, the tenants were expected to look after the property and pay their rent. She collected the rents herself, often finding her way through dark courtyards among drunken and brawling men. She treated her tenants with respect: she would not enter their homes uninvited, but she often became a friend and confidante. Gradually she taught them to look after the property, paying the men to do small repairs, and helping the families to budget in order to pay their rent. Persistent defaulters were evicted, and she required references for new tenants. She organized a playground for the children: Ruskin sent flowers and plants, and volunteers came to teach the children games and dances as an alternative to squatting listlessly in dirty courtyards.

In 1868, the Charity Organisation Society was founded. Ruskin paid two-thirds of its original costs. Octavia became a district visitor, a liaison officer, and eventually one of the most influential members of its Central Council. Its principles were very much her own – 'Not alms, but a friend'. She found fellow-spirits in *Samuel and *Henrietta Barnett, and took over properties in their Whitechapel parish. In 1884, the Ecclesiastical Commissioners asked her to manage their properties in Deptford, and then Southwark. The Women's University Settlement in Southwark became the centre for training in housing management, where students were taught human relations, accounting and a very useful knowledge of drains, plumbing and the law of landlord and tenant. Similar training centres were started in Leeds, Liverpool and Manchester, and the system was taken up in Germany, Holland and the United States.

Octavia's interests became wider: she became the champion of open spaces in crowded London, campaigning for 'the healing gift of space', 'open air sitting rooms' for Londoners. Funds poured in to save Parliament Hill Fields and Vauxhall Park – but she failed to save Swiss Cottage Fields, which became FitzJohn's Avenue, Hampstead. She gave evidence to the Royal Commission on Housing in 1878, and turned to writing, urging the privileged occupants in central London squares to throw the squares open to the public. She was a founder member of the National Trust, and the policy of creating Green Belts round the cities owes much to her efforts.

Octavia Hill became as celebrated as her contemporary, *Florence

Nightingale. Peers and cabinet ministers called on her, bishops and royalty supported her work. Like Florence Nightingale, she avoided publicity and public speaking. She lived quietly and modestly, and she rejected the suggestion of a state funeral in Westminster Abbey.

C. E. Maurice (1914); E. Moberly Bell (1941); W. T. Hill (1956); *Far Above Rubies*, pp. 23–44. Writing: *Homes of the London Poor* (1883, repr. 1970).

14. Maximilian Kolbe (1894–1941)   *[Commem.]*

Maximilian, born near Lodz in Poland, grew up under the Russian domination of his country. His parents were devout Catholics and patriots. Both became Franciscan Tertiaries, and in later life entered monastic communities for a time. His father, who went on to manage a bookshop at the national shrine of the Virgin Mary at Czestochowa, fought against the Russians in 1914. He was captured and executed.

By that time, Maximilian had entered the Franciscan Order. After studying in Rome, he was ordained in 1919, and taught Church history in a seminary before coming to the conclusion that he must find a way of disseminating the faith more widely. With a group of other Franciscans and lay brothers, he published a magazine in Cracow which soon had a circulation of 45,000.

The community which he founded had a unique blend of Franciscan principles combined with publishing and marketing skills. They produced a variety of weekly and daily newspapers which were highly successful. Despite two serious attacks of tuberculosis, he went on to found a Franciscan community on similar lines in Japan – at Nagasaki – before returning to Poland in 1936 as prior of a large community at Niepokalanow, where there were nearly eight hundred friars.

In 1939, Germany invaded Poland. The friars continued their publishing work as long as they could, taking a patriotic and independent line, and making no concessions to the invaders; but many were forced to leave, and those who remained organized a refugee camp for thousands of displaced Poles and Jews. In May 1941, the Gestapo arrived. Father Kolbe and four other brothers were sent to the concentration camp at Auschwitz.

It was a life of heavy labour, near-starvation and constant fear. Kolbe was intelligent and resourceful, and he learned that there were ways of surviving: keeping fit, working hard, avoiding the eyes of the guards; but he continued to exercise his ministry as a priest, celebrating the Eucharist in secret, hearing confessions and showing compassion towards his fellow-prisoners. He was beaten for it, and set to shovelling manure. He had been in Auschwitz for four months when a prisoner from his block escaped. The 600 men in the block were paraded, and forced to stand all day in the hot sun. Some fainted, and were left where they lay. At length ten men, selected at random, were sentenced to die by starvation in reprisal. One of them was a sergeant named Francis Gajowniczek, who asked for mercy in the name of his wife and his children. Maximilian Kolbe picked his way through the ranks, saying, 'Herr Kommandant, I have a request.' He went on, 'I am a Catholic priest. I wish to die for that man. I am old, he has a wife and children.'

The condemned prisoners were stripped naked and taken to the death cell. There was a prisoner-interpreter with them, who later left sworn statements of what happened in this dreadful place, where men were shorn of all human dignity. Father Kolbe led the others in prayer and prepared them for death. Two weeks later, he was one of only four who were still alive. He was executed by a lethal injection. The story of his death was carried to the other camps, and out into Poland where a young man named Karol Wojtila was working in a stone quarry, and secretly studying for the priesthood.

On 10 October 1982, Maximilian Kolbe was declared a saint by Pope John Paul II, the former Karol Wojtila. The man whose life he saved was present at his canonization.

Patricia Treece, *A Man for Others: Maximilian Kolbe in the words of those who knew him* (1982); G. Bar (1972); Diana Dewar, *Saint of Auschwitz* (1982); D. Forrestal (1987); Roman Komaryczko in Chandler, pp. 46–65.

15. The Blessed Virgin Mary   Festival

Two problems arise in writing about the mother of Jesus: first, Mary became known in the Christian Church as *Theotokos*, the Mother of God, and the focus of many cults seeking to pay her honour; for men, she was the ideal woman; for women, she was the greatest of all women, who understood their problems. Second, in reaction against the legends and accretions which came from this process, the ecclesiastical reformers of the sixteenth and seventeenth centuries stressed the danger that Mary herself might come to be regarded as divine, and that this would reflect on the true humanity of Jesus. The Anglican Communion has generally avoided extreme views of either kind, while seeking to pay due respect to the mother of our Lord.

The only biblical evidence we have on the life of the Virgin Mary (or Miriam in Hebrew) is that given in the four Gospels, and there are marked differences of emphasis. *Matthew is writing for Jewish Christians. He starts in chapter 1 with the genealogy of Joseph, and describes his dilemma: he is 'a righteous man', and cannot accept an illegitimate child, but at the same time, he is kindly and considerate. He does not want to expose Mary to public disgrace, and plans to 'dismiss her quietly' until he receives a message from God telling him of her high destiny. Then he takes her home with him, cares for her and protects her, and does not have intercourse with her until after her son is born (Matthew 1:18–25).

*Luke the physician is much more interested in Mary's reaction to her pregnancy. It is he who tells us about the Annunciation, and how Mary was 'deeply troubled' until she was reassured that the child came from God, and that she would have company: her elderly relative Elizabeth, long past childbearing, was also pregnant (Luke 1:26–38). Luke goes on to recount the story of Mary's Visitation to Elizabeth, and her great hymn of thankfulness (the Magnificat), before going on to parallel the events of the birth of *John the Baptist and the Nativity of Jesus.

Neither *Mark nor *John records any of these events: Mark starts his narrative from John the Baptist's time in the wilderness, and John begins with the superbly poetic theology of the Prologue, the account of the Word made flesh, rather than the birth of a child.

In the accounts of the Nativity, Matthew is concerned with Jewish politics: the foreign astrologers who come seeking the child born to be king of the Jews, Herod's reaction, the massacre of the *Innocents in Bethlehem (Matthew 2:1–16). Luke again concentrates on human situations – the local shepherds who came to see the child and spread the story through the district (Luke 2:8–18), and the presentation in the Temple, where Simeon and Anna see the child and give thanks for him. Mary and Joseph were 'full of wonder at what was being said about him', and Mary 'treasured all these words and pondered them in her heart' (Luke 2:21–40). Luke's picture of Mary is of a thoughtful and sensitive young woman.

Luke goes on to say that the family 'returned to their own home' in the town of Nazareth (Luke 2:39). Matthew, again concentrating on the interests of his Jewish readers, gives the story of the flight into Egypt (which would have suggested parallels with Moses) and suggests that Nazareth was not their previous home: they went there to fulfil the prophecy that the child would be a Nazarene.

We have only two more glimpses of Mary before the Crucifixion: Luke describes how the twelve-year-old Jesus was lost on the way back from their trip to Jerusalem for the Passover, how his frantic parents found him still in Jerusalem, listening to the elders and asking them questions; and how Mary, like any mother in the circumstances, said, 'Why have you treated us like this? Look, your father and I have been searching for you in great anxiety' (Luke 2:41–52). Again, Mary meditated on what had happened, and 'treasured all these things in her heart'.

John tells us about the wedding feast at Cana of Galilee, and how Mary, understanding the embarrassment of the bridegroom's family which was responsible for the catering, told her son that the wine had given out. The Authorized Version's translation of Jesus's reply, 'Woman, what have I to do with thee?' (which probably reflects the comparative harshness of Hebrew expressions) is softened in the New R.S.V. to 'Woman, what concern is that to you and me?' (John 2:1–11); but Mary tells the servants to do what he says, and the water becomes wine. Many explanations have been offered for this occurrence, but the important facts are the trust and understanding between mother and son, and the benediction on marriage.

So Jesus comes to the Cross, and Mary is there at the last. The synoptic Gospels do not mention her specifically, but the Gospel according to John records how she is commended to the Beloved Disciple, who is to care for her as a son from that time on, 'and from that hour, the disciple took her into his home' (John 19:25–7). Mary appears once more in the Acts of the Apostles: she is present when the disciples choose Matthias to replace Judas; and we can assume that when 'they were all together in one place' on the day of Pentecost (Acts 1:14 and 2:1) she was there to receive the Holy Spirit.

The New Testament accounts necessarily deal with Mary only in circumstances where she is in contact with her son: the Gospel writers knew about the contact and it has significance in the story they have to tell about Christ's deeds and his message. He is the focus, she is not. None of the Gospel accounts makes any attempt to give a biography of

Mary. There is much about her earthly life which we do not know, and perhaps are not meant to know.

Through the centuries, doctrines like that of the Immaculate Conception, the Assumption and the Ever-Virginity of Mary have developed among some devout people in order to give greater honour to the Mother of our Lord, though they have often been the subject of much debate. For instance, neither *Bernard of Clairvaux nor *Thomas Aquinas accepted the doctrine of the Immaculate Conception. The Anglican Calendar has four festivals of the Virgin Mary: her main feast on 15 August, and three lesser festivals for her Conception (8 December), her Birth (8 September) and her Visitation to Elizabeth (31 May). The same feast days are kept in the Roman Catholic and Eastern Orthodox Churches, though with varying doctrinal emphases, and others are added.

There are over seventy pages of references to publications on the Blessed Virgin Mary in the British Library catalogue, including devotional and exegetical works. Among important modern publications are *Mary in Doctrine and Devotion: papers of the 1959 Conference of the Ecumenical Society of the Blessed Virgin Mary*, ed. Alberic Stacpoole et al., and *Occasional Papers* of the same Society, 1970–80, both published by the Columba Press, Ireland. Roman Catholic views are summarized in N.C.E., 9, pp. 335–87, with extensive bibliographies.

20. Bernard of Clairvaux (1090–1153)   [L.F.]

Bernard was known in his own day as 'the oracle of Christendom'. He was the son of a nobleman who fought in the First Crusade, and was barely twenty-two when he entered the monastery at Cîteaux with thirty-one companions, including two of his brothers. Bernard seems to have been the moving spirit behind this influx, which completely transformed a small, rather run-down Benedictine monastery. In 1115, he became abbot of a new foundation, Clairvaux, in Champagne.

At first, he introduced an extremely severe régime. The monks are said to have lived on barley bread and beech leaves, and their physical stamina was tried to the limit by vigils and penances. The bishop induced Bernard to relax the Rule to some extent, and it was then adopted by a number of other foundations. Benedictine monasteries had often become lax and places of luxurious living, and Bernard's call to simplicity, piety, and seclusion from the world came at the right time. Bernard had a considerable influence on church architecture and furnishings: he was opposed to the elaborate decoration and stained glass of his day, and preferred simple churches: bare stone, white walls, plain glass.

Bernard himself was anything but secluded from the world. He became very influential in Church affairs. Among many other activities, he secured recognition from the Council of Troyes for the Knights Templar, who were established to defend sick people and pilgrims on the routes to the Holy Land, and wrote their Rule himself. He attacked the monks of Cluny, who were Benedictines, for their worldliness. He marshalled his forces to defend Pope Innocent II against the anti-pope Anacletus, and reached his highest point of influence when one of his own monks became pope in 1145 as Eugenius III.

Bernard's influence was exerted through incessant travel (despite a painful illness, probably a gastric ulcer) and correspondence. He is said to have been able to dictate two letters at once, and he wrote many letters of advice to those who asked for his counsel – from popes, bishops and kings to humble people of no worldly importance. When he travelled, people clogged his progress and waited outside the windows of his lodging, asking for the laying on of hands. Bernard was always careful to tell them that any cure would be a result of their own faith, not of his ministrations.

He wrote endlessly in fluent and stylish Latin, and his works fill four volumes of the *Patrologia Latina*. His writing indicates a man with a very wide emotional register: he could be violently angry, using stinging sarcasm and blunt invective – as when he told Pope Eugenius II that Bishop Henry of Winchester, a particularly worldly Benedictine, was 'the enem . . . the man who walks before Satan, the son of perdition, the man who disrupts all rights and laws'. He could also be so gentle and kindly that he earned the title of *Doctor mellifluous*, the honey doctor. His sermon on the death of his brother Gerard, who was also a monk at Clairvaux, shows a great capacity for tenderness and affection. His devotion to the *Virgin Mary, though expressed in terms which are sometimes startling to modern readers, was undoubtedly deep and genuine. His treatise *On the Love of God*, which insists on 'the sweetness of God', is an outstanding example of his mystical theology.

Bernard preached peace, compassion and self-denial. He was insistent that the Jews should not be persecuted, saying, 'The Jews are for us the living words of Scripture.' His influence on the development of monasticism was enormous: there were over 400 Cistercian monasteries when he died, including fifty in England.

AA.SS., Aug., 4, pp. 101–369; *P.L.*, vol. 182 (Lives) and 183–5 (Works); W. Williams (1935); I. Schuster, trans. G. J. Roettger, *Saint Bernard and his Times* (1951); A. Walker (1960); E. Gilson, *The Mystical Theology of St Bernard* (1940); B. P. Maguire, *The Difficult Saint* (1991); *Butler*, Aug., pp. 193–202. Works: *On the Love of God* (trans. E. Conolly, 1937); Letters in J. Cumming, ed., *From Saints to Sinners* (1995).

William Booth (1829–1912)
and Catherine Booth (1829–90)   [*Commem.*]

William Booth's father died when he was in his early teens, and he was apprenticed to a local pawnbroker. He learned about violence and drunkenness and shame and misery from the lives of the poor, and had a religious experience which led him to give his life to preaching repentance and salvation. He moved from Nottingham to London when he was twenty, and joined the Methodist New Connexion at Camberwell, as a lay evangelist. He studied the Bible and became a powerful preacher. In 1855, he married Catherine Mumford, who was to be his partner in the foundation and building up of the Salvation Army.

He embarked on preaching tours in the cities of the north and east of England. He took seriously Wesley's injunction that 'You have nothing to do but save souls', and he went into the poorest areas, the 'dark ocean of human wrecks', to find his converts. His methods were unorthodox: he gave out handbills for his meetings, inviting people to 'Come, drunk or sober.' He took crowds of poor, ill-dressed and often unwashed converts into the Methodist chapels, where they were not always welcome. When the New Connexion tried to restrain his zeal by confining him to a particular circuit, he resigned, and set up his own Christian Mission in the East End of London.

By this time, he and Catherine had four children. Catherine insisted that women could preach as well as men, and women always played a full part in the Mission's work, the lady preachers being popularly known as 'Hallelujah Lasses'. Some of them, like 'Happy Liza' and 'Hallelujah Abbie', became popular figures with the East Enders. Seventy years before the foundation of Alcoholics Anonymous, the Booths organized their 'shock troops' to combat alcoholism. The mission became the Salvation Army – 'an Army terrible with banners' – with William Booth as its General.

Members of this new army adopted military terminology: their mission halls were 'citadels' or 'forts'. They practised 'knee-drill' when they knelt in prayer. 'Fix bayonets!' was a request for hands to be raised in assent and acclamation. Their brass bands attracted the crowds and drowned the jeers and cat-calls of their opponents. They adapted the popular songs of the day to new words (a technique practised by *Ambrose, *Francis Xavier, *Ignatius of Loyola and *John of the Cross among others). 'Here's to good old whisky' became 'Storm the forts of darkness, bring them down'. Their motto, shown on the flag, was 'Blood and Fire' – the Blood of the Lamb and the Fire of the Holy Ghost. These words are still engraved above the lintels of many Salvation Army citadels; and the flag has never flown at half-mast.

A uniform was devised for the 'shock troops', and William Booth wrote *Orders and Regulations for the Salvation Army* on the lines of a well-known manual for the Armed Forces. His troops needed both faith and stamina: they were often pelted with rotten eggs or fish refuse, and sometimes with stones. The women's hats had 'broad missile-resistant brims'. In 1879, the *War Cry* began publication – four pages, weekly, a ha'penny a copy – and they sold it on street corners and in the public houses.

There was active opposition – often inspired by brewers or publicans – and the police frequently turned a blind eye to attacks. In 1882 alone, 669 of these Christian soldiers were assaulted, and sixty buildings wrecked; but the movement prospered, and spread with remarkable speed: to the United States, to Canada, Australia, India and other countries. The local mission had become an international movement.

In 1881, the Salvation Army moved its headquarters to central London, and William Booth met a deputation from the Church of England, headed by the archbishop of York, to discuss joining forces; but Booth decided that his Army must keep its original character. The Church of England set up its own body, the Church Army (see *Wilson Carlile), and the Salvation Army continued its independent work.

Catherine Booth, 'the Mother of the Salvation Army', died in 1890. She had raised seven children. One died, and the other seven, Bramwell, Kate, Herbert, Ballington, Emma, Lucy and Evangeline (Eva) were to play a major part in the Army's work. She had lived in a house 'like a railway station', where the work of evangelism went on continually; and she had preached her own message unflinchingly. William continued alone for another twenty-two years, all devoted to his work. In 1890, he published his major work *In Darkest England: or, the Way Out.* Henry Stanley's dramatic encounter with David Livingstone on the borders of the Congo, and his book *Darkest Africa,* had attracted great public attention. Booth revealed the horrors of 'darkest England' – the 'submerged tenth' of the population which still lived in unimaginable squalor and misery on his readers' doorsteps. The Salvation Army was pioneering in many fields of social reform – child prostitution, labour exchanges, legal aid for poor clients, a missing persons' bureau. Though the Charity Organisation Society insisted that 'the hunger of the mass can only be met by their own exertions' and *Punch* satirized 'Field Marshal von Booth', William Booth's efforts, in England and abroad, were unsparing. By the time he died at the age of eighty-three, he had travelled five million miles, preached nearly 60,000 sermons, and seen the Salvation Army established in fifty-eight different countries. As he said of himself, he was a fighter to the very end.

William Booth: F. Booth-Tucker (1898); G. Railton (1912); H. Begbie (1920); St John Ervine, *God's Soldier* (1934); R. Collier, *The General Next to God* (1965); Roy Hattersley, *Blood and Fire* (1999).Works: *How to reach the Masses with the Gospel* (1872); *Doctrine and Disciplines of the Salvation Army* (1872); *In Darkest England, or the Way Out* (1980). Catherine Booth: Catherine Bramwell-Booth, (1970); *Great Christians*, pp. 53–66; *Far Above Rubies*, pp. 245–9.

24. Bartholomew   Festival

In the synoptic Gospels, Bartholomew's name is given as one of the twelve apostles (Matthew 10:3; Mark 3:18; Luke 6:14), but there is no other reference to him. In the Gospel according to *John, there is a detailed reference to Nathanael, who has been identified with Bartholomew. The reasons for concluding that they are the same person are first, that Bartholomew means 'son of Tolmar'; it is a patronymic, not a personal name. Second, both names are associated with *Philip, who in John 1:45 is said to have found Nathanael. Third, the synoptic Gospels mention Bartholomew, but not Nathanael, as one of the twelve apostles, while John mentions Nathanael, but not Bartholomew.

In John's narrative, Philip asks Nathanael to come and see the prophet from Nazareth. His response is, 'Can any good come out of Nazareth?' Philip insists, and Jesus says of the new recruit, 'Here is truly an Israelite in whom there is no deceit.' Nathanael asks, 'Where did you come to know me?' and Jesus says, 'I saw you under the fig tree before Philip spoke to you.' Nathanael replies, 'Rabbi, you are the Son of God, you are the king of Israel.' Jesus says, 'Do you believe because I saw you under the fig tree? You will see greater things than that', and promises him that he will see the heavens open, and God's angels ascending and descending on the Son of Man.

Bartholomew/Nathanael was a fisherman from Galilee. In John 21:2 he is described as coming from Cana, and he and Peter and Thomas and the sons of Zebedee toil together all night without a catch – to find Jesus standing on the shore and saying 'Let down the nets on the other side.' In the Acts of the Apostles, he is with the others after the Ascension (Acts 1:13).

There is no further mention of him in the New Testament, but the historian Eusebius of Caesarea, writing in the early fourth century, has an interesting story to tell. He says that St Pantenus of Alexandria, a century earlier, had found in 'India' people who already knew of Christ through Bartholomew's preaching. They showed him a Gospel of *St Matthew written in Hebrew, which Bartholomew had brought with him and left behind. At this time, 'India' was often used by Greek and Latin writers for territories in Arabia or Ethiopia, so Bartholomew may have gone south to carry out his own mission. *St John Chrysostom says Bartholomew taught the people in Lycaonia (Asia Minor).

The Roman Martyrology compiled by Cardinal Baronius in the sixteenth century says that he carried out missions in India and Armenia, and that he was martyred, being flayed alive and beheaded at Albanopolis (now Derbed) on the west coast of the Caspian Sea. The church of St Bartholomew in Rome claims his relics.

Eusebius, *H.E.*, 5, ch. 9.1; *AA.SS.*, Aug., 5, pp. 7–108; *O.D.S.*, p. 39; *Butler*, Aug., pp. 232–3. (24 Aug. in Roman Calendar.) Fragments of an apocryphal *Gospel of Bartholomew* and a Coptic *Acts of Andrew and Bartholomew* still exist: see *Anal.Boll.*, 14 (1895), pp. 353–60. *O.C.B.*, p. 75.

27. Monica (332–87)   [L.F.]

Monica was the mother of *Augustine of Hippo, and our knowledge of her comes from Augustine's *Confessions*: a very frank account of a difficult but rewarding mother–son relationship. They lived in Tagaste, in what is now Algeria. Monica was a Christian, but she was married at the age of fourteen to a man named Patricius, who was not. He was unfaithful to her, and frequently flew into violent rages, but she bore his failings patiently, and brought their children up as Christians. Augustine was sent to study in Carthage. For a time, he mixed with unsuitable friends; he took a mistress, and became a Manichaean and therefore a heretic.

Monica wept over him. She took advice from a bishop who recommended that she should 'let him be where he is', because he would find his own way to the faith, and her prayers would not be in vain. She found this very hard to accept. In 382, when he wearied of the uncouth students of Carthage, and decided to teach in Rome, Monica determined to go with him; but Augustine sailed for Italy with his mistress and their son, leaving his mother at her prayers in a chapel at the port of embarkation.

Monica was evidently a very possessive mother. Augustine wrote that he thought there was 'something unspiritual' in the way she clung to him. She followed him to Rome, only to find that by the time she arrived, he had gone to Milan. She went on to Milan, where *Ambrose was bishop. Augustine, inspired by Ambrose, was finding his way to Christian faith, but Monica was still trying to control his life. She succeeded in getting him to send his mistress back to North Africa, keeping their child Adeodatus. She tried to arrange a wealthy marriage for him to an heiress; but he had decided on ordination and celibacy. She went with him to live in community with some male Christian friends, acting as their housekeeper. She had a very strong Christian faith, but she was not educated, and probably could not read or write. She must have wondered why it took these theologians so long to come to conclusions which she had accepted by rote.

At last in 387 they both decided to go back to North Africa. Augustine had been baptized by Ambrose, and had wearied of the teaching of rhetoric. They got as far as Ostia, the port for Rome, where they came at last to a deep personal understanding. Monica had prayed unremittingly for Augustine's conversion. He, making his own decisions in his own very different way, had come to the same conclusion. They were finally at peace together, and they spent some time talking about the mysteries of the universe and God who made it, leaning on a window sill overlooking a garden. It was a time of tranquillity and mutual sympathy.

Five days later, Monica collapsed. She had been kind to the boy Adeodatus, and he wept at her bedside. When she was dying, she called Augustine (then thirty-three years old) 'a dutiful child'; but he was by then sufficiently mature to be able to accept that to her, he would always be the child she loved rather than the great bishop he was about to become. The Augustinian canons, named after her son, have long kept her memorial.

Augustine, *Confessions*, World's Classics, trans. Henry Chadwick, (1991), esp. Books 3, 6, 9; L. André-Delastre (1960); V. E. Bougaud, trans. Lady (Mary Elizabeth) Herbert (1894); M. E. Procter (1931); W. Sherren (1949); *D.A.C.L.*, 11, 2, cols 2232–56.

28. Augustine of Hippo (354–430)   [L.F.]

Augustine was a man of outstanding intellect, strong physical desires, and great spiritual insight. In his *Confessions*, he gives a detailed and almost brutally honest account of how these different elements warred in him, and of his long struggle to find God. He was brought up a Christian by his mother *Monica, but not baptized. As a student at Carthage, he found himself among others who were 'foul and uncontrolled' and who showed 'an astonishing mindlessness'. He retreated by joining a circle of world-weary and degenerate cynics. He writes, 'All around me hissed a cauldron of illicit loves,' and he retreated again by taking a mistress, a young local girl of low social standing and no education. This was a common practice at the time for young men who wanted to settle down and concentrate on their studies. He was faithful to her for fifteen years. By his mid-twenties, he had become a brilliant teacher with his own schools of rhetoric and grammar in Tagaste and Carthage.

In his search for a faith to live by, he joined the Manichaeans, then the chief rivals to the Christian Church. They dealt with the problems of sin and suffering by holding that good and evil were equal and conflicting forces, and so denied the Christian doctrine of the Trinity, the omnipotence of God, and the divinity of Christ. To the Christians, they were heretics; but they had their own clergy and bishops, their rituals and services and their missionary activities. Augustine bombarded them with theological questions, but could find no answers.

At this time, he was severely depressed, and in great spiritual confusion. He resolved to go to Rome, and took his mistress and their child with him leaving his mother behind 'crazed with grief'. In Rome, he was seriously ill, and though the Roman students came to his lectures, they failed to pay the fees. He heard that there was an appointment to teach logic in Milan, and he went there, to meet *Ambrose, who was then archbishop. Ambrose was friendly to the young scholar from North Africa, and Augustine, listening to his sermons, began to find the truth he had been so long seeking. He was being driven remorselessly towards God – reading, meditating, discussing the Christian faith.

His mother arrived in Milan, and with the best of intentions, tried to reorganize his life. His mistress was sent back to Carthage. He promptly took another mistress. A marriage was arranged for him to an heiress. For a time he was tempted by 'honours, money, marriage', but he was increasingly drawn to the priesthood and the sacrifices involved in celibacy.

At Easter 387, Ambrose baptized him, and he determined to return to North Africa. After his final reconciliation with Monica and her death, he left Italy, and lived for a time in a semi-monastic community in North Africa, still reading, meditating and discussing his faith. He was ordained priest in 391, and became bishop of Hippo in 396, remaining in that office until his death in 430. He was an excellent bishop, maintaining law and order in a fast-disintegrating society, holding fast to the eternal certainties, preaching assiduously and caring for the poor. By the time he died, the Vandals were poised to conquer North Africa, but his writings were to reach readers all over Christendom.

In addition to the *Confessions*, Augustine's works on the Trinity, his sermons on the Gospel according to *John, and above all the *De Civitate Dei*, written in his later years, have become classics. In the *De Civitate Dei*, he describes the City of God, standing four-square as a bastion of Truth, the perfect society in opposition to the secular world. His expositions of the doctrines of grace, creation and the nature of the sacraments have become part of the Christian heritage. In addition, he wrote much that was influential in his own day, chiefly on doctrinal controversies with the Manichaeans, the Pelagians and the Donatists.

Commentators have criticized him for his extreme doctrines on predestination, which involved the view that the unbaptized could not be saved; and also for his contention that sexual intercourse was only permissible for the purpose of generation. More recently, some commentators have objected to the way in which he appears to have disposed of his mistresses and his fiancée as mere obstacles to celibacy. He does not even tell his readers their names; but this may be no more than reticence in a man who was struggling to lead a celibate life.

Augustine remains a towering influence on the development of Christianity. With *Jerome, *Ambrose and *Gregory the Great, he is recognized as one of the four great Latin Fathers of the Church. His work is still essential reading for any student of theology, and for many other Christians.

Ancient Life by Possius of Calama in *The Western Fathers*, pp. 191–244, *AA.SS.*, Aug., 6, pp. 213–460; Lives by E. Gilson (1943); G. Bonner (1963); P. R. L. Brown (1967); D. Bentley-Taylor (1980); A. Mandouze (1987); H. Chadwick (1986). Works in *P.L.*, vols 22–47; Eng. trans. in the Fathers of the Church Series, various authors, Catholic University of Washington, D.C. *Confessions*, trans. and ed. Henry Chadwick (1991); *Later Christian Fathers*, pp. 191–251. See also Jostein Gaarder, *Vita Brevis: A Letter to Augustine* (1998).

30. John Bunyan (1628–88)   [L.F.]

Bunyan was born at Harrowden in Bedfordshire, the son of a brazier and tinker. He says of himself that he was 'born in a base and low estate' for tinkers were travelling men, and often treated as vagrants. He went to a charity school, and learned to read and write, but probably the only book available to him was the Bible. At the age of sixteen, during the Civil War, he joined the Army, perhaps because he was unhappy at home. His mother and sister had died, probably in an epidemic, and his father married again only a month after his mother's death. It has generally been assumed that he joined Cromwell's New Model Army and served in the Newport Pagnell garrison, but his name was a common one, and he may have been mustered for the King's Forces. The New Model Army was seething with religious controversy, and he showed no sign of conversion at the time. He probably saw no action, though a comrade was killed by an unlucky musket shot.

At nineteen, he went home again, a strong big-boned peasant with a ruddy complexion and reddish hair. He took up his father's trade, striding from village to village carrying his anvil and tools: he knew about heavy burdens, and the relief when they rolled off his back. He and his wife Mary were desperately poor, 'not having as much household stuff as a dish or a spoon', and their first child, a girl, was born blind. He drank heavily, swore like the trooper he had been, and broke the Sabbath by playing games on the village green; but he had an increasing sense of guilt. He was playing tip-cat with his friends when he heard a voice from heaven saying, 'Wilt thou leave thy sins and go to heaven? Or have thy sins and go to hell?' He went to church, and the vicar preached against Sunday games. In Cromwell's England, even 'vain and profane walking' on the Sabbath was forbidden.

He resolved to lead a better life, and began to study the Bible earnestly. Like many Puritans, he was attracted to the dramatic events of the Old Testament, and the vengeful God who punished people for their sins. He had no education to guide him, and he took every text literally, applying it to his own condition. Sometimes a phrase would reverberate in his mind for weeks as he went from village to village, wrestling with what he had read. The influence of *John Calvin was strong in England, and he doubted whether he was one of the elect. If not, it seemed to him that he might as well go back to his old ways, for there was no hope for him. He alternated between fits of religious excitement and despair. He learned from *St Paul that faith was a gift: but would God give him the gift? He prayed for a sign, asking God to dry up the puddles in the road to assure him of salvation; but the puddles remained.

He doubted the existence of God, and the goodness of God. His mind filled with blasphemies, and he longed to commit 'the sin against the Holy Ghost', though he was not sure what it was. The mood-swings continued; but the phrase 'My grace is sufficient' came into his mind. When he and his family moved to Bedford in 1653, he began to attend the Bedford Meeting of Independents or Dissenters. Before long, he began to preach and wrote his first tract: he had discovered the gift of words.

The vicar of Bedford was a man of broad sympathies. He took Prayer Book services in his church, but also conducted non-conforming services for the Independents. All went well until the Restoration of Charles II in 1660, when many Royalists tried to put the clock back, and perhaps to pay off old scores. A new vicar no longer took services for the Independents, and a warrant was issued for Bunyan's arrest. The justices enquired whether he and his companions at the Bedford Meeting were armed, but the constable gave evidence that 'there was only a few of them met together, to preach and hear the Word'. Their only ammunition was the Bible.

Bunyan was charged with having 'devilishly and perniciously abstained from coming to church' and described as 'a dangerous and notorious Dissenter'. He refused to give sureties that he would no longer preach, though friends would have provided the money; and he was consigned to the small, crowded county gaol with a mixture of felons and political prisoners.

Bunyan's first wife had died soon after they settled in Bedford, and he had married again. His second wife, Elizabeth, was pregnant with her first child when he was arrested. She went into premature labour, and the child was born dead. The sufferings of his family weighed heavily on him, and he knew that he faced the danger of transportation or even execution. Elizabeth energetically campaigned on his behalf, arguing that he had been arrested two years before the passing of the Act of Uniformity of 1662, and that his detention was therefore illegal. She even went to London and presented a petition to the House of Lords, but without effect. He stayed in prison for twelve years, from 1660 to 1672.

In the noise and confusion of the county gaol, he began to write. He had no privacy for writing, but the gaoler did find him a small table. He wrote *Grace Abounding*, an autobiographical account of his own life and conversion, and then began to write a more allegorical account of the Christian journey: 'As I walked through the wilderness of this world . . .'. The first part of *Pilgrim's Progress* has enriched English literature and English spirituality with so many images: the Slough of Despond, the Valley of Humiliation, Doubting Castle, the Hill of Difficulty and many more. It is written in the incomparable English of the Authorized Version of the Bible. If Bunyan had had more education, it would probably have been embellished with Greek and Latin tags, and the worse for it. He said afterwards, 'I did it mine own self to gratify', and was doubtful whether he should publish a work of fiction. A local bookseller eventually had it printed, and sold it for eighteen pence.

Bunyan was not released from prison until 1672, and was confined again in 1676–7; but by this time, public animosity against the Dissenters had died down. He became a local hero, and in great demand as a preacher. Some called him 'Bishop Bunyan'. He went on to write the second part of *Pilgrim's Progress*, then *The Life and Death of Mr Badman*, and *The Holy War*, but none of his later works reached the powerful simplicity of his prison writing. He died suddenly on a visit to London in 1688, the year in which the Revolution Settlement of William III and Mary II brought toleration for the Dissenters.

William York Tindall, *John Bunyan, Mechanick Preacher* (1934); Roger Sharrock, *John Bunyan* (1954); Monica Furlong, *Puritan's Progress* (1975); Christopher Hill, *A Turbulent, Seditious and Factious People: John Bunyan and his Church* (1988). Works: *Grace Abounding, Pilgrim's Progress, The Life and Death of Mr Badman* and *The Holy War*, all in many editions.

31. Aidan of Lindisfarne (d. 651)   [L.F.]

Aidan was a monk of Iona, after the time of *Columba, when Segenus was abbot. *Bede describes how King *Oswald of Northumbria asked for a monk to christianize his kingdom, and Aidan was sent. The earlier Christian mission established by *Paulinus had collapsed when Paulinus went south. Oswald defeated Penda in 633, and became king of Northumbria. He had taken refuge in Iona during Edwin's reign and had become a committed Christian according to the Celtic rite, so he asked the monks of Iona rather than those of Canterbury for a new mission.

The first to be sent to Northumbria was a monk of 'austere disposition'. He returned to Iona saying that the English would not listen to him, and that they were 'an ungovernable people of an obstinate and barbarous temperament'. Aidan, who was present at the gathering to hear the monk on his return, told him that he should have begun as the apostles did, and given the Northumbrians 'the milk of simple teaching', gradually nourishing them with the word of God. It was decided that Aidan should take on the mission. He was consecrated bishop, and sent to instruct the ignorant and unbelieving.

He chose the island of Lindisfarne, now known as Holy Island, as his base. It lies only two miles from the mainland, and is accessible on foot at low tide. Like all the monks of the Celtic tradition, Aidan needed a place where he could be alone, in touch with the natural world. Lindisfarne was close to the royal palace at Bamburgh, which provided protection for the monastery, but he was able to withdraw from the court for prayer and meditation. He would dine with the king, eat sparely, and leave early to go back to his island retreat. Other monks came to join him, and later hermits settled on the Farne Islands to the south of Lindisfarne.

Bede has nothing but good to say of Aidan. He says that 'the highest recommendation of his teaching to all was that he and his followers lived as they taught'. He was above anger and greed, and despised pride and conceit. If wealthy people gave him gifts, he gave them away to the poor. For most of his ministry, he went on foot. When he was old and found travelling difficult, King Oswin of Deira gave him a good horse, but he gave it away to the next poor man who had need of it.

Except when rebuking the mighty, Aidan was a gentle and moderate man, of discretion and wisdom. He talked to everybody he met, rich and poor alike. He strengthened the faith of the baptized, and spoke of the gospel message to those who were not. At this time, there were many slaves in England, the majority of them captives from the wars between the kingdoms. Aidan made a practice of ransoming slaves, and sending them home. He so ordered his monastery that it was an example to all in the regularity and order of worship, teaching his monks to study the Bible and learn the Psalms by heart. He set up a monastic school for twelve boys: among them were *Chad and *Cedd, who became missionaries in turn. He encouraged the ministry of women, first sending a woman named Heiu to form a small community at Hartlepool, and then sending *Hilda to follow her and found the abbey at Whitby. He was a constant pastoral visitor to both communities.

Aidan and his monks lived very simple and holy lives in the Celtic tradition. They built no elaborate buildings, and devised no elaborate rites. At the Synod of Whitby in 664, Aidan argued long and earnestly for the maintenance of the Celtic rite against the more sophisticated representatives of the Latin rite and papal authority; but he and his supporters were defeated by the advocacy of *Wilfrid and the successors of *Augustine.

Oswald and Aidan worked together as friends and allies. When Penda attacked Bamburgh, Aidan was on Lindisfarne. He saw the flames and smoke from his monastery across the causeway, and prayed that the city might be saved. Bede recounts that the wind changed direction, and Bamburgh was spared. The king and his bishop died within eleven days of one another in 653.

Lindisfarne was sacked by Viking raiders in 793. Nothing remains of Aidan's monastery, though many pilgrims go to Holy Island and find it still a place of great calm and holiness. The adoption of the Latin rite in the north of England, together with the lack of visible reminders such as ruins and tombs, somewhat eclipsed Aidan's reputation, but Bishop Lightfoot insists that it was 'not Augustine but Aidan who was the true apostle of England'.

AA.SS., Aug., 6, pp. 688–94; Bede, *H.E.*, bk 3, chs 3—6, 15—17, 26. *Men.E.W.*, pp. 429–30; *N.C.E.*, 1, p. 224; J. B. Lightfoot, *Leaders in the Northern Church* (1890); J. Godfrey, *The Church in Anglo-Saxon* England (1962), pp. 102–11; *D.N.B.*, 1, pp. 182–3; Mayr-Harting, pp. 94–113.

September

1. Giles of Provence (eighth century) [Commem.]

Legends surround the name of Giles (Aegidius in Latin), a hermit who lived in a remote area of Provence near the mouth of the river Rhône. A tenth-century biography gives the earliest account of him: he came from Athens, landed at Marseilles, and stayed with Caesarius of Arles for two years. Caesarius asked Giles to found a monastery. Giles was much loved, and had a reputation as a healer. He healed a beggar by wrapping him in his own cloak; and he alone knew of Charlemagne's 'secret sin', which was revealed to him at Mass by an angel bearing a scroll.

In fact, Caesarius was a monk of Lérins who became archbishop of Arles and died in about 543, while Giles is thought to have died in 710; and Charlemagne was not born until 747, so either the Caesarius story or the Charlemagne story, or both, must be discounted; but whatever the facts behind the legends, the hermitage became a monastery, and the monastery became a celebrated mediaeval pilgrimage site where pilgrims from England and northern Europe stayed on their way to Compostela, Rome or the Holy Land. It was well situated geographically for all three, since Marseilles was the main port from which pilgrims sailed for Jerusalem. Giles became one of the Fourteen Holy Helpers traditionally celebrated on 8 August in Germany before the Reformation, the only one who was not a martyr.

He was known as the patron of the lame and halt, of nursing mothers and of lepers. Since lepers were not allowed to enter mediaeval towns for fear of contagion, small leper settlements often developed outside the walls, and churches were built by those who cared for them. In England, 162 churches had dedications in Giles's name, and St Giles's Fair was celebrated annually at Winchester and Oxford. The latter survives in the form of a fun fair, and St Giles is the thoroughfare which runs from St Giles' church to the much later Martyrs' Memorial. St Giles' cathedral, Edinburgh also perpetuates the name of this ancient saint.

AA.SS., Sept., 1, pp. 284–304; N.C.E., 6, p. 483; O.D.S., pp. 206–7; E. C. Jones, *Saint Giles* (1912); F. Brittain (1928); *Anal.Boll.*, 8 (1889), pp. 103–120; *Butler* (1956), 3, pp. 457–8; *P.B.*, 10, pp. 404–6 for the legends.

2. The Martyrs of Papua New Guinea (1901 and 1942)
[Commem.]

Papua New Guinea is the southern part of the large tropical island of New Guinea to the north of Australia. It was first explored by the British in the eighteenth century. At the end of the nineteenth century, the London Missionary Society sent out two missionaries, James Chalmers and Oliver Tomkins, who were killed with some companions by tribesmen in 1901. Their martyrdom led to a great increase in missionary activity in the area, and by the time of the Second World War there were over a million Christians, the majority of them Anglicans or Methodists.

When the Japanese invasion began in 1942, many Christians escaped into the deep forests, but two Gona sisters, Mavis Parkinson, a teacher, and May Hayman, a nurse, were bayoneted to death by Japanese troops. Father Henry Holland, a priest who had been in Papua for twenty-five years, and his colleague John Duffill were both killed, their mission station looted, and Father Holland's translations of the Scriptures into Orokaiva, the local language, lost. Father Vivian Redlich, Lucian Taipiedi, evangelist, and two women teachers, Lilla Lashman and Margery Brenchley, were all killed in the Orokaiva area of North Papua, and John Barge, an evangelist in a very remote area who had stayed at his station, was forced to dig his own grave before being shot.

In all, 333 Christians of all denominations lost their lives, and the Martyrs' School perpetuates their memory. Lucien Taipedi is one of the twentieth-century martyrs whose statues stand on the west front of Westminster Abbey. His killer subsequently became a Christian, adopted Lucien's name, and built a church at Embi.

Dorothea Tomkins and Brian Hughes, *The Road from Gona* (Sydney, 1969);

David Wetherell, ed., *The New Guinea Diaries of Philip Strong* (Melbourne, 1981); Errol Hodge in Chandler, pp. 66–80.

3. Gregory the Great (c.540–604)   [L.F.]

Gregory was a wealthy man of distinguished lineage, the son of a Roman senator. His own standing in Rome was so high that in 373 he became prefect of the city; but within a few months, he reacted against the luxury and political intrigue of high office. He sold all his estates, founded six monasteries in Sicily, and turned his palatial family mansion in Rome into a seventh, St Andrew's on the Coelian Hill, where he entered monastic life himself. He was called out of the monastery to be one of the seven deacons of Rome, and then to be the pope's representative in Byzantium. There are signs that he disliked this appointment. The Church of Rome and the Byzantine Church were already quite far apart in doctrine and liturgical practice. He never learned Greek, and he refused to answer letters written in Greek.

After six years, he was called back to be abbot of St Andrew's. It was during his time as abbot that he is said to have seen flaxen-haired slaves in the market, and enquired who they were. The story was probably embroidered: in the popular version, Gregory not only said 'Not Angles but angels'; when told that they came from Deira (England from the Humber to the Scottish border), he said that they should be saved *de ira* – from the wrath of God; and that the name of their king, Aelle, signified that the land should resound with Alleluias. One account is that Gregory intended to lead a mission to England himself: he asked Pope Pelagius II for permission to do so, and was refused, because the people of Rome clamoured for him to stay with them. The intention had to be abandoned when in 591, Pope Pelagius died, and Gregory was elected in his place.

Throughout his thirteen-year pontificate, he had much to occupy him in Italy – floods, famine, plague, and the Lombard hordes almost at the gates of Rome. He had to struggle for the survival of the city at a time when the Imperial power was very weak, and the exarch of Ravenna exercised civil power on behalf of the emperor in Byzantium. *Bede says that a group of monks from St Andrew's went with him to the Vatican, and 'their example proved an anchor-cable that held him fast to the peaceful shore of prayer while he was tossed on the restless waves of worldly affairs'. Even when he became pope, he ordered his house as a monastery; but he was primarily a man of action – politically aware, swift to make decisions, intelligent in his judgements.

Gregory was a prodigious writer, but not a scholar or a contemplative. His books were pastoral and exegetical works for the guidance of his bishops and clergy, including *The Pastoral Office*, which told the clergy how they should live; the *Synodical Book*, which set out the administration of the Church; forty *Homilies on the Gospels*; four books of *Dialogues*; and a number of biblical commentaries. As a letter writer, Gregory rivalled *St Paul – he too had 'the care of all the churches', and took it very seriously. Many of his letters of instruction and answers to pastoral problems survive. Gregory sent *Augustine's English mission important letters of support and guidance. It is not too much to say that he master-minded the mission – both Bede and the *Whitby Life* term him 'the Apostle of the English'.

Gregory was the first pope to term himself 'the servant of the servants of God', and there is every indication that he meant it. His life was one of constant toil and effort on behalf of his clergy and the people of Rome. On his death, he was buried in the basilica of St Peter's on Vatican Hill with an epitaph which included the following:

> Wisdom was in his words, and all he wrought
> Was as a pattern, acting what he taught.
> To Christ he led the Angles, by God's grace
> Swelling faith's armies with a new-won race.

Bede, *H.E.*, bk 1, chs 23—33, bk 2, ch. 1; *The Whitby Life of Gregory the Great* (about 713), ed. B. M. Colgrave (1968); F. A. Gasquet (1904); F. H. Dudden (2 vols, 1905); J. Richard, *Consul of God* (1980); G. R. Evans, *The Thought of Gregory the Great* (1986); Mayr-Harting, ch. 3; *O.D.S.*, pp. 211–13.

4. Birinus (d. 650)   [Commem.]

Birinus, who is known as 'the Apostle of Wessex', was an Italian Benedictine monk sent to Britain about the year 635 by Pope Honorius I. Gregory the Great had sent Augustine's mission in 596, but that mission had not penetrated into Wessex. Bede tells us that Birinus was consecrated bishop by Asterius, bishop of Genoa, before he left Italy, and commissioned to 'scatter the seeds of the holy faith in the remotest regions of England where no teacher had been before'. There is no record of any contact between him and Canterbury. In the *Anglo-Saxon Chronicle*, he is called 'the Romish bishop', which suggests that his presence and his independent episcopal status were somewhat resented.

Birinus could not go further north than Wessex, for the Midlands were the territory of the powerful and anti-Christian King Penda of Mercia. In Wessex, he converted Cynegils, king of the West Saxons, and baptized him and his household. He was with the royal family when *Oswald of Northumbria came to seek Cynegils' daughter as his wife – though it was *Paulinus, one of the Canterbury priests, who went back to Northumbria to evangelize that difficult and dangerous kingdom. Cynegils gave Birinus the city of Dorcic (Dorchester), an important and comparatively large settlement since Roman times, as an episcopal seat. He remained there for fifteen years, founding many churches in the area, including one at Winchester which was later to become the royal capital of Norman England.

When Birinus died about the year 650, a successor was sent to continue his work; but there is no record of Wessex bishops at Dorchester after 660. The district was absorbed into the kingdom of Mercia, Dorchester became no more than a village, and the southern province established at Canterbury absorbed the diocese.

Berin's Hill, near Dorchester, preserves the name of Birinus, as does the village of Berinsfield. His shrine in Dorchester was much visited by pilgrims in the Middle Ages, and has recently been restored.

Manuscript Lives listed in T. D. Hardy, *Catalogue of Materials, History of Great Britain and Ireland* (R.S. 26), 1, pp. 235-9. See also Bede, *H.E.*, bk 3, ch. 7; *A.S.C.* for 635 and 650; J. E. Field, *Saint Berin of Wessex* (1902); T. Varley, *St Birinus and Wessex* (1934); *N.L.A.*, 1, pp. 118-22; *D.N.B.*, 2, pp. 542-3; *D.H.G.E.*, 8, pp. 1530-1; *Men.E.W.*, pp. 581-2.

6. Allen Gardiner (1794–1852)   [*Commem.*]

As a lieutenant in the Royal Navy, Allen Gardiner saw action against the French fleet in ships with stirring names – HMS *Fortune*, *Ganymede*, *Leander* and *Dauntless* – in the years before Napoleon's final defeat at Waterloo; but the end of hostilities was followed by a period of retrenchment, and there was no further appointment available to him. A man of deep Evangelical conviction, he turned to mission work. In 1831, he was in Africa, exploring Zulu territory, and he set up a mission station at Port Natal. From 1838 to 1843, he worked in the islands of the Indian archipelago. He first visited Tierra del Fuego when his schooner dropped anchor there on the way from the Falklands. He made requests to the major missionary societies to fund an expedition to Patagonia, the remote and barren plateau at the southernmost tip of Argentina and Chile, but none of them were able to do so. He organized a mission of his own, but it failed, and the party endured great hardship before they were finally rescued by ship. On a second expedition, he was accompanied by a Spanish Protestant who could communicate with the American Indians of the area, and they distributed Bibles. Roman Catholic missionaries in the area were opposed to their work, and again they had to withdraw.

Allen Gardiner returned to England, and attempted again to raise funds. At last an unknown lady from Cheltenham donated £700, and he set out for a third time, accompanied by a surgeon, a carpenter, a catechist and three Cornish fishermen. He and his companions landed on Picton Island to endure windstorms and bitter cold. The Fuegans were hostile and stole their supplies. They waited in vain for further supplies, which were delayed in the Falklands for lack of a ship to transport them.

They died of starvation. Allen Gardiner and Richard Williams had kept journals, which suggested that Allen Gardiner was the last survivor, and that he died on 6 January 1852. When two rescue ships finally arrived, all that they could do was to bury the bodies, and bring the journals back to England.

The fate of the party was widely reported in the English press, and several books were published to commemorate a brave, if possibly ill-organized, venture. A missionary ship was named after Allen Gardiner, and his son subsequently became a missionary in Patagonia.

George P. Despard, ed., *Hope Deferred, Not Lost* (extracts from the diaries of Allen Gardiner, Robert Hunt and Richard Williams, 1852); *Gentleman's Magazine*, July 1852; *Illustrated London News*, 1 and 8 May, 1852; J. W. Marsh, *A Memoir of Allen Francis Gardiner* (1857); J. W. Marsh and W. H. Stirling, *The Story of Commander Allen Gardiner* (1867); Jesse Page, *Captain Allen Gardiner, Sailor and Saint* (1897); D.N.B., 7, pp. 850–1.

9. Charles Fuge Lowder (1820–80)   [*Commem.*]

Charles Lowder (Fuge was his mother's family name) was a Londoner, the son of a businessman. During his university career at Oxford, he joined the Tractarian movement. He returned to London in 1851 to become a curate at St Barnabas, Pimlico. At this time, there was a public reaction against the innovations in ritual which had become High Church practice. Windows were smashed, hooligans were paid to disrupt services, and clergy were sometimes physically attacked. After five years at St Barnabas, Lowder moved to St George's-in-the East in the London Docks, to take charge of a small mission house. The parish was an area of bars and brothels, of drunken sailors and prostitutes, and of much human misery, where he visited and ministered with devotion.

There were two mission houses, fortunately not consecrated as churches, which meant that Lowder and his fellow-curate Alexander Machonockie could issue tickets for admission, and keep out the rowdy element; but there were no barriers to admission at St George's, where the two curates assisted the vicar, Bryan King. The clergy wore vestments, there were two lighted candles on the altar, and the service was intoned. In 1859–60, there was hissing and cat-calling at services in the packed church, choirboys were spat upon, fireworks were set off, and cushions and other missiles were thrown at the altar. The police were reluctant to intervene, but eventually seventy-three policemen were sent every Sunday to keep order. They failed; and in 1859, the bishop of London, A. C. Tait, closed the church for two weeks. When it reopened, Anglo-Catholic gentlemen from all over London came to protect their own. They included a very useful amateur boxer.

St George's became the focus of the battle for and against the Catholic wing of the Church of England. The clergy were jeered at, threatened and pelted in the streets. Father King found the strain so unbearable that he left for a protracted rest, and finally resigned. Father Lowder and Father Machonockie stayed on.

Father Lowder became the most celebrated of the London priests of the slums, teaching in the schools, visiting crowded and squalid tenements in cholera epidemics, and founding an orphanage. When Anglo-Catholics contributed money to support his work, he was able to make the dilapidated church of St Peter, London Docks fit for worship, and he ministered from there. He was appointed curate in charge, but never held a living. He was one of the founders of the Society of the Holy Cross, and founder of the Confraternity of the Blessed Sacrament.

The Anglo-Catholics were convinced that they were fighting irreverence and near-blasphemy. The opposition came not from the Evangelical movement and the Free Churches, but from a mob reaction to 'Romish' ways. While it lasted, it was a notable confrontation.

Maria Trench (1881); *The Times*, 12 Sept. 1880; *Church Times*, 17 and 24 Sept. 1880; *D.N.B.*, 12, p. 187; *Victorian Church*, 1, pp. 497–501.

13. John Chrysostom (347–407)   [L.F.]

John's father, an Army officer, died when he was young, and he was brought up in Antioch by his widowed mother. Antioch was one of the two great centres of learning in the Eastern Empire, the other being Alexandria. John had an excellent education in oratory and law. In 373 he became a monk, and went to live as a hermit in a cave outside the city. Poor diet and a damp cave damaged his health, and he returned to Antioch in 381, to become a deacon in the Church. He was priested in 386, and became the bishop's special assistant, with responsibility for preaching to the poor and distributing alms.

He was called to be archbishop of Constantinople in 398.

John was an austere man. He reduced the expenditure of his own household sharply, to have more money to devote to the poor and the foundation of hospitals. He censured corrupt clergy and those with low standards of personal morality. He launched an attack on the morals of the court which particularly incensed the empress, Eudoxia. He criticized the women of the court – their extravagant clothes, their cosmetics, their jewels, their failure to observe holy days. Eudoxia retaliated by having a statue of herself placed outside his cathedral, Hagia Sofia, in Constantinople, and by organizing races and games on Good Friday and Holy Saturday. John Chrysostom preached about Jezebel, and the empress took this as a personal insult.

Opposition was stirred up against him. Theophilus, patriarch of Alexandria, organized a hostile group of bishops, and he was summoned to attend a council at Chalcedon. The historian Sozomen says that he refused to attend, saying that he was not insane enough to appear before his enemies, and that if they made specific charges, he would answer them. Charges were trumped up, so that he could be condemned in his absence and exiled.

After John left Constantinople, there were riots in the streets, and Hagia Sofia was burned down. The Christians were accused of burning it down themselves. Olympias, a wealthy elderly deaconess who had supported John in his work, was actually accused of this crime. She was heavily fined and driven out of Constantinople. What we know of John's life in exile comes from his letters to her, of which seventeen are accessible. These are pastoral letters: he is greatly concerned for Olympias, and says little about his own sufferings. Only later does it emerge that he has been taken to a very dangerous region of Armenia, where people are afraid even to talk to him, and the threat of attack from the hostile Isaurians is strong. He remembers a terrible sea voyage, and the sight of wrecked ships and drowned sailors; but he tells Olympias that as God calmed the storm, so he will calm the storms in their lives.

Olympias sent him money, and was able to lessen the severities of his exile for a time. The pope, Innocent I, made representations on John's behalf, and tried to induce the emperor to recall him; but the emperor sent soldiers to take him to a more remote place of banishment. Frail and exhausted, he was forced to journey further and further into exile despite frequent pleas for rest, and he died in Pontus in Asia Minor.

John is celebrated in the Eastern Church as one of the Three Holy Hierarchs and Universal Teachers, and in the Roman Catholic Church as one of the four Greek Doctors (with *Basil, *Gregory of Nazianzus and *Athanasius). His writings contain some of the most powerful defences of the Christian message and God's purpose in the world.

Sozomen, *H.E.*, 8, pp. 2–28; Socrates, *H.E.*, 6, pp. 2–23 (both in *N.P.N.F.*). The Life by Palladius was published in *Anal.Boll.*, 15 (1896), pp. 400–23. Modern Lives: A. Moulard (1941); D. Attwater (1959); C. Baur (2 vols, Eng. trans. 1959–60). A. Moulard, *Lettres à Olympias* (Fr. trans. 1949); E. A. Clarke, *Jerome, Chrysostom and Friends* (1979); Attwater, pp. 59–66. Works: *Later Christian Fathers*, pp. 169–76; J. d'Alton, *Selections from St John Chrysostom* (1940).

15. Cyprian of Carthage (*c.*200–58) [L.F.]

Cyprian was bishop of Carthage, and is thus sometimes misleadingly referred to as an 'African bishop'. In his time, much of north Africa was in Roman hands, though ecclesiastically it was regarded as something of a colonial outpost, and the 'African bishops', though of Roman blood, did not always see eye to eye with the bishop of Rome.

Cyprian was a public orator, a teacher of rhetoric and an advocate. He was converted to Christianity about the year 225, becoming a disciple of Tertullian, and thereafter gave up all classical study, concentrating on the Scriptures and the works of the early Fathers of the Church. He became a priest, and bishop of Carthage in 248.

During the persecutions of Decian, he left his see, but kept in touch with his people by letter. When the persecutions were over, he was faced with a problem of Church discipline: the imperial officers had demanded that Christians should sacrifice to the Roman gods. Some refused, and were martyred. Some complied, though with mental reservations, and some purchased false certificates which purported to show that they had complied. The last two groups were known as the *Lapsi*. The Church honoured the martyrs, but what was to be done with the *Lapsi*? Could they be accepted back, or had they for ever lost their chance of salvation? One priest welcomed them back without penance, while another took the view that they could not be absolved. Cyprian, more moderately, laid it down that penances should be imposed, but that they could be readmitted to the congregation after a suitable period of time.

Cyprian led the 'African bishops' in a controversy with Pope Stephen II concerning the validity of baptism. The papal view was that baptism could be regarded as valid even if it was performed by those who were not wholly orthodox in their views. In north Africa, some doctrines mixed with Gnostic and neo-Platonic views were gaining many adherents, and the bishops took a harder line.

In the persecutions of Valerian, Cyprian was exiled for a time, but he returned to Carthage, and faced his own martyrdom in 258.

AA.SS., Sept., 4, pp. 191–348; H. Delehaye, *Les passions des martyrs et les gens littéraires* (1921), pp. 82–104, and *Légendier*, pp. 174, 177. Modern Lives by E. R. W. Benson (1897); P. Monceau (1914); J. H. Fichter (1942); P. Hinchcliff (1974). Works: *Letters*, trans. R. B. Donna (1964); *Lapsi, and the Unity of the Catholic Church*, trans. M. Bevenet (1957).

16. Ninian (fifth century) [L.F.]

*Bede writes of Ninian in a chapter of his *Ecclesiastical History* concerned with how the Picts received the Christian faith. He says that when *Columba came to the 'northern Picts' in the Highlands of Scotland, the southern Picts had already been evangelized by Ninian, 'a very reverend and holy man of British race'. He became bishop of the area, and his see, named after *St Martin of Tours (316–97), was 'famous for its stately church', where his body rested. Bede mentions that the place was called *Candida Casa*, the white house.

There has been considerable discussion among scholars on the accuracy of Bede's account, but it has received support from archaeological excavations at Whithorn in southern Scotland, where stones of an early church painted white have been found. Stones bearing Christian inscriptions show traces of a monastic community.

It is not clear what Bede means by 'Picts'. He seems to use the term to cover the tribal kingdoms of south and west Scotland which the Anglo-Saxons called ' the province of Bernicia', a term later restricted to Northumberland and Durham. Since he was writing in Northumbrian Jarrow in the seventh century, he would have had a good knowledge of the traditions of two centuries earlier. In his day, and until the sixteenth century, Whithorn was a popular place of pilgrimage to visit Ninian's shrine.

There were many church dedications in southern Scotland to St Ninian, and there is a place near Stirling which bears his name.

Bede says that Ninian was 'regularly instructed in the Christian faith in Rome' and that he brought back a relic of St Martin for his church. If he travelled to Rome, it is very likely that he visited Tours on the way, and that he returned to Scotland with a devotion to the soldier-saint.

Bede, *H.E.*, bk 3, ch. 4; Life by Aelred of Rievaulx in A. P. Forbes, *Early Historians of Scotland* (1874); *L.S.S.*, pp. 1–28; A. O. Anderson, *Early Sources of Scottish History* (1922); W. D. Simpson, *Saint Ninian and the Origins of the Christian Church in Scotland* (1940). See *O.D.S.*, p. 358 for recent journal articles.

Edward Bouverie Pusey (1800–82) [Commem.]

*John Keble and *John Henry Newman were the founders of the Oxford Movement. Pusey, also a Fellow of Oriel College, joined them about two years after Keble's Assize Sermon, and wrote a number of *Tracts for the Times*. Academically senior to both, he was a great asset to the movement: he was a patrician (Eton and Christ Church, with a viscount for his grandfather), and a heavyweight scholar, already renowned as an orientalist.

He had spent nearly two years in German universities – Göttingen, Berlin and Bonn – in oriental and biblical studies. He worked in Hebrew, Syriac and Arabic; and so great was his reputation for learning that when he was ordained in 1828, the Prime Minister, the Duke of Wellington, recommended his appointment as Regius Professor of Hebrew, with a canonry at Christ Church. He was still only twenty-eight years old. He had been greatly alarmed at the rationalist tendencies in German biblical studies, and was determined to defend the Anglican Church against non-conformity and atheism.

The Oxford Movement, sometimes referred to by its opponents as 'Newmania', soon became known as 'Puseyism'. It was Pusey who founded the Oxford Library of the Holy Catholic Church anterior to the division of East and West, which was to run to forty-eight volumes in all. He was an earnest preacher, believing in the essential unity of the Catholic Church despite its divisions; but he clearly distinguished the Anglican position from that of Rome, holding that Anglicanism was the old faith, the faith of the early Church, before Roman claims to supremacy split Christendom.

When Newman agonized and Keble returned to parish life, Pusey, by nature a timid and somewhat absent-minded man, found himself the leader of the Oxford Movement. Within the university, he faced considerable opposition, and in 1843, a commission of inquiry led to his suspension as a university preacher for two years on the grounds of 'heresy'; but he took the movement far beyond the confines of the university. He founded the Anglo-Catholic church of St Saviour's, Leeds – and paid £6,000 for its building out of his own income. He revived the idea of women's religious communities, and was involved in the foundation of sisterhoods in London, Devonport (see *Priscilla Lydia Sellon), Clewer (see *Harriet Monsell) and Wantage. He revived the practice of private confession, and encouraged the use of ritual in church services, though he used little himself.

The restoration of the Roman Catholic hierarchy in England in 1850 brought attacks from both sides. A number of Anglo-Catholics, including Archdeacon Manning of Chichester and the clergy of St Saviour's, Leeds, followed John Henry Newman in joining the Roman

Catholic Church, and some of Pusey's former colleagues accused him of 'cowardice' for not doing the same; while a number of Anglicans suspected him of 'Romish tendencies'. Bishop Blomfield of London openly attacked him in a charge to the London clergy, and the bishop of Oxford forbade him to preach in the diocese.

Pusey stood firm, pursuing his own vision of Church reunion on the lines of early Christianity. He tried to discuss the possibilities of reunion with Methodists, and with the Eastern Orthodox Church, but they were unwilling to engage in debate. He wrote to the Vatican, asking the exact meaning of the term 'papal supremacy': his letters were returned unopened. In Oxford, he engaged in bitter debates with Dr Jowett of Balliol, whom he considered 'a latitudinarian', and actually charged Jowett before a consistory court with teaching opinions 'not in accordance with the teaching of the Church of England'. The court threw the case out. He defended the Athanasian Creed against Archbishop Tait.

Dr Pusey was a man of deep learning, great sincerity and firm views. Pusey House, Oxford was founded in his memory, and acquired his considerable library.

The standard work on Pusey is H. P. Liddon (4 vols, 1883–7). See also G. W. E. Russell (1907); G. L. Prestige (1933); Perry Butler, ed., *Pusey Rediscovered* (1983); George Herring, *The Oxford Movement* (2000); *Victorian Church*, 1, pp. 167–231, 298. There is a full bibliography of Pusey's works in Liddon.

17. Hildegard of Bingen (1098–1179)   [L.F.]

Hildegard tells us that from early childhood, she saw the whole world as a reflection of the 'living Light' of God. She was the tenth and last child of Hildebert of Bemersheim and his wife Mechtild, and at the age of eight, she was sent to be taught by Jutta of Disibodenberg, a recluse who lived near a Benedictine monastery between Mainz and Trier in the Rhineland. Jutta became her foster-mother, her teacher and her spiritual guide. Hildegard said of her, 'This woman overflowed with the grace of God like a river fed by many streams.'

In 1112, when she was fifteen years old, Hildegard became a nun. She continued to live the dedicated life of the Benedictine Rule with Jutta until her mid-forties. As other women came to join the two, the enclosure developed into a women's monastery. When Jutta died in

1136, Hildegard became prioress. She became increasingly convinced that she must write down her visions, and a monk named Volmar was allowed to help her. With Volmar's help, she began work on *Scivias*, an abbreviation of *Nosce Scivias Domini*, or 'Know the ways of the Lord'. The archbishop of Mainz, *Bernard of Clairvaux and eventually Pope Eugenius III (who had been one of Bernard's monks) approved of her work, though she was always very hesitant in letting it be known outside the monastery, and was apt to describe herself as '*paupecula feminea forma*', a poor little woman.

In *Scivias*, she makes it clear that her visions are not hallucinations: she did not perceive them 'in a dream nor when asleep nor in a delirium nor with the eyes and ears of the body'. They had come to her 'when she was awake, and looking around with a clear mind, with the inner eyes and ears, in open places according to the will of God'. She remained in her enclosure, recording her visions, expressing the glory of God in music and poetry, and writing to her many correspondents.

She reports thirteen visions which describe the essential and dynamic unity of all living things under God: the heavens and the earth, the elements, mountains, rivers and seas, plants and trees. She sees the Holy Trinity like a flame: the shining brightness represents the Father, the 'purple vigour' represents the Son, and the fiery glow is the Holy Spirit, poured into the heart of believers.

In *The Book of Divine Works*, completed in 1174, Hildegard tells how her voice from heaven told her: 'I am Life, without beginning and without end . . . I flame above the beauty of the fields, I shine in the waters; in the sun, the moon and the stars, I burn.'

Hildegard's poetry has been compared to that of Dante or Blake. Her seventy-seven pieces of strikingly original church music, including many dissonances and passages in a minor key, were written for her nuns to sing in church and echo the melodies of heaven. She wrote many letters of advice and counsel to prominent people, including four popes and the emperor Frederick I (Barbarossa). Before the murder of *Becket, she wrote to King Henry II of England, warning him about the abuse of power. Her letters were always accompanied by protestations of her own unworthiness, but written with authority and clarity: 'Thus saith the Lord.'

Hildegard's monastery became too large for its site at Disibodenberg, and she was forced to move it to Bingen. She was over sixty when she felt called to leave her enclosure and preach in other monasteries. She undertook four trips through the Rhineland in all, speaking to the monks and nuns who crowded into their chapter houses to hear her. She died at the age of eighty-one. More than nine hundred years later, her works are still being published, and her music is widely available on tape and compact disc.

Lives by Gottfried of Disibodenberg and Dieter of Echtenberg, with additions by Guibert of Gembloux (all three were contemporaries): *P.L.*, 197, 91–130. This volume also includes *Scivias* and other works, and a number of letters. The *Acta Sanctorum* version of the Life (*AA.SS.*, Sept., 5, pp. 629–701) has been translated into English by J. H. McGrath as *The Life of the Holy Hildegard* (1980). Modern Lives and commentaries: S. Flanagan (1989); B. Newman, *Sisters of Wisdom: St Hildegard's Theology of the Feminine* (1987); F. Bowie and O. Davies, eds, *Hildegard of Bingen: an anthology*, with new translations of her writings by R. Carver (1990); *Hildegard of Bingen's Scivias*, trans. B. Hozeski (1986). There are many audiotapes of her music for women's voices.

19. Theodore of Tarsus (602–90) [*Commem.*]

Theodore came from *St Paul's city in Asia Minor. We know very little about his early life. He studied in Tarsus and in Athens, at two renowned schools of theology. He was a refugee from Islam who worked as a Greek scholar in Rome and Naples. In 668, at the age of sixty-six, he was Pope Vitalian's unexpected choice as archbishop of Canterbury.

The Church in England had been in a parlous state since the Synod of Whitby four years earlier. It was still rent by dissension between the Latin and Celtic monks, a plague had all but wiped out the episcopate, and many of the people had relapsed into heathenism. Pope Vitalian decided that, to avoid controversy, the new archbishop must come from outside both the Latin and Celtic traditions. Like the Celtic monks, the Eastern Orthodox also had problems with the Latin rite, the date of Easter and the form of the tonsure.

Like many Greek monks of the time, Theodore was not in Holy Orders, so he had to become sub-deacon and then deacon, priest, bishop and archbishop very quickly. He had to wait in Rome for a month for his hair to grow, so that he could be tonsured in the Latin fashion. When these matters had been attended to, he set out, staying at Frankish monasteries on the way, learning the English tongue and the ways of the Western Church. It took him and his party a year to make the journey via Marseilles and Paris.

Once in England, Theodore acted decisively. He set up a cathedral school in Canterbury, and appointed *Benedict Biscop, who had accompanied him, as abbot of the monastery of St Peter and St Paul, set up by *Augustine of Canterbury. *Bede says that Theodore 'visited every part of the island'. This probably meant no more than visiting the kings and courts of the small kingdoms, and the clergy attached to them; but he was certainly 'the first archbishop whom the entire Church of the English obeyed', though some of them came to obedience slowly.

He called an episcopal synod at Hertford in 672 or 673. Only four bishops attended – Wini of London stayed away, and so did *Wilfrid of York, though he sent representatives. Undeterred, Theodore presented the synod with an agenda. Ten canons or decrees were agreed and written down, and the bishops present signed them. Bede gives them in full: they included confirming the Latin date of Easter, specifying that bishops were to stay in their own dioceses and not to go about preaching all over England, and distinguishing the responsibilities and powers of bishops and abbots. It was proposed 'that more bishops should be consecrated as the number of the faithful increases', but the synod evidently could not agree about that, as the issue was deferred. In 679 or 680, another synod, better attended, was held at Hatfield. This time the agenda was theological: it was necessary to confirm the decisions of the Church in Rome against the Monothelite heresy.

Meanwhile, Theodore proceeded, with or without synodical approval, to reorganize the dioceses and appoint new bishops, very much on the lines proposed by *Pope Gregory before Augustine's mission. He decided that each of the kingdoms should contain two or more dioceses, so that the link between king and bishop was not too close; but no diocese should cross the boundaries between kingdoms. East Anglia was divided into two dioceses, one for the North-folk and one for the South-folk. Mercia was split between Lichfield and Leicester. Northumbria, Wilfrid's enormous and unwieldy diocese, administered from York, was cut into three, and Wilfrid retained only the smallest area. There seems little doubt that, though the administrative changes were necessary, Theodore took the opportunity to deflate the ambitions of Wilfrid, who may have had ambitions to become archbishop of the north. Wilfrid, who had not been consulted, took his grievance to Rome, but papal decrees restoring Wilfrid to his see were simply ignored. Reconciliation with Wilfrid was one of Theodore's last acts, shortly before his death at the age of eighty-eight.

Theodore was a modernizer, and an administrator of remarkable calibre. He was not a particularly tactful one. He could be ruthless when he thought it was necessary; but he took a disorganized and disheartened scatter of missionaries, and turned them into something recognizable as the English Church.

Bede, *H.E.*, bk 4, chs 1–2, 5, 6, 12, 17, 20, and bk 5, ch. 8; *AA.SS.*, Sept., 6, pp. 55–82; G. F. Browne, *Theodore and Wilfrid* (New York, 1897); J. Godfrey, *The Church in Anglo-Saxon England* (1962); Michael Lapidge, ed., *Archbishop Theodore: commemorative studies* (1995); *Cantuar*, pp. 16–21; Mayr-Harting (many refs, see index); *N.C.E.*, 14, p. 17; *O.D.S.*, pp. 451–3.

20. John Coleridge Patteson and his Companions (d. 1871)
[L.F.]

As a result of the pioneer work of *Bishop George Augustus Selwyn, John Coleridge Patteson, a fellow Old Etonian, joined him in his missionary work in Melanesia. He was the curate of Ottery St Mary, his home parish in Devon, and he had a gift for languages. Patteson sailed the islands, learned the island languages (he was later said to speak twenty-three different tongues) and developed a scheme for a school for Melanesian boys. After some trials, this was established on Norfolk Island, where the inhabitants included Pitcairners, the descendants of the mutineers of the *Bounty* and their Tahitian wives. The boys came for a year with their parents' permission before returning to their own islands, and it was said that Patteson treated them exactly like Etonians.

In 1861, he was consecrated bishop of Melanesia, and took sole direction of the Melanesian Mission. The work was supported by the income from his fellowship at Merton College, Oxford, which he retained, and by his inheritance from his father, who died in 1861. There was also a Melanesian Society at Eton, and an association in Australia. The Pitcairners supported him, and some of the pupils from the school on Norfolk Island went on to ordination. It was all a glorious and successful adventure, and Bishop Patteson was a man at the peak of his powers – working incessantly at whatever came to hand, preaching, converting, confirming, building churches, cooking, sailing. He was enthusiastic about Bishop Selwyn's scheme for synodical government. Then he encountered the slave traders.

These were planters in Fiji and Queensland, who wanted labourers for their plantations. They made a practice of visiting the islands and luring the young men away with false promises. Few of them were able to return, and the islands were becoming depopulated, so great was the trade. The planters even used Bishop Patteson's name to further their ends: he protested vehemently, and helped to bring some of them to court in an effort to stop the abuses.

On 16 September 1871, he and a small party visited the island of Nutapu, unaware that the traders had raided it and killed five islanders. He landed alone and unarmed, and was not recognized. The rest of the party wanted to follow, but were met by a hail of arrows. Later, a canoe was pushed out towards them. It contained Bishop Patteson's body covered by a palm frond bearing five knots – signifying revenge for five deaths. With him are commemorated three of his companions who died from tetanus as a result of poisoned arrows: Fisher Young and Edwin Noble in an attack in 1864, when Patteson escaped, and Joseph Atkins, who died in the incident when he was killed.

In the year after his death, the British parliament regulated the labour trade in Melanesia. The second bishop of Melanesia was John Selwyn, son of Archbishop Selwyn, who braved considerable danger to visit Nutapu and make the islanders understand the nature of the tragedy which had occurred. A cross was erected on the spot where John Coleridge Patteson had died.

Lives by Jesse Page, *Among the Maoris: daybreak in New Zealand* (1894); Charlotte M. Yonge (2 vols, 1873); Mary H. Debenham (1921); Elizabeth W. Grierson (1927); Norman T. Davidson (1931); Charles E. Fox, *Lord of the Southern Isles: the story of the Anglican Mission in Melanesia, 1849–1949* (1958), pp. 12–27; Robert C. Finney, *I'll Have a Hurricane* (1955); D.N.B., 15, pp. 498–501.

21. Matthew, Apostle and Evangelist   Festival

Matthew was a Jew who collected taxes for the Romans. The tax collectors were regarded with scorn by other Jews, because they worked for the occupying power. Matthew was sitting at his tax booth, receiving taxes, when Jesus said to him 'Follow me'; and he left his booth and he followed (Matthew 9:9). Afterwards Matthew, who must have been fairly prosperous, gave a banquet for Jesus at his house, and many other tax-collectors and sinners – the two were considered almost synonymous – came. The Pharisees, predictably, were horrified, and asked themselves what sort of man was prepared to mix with tax collectors. Jesus used this occasion to demonstrate that he had not come to call only the righteous, but to call even the most unpopular and stigmatized.

The indications are that his meeting with Matthew was no casual encounter. *Mark and *Luke both tell the story (Mark 2:14; Luke 5:27), and Mark adds 'son of Alphaeus'. Matthew is also called Levi – an honoured name in Jewish tradition. The Levites were the priestly caste: the Old Testament Book of Leviticus is devoted to the religious observance for which they were responsible. Matthew was probably a man deeply ashamed of his occupation, and on the verge of conversion. The confrontation at the tax booth provided the occasion. Thereafter, his commitment was whole-hearted. He is named as one of the Twelve (Matthew 10:3; Mark 3:18; Luke 6:15) and as one of the group in the Upper Room 'constantly devoting themselves to prayer' after the Crucifixion.

Matthew is identified as the author of the First Gospel, who is closely associated with Jewish tradition. While Mark begins with an account of *John the Baptist preaching in the wilderness, Luke with the pregnancies of Elizabeth and *Mary, and *John with the eternal significance of the Word made flesh, Matthew begins in the Jewish patriarchal tradition with a genealogy of Joseph, the Christ-child's adoptive father. He anchors the story in Jewish history from the time of Abraham, twenty-eight generations earlier: fourteen generations to the Babylonian Captivity, and fourteen since, covering the whole history of his people.

The Gospel according to Matthew was written in the second half of the first century. Content analysis shows that it draws in part either on Mark's Gospel or on a source, known as 'Q', which was common to both, but the genealogical material is his alone.

Christian tradition is that Matthew was martyred. *Jerome's martyrology gives the place as Tatrum in Persia, but the Roman Martyrology of Cardinal Baronius records that it occurred in Ethiopia. Matthew is frequently depicted in mediaeval paintings, sometimes with a money-box, and often with spectacles, which he presumably needed for studying his account books.

AA.SS., Sept., 6, pp. 194–227; Anal.Boll., 80 (1962), pp. 82–110; N.C.E., 9, pp.

490–1; *O.D.S.*, p. 331. Modern commentaries: M. J. Lagrange (1948); F. W. Filson (1960); J. C. Fenton (1963); J. D. Kingsley (1986); *D.A.C.L.* (H. Leclercq) 10, 2, cols 2682–3; *O.C.B.*, pp. 501–7.

25. Sergei of Radonezh (?1314–92)   *[Commem.]*

Sergei (Sergius) is recognized as a saint in both the Eastern Orthodox and the Western Church. His modern biographer, Nicholas Zernov, calls him 'Russia's tutor in Christ'. He was born near Rostov of a noble Christian family at the time of the Tartar invasions of Russia. His baptismal name was Bartholomew. As a boy he had difficulty in learning, but he is said to have taken home an old hermit, who prophesied that he would serve the Holy Trinity.

Tartar attacks on Christians in Rostov led to his family's financial ruin, and they were forced to move to a small farm, where Sergei, the only unmarried son, had to engage in hard manual work to support his parents. In 1335, when he was in his early twenties, they died, and he and his brother Stephen, whose wife had also died, went to lead a life of seclusion in the forest. They built themselves a chapel which was consecrated by the bishop of the area, and dedicated to the Holy Trinity at Stephen's suggestion; but Stephen found the solitary life too hard and too dangerous, and went off to join a regular monastic community, leaving his brother, who had taken monastic vows and the name of Sergei, alone. For two or three years, Sergei stayed in the forest, leading a life of prayer and contemplation. He grew his own food, subsisting on bread cakes from his own corn and root vegetables through the bitter Russian winters. He often endured hunger, and it was said that he could go for days without food. Though there were bears and wolves in the forest, he respected them, and shared his meagre food with them. After a time, visitors came to see the holy man of the forest, and some stayed, building cells near his. When there were a dozen or more, the bishop ordered him to become their abbot, and he reluctantly agreed. They met only for worship. Sergei insisted that each man should till his own field, and live by his own labour. He would not allow begging, and often they could not even keep to their practice of a daily celebration of the Eucharist, because they had no money for bread and wine. They could not afford books, and many manuscripts were copied on to birch bark (which was plentiful) so that they could build up a library.

After a dispute with his brother, who had returned to the monastery, Sergei became a <u>hermit</u> for a time. Then he returned to the monastery under another abbot to continue his humble life of prayer and manual labour. The house of the Holy Trinity became celebrated as a place of pilgrimage, and many people, from princes to peasants, came to consult Sergei, drawn by his warmth, simplicity and wisdom. Moscow was becoming the centre of Russian resistance to the Tartars, but the princes were warring among themselves, and on several occasions Sergei undertook long journeys in the cause of reconciliation. In 1380, the Moscow princes joined together to face the Tartar armies, and Prince Dmitri, their leader, went to ask Sergei if it was right to attack the invaders. The man of peace said, 'Go forward and fear not. God will help you.' He sent two monks back to the battle lines with Dmitri, and gathered the other monks to pray for the souls of those who would die in battle. Some 150,000 Russians, under the sign of the three-barred Eastern cross, faced about 400,000 Tartars, under the sign of the crescent; and the Russians were victorious. This great battle of the Kulivoko Polik was a turning point in the freeing of Russia from Moslem domination.

When the Metropolitan Alexei was dying, he nominated Sergei as his successor; but Sergei refused the honour, and went quietly back to Holy Trinity. Many new monasteries, all adhering to an ascetic way of life, were developed by the Holy Trinity monks on his inspiration. Sergei was known to have intense spiritual experiences and the power of healing, but only those closest to him knew about his gifts, and they were charged not to mention them to others. He died very peacefully at the age of about seventy-eight after receiving the Eucharist. He was already recognized as a saint in the first half of the fifteenth century.

A translation of a contemporary Life by Epiphanius, a monk of Holy Trinity, is included in Nicholas Zernov, *St Sergius, Builder of Russia* (1938). See also *N.C.E.*, 13, p. 114; *O.D.S.*, pp. 431–1; P. Kovalevsky, *St Serge et la spiritualisme russe* (Paris, 1958).

Lancelot Andrewes (1555–1626)   [L.F.]

Andrewes was ordained in 1580, and became a prebendary of St Paul's in 1589. It is said that his preaching 'brought over many recusants to the Protestant religion', and T. S. Eliot regards him as one of the chief founders of the Anglican tradition. Queen Elizabeth I was said to be fascinated by his sermons: he combined great scholarship with an effective and charming delivery. He became dean of Westminster in 1601 and bishop of Winchester in 1619.

There are five volumes of Andrewes' sermons in the Library of Anglo-Catholic Theology. His prose style is precise and clear, and Eliot rates him 'the first great preacher of the English Catholic Church'. Though his style is often somewhat dry for modern readers, he shows a breadth of culture, and a remarkable felicity with words. It was Andrewes who first wrote of the Magi:

> A cold coming they had of it, at this time of the year, just the worst time to take a journey, and specially a long journey . . . the ways deep, the weather sharp, the days short, the sun farthest off . . . the very dead of winter.

Andrewes was responsible for much of the translation of the Authorized Version of the Bible, approved by King James I in 1611. His *Private Prayers (Preces Privatae)* were first written in Latin, then translated by him into Greek. In English translation, they have become spiritual classics. He is said to have spent five hours a day in private prayer, in addition to public worship. He was an excellent pastor, and an able theologian who maintained the Anglican position in debate with Cardinal Bellarmine, head of the Vatican Library and spokesman for the papacy in the debates which followed the Reformation. Lord Clarendon, in his *History of the Rebellion*, regretted that Andrewes was not appointed archbishop of Canterbury, speculating that reunion with Rome might have been possible if he had carried the authority of this office.

Henry Isaacson (1650, repr. Newcastle 1817); F. E. Brightman, (1926); *D.N.B.*, 1, pp. 401–5; T. S. Eliot, *Selected Essays* (1982), pp. 341–53, reproduces a study of Andrewes' writings first published in 1926. Eng. trans. of *Preces Privatae* by Dean Stanhope (1913); J. H. Newman and J. M. Neale (1920). Works in the Library of Anglo-Catholic Theology, ed. J. P. Wilson and J. Bliss (1841–54, 11 vols).

26. Wilson Carlile (1847–1942)   [Commem.]

Wilson Carlile was born in Brixton when Brixton was a prosperous upper-middle-class suburb of London. His father was a merchant in the City of London, and his mother, Maria Louisa Wilson, the daughter of the master of the Haberdashers' Company. The eldest of twelve children, Wilson was sent to private schools because he was delicate, and entered his grandfather's silk firm when he was thirteen years old. By this means he acquired an unusual education: he spent a year at Lille, travelled on business in both France and Germany (including a period during the Franco-Prussian War, when he was able to profit from the dislocation in the silk market) and learned to speak fluent French and German. He inherited his grandfather's business, but lost it in the depression of 1873, and was seriously ill for a time. Perhaps as a result of these experiences, he turned to religion. Though his family were Congregationalists, he was confirmed in the Church of England; but he retained his links with the Free Churches, acting as organist for Ira Sankey of Sankey and Moody during one of their English missions.

In 1878 he decided to seek ordination, and went to St John's College, Highbury, a leading Evangelical theological college. He became a deacon in 1880 and was priested in 1881, by which time he was a curate at St Mary Abbots church at Kensington. The vicar then had twelve curates; but St Mary's was a fashionable church for the well-to-do, and Wilson Carlile felt that it was out of touch with the working classes. He was a powerful preacher. He began to hold open air meetings, and attracted crowds so large that he caused traffic obstructions, and was asked to give them up.

• The Salvation Army was organized by 1878. Four years later, Wilson founded the Church Army as the Anglican equivalent in the slums of Westminster. There were violent brawls at his meetings, and on two or three occasions he was quite seriously injured. Many people in the Church disliked his unconventional methods; but he persisted, and in 1884 was able to found the Church Army Training College at Oxford, training evangelists. In 1897, they were accorded recognition by an Order of Convocation as 'full-time Evangelists in the Church of God'. The founder's sister, Marie-Louise Carlile, founded a similar training college for women, though they did not win recognition as Evangelists until 1921.

In 1889 the first of the Church Army homes, for homeless men and ex-prisoners, was instituted, and Wilson Carlile, accompanied by his officers, spent two or three nights a week on the Thames Embankment in London, where as many as 2,000 destitute people were often seeking food and shelter. In 1891, he became rector of St Mary-at-Hill, a redundant City church which he filled and made the centre of his ministry. In 1906, he became a prebendary of St Paul's Cathedral. In the First World War, he was at the front in France and Belgium, where his ministry was needed most. He became a Companion of Honour in 1926, and lived through to 1942, to see the Church Army become the largest lay society in the Church of England.

A. E. Reffold, *Seven Stars* (1931) and *The Audacity to Live* (1938); Sidney Dark, *Wilson Carlile* (1944); Edgar Rowan, *Wilson Carlile and the Church Army* (5th edn, 1955); D.N.B., *1941–50*, pp. 134–6.

27. Vincent de Paul (1580–1660)   [L.F.]

Vincent came from a peasant family in Gascony. He was educated by the Franciscans, ordained at the early age of twenty, and after a period as chaplain to a noble family became a court chaplain. In a society where rich and poor were far apart, he was unique in his ability to minister to the wealthy and celebrated while devoting himself to the cause of the poor and oppressed. He worked with prisoners in the galleys at Bordeaux, and with convicts. In 1625, he founded a brotherhood of priests who renounced all preferment and carried out an apostolate to the smaller towns and villages, remote from the world of the court and the nobility. Eight years later, he was given the church of St Lazare in Paris which served a large institution for the sick poor.

Vincent's devout nature and the strength of his faith led many of the nobility to seek his spiritual direction. He often found work for them to do in assisting his many charitable causes. He formed a group named the Ladies of Charity to do nursing and sick visiting, but found that, while his wealthy ladies were willing enough to give money, they lacked the practical skills in nursing and sick visiting which were required. One of the ladies under his direction, Louise de Marillac, collaborated with him in founding the Daughters (later Sisters) of Charity, sturdy young peasant girls of good character. They were taught prayer, meditation, basic nursing and the care of the destitute. Records exist of the 'conferences' or training sessions which Vincent de Paul and Louise held for them – long discussions on spiritual matters in which they would exchange ideas, but be careful that even the slowest and most timid of their students was drawn into the conversation.

Vincent was very influential at the French court during the rule of

Anne of Austria, regent for her young son Louis XIV, though he was opposed to the machinations of her Italian favourite, Cardinal Mazarin. He was a close friend of *Francis de Sales, through whose recommendation he became chaplain to the Paris house of the Visitandines, another celebrated religious community for women. He was a very hard worker and an excellent organizer, initiating plans for new seminaries and missions, and developing a brotherhood of priests who were prepared to take on the most difficult kinds of work – in prisons and the galleys, on the field of battle and in hospitals.

The Order he founded was one of the many religious casualties of the French Revolution, but it was re-founded as the Society of St Vincent de Paul in 1833 by the Catholic scholar Antoine Frédéric Ozanam.

Lives: L. Abelly (1664); P. Coste (3 vols, 1932, Eng. trans. 1934–5); J. Calvet (1948, Eng. trans. 1952); M. Purcell (1963). For political and religious background, see H. Brémond, *Histoire littéraire du sentiment religieux en France*, 3 (Paris, 1921), *passim*. The Conferences of St Vincent de Paul to the Sisters of Charity, ed. P. Coste, trans. J. Leonard (4 vols, 1938–40). N.C.E., 14, pp. 682–4.

30. Jerome (c.342–420)   [Commem.]

Jerome was a man of great learning, and his life was dominated by a single idea: to translate the Bible accurately from the original Hebrew and Greek into Latin. He translated all, or nearly all, of both the Old and New Testaments. There were many other partial translations in his time, but they were often translations of translations. He insisted that the texts must be studied in the original tongues. He brought to the work of biblical translation a new thoroughness, accuracy and breadth of scholarship. His version formed the basis of the Vulgate, which was subsequently used in many countries for translations into the vernacular.

Jerome's full name was Eusebius Hieronymus Sophronius, and he was born in Strido, near Aquileia in Dalmatia, the son of wealthy parents. He studied in Rome, and visited the churches and catacombs assiduously. He was baptized before he was twenty-five. He travelled widely, decided to become a monk while he was in Trier (then the Imperial city for the western borders of the Empire) and went to Palestine. There he abandoned his classical studies for biblical study, and spent five years in the desert as a hermit. He was ordained priest in Antioch, and studied in Constantinople under *Gregory of Nazianzus. In about 381, he went back to Rome, and became secretary to the aged Pope Damascus for the last three years of his pontificate.

Damascus commissioned Jerome's work on the Bible texts and commentaries. He also sought Jerome's assistance in his task of opening up the catacombs, identifying the remains of martyrs and writing inscriptions for their shrines. Jerome became very influential in papal circles, and his influence was much resented. He was a testy man – overbearing, impatient and sarcastic. When Pope Damasus died, he was a possible candidate for the papacy, but he had made many enemies. The supporters of rival candidates bribed slaves to make unfounded allegations against him, and Siricius was elected pope instead.

Jerome defended himself energetically, but though he won his case, he had to leave Rome. He went back to Palestine. He settled in a cave in Bethlehem next to the cave of the Nativity until he became abbot of a monastery founded by Paula, one of the wealthy Roman noblewomen whose spiritual direction he had undertaken. He remained there, writing his translations and commentaries, until his death in 420.

Many paintings, including a celebrated one by Albrecht Dürer, show 'St Jerome in a rocky landscape', with a cardinal's hat and an attendant lion. In fact, there were no cardinals in Jerome's day, and the artistic consensus is that Dürer (1471–1528) had never seen a lion, since the animal is a large dog with a cat's face. Jerome did not live as a hermit in Bethlehem, but worked in collaboration with a group of literary assistants, transcribers and copyists. He is widely considered to be the most eloquent and scholarly of the four Latin Doctors of the Church, the others being *Ambrose, *Augustine of Hippo and *Gregory the Great.

F. X. Murphy, ed., *A Monument to St Jerome* (1952); H. F. D. Sparks, 'Jerome as Biblical Scholar', in *The Cambridge History of the Bible*, 1 (1970), pp. 510–41; J. N. D. Kelly (1975); Works in *P.L.*, vols 22–30; Eng. trans. in *N.P.N.F.*, vol. 6; *Later Christian Fathers*, pp. 187–90.

October

1. Remigius (d. 533)

Remigius or Rémi was bishop of Rheims during the reign of Clovis I, king of the Franks. He is best known for the part he played in the conversion of Clovis. This led to the acceptance of Christianity throughout the Frankish kingdom, and Remigius is known as 'the apostle of the Franks'.

Clovis was a battle-hungry heathen, but his wife Clothilde was a Christian who relied on the spiritual guidance of Bishop Remigius. When her first son was born, she insisted on having him baptized – and the child died. When her second child was born, she risked Clovis's wrath by again insisting on baptism. There was alarm in the court when this baby also became ill, but Clothilde stood firm, and the child survived. Clovis was fighting the German tribes, and when he was hard pressed, he prayed to 'Clothilde's God', promising that if he was victorious, he would become a Christian.

His troops won the day, and he was as good as his word. Clothilde asked Remigius to come and instruct the king in the Christian faith. Remigius undertook this personally, and told Clovis the whole story of the life of Christ. Clovis was amazed at his account of 'this unarmed God who was not of the race of Thor or Odin'. When Remigius came to the Crucifixion, Clovis said, 'Hah. Had I and my faithful Franks been there, the Jews had not dared to do it.' So, in the words of Remigius, the king came 'to adore what he had burnt and to burn what he had adored'.

In 496, Remigius baptized the king in Rheims cathedral in a splendid ceremony. There were banners and processions in the streets, the cathedral was draped in white, and Clovis went forward to his baptism in clouds of incense, surrounded by a forest of perfumed tapers. The fifteen-hundredth anniversary of this occasion was celebrated by a papal Mass in Rheims cathedral on 22 September 1996.

Clovis's family and three thousand of his faithful Franks also became Christians. Under the king's protection, Remigius was able to establish bishoprics and to build churches, and Gaul became Christian. At this time, the other kings in Italy, France, Spain and North Africa were all Arians, so Clovis became the only monarch in Europe to uphold the Athanasian Creed. Remigius died in Rheims on 13 January 533.

AA.SS., Oct., 1, pp. 59–187; E. d'Avenay (Lille, 1896); A. Haudecoeur (1896); Gregory of Tours, *History of the Franks*, trans. and intro. H. M. Dalton (1967), 2, pp. 67–9, 88, 102, 106; *P.B.*, 9, pp. 587–93; Lewis Thorpe (1974), pp. 163–4; H. Leclercq in *D.A.C.L.*, 14, 2, cols 2231–7. For background, see Edward James, *The Franks* (1988).

Anthony Ashley Cooper (7th Earl of Shaftesbury) (1801–85)
[Commem.]

The first-born sons of the earls of Shaftesbury have traditionally received the names of Anthony Ashley, and borne the title of Lord Ashley while their fathers held the earldom. The commemoration on this day refers to the Lord Ashley who succeeded as the seventh earl in 1851.

He was born in 1801, lived until 1885, and was a man of very strong convictions: a fervent Christian who strongly attacked both the Tractarians and the Salvation Army; an aristocrat who was happiest in the company of pickpockets and shoeblacks; a Conservative who fought for social reform, but opposed trade unions and the extension of the franchise; the landlord of a huge estate who could not afford to repair his labourers' cottages; a shy and reserved man who drew thousands of the poor to him in sheer affection, refused a post at court, and told Queen Victoria to her face that she should not take the title of Empress of India.

He had a very unhappy childhood. His parents took the view that 'to render a child obedient, it should be in constant fear of its father and mother', and his only solace was the love of an elderly servant, Maria Millis, who taught him her own strict Evangelical faith. He wasted his time at Harrow, but worked at Oxford, and took a First in

Classics. At the age of twenty-five, he became a member of parliament in the unreformed House of Commons, taking the pocket borough of his uncle the duke of Marlborough.

For nearly all of the next sixty years, until his health failed, he was involved in legislation to improve the condition of lunatics, to prevent the abuse of women and children in the factories and the mines, to protect the 'climbing boys' or chimney-sweeps, and to improve public health in the disease-ridden towns. This parliamentary activity – the long hours of debate, the speeches, the investigations, the drafting of new laws, the endless committees and membership of regulatory bodies – he felt to be his public duty; but he was equally active in the Church and in the field of voluntary social service. He was the leader of the Evangelical movement in Parliament. He chaired the Lord's Day Observance Society, supported the foundation of SPCK and the YMCA, took part in Evangelical rallies, and whole-heartedly opposed Christians with different views. He went once to St Alban's church in Holborn, and described its Anglo-Catholic ritual as 'the worship of Jupiter and Juno'. He was equally horrified when the archbishop of Canterbury sent William and Catherine Booth the sum of £5, commenting that 'the Salvation Army' was 'a haughty title', and that religion could not be made 'easy and jocular'. When Lord Palmerston became prime minister in 1855, knowing little or nothing of ecclesiastical affairs, he turned to Shaftesbury, to whom his wife was related by marriage, for advice on appointments. In the following ten years, Shaftesbury virtually appointed five archbishops, twenty bishops and thirteen cathedral deans, all Evangelicals. The 'Puseyites' were outraged, and Bishop Wilberforce called them all 'wicked appointments'.

But if Shaftesbury's mind was closed on ecclesiastical issues, his heart was wide open to suffering. His work with the Ragged Schools, with the training and education of homeless children in the National Refuges, later called the Shaftesbury Homes (the training ship was the Arethusa), with the regulation of common lodging houses, the protection of young girls, and many other causes, was tireless. He wrote in his diary, 'I cannot bear to leave the world with all the misery in it.' At his funeral in 1885, over two hundred voluntary associations with which he had worked were represented, as well as the great and powerful, and the poor of London lined the streets to watch his coffin pass.

E. Hodder, *The Life and Times of the Seventh Earl of Shaftesbury, K.G.* (3 vols, 1886); J. L. and Barbara Hammond, *Shaftesbury* (1923, repr. Penguin, 1939). *Victorian Church*, 1, pp. 440–55, 468–75.

4. Francis of Assisi (1181–1226)   [L.F.]

Francis was the son of a wealthy cloth merchant of Assisi, brought up to follow his father in the business. He had little formal education, and probably started buying and selling cloth when he was in his mid-teens. He lived the life of a young man about town, spending lavishly – though it was noted that he was always generous to the poor. At the age of twenty, he took up arms when Assisi went to war with Perugia, and was a prisoner of war for a year. Afterwards, he was seriously ill: his experiences had scarred him deeply. He had a dream in which he was told, 'Follow the master, and not the man.' When he met a leper, he dismounted from his horse, gave the man some gold, and kissed his hand. He said afterwards that this was the moment at which he 'left the world'.

Some time later, he was praying at the church of San Damiano in Assisi when he heard a voice telling him to repair the church. He set to work, and sold some of his father's cloth to help raise the money. For his father, this was clearly the last straw. He took this recalcitrant son before the bishop of Assisi to recover the money. The bishop told Francis that he must return his father's property, and there ensued one of the most dramatic father-and-son conflicts ever recorded. Francis returned the money, then stripped off his clothes, threw them before his father, and renounced his inheritance.

For two years, he wandered about Assisi begging alms for the poor, and spent much of his time re-building three churches in the city – San Damiano, San Petro and the Portiuncula. While at Mass in 1208, he heard the Gospel reading of Christ's sending out the disciples without money or luggage or shoes (Matthew 10:5–20): he took it literally, and began to preach the original Christian message in a world grown complex, venial and violent.

Other men came to join him – a prosperous merchant, a canon of the cathedral. When there were about a dozen, they called themselves 'the lesser brothers', or *fratri minori*, hence their present title of Friars Minor. Francis drew up a Rule, and took it to Rome for approval. He always worked within the structure of the Church: he did not protest

at institutional structures, but appealed directly to the human heart.
• He was made deacon, but he had such a respect for the priesthood that he never became a priest. He founded an Order for women with *Clare of Assisi. He also developed an Order of Tertiaries: people of both sexes who would live 'in the world', but accept a framework of prayer and commitment for a deeper spiritual life.

The movement grew rapidly. By 1220, there were over five thousand friars, divided into provinces and held together by an annual Chapter. When Anthony of Padua first encountered the Franciscans at the Great Chapter of 1221, he found Brother Elias in the chair, and Francis, still a deacon, sitting humbly at his feet. Francis was involved in the framing of a more detailed Rule, approved by Pope Honorius III in 1222, but he had no wish to be treated as a celebrated founder.

He had a very strong sense of mission. In 1212, he attempted to go to the Holy Land and preach to the Saracens, but his ship was wrecked before it left the Adriatic. In 1214, he set out for Morocco, but became ill in Spain, and had to return to Assisi. In 1219, he went to Egypt, where a force of Crusaders was besieging Damietta; but he thought the Crusaders much in need of Christian teaching, while the Sultan received him most courteously and allowed him to preach. The first Franciscan martyrs died in Morocco in 1227, and later there was a strong Franciscan presence in China and the Far East. Francis was only forty-five when he died. He was buried in the church at San Damiano – now the magnificent basilica damaged by an earthquake in 1998.

Popular devotion to Francis has sometimes been sentimental, seeing him only as a gentle and loveable character who talked to the birds, tamed a wolf, wrote the *Fioretti*, or 'The Little Flowers of St Francis', and was on familiar terms with Brother Son and Sister Moon, rather than as the founder of a world-wide missionary movement. The popular 'Prayer of St Francis' is a compilation, though some of the phrases are his.

AA.SS., Oct., 2, contains the two Lives by Thomas of Celano, which provide the best contemporary accounts. For modern accounts, see J. R. H. Moorman, *Richest of Poor Men: the Spirituality of St Francis of Assisi* (1977); R. D. Sorrell, *St Francis of Assisi and Nature* (1988). Works trans. and ed. L. Sherley-Price (1959); B. Fahy (1964). *The Little Flowers of St Francis* is available in several editions.

6. William Tyndale (c.1494–1536)   [L.F.]

Tyndale came from the borders of Wales, and is thought to have been born some time after 1490. He studied at both Oxford and Cambridge, and complained that scholars were steeped in 'heathen learning' and taught false principles by which they were 'clean shut out of the understanding of the Scriptures'. There were partial translations of the Bible into the vernacular, such as those of John Wyclif, but they had all been taken from the Latin Vulgate, based on *Jerome's work of many centuries earlier. Tyndale's aim was to make a translation direct from the Greek into English. When clergy told him that this was forbidden, he told them that he 'cared not for the pope's laws', but that he would 'cause a boy that driveth the plow' to know more of the Bible than they did.

He took his project to Cuthbert Tunstall, bishop of London, but was rebuffed. In 1524 he went to Germany to work with Reformation scholars. Their life was hazardous, and he had to move from place to place to evade capture; but he worked steadily on his text. He met *Martin Luther at Wittenberg, and absorbed his ideas. He supplemented his own knowledge of New Testament Greek with Erasmus's translations from Greek into Latin and Luther's translations from Latin into German. His versions of the Gospels according to *Matthew and *Mark were printed in Cologne, but the printer's shop was raided, and he had a narrow escape. The whole text was printed in Worms in 1526, under a pseudonym, though his identity was soon discovered. Copies were smuggled into England, where they caused an uproar. Lollards and Lutherans were still being energetically hunted down and imprisoned. Bishop Tunstall denounced Tyndall's text, and copies were publicly burned in Cardinal Wolsey's great book-burning of 1526. Tyndale had translated *presbyterus* as 'senior' or 'elder' rather than 'bishop', *ecclesia* as 'congregation', not 'church', and *caritas* as 'love', not 'charity'.

Tyndale had been learning Hebrew for some years. In 1530–1, he published his translation of the Pentateuch, the first five books of the Old Testament. This was revised in 1534, and one copy, inscribed on vellum, went to Anne Boleyn, who was known to have Protestant sympathies, about the time of her coronation as Queen of England.

Tyndale laboured over his work, believing that the Scriptures were the one source of truth in a confused and contradictory world. He met

Miles Coverdale, who was making his own translations, but for the most part he worked alone. He was known as 'a man very frugal and spare of body, a great student, an earnest labourer in the setting forth of the Scriptures of God'. For the last few months of his life, he found a safe haven in the English House at Antwerp, with the merchants who enjoyed some immunities from arrest; but in May 1535 he was lured out of safety, charged with heresy, and imprisoned in the great castle-prison of Vilvorde, near Brussels. There is a letter extant in which he asks for warm clothes to keep out the cold and damp, and for his Hebrew Bible, grammar and dictionary, so that he can continue his studies. In August 1536, he was condemned and delivered to the secular authorities. On 6 October, he was placed on a pyre, strangled and then burned. John Foxe says that his last words were 'Lord, open the king of England's eyes.'

Within a few years of his death, his work was accepted and celebrated in his own country. Cranmer's Great Bible of 1539 was a combination of the work of Coverdale and Tyndale. Coverdale, who survived persecution, undertook the final revision. The Old Testament text was Tyndale's as far as II Chronicles, then Coverdale's. Some marginal comments, such as 'There is a lesson for the pope' written against a passage in Exodus were removed. The New Testament was entirely Tyndale's. Tyndale wrote in plain, vigorous English, very different from the stilted, latinized prose of the academics of his day: he was writing for the laity. It is generally agreed by biblical scholars that he was responsible for most of the New Testament and some of the Old Testament work for the Authorized Version of the Bible of 1611. He gave theologians words like 'passover', 'atonement' and 'mercy seat'. He gave the English people the first printed version of the New Testament in their own language, with a matchless sense of poetry and cadence. His translation of the opening of 1 Corinthians 13 is: 'Though I spake with the tonges of men and angels, and yet had no love, I were even as sounding brasse: or as a tynklynge Cymball.'

Foxe, pp. 117–31. Lives by R. Demaus (1886); J. Mozley (1937); S. L. Greenslade (1938); G. M. Houghton (1985). Loane, pp. 45–85. *D.N.B.*, 19, pp. 1351–8. Works: Parker Society edition, ed. and intro. G. E. Duffield (1964–). N.T. published as *The newe Testament of our Savyoure Jesus Christ* (1549); facsimile edition, The British Library (2000).

9. Denys of Paris and his Companions (d. *c*.250) [*Commem.*]

Denys is thought to have been an Italian, one of six missionary bishops sent to evangelize Gaul towards the middle of the third century. He and two companions, a priest named Rusticus and a deacon named Eleutherius, established a Christian centre on an island in the Seine, and began their work of converting the local population; but they were captured by a pagan tribe, imprisoned for a long period, and finally beheaded. Their bodies were thrown into the Seine, but recovered by Christians, and buried on their island.

In the seventh century, the Merovingian king Dagobert built the abbey of Saint-Denis over their graves. This became the burial-place of the French kings, and for some centuries the place where they were crowned: the importance of capturing Saint-Denis so that the coronation of the Dauphin could take place is stressed in the historical records of *Joan of Arc.

In order to spread the fame of his patron, a ninth-century abbot of Saint-Denys, Hilduin, wrote a work entitled *Areopagitica*, in which he identified Saint Denys with Dionysius the Areopagite, converted by St Paul at Athens (Acts 17:13–34), claiming that the first-century *Pope Clement had sent him to convert France. French hagiography is particularly rich in claims of first-century links with the apostles (see *Mary, Martha and Lazarus). Hilduin then identified this compound personality with Pseudo-Dionysius, the fifth-century neo-Platonist philosopher. This conflation of three distinct traditions was embellished with legends about the death of the martyr, and became immensely popular, but is totally lacking in historical foundation.

Denys is commemorated as the first bishop of Paris and the principal patron of France.

AA.SS., Oct., 4, pp. 865–987; D.A.C.L., 4, cols 558–606 (H. Leclercq); O.D.C.C., p. 105; D.H.G.E., 14, 263–5. For the legends, see P.B., 12, pp. 192–208.

Robert Grosseteste (*c*.1170–1253)   [*Commem.*]

Very little is known about the life of this remarkable theologian and scholar before he became bishop of Lincoln in 1235, when he was well over sixty years of age. Historians agree that he was of humble birth, and born in Suffolk. He had a sister named Juetta, who became a nun.

He was a clerk in the households of the bishops of Lincoln and Hereford (which would have given him access to great libraries). He studied at Lincoln, possibly Cambridge, possibly Oxford, and then somewhere in France, probably not Paris, during the papal interdict of 1209-13. He went (or returned) to Oxford about 1225 to teach theology at the newly established Franciscan house of studies, and had an astonishing literary output. He translated Greek classical and theological works, produced biblical commentaries, wrote on astronomy, and natural science, and studied canon law and medicine. His work excited the admiration and imitation of that later thirteenth-century Oxford polymath, Friar Roger Bacon.

• Grosseteste was elected chancellor of the University of Oxford, and held many preferments; but when he was appointed bishop of Lincoln, he resigned all his other offices, and devoted the remainder of his life to attacking abuses in the Church. Power came to him late in life, and he used it. Lincoln was the largest and richest diocese in England, and it gave him an excellent platform. He proceeded to do battle with lax or absentee diocesan clergy, the monasteries, the cathedral clergy, the English judicial system, and the ecclesiastical authorities in Rome.

He investigated everything, and he was nothing if not thorough. He made an extensive visitation of his whole diocese, and in 1240-3 drew up his *Constitutions*, which told the parish clergy in great detail what they must know and do. This was not unusual for a conscientious diocesan, but Grosseteste wanted immediate results: he was not prepared to tolerate delay or compromise. He rigorously visited monasteries and convents in his diocese, alarming monks and nuns, according to the chronicler Matthew Paris, by his search for evidence of sinful behaviour. He embarked on reform of the cathedral chapter. When the dean and chapter contended that they were independent of episcopal jurisdiction, he took the matter to Rome, and obtained a papal Bull in 1245 which gave him the power he wanted.

He believed that 'the sacerdotal power is greater and more dignified than all secular power'. In 1237 he urged the papal legate, Otto, to demand ecclesiastical liberties from King Henry III. He took the rigorist view that ecclesiastics should not hold any office of state, and that the ecclesiastical courts should be totally free from all secular interference. There were constant battles with the secular authorities over benefit of clergy (which gave some fairly dubious people the right to have their cases remitted to the ecclesiastical courts), over appointments to benefices and the payment of tithes, and other issues.

Grosseteste argued that the king 'impedes and perturbs the ecclesiastical process . . . to the great detriment of souls'. His list of grievances grew, and was repeatedly expressed.

In 1250, Grosseteste went to the Council of Lyons, and delivered before Pope Innocent IV and the cardinals a stinging condemnation of the abuse of power by Rome, describing the 'diminution in the numbers of good shepherds of souls, the increase of wicked shepherds, and the circumscription of pastoral authority and power'. The result was 'unbelief, division, heresy and vice', and the responsibility lay with the Roman Curia, which granted English benefices to Romans who drew the revenues but left the care of souls to poorly paid English curates, 'handing over many thousands of souls to eternal death'. The result of this speech was a temporary suspension from his bishopric, and a continuing threat of excommunication.

In the last year of his life, Grosseteste was told to promote the pope's nephew to a canonry. He refused. It is not clear whether Innocent IV actually excommunicated him, but he continued to administer his bishopric until his death on 9 October 1253 at Buckden, near Huntingdon. A century later, *John Wyclif and the Lollards saw him as a heroic anti-papal figure. Foxe's *Book of Martyrs* celebrated him as 'the great mauler of the Romans', and in the nineteenth century the constitutional historian Bishop Stubbs, who read his own Victorian ideal of democracy back into many mediaeval texts, regarded him as a champion of the liberties of the Church. Among more recent historians, some regard him as a central figure in the development of thirteenth-century ecclesiastical thought, while others have stressed his tempestuous unorthodoxy; but there is general agreement that he was a man of great intellectual power and original thought who abandoned prudence in his later years for devastatingly plain speaking on the authority and responsibilities of the priesthood.

There are no reliable contemporary biographies. Of the modern studies, B. C. Boulter, *Robert Grosseteste: the Defender of our Church and Liberties* (1936) is now very dated. *Robert Grosseteste, Scholar and Bishop: Essays in Commemoration of the Seventh Century of his Death*, ed. D. A. Callus (1953), takes the 'Powicke' or consensual view: see Powicke, pp. 70–2, 450–66. J. McEvoy, *The Philosophy of Robert Grosseteste* (1982) and R. W. Southern, *Robert Grosseteste: the Growth of an English Mind in Mediaeval Europe* (1986, repr. 1988) stress the originality of Grosseteste's thinking. Both contain full bibliographies. Works: S. Harrison Thomson, ed., *The Writings of Robert Grosseteste* (1940).

10. Paulinus, Bishop of York (d. 644) [L.F.]

Paulinus came to England with the second party of the Augustinian mission, headed by *Mellitus, in 601. At that time, *Augustine was established in Canterbury, but had not extended his work outside Kent. In subsequent years, the mission developed in the south of England and East Anglia, but the north remained unknown and unexplored territory.

An opportunity to extend the mission came when King Edwin of Northumbria sent emissaries to the king of the Kentish folk asking for the hand of his sister, Aethelburh or Ethelburga, in marriage. He received the reply that 'it was not permissible for a Christian maiden to be given in marriage to a heathen husband, lest Christ and his sacraments be profaned by her association with a king who was wholly ignorant of the worship of the true God'. Edwin agreed to allow Ethelburga and her household to practise their faith, and to accept it himself if 'on examination, his advisers decided that it appeared more holy and acceptable to God than their own'. His bride went north accompanied by Paulinus, who had been consecrated bishop (not yet archbishop) of York. The date is disputed: though her marriage was traditionally thought to have taken place in 625, there is some evidence that it may have been as early as 619. Edwin, a thoughtful and honourable man, held a council of wise men, and after much discussion, he and all his household were baptized. Among them was the thirteen-year-old *Hilda, future abbess of Whitby. Many of the nobility and their households followed suit. The Latin monks put their case so well that Coifi, the chief priest, destroyed all his own altars and also became a Christian.

A wooden church was hastily built at York, and dedicated to St Peter. Edwin determined to build a stone church, a worthy centre for the northern province, and the walls began to rise round the small wooden building. Missions were undertaken in places which have been identified as Doncaster, Leeds and Catterick, and across the Humber into Lincolnshire. A stone church of fine workmanship was built in Lincoln.

Edwin's territories became peaceful and law-abiding, and the Church became well established; but in 633, disaster came when Edwin was killed in battle at Hatfield Chase, and the pagan forces of Penda of Mercia and Cadwalla of Wales ravaged the area. There were appalling massacres. Paulinus escorted Ethelburga and her daughter back to Kent, and became bishop of Rochester. Only his assistant, *James the Deacon, stayed in the north.

A year later, Christianity came back to Northumbria, but in a different form, with the accession of *King Oswald, who called on the Celtic monks of Iona to establish a mission; but the Latin mission established by Paulinus was not resumed until after the Synod of Whitby in 664.

Bede, *H.E.*, bk 2, chs 9—20; bk 3, ch. 14; Stenton, pp. 113–16; D. P. Kirby, 'Bede and Northumbrian Chronology', *English Historical Review*, 88 (1963), pp. 514–27; Mayr-Harting, pp. 66–8, 75–6; *N.C.E.*, 11, p. 29.

Thomas Traherne (?1636–74)   *[Commem.]*

The literary scholar Bertram Dobell said of Traherne in 1903, 'The centuries had drawn their curtains around him.' He was almost unknown until Dobell undertook critical analysis of a hand-written manuscript of poems found on a London bookstall, and purchased for a few pence. The poems were at first attributed to Traherne's near contemporary, Henry Vaughan, who is often rated as the best of the later metaphysical poets, but analysis of the author's ideas, rhythms and use of words in comparison with two prose works of Traherne, then known only as an obscure seventeenth-century divine, was convincing evidence that Traherne was the author. The discovery that one poem was repeated in two of the prose works was conclusive. The poems were published by Dobell in 1903, and since then, Traherne's prose works have also been revaluated.

Traherne, the son of a shoemaker, was probably born in Hereford or Ledbury. He went to the local grammar school in Hereford. He proceeded to Brasenose College, Oxford, took Holy Orders, and became curate, perhaps later vicar, of Credenhill. He ministered there for nine and a half years before Sir Orlando Bridgman, a prominent lawyer and statesman, was appointed Lord Keeper of the Seals to Charles II, and invited him to become his private chaplain. He must have met many famous people at court (that inveterate gossip John Aubrey knew him), but when Sir Orlando fell from favour he retired to his private estates at Teddington, taking Traherne with him. Traherne died at Teddington three months after his patron, at the age of about thirty-eight or -nine.

Traherne, like other religious poets of the time, was overwhelmed by the majesty and grandeur of the universe being revealed by science. He writes of mankind coming into the inheritance which God has provided: 'You never enjoy the world aright until the sea floweth in your veins, till you are clothed with the heavens and crowned with the stars . . . till you delight in God for being good to all, you never enjoy the world'. He writes (long before Rousseau or Wordsworth) about the innocent wonder of childhood, and the way in which it is corrupted by the 'customs and manners' of the world: 'It was a difficult matter to persuade me that the tinseled ware upon a hobby horse was a fine thing. . . . And to teach me that a purse of gold was at any value seemed impossible.'

Some commentators have suggested that Traherne was influenced by neo-Platonism or Gnosticism in his rejection of the material world; or that he was a Pelagian because he emphasized the innocence of childhood, and thereby denied the doctrine of original sin; but such ideas were common currency among philosophers and divines in the seventeenth century, and they do not invalidate the intensity and beauty of his vision of the glory of the Creator, manifest in his works.

B. Dobell, ed., *The Poetical Works of Thomas Traherne, B.D., now first published from the Original Manuscript, with a Memoir of the Author* (1903); G. I. Wade's Life (1944) includes a bibliography of criticism. Dick Davis, ed., *Thomas Traherne: selected writings* (1980, 1988). Prose works of Thomas Traherne: *Centuries of Meditations*, parts of which were previously known in anthologies; ed. B. Dobell (1908); *Roman Forgeries* (1673); *Christian Ethicks* (1675).

11. Ethelburga of Barking (d. *c.*675)   *[Commem.]*

Ethelburga was the sister of Erconwald, whom *Theodore of Tarsus appointed bishop of the East Saxons, with the city of London as his see. They were probably of noble blood, and there is a tradition that they were members of the royal family. Before he became bishop, Erconwald had built two monasteries, one at Chertsey for himself, and one at Berecingum or Barking for his sister. The monastery at Barking was a double monastery (see *Hilda of Whitby), and Ethelburga was installed as abbess and head of both communities. This may have been her introduction to monastic life, for it is said that Erconwald appointed a French nun as prioress, to teach her the Benedictine tradition. *Bede knew of her, and recorded that she 'always bore herself in a manner worthy of her brother the bishop, upright of life and constantly planning for the needs of her community'. He says of her death, 'God's beloved Ethelburga, the Mother of the Community, was set free from her bodily prison. And none who knew her holy life can doubt that when she departed this life the gates of our heavenly home opened to her.'

Though little is now known about her life, there are traces of a liturgical cult, as her name appears in some mediaeval calendars of saints and prayers.

Bede, *H.E.*, bk 4, chs 6 and 9; *AA.SS.*, Oct., 5, pp. 648–72 ; the Life by Goscelin of Canterbury is published in *Anal.Boll.* 58 (1940), pp. 101–6. See also *Butler*, Oct., p. 81.

James the Deacon (seventh century)   *[Commem.]*

There is no information available on when James the Deacon was born, or where he came from. Since he came to England with *Paulinus in 601, he was probably Italian, and probably from a Roman monastery. He assisted Paulinus during his time in the north of England, and was very energetic and active in conversion. When Paulinus went south after the death of King Edwin in 633, he stayed and managed to survive the year of bloodshed which followed. He may have been living outside York: one of the regular places for baptisms was on the River Swale, near Catterick, and *Bede says that a village near Catterick bore his name.

When the Celtic monks from Lindisfarne came to Northumbria, James simply carried on quietly with his own ministry in Swaledale, keeping to the Latin rite, and singing Gregorian chant. He 'kept the true and Catholic date of Easter with all whom he could persuade to adopt the right observance'. He seems to have been the only chanter in the north of England until *Wilfrid brought Eddi (Eddius Stephanus), and *Benedict Biscop brought John the Chanter from Rome.

More than thirty years later, James, by that time a very old man, was present at the Synod of Whitby. It must have been like coming home. He was the only one of Paulinus' original party of thirty to see their work restored in the northern province.

Bede, *H.E.*, bk 2, chs 16, 20; bk 3, ch. 25; bk 4, ch. 2. *Men.E.W.*, pp. 302–3; Mayr-Harting, p. 42; *O.D.S.*, pp. 249–50.

12. Wilfrid (*c*.633–709) [L.F.]

*Bede says of Wilfrid that he was 'the first bishop of English blood to teach the Church of the English the Catholic way of life'. He was the son of a Northumbrian nobleman. He went to Lindisfarne at the age of fourteen, and studied there for about four years before deciding to make a pilgrimage to Rome. At the court of the king of Kent, he met *Benedict Biscop, and the two young men travelled across France together, staying in monasteries. At Lyons, they parted company: they were very different in temperament. Wilfrid was greatly impressed by the status and magnificence of the Frankish bishops, so different from the homespun and simple ways of the Celtic bishops. He visited Rome, but spent most of the long period of his absence from England with Bishop Annemundus of Lyons, who ordained him.

When he returned to Northumbria, Wilfrid became abbot of Ripon, where he introduced the Benedictine Rule and the Latin date of Easter. At the Synod of Whitby in 664, he must have been one of the younger participants, but he was asked to speak for the Latin case, and he seized his opportunity. He poured scorn on the traditions of *Columba and the Celtic monks, and asked whether these few men on a small, remote island could set themselves up against *Peter, the Prince of the Apostles, to whom Christ had committed his Church. He successfully led the case for the introduction of the Latin rite and Latin practices against his former teachers.

He was appointed bishop of York, and went to Gaul to be consecrated. Twelve Frankish bishops participated, and in a magnificent ceremony [Wilfrid was carried into the sanctuary shoulder-high in a golden chair.] He was away for a year or more on this occasion, and he returned to find that *Chad, abbot of Lastingham, had been nominated in his place by *King Oswald of Northumbria, and consecrated by English bishops. Wilfrid retired to Ripon for a time, and appealed to the pope. The pope supported him, but it is not clear what happened next: some writers follow Eddi, Wilfrid's companion and very partisan biographer, in insisting that he was fully restored to the control of the whole of Northumbria from York to the Scottish border on the pope's command. Others are equally insistent that he was unacceptable in Northumbria, and spent most of his time travelling elsewhere. *Theodore of Tarsus, archbishop of Canterbury, divided the Northumbrian diocese into three in 678, and into five in 681, leaving

Wilfrid with only a very small diocese. He appealed to the pope again, and went to Rome himself. He was shipwrecked off the coast of Frisia (now Holland), Bede says that he was 'honourably received by the barbarous people' and spent a year converting the Frisians.

When he returned with the pope's approval, King Egfrith of Northumbria not only refused to accept the decision, but had Wilfrid cast into a very unpleasant prison. He was only freed on his promise to leave the kingdom. He was reinstated for a time, but after a series of disputes with the new king of Northumbria, Aldfrith, he went to Mercia, and acted as a bishop in the Leicester area. In 703, a synod presided over by Theodore's successor as archbishop of Canterbury decreed that he should resign his see. Again he appealed to the pope, but had to accept the small diocese of Hexham, keeping control of the monasteries which he had set up in various parts of the country. He died at the age of seventy-six in a monastery at Oundle.

Wilfrid's life was a stormy one: he attracted loyal followers, including some who followed him on his many travels, but he also stirred up determined opposition. He lived, like the Frankish bishops he admired, as a prince of the Church, with a large household, a bevy of retainers and extensive patronage. He amassed a large fortune, and left some of his wealth to the abbots of his monasteries 'so that they could purchase the friendship of kings and bishops'.

The English Church has never found Wilfrid a sympathetic character. He was too worldly, too ambitious, too closely tied to Rome; but he was a pioneer, a man of much energy and vision; and we may wonder what would have become of the English Church if the decision had gone the other way at Whitby.

Eddius Stephanus, *passim*; Bede, *H.E.*, bk 3, chs 13, 25, 28; bk 4, chs 2, 5, 13, 15, 19; J. Godfrey, *The Church in Anglo-Saxon England* (1962); many refs in Mayr-Harting, esp. pp. 107–87; *O.D.S.*, pp. 492–4; *D.N.B.*, 1, pp. 1324–6.

Elizabeth Fry (1780–1845)   [*Commem.*]

By the late years of the eighteenth century, the Quakers, rebels and zealots in *George Fox's time, had become highly respected and often very prosperous members of the community. Elizabeth was one of the seven daughters of the banker Joseph Gurney of Earlham Hall in

Norfolk. She went through a conversion experience when she heard an American visiting preacher, William Savery, address one of the Norwich Meetings. She wrote in her journal, 'I have *felt* there is a GOD.'

She married Joseph Fry, a member of another banking family, when she was twenty. The Frys were 'plain Quakers', who kept to the sober Quaker dress, used the distinctive Quaker speech of 'thee' and 'thou', and disapproved of music, dancing, cards and theatres. For some years, Elizabeth was absorbed in child-bearing – the Frys had eleven children in all – and in running a large London household close to the Bank of England and the Guildhall. In 1811, she became a Quaker preacher. One of her sisters married Fowell Buxton, and another married Samuel Hoare. Both men were members of the Clapham Sect (see *Venn, *Wilberforce), bankers, members of parliament and prison reformers. It was with Anna Buxton that she first visited the women's section of Newgate prison in 1813. She was shocked at the state of women 'reduced to the level of wild beasts'; but she talked to them, and found them responsive. Perhaps her Quaker dress and her gentle, old-fashioned speech helped.

Four more years passed before she was able to get permission to go into Newgate to set up a school for the children of prisoners and for juveniles. She met the governor of Newgate, and the two sheriffs of London. They were unanimous that a lady could not work with these incorrigible and degraded females. She used quiet persistence; the women asked for her to be allowed to help them, and at last a school was set up for the children, with a paid teacher. Then the women prisoners asked for occupation and employment for themselves. Elizabeth pressed for the setting up of a workshop, and for a woman matron to be employed. Her requests were brushed aside until Joseph Fry supported his wife by inviting the governor and the two sheriffs to dinner. The evident wealth and social standing of the Frys made its impression, and permission was given. Elizabeth organized the women into groups, each with a monitor elected by themselves, and obtained materials for sewing and knitting. She read the Bible to them, and they listened. The Governor was so impressed with the results that he found better accommodation, and had it whitewashed and fitted out as a workroom.

Elizabeth found outlets through her Quaker connections for the goods made by the prisoners, and noted in her diary, 'Already, from being wild beasts, they appear harmless and kind.' In February 1818, she was called upon to give evidence to a Select Committee of the House of Commons on London Prisons. She gave her evidence quietly and composedly, insisting that there should be separate women's prisons, with women staff, proper employment and recreation. This was the first of many contacts with ministers and members of parliament, in which she became the leading expert on women prisoners.

She found much more to do. She visited and organized the convict ships which carried women prisoners to the colonies, and persuaded the governor not to send the women to the docks shackled, in open carts. She asked what happened to them when they arrived in Australia, and was instrumental in ensuring that there was proper accommodation for them. She sat with women condemned to death through their last hours, and prayed with them. She started a 'nightly shelter for the homeless' in London, where both men and women could find bread and soup and simple accommodation for the night. She made recommendations for the care and occupation of women patients in the county asylums which were then being built. She visited France and Germany, and was listened to with respect and admiration by social reformers in these countries. She went to Kaiserswerth (see *Elizabeth Ferrard), where Pastor Fliedner adopted her prison visiting system, and taught her in return his own techniques for training teachers and nurses. When she returned to England in 1840, she made plans for a nurses' training establishment in London. *Florence Nightingale took several Fry nurses to Scutari with her in 1854.

Elizabeth led a very busy life – supporting her husband, bearing and raising her children, managing a large establishment, acting as a London hostess. Her deep and sincere Christian commitment and her ability to relate to poor and vulnerable women gave her life another dimension as a pioneer of social reform.

Memoirs by her daughter, R. E. Cresswell (1845 and 1847), and by Thomas Timpson (1847). Georgina K. Lewis (1903); Janet Whitney, *Elizabeth Fry, Quaker Heroine* (1937); W. Monro (1940); P. Pringle, *The Prisoner's Friend* (1953); J. H. Kent (1962); S. Pitcher, *The Making of a Social Worker* (1987); *Far Above Rubies*, pp. 227–37.

Edith Cavell (1865–1915)   [*Commem.*]

Edith was the eldest daughter of the Revd Frank Cavell, vicar of Swardeston, Norfolk. She was educated at home, at school in

Somerset, and in Brussels. When she inherited what is described as 'a modest competence', she travelled on the Continent, and visited a free hospital in Bavaria, where she established a fund for medical instruments. In 1895, at the age of thirty, she enrolled as a probationer at the London Hospital, qualified, and became a staff nurse before moving to Poor Law nursing in Highgate and Shoreditch infirmaries in London.

She had kept her links with Brussels, and in 1906 she moved there to help in setting up a new training school for nurses on the English pattern with a Dr Depage. This became the Berkendael Medical Institute, which was given official recognition and state funding by the Belgian government. In 1907, she became the matron.

In August 1914, the Germans invaded Belgium. Dr Depage went away to organize military hospitals, and Edith was left to run a Red Cross hospital under German occupation. The hospital accepted wounded French, Belgians, British and Germans alike. Edith helped Allied soldiers who had been cut off from their units in the retreat to escape: they faced summary execution if caught by the German military administration. On 5 August 1915, she was arrested and court-martialled.

The United States was a neutral power. The American ambassador in Brussels made repeated representations on her behalf, protesting that the trial took place in German, with only a French interpreter, but she was found guilty, allegedly on the basis of a confession that she had helped 130 men of military age to escape, and thus to go back to the front. Had she been charged with merely *attempting* to 'conduct soldiers to the enemy', that would have been a comparatively minor offence. It is not clear whether she confessed freely in the conviction that she was morally in the right, whether she was confused by language difficulties, or whether nine weeks of solitary confinement when no adviser was allowed to visit her led her to make the admission; but at the trial, she said openly that she had received letters of thanks from men who had escaped to freedom. The sentence was death.

The US legation was given three hours' notice that she was to be executed at two o'clock in the morning, and Edith Cavell faced a firing squad. In Britain, her death was regarded as an atrocity, an act of judicial murder. British tribunals did not pass a sentence of death on women even if they were convicted of espionage, and she was not a spy: she was a nurse, acting with Christian charity and humanity to young men in desperate need. Her statue north of Trafalgar Square bears her message: 'Patriotism is not enough.'

[Foreign Office] *Correspondence with the U.S. Ambassador respecting the Execution of Miss Edith Cavell at Brussels*, Cd. 8013 (H.M.S.O., 1915); *Face à la mort*, from the diary of Philippe Baucq, who was executed with Miss Cavell (Paris, 1924); H. Leeds (1915); Paul Painlevé, ed. and intro., *La vie et la mort de Miss Edith Cavell* (1915); H. Judson (1941); *D.N.B.*, *1912–21*, pp. 100–1.

13. Edward the Confessor (?1004–66)   [L.F.]

The date of Edward's birth is uncertain; but he was still a child in 1013 when the Danes conquered most of southern England, and his parents fled with him to Normandy. His father, Ethelred 'the Unready', went back to England to do battle with the Danes, and died there in 1016. His Norman mother, Emma, went to England later to marry Canute; but Edward stayed with her brother, Duke Robert of Normandy. He lived at the duke's court for twenty-five years before the Danish line died out, and he was called back to be king of England. After that, he ruled England for a further twenty-five years before his death.

This interlude between the Danish kings and the Norman kings was a time of peace and stability. Edward's reputation for holiness (which may have earned him the title of 'the Confessor', that is, a person honoured by the Church for Christian witness) rests on <u>three</u> main features of his reign: he strengthened links with the papacy; he promoted many Norman knights to high office in England, and Norman clerics to bishoprics; and he re-founded Westminster Abbey. The first and second of these were probably consequences of his Norman upbringing. The Normans were notably closer to the papacy than the Anglo-Saxon kings, and he relied on the papacy to validate his claim to the throne. The Normans he appointed to high office were generally shrewd and competent men with a wider experience than their Anglo-Saxon counterparts.

He re-founded an old monastic house in London on the north bank of the Thames, devoting ten per cent of his income for some years to the building of a new church, in addition to endowing the monastery with many grants of land. The church became Westminster Abbey, the abbey church of St Peter. It was planned as a place of coronation and burial for the kings and queens of England, and finished and consecrated in Edward's lifetime, though he was too ill to attend the ceremony. He was the first monarch to be buried there.

Much of the interest of Edward's reign focusses on his last few months, and the determination of the succession. The choice was between his Norman cousin William and his brother-in-law Harold Godwinson. In England, the nobles preferred Harold, a warrior they knew, the son of England's premier earl; but Edward, himself brought up in Normandy, may well have preferred a successor of his own blood. The evidence is lost in claims and counter-claims about oaths and death-bed pronouncements.

Edward the Confessor died on 5 January 1066. He was buried in his abbey church on the following day. Harold died at Battle, which the Normans called Senlac, or lake of blood, nine months later, and William became king. Edward's reputation was greatly enhanced after the Norman Conquest. He could be regarded as the last of the Anglo-Saxon line, a great king who ruled in a golden age; but he could also be regarded as the first of the Norman modernizers, succeeded by the rightful heir. So both sides combined to praise him, and to keep his memorial. It was said that he was accessible to the people, and generous to the poor. Many miracles and cures were attributed to him, and he became a very popular saint. He appears in the Wilton Diptych with *Edmund of East Anglia, presenting the young King Richard II to the Madonna and Child, and is the subject of many paintings and church dedications.

AA.SS., Jan., 1, pp. 4–5; A.S.C., 1042–66; H. R. Luard, ed., *Lives of Edward the Confessor*, R.S., no. 3 (1858); Men.E.W., pp. 4–5; *The Life of the King who rests at Westminster*, ed. F. Barlow (1962); Stenton, pp. 423–9, 568–9, 580; O.D.S., pp. 149–51; *Butler*, Oct. pp. 82–4.

15. Teresa of Avila (1515–82)   [L.F.]

Like *John of the Cross, Teresa de Ahumada y Cepeda came of the stock of the Toledo weavers, a wealthy group of Jewish ancestry; but she was brought up a Christian, and educated by Augustinian nuns. She was a romantic and impetuous child. When she was seven, she and her brother Rodrigo ran away from home so that they might be killed by Moors and become Christian martyrs. She was fifteen when she had a serious illness – probably a severe form of malaria, which recurred in later life. She was given the Letters of *Jerome to read, and decided not to marry. In 1536, against her father's will, she entered a nearby Carmelite convent.

The convent was large and noisy, the Rule was lax, and the nuns were worldly. Social status counted for much, they were allowed their own servants, and they entertained many visitors from the outside world in commodious quarters. Teresa was not happy there. She was ill again, and thought to be near death; but it was over twenty years before her ideal of a small, simple community living a life of prayer and sacrifice became a reality. It was a time for Church reform. Though Protestantism did not cross the Pyrenees, and the grip of Catholic orthodoxy tightened in Spain, new initiatives were possible. In 1562, she founded the convent of St Joseph at Avila, originally with four companions. Her aim was to return to the purity of the primitive Rule with its emphasis on contemplation, silence and poverty. Her nuns, who came mainly from noble Spanish families, wore plain habits and rough leather sandals. They became known as the Descalzas, Discalced or 'shoeless'. Teresa told them that 'the Lord walks among the pots and pans', and they responded to her homeliness and simplicity.

In 1567, the Father-General of the Carmelite Order gave her permission to found other houses for women, and two for men. She chose two Carmelite monks to develop the male side of the Order, one of whom was *John of the Cross. He became her confessor and in some respects her teacher, in spite of their difference in age. Together they read the first full Spanish version of the Bible, published in 1569. Much of Teresa's writing is rooted in the Scriptures.

When John was imprisoned by the unreformed Carmelites, Teresa wrote to Philip II of Spain, and later had an audience with him. She remained under his protection, and her work grew. She spent the last thirteen years of her life travelling indefatigably in spite of increasing illness and weariness, crossing the high plateau and the mountain passes of Spain in extremes of heat and cold. She often faced rejection by the unreformed Carmelites, and suffered great distress; but she founded twelve houses for women, kept in touch with them all, and saw the Order for men develop in parallel. In 1550, the 'Discalced' Carmelites were granted a separate jurisdiction of their own, and in 1594, after Teresa's death, they were to become a separate Order.

Teresa combined an active life of great effort and achievement with a contemplative life of deep spirituality. Her writings, particularly *The Way of Perfection*, *The Interior Castle*, her autobiography and her Letters, have become classics of the spiritual life, as relevant today as in sixteenth-century Spain. Her devotion was centred on the humanity of Christ and his sacrifice for humankind. She would tell her nuns,

'Look at the crucified one.' She saw the human soul as a castle of seven mansions, where God himself, 'His Majesty', lives in the innermost mansion; or as a garden. Her analogies are always simple and direct, yet they contain a depth of contemplative experience to which other Christians are able to relate.

Teresa died of exhaustion at Alba de Tormes on 4 October 1582, on her way back from Medina to Avila. She was sixty-seven years old. Her feast is observed on 15 October because on the day after she died the new Gregorian calendar was adopted in Spain, and eleven days were omitted from that year. There is a contemporary portrait of her at Avila, a Bernini sculpture in the church of Santa Maria della Vittoria in Rome, and a painting by Rubens now in the Metropolitan Museum of Art in New York.

AA.SS., Oct., 7, pp. 109–570; E. Allison Peers, *Mother of Carmel* (1945); E. Hamilton, *The Great Teresa* (1960); S. Clissold (1975); S. du Boulay (1991); *Dict. Spir.*, 15, cols 611–58; *Butler*, Oct., pp. 94–101. Works: the edition of Silverio de Santa Teresa is the basis of the translations by E. Allison Peers, *The Complete Works of St Teresa of Jesus* (3 vols, 1946) and *The Letters of St Teresa of Jesus* (2 vols, 1951). *The Interior Castle* and *The Way of Perfection* are available in paperback.

16. Hugh Latimer (c.1485–1555)   [Commem.]

In the events which led up to his death, Hugh Latimer was repeatedly referred to as 'old Father Latimer'. He must have seemed immensely old to his accusers. He was born about the time when Richard III died on Bosworth Field, a survivor who had lived through the reigns of Henry VII, Henry VIII and Edward VI to be accused of heresy in the reign of Mary Tudor. He came of a Leicestershire family in what had been Lollard country a century earlier; but at Clare Hall, Cambridge, he was trained in the theology of Aristotle and the mediaeval schoolmen. He said loudly that he understood no Greek, and had no time for the new-fangled study of the New Testament. He made a vehement attack on *Luther's colleague Melanchthon, and seemed to be one of the soundest of the old-style theologians.

About 1524, he began to change his mind. He was opposed to the many forms of corruption he saw in the Church, and to the superstitions which had become associated with the Mass and the veneration of holy relics. He came to believe that the Scriptures should be published in English, so that people could interpret them for themselves. He spoke out: for a time he was suspected of heresy, and lay low in a country parish in Wiltshire; but he rose with *Thomas Cranmer. In 1535, he preached before Henry VIII's court for six weeks. In September of the same year, he was consecrated bishop of Worcester. He embarked on the hard work of reforming a run-down diocese where most of the livings provided revenues for absentee Italian prelates, many clergy did not own a Bible or a New Testament, and parishioners often had no idea of the meaning of the Lord's Prayer. In the following year, he was invited to preach to Convocation, and he delivered a forceful sermon on the evils of 'purgatory pick-purses' and 'mass priests' who took money from the poor by preying on their fear of judgement; but by this time, his views were too Protestant for Henry VIII. He was relieved of his bishopric, and spent some time in prison for helping a Protestant to escape abroad.

In the short reign of Edward VI, he was not only released, but restored to favour. He refused to take up his bishopric again because of failing health, but was much in demand as a preacher. His plain, homely sermons were delivered forcefully, and with great conviction. When Mary Tudor succeeded, he was old and sick and might have been left in obscurity, but his preaching had been so powerful that he was arrested and sent to the Tower of London with *Cranmer and *Nicholas Ridley, bishop of London. He was not a learned man: while Cranmer and Ridley defended their theological position with scholarship and subtlety, he simply clung to his views stubbornly and wearily. In the great theological disputation at Oxford, all three were arraigned. 'Last of all came Master Latimer,' says John Foxe, 'with a kerchief and two or three caps on his head, his spectacles hanging by a string at his breast, and a staff in his hand.' He looked so old and broken down that a chair was found for him. Among jeers and cat-calls, he told his questioners that he could not reply to their questions in Latin: he had not much used the Latin tongue in the past twenty years. He agreed that he had read the New Testament: he had read it through seven times in captivity, and he could not find a Mass in it. Christ had made one perfect sacrifice for the whole world, 'neither is there any propitiation for our sins save his Cross only'. The service of Holy Communion was a memorial: 'The bread is still bread and the wine still wine, for the change is not in the nature but in the dignity.'

Old Master Latimer was sent back to prison, where he awaited his end philosophically: 'Die we must: how and where we know not.

Happy are they to whom God giveth to pay nature's debt (I mean, to die) for his sake. Here is not our home.' On 16 October 1555, he was taken to his place of execution in Oxford. When Nicholas Ridley joined him and embraced him, he produced his most memorable sermon: 'Be ye of good cheer, Master Ridley, and play the man. We shall this day light such a candle by God's grace in England as shall never be put out.'

Foxe, pp. 290–312; W. Gilpin (1755); R. Demaus (1881); H. S. Darby (1953); A. G. Chester (1954); Loane, pp. 86–132.

Nicholas Ridley (1500–55) [Commem.]

Ridley, about fifteen years younger than *Hugh Latimer, went to Cambridge when the New Learning was sweeping the university. He studied the New Testament in Greek, and when he went on to the Sorbonne, he found the teaching in Paris distinctly old-fashioned, and spoke sardonically of 'Sorbonian clamours'. He went back to Cambridge, took his doctorate in Divinity, and became Master of Pembroke Hall. He was highly thought of by *Cranmer as one of the 'new men', but a moderate.

In 1538 he retired to a country living in Kent, and there he had a theological revelation. He came across a text by Bertram or Ratramn, a ninth-century monk of Corbey, entitled *De Corpore et Sanguine Domini* which argued that Christ's words used in the consecration of the elements at Communion were allegorical, and not meant to be taken literally. The book had been written at the request of the pope, and could therefore be taken to be unquestionably orthodox. Ridley came to the conclusion that the current Roman doctrine of the Mass was neither scriptural nor primitive, but blasphemous and dangerous, and he preached widely on this theme.

In the reign of Edward VI he became Cranmer's right-hand man. In 1552, he was consecrated bishop of Rochester. He insisted that the laity should receive both bread and wine in the Communion service, and was a member of the Commission which authorized the Prayer Book of 1549. When Edmund Bonner, bishop of London, refused to use or approve the new Prayer Book, he was deprived of his see, and Ridley was installed in his place. He carried out a stringent visitation of his diocese, ensuring that Mass was not being said in the old style, and that altars were everywhere replaced by tables. The Communion service was not 'an altar sacrifice offered God-ward, but a sacrament delivered from God man-ward'. Clergy were told to wear a plain rochet, not elaborate vestments.

When Mary Tudor became queen, Ridley warned his friends to fly, but said that he thought it right to stay and 'die for the Truth's sake'. He was deprived of the bishopric of London, and sent to the Tower of London, where he spent some time imprisoned with Cranmer and Hugh Latimer. Of the three, he was the most learned, and the sharpest in debate at the great Disputation in Oxford. He said: 'I fight in Christ's quarrel against the Mass, which doth utterly take away and overthrow the ordinance of Christ.'

He refused to recant, saying that he preferred the antiquity of the Primitive Church to the novelty of the Romish Church; and he went proudly to his death, wearing the undress (i.e. everyday) robes of a bishop. He ran to greet Latimer at the pyre, and embraced the old man, replying to his greeting: 'Be of good cheer, brother, for the Lord will either assuage the fury of the flames or else strengthen us to abide it.' He began to speak to the crowd, but the bailiffs put their hands over his mouth; and he died, calling on God to receive his spirit.

Ridley Theological College, Cambridge, bears his name.

Foxe, pp. 290–312; G. W. Bromley (1951); Loane, pp. 137–76; D.N.B., 16, pp. 117–205. Works: Parker Society (1843).

17. Ignatius of Antioch (c.37–107)   [L.F.]

Ignatius may have been a member of the earliest Christian community in Antioch in Syria, which was one of the great metropolitan centres of the Eastern Mediterranean. *Peter and *Paul both preached there, and there is a tradition that Ignatius was a disciple of *John the Evangelist. He is thought to have become bishop of Antioch about the year 69, when there would have been much discussion about the martyrdom of Peter and Paul in Rome only some five years earlier; but there is no definite information about his life and work until his final journey from Antioch to Rome under guard: he had been sentenced to death in the persecutions of Trajan, who was emperor from 98 to 117.

At Smyrna, he was received with honour by *Polycarp and members of the church, and he wrote letters to the churches of Ephesus, Magnesia, Tralles and Rome. At Troas, he wrote to Polycarp, and to the churches of Smyrna and Philadelphia. These seven letters are still extant. It seems evident that he was a leading figure in the churches of Asia Minor, and that he had a very active ministry. When he and his guards approached Rome, the Christians came out to welcome him, but he urged them not to stand in the way of his going to the Lord. He was taken to the Colosseum, thrown to the lions, and died almost at once.

The letters provide a valuable insight into the theology of the early Church. Bishop Ignatius tells the churches that the Church was founded by Peter and Paul, and describes himself as a disciple of Christ and a bearer of God (*theophorus*). He urges Christian communities to work together, and stresses the importance of the Eucharist in their worship. It is 'the medicine of immortality, the antidote against death which gives eternal life in Jesus Christ'. They must support their bishops, who are given grace to direct them. He is not only prepared for martyrdom but seeks it, writing, 'Even if I do suffer, I shall do so as a freedman of Christ. In Christ, I shall rise again as a free man. Now, in my bondage, I must learn to forget all my desires.' He prays for unity, for love between Christians, and for an end to persecution.

Though some doubt has been cast on the authorship of three of the seven letters, four are certainly authentic, and recent authorities consider all seven to be written by Ignatius.

AA.SS., Feb., 1, pp. 13–37; C. C. Richardson, *The Christianity of St Ignatius of Antioch* (1935); V. Corwin, *St Ignatius and Christianity in Antioch* (1960); J. Rius-Camps, *The Four Authentic Letters of Ignatius* (1980); C. Trevett, *A Study of Ignatius of Antioch in Syria and Asia* (1992). See also Delehaye, pp. 56–7; *Dict. Spir.* 7, 2, cols 1250–66; *O.D.S.*, p. 241; *Butler*, Oct., pp. 115–16. Letters in *Early Christian Fathers*, pp. 74–120.

18. Luke the Evangelist   Festival

The Gospel according to Luke and the Acts of the Apostles come from the same author. In the Gospel, he tells the story of the earthly life of Christ up to the Crucifixion and the Resurrection appearances. In the Acts, he refers to that story as the first part of his work, and continues with an account of the foundation and early work of the Church. Early traditions say that he was a Hellenic Jew from Antioch, and that he lived to the age of eighty-four. *Paul refers in his Letter to the Colossians to 'Luke, the beloved physician' (Colossians 4:14).

In the Prologue to his Gospel narrative, Luke tells his readers why he is writing. There are many accounts being written of 'the events which have happened to us'. He has gone over the whole story in detail, talked to eye-witnesses (of whom he is evidently not one) and proposes to set down an orderly and connected account. He is evidently a man of education: he writes in good classical Greek, lapsing into demotic Greek for reported speech. He has a detailed knowledge of synagogue practice, and can write in Septuagint Greek when required, so he is probably a Jew; but he is writing for non-Jews, insisting that Christ's life, teaching and sacrifice are for everyone. He suits the style to the subject, and is a skilled story-teller with a good eye for significant detail. He relates thirteen parables which are not in the other Gospels, and gives some vivid thumbnail sketches, such as those of the Unjust Steward and the Prodigal Son.

Luke alone tells the story of the Annunciation, the Visitation to Elizabeth, and the visit of the local shepherds to the Christ-child in detail. Earlier commentators assumed that he had heard of these events from *Mary the mother of Jesus herself, but it is now thought probable he learned of them from a group of women disciples. Luke related well to women. It is he who tells his readers the stories of *Mary and Martha, of the widow of Nain (7:11-15), of the woman who was a sinner (7:37-50), and of the 'daughters of Jerusalem' who wept at the Crucifixion (23:27-31). He also has a feeling for stigmatized people: the unpopular little tax collector Zacchaeus who climbed a tree to see Jesus (19:1-10); Lazarus the beggar in Christ's parable (16:19-31); the penitent thief (23:39-43).

The Acts of the Apostles provide the principal source of information about the life of the early Church, and the personalities of the apostles. In the account of the coming of the Holy Spirit at Pentecost, Luke writes a superb account of the fulfilment of Christ's promise to the disciples: to him, the Spirit is a palpable force, inspiring and energizing the whole Christian community. He goes on to describe the early points of decision: the first healing at the Gate called Beautiful and the confrontations with the high priest and the elders, the holding of all property in common, the stoning of *Stephen, the conversion of *Paul, the debates about the status of the Gentiles, the first persecution, the move into mission. He reconstructs speeches, notably those by Stephen and *Peter, and it is notable that Peter's speeches include semitic idioms, which suggest that they were fairly close to what Peter actually said.

The second part of the Acts of the Apostles, which is mainly concerned with the journeys of Paul and his companions, reads like a diary; and from chapter 16, the author begins to say 'we' rather than 'they'. Though some commentators have raised the question of whether Luke the writer is the same person as Luke the missionary, there seems no reason to doubt this. Admittedly his name was a fairly common one in the first century, and Paul, who says he is a physician, does not mention that he was also a writer; but the switch from 'they' to 'we', and the continuity of style and expression are convincing. Paul, overwhelmed by his own urgent and taxing mission, may not have been particularly interested in his companion's scribblings. Luke was with Paul in Macedonia (Acts 16:10) and Troas (20: 6) and set sail with him for Italy (27:1—28:15). These accounts fit with those of Paul in his Letters.

Luke's story ends with Paul 'teaching about the Lord Jesus Christ with all boldness and without hindrance', for two years after his first house arrest. This suggests that the narrative ends before the year 65, and commentators have asked why Luke did not continue it up to the time of the deaths of Peter and Paul. The answer must be either that Luke died, or that he went back to Jerusalem. Perhaps he left the manuscript behind, so that he was unable to complete it; but the fact that it is not rounded off strengthens the view that it came from this single and inspired author.

AA.SS., Oct., 8, pp. 283–313; A. Harnack, *Luke the Physician* (1907); A. T. Robertson, *Luke the Historian in the Light of Research* (1920); C. K. Barrett, *Luke the Historian in Recent Study* (1961); P. Ester, *Community and Gospel in Luke-Acts* (1987); O.C.B., pp. 469–74 and 6–10.

19. Henry Martyn (1781–1812)   [L.F.]

As a student at Cambridge, Henry Martyn came under the influence of the celebrated Evangelical *Charles Simeon. He was ordained, and became Simeon's curate at Holy Trinity. He felt called to the mission field, but the Church Missionary Society was in its early days, and had no funds to support him. When his father's business at the tin mines in Truro failed, Martyn accepted a chaplaincy to the British community of the East India Company in Bengal as a means of support; but he was not content to confine his ministry to his fellow-countrymen. He lived alone in a small bungalow, and took no part in their social life. He learned the local languages, conducted services for Indians, and taught in mission schools. He visited Hindu temples, and explained to the Brahmins 'the history of redemption'. To the surprise, and probably the alarm, of the English *mems* and *sahibs*, he went out and preached to the beggars on the streets. This was not approved of by the Company officials: the fear of insurrection by the 'natives' was so strong that Anglicans were forbidden even to sing the Magnificat, lest the idea of 'putting down the mighty from their seat' might lead to riots against British rule.

Martyn, originally a mathematician and Senior Wrangler at Cambridge, developed a gift for languages, and turned it to scholarship. He translated the New Testament and the *Book of Common Prayer* into Hindustani. He learned Arabic script, and went on to translate the New Testament into Arabic and Farsi, the language of Persia (Iran) and Afghanistan. He travelled in Persia, meeting Moslem scholars in Shiraz and Tabriz, and debating with them the central tenets of the Christian and Islamic faiths. He tried to present the Shah with a copy of his Farsi New Testament, but was unsuccessful. It was finally printed in St Petersburg.

A frail young man, thought to be consumptive, Henry Martyn died at Tokat in Armenia, among strangers, at the age of thirty-one. His letters and journals, edited by Bishop Samuel Wilberforce, have left a remarkable record of a lonely mission by an Evangelical pioneer.

Charlotte M. Yonge, *Pioneers and Founders* (1871), pp. 81–95; Charles D. Bell (1880); E. T. Butler (1921); C. E. Padwick (1922, repr. 1953); Jesse Page (1930); A. G. Pouncy (1947); *D.N.B.*, 12, pp. 1200–2. *Journals and Letters*, ed. Samuel Wilberforce (1831). The British Library has Henry Martyn's translations of the New Testament in Hindustani and Farsi.

25. Crispin and Crispinian, Martyrs (*c.*305)   [*Commem.*]

The battle of Agincourt was fought on 25 October 1415, and in Shakespeare's version Henry V invoked 'Crispin Crispian' before it took place. The two saints were well known in Europe in the Middle Ages, and are thought to have been Roman noblemen. According to one tradition, they were executed in Rome during the persecutions of Diocletian. According to another they travelled to Gaul to spread the

Gospel, and settled at Soissons, where they earned their living as shoe-makers (St Crispin is the patron saint of cobblers), much as *St Paul supported himself by making tents. They lived in Soissons for a number of years, but were reported to the authorities as Christians during the persecutions of Maximian, tortured and executed there. Bishop Gregory of Tours (539–94) mentions them in his writings, and Bishop Eligius of Noyon (c.588–660), who was a goldsmith of great skill, enriched their shrine. Some accounts say that they died in Rome and their relics were taken to Soissons, others that they died in Soissons and their relics were taken to Rome.

England also claimed them: the story is that they fled from the perse-cutions in Gaul and settled at Faversham in Kent, where they con-tinued to work as shoemakers in a house on the site of the Swan Inn at the bottom of Preston Street. A Mr Southouse, writing about 1670, noted that this house was visited by many pilgrims. There is an altar in their honour in Faversham church.

Relics were greatly prized in the Middle Ages, both as a focus for devotion and as a means of attracting pilgrims and so raising church funds. It is quite possible that different relics were held in Rome, in Soissons and in Faversham, and that stories tying them to particular localities developed later, to stress their local importance.

AA.SS., Oct., 11, pp. 495–540; N.C.E., 4, pp. 461–2; Delehaye, pp. 128–9, 132–4; L. Duchesne, *Fastes Épiscopaux* (1908), 3, pp. 141–52; O.D.S., p. 114.

26. Cedd (d. 664)   *[Commem.]*

Cedd and *Chad were brothers. They were among the twelve boys who were the first pupils in *Aidan's monastery school at Lindisfarne. They had two brothers, who also became priests. Cedd was one of four missionary monks sent to the Midlands when Penda, king of Mercia, finally allowed Christians into his kingdom. Though Penda never became a Christian, his son Pendea did, and a daughter became an abbess.

In about 650, Cedd was sent to the land of the East Saxons (Essex) with a single priest. Earlier attempts by the Canterbury monks to evangelize this region said to be rife with witchcraft and superstition had been unsuccessful, but Cedd's mission was so successful that he 'returned home to Lindisfarne', as *Bede puts it, to be consecrated bishop of a new diocese. He founded monasteries at Tilbury and Bradwell-on-Sea. His church at Bradwell, founded in 653, still stands. Cedd frequently went back to Northumbria. On one visit north, he was offered land for a monastery. He chose a site on the North Yorkshire moors 'among deep and remote hills which seemed rather to contain the dens of robbers and the lairs of wild beasts than the habitations of men', and here at Lastingham he prayed and fasted long through Lent before taking further action. Each day he ate only a little bread, one hen's egg, and milk mixed with water. There were ten days of Lent left when he was summoned to the king, and his brother Cynibill came to complete the fast for him.

Cedd was an interpreter at the Synod of Whitby in 664, when many of the Latin contingent arrived with little knowledge of English. Bede says that he listened to the debates very carefully, and became convinced of the necessity of changing the date of Easter, though in other ways he remained a monk of the Celtic tradition.

He died at Lastingham, it is said of a plague, soon after the Synod ended, and was buried in the sanctuary of his church.

Chad (Ceadda) (d. 672) may also be celebrated on this date. See 2 March.

Bede, *H.E.*, bk 3, chs 21—6; bk 4, ch. 3; *Men.E.W.*, pp. 95–6; *N.C.E.*, 3, p. 361; Mayr-Harting, pp. 101–2; Stenton, p.121; *D.N.B.*, 3, pp. 1322–3; *O.D.S.*, p. 92.

Alfred the Great (849–99)   [L.F.]

Alfred was the fifth and youngest son of Aethelwolf, King of Wessex, and his wife, who came from Jutland. The Wessex court was Christian, and evidently in touch with Continental culture: when Alfred was four, he was taken to Rome, to be confirmed by Pope Leo IV, and he subsequently visited the court of the Frankish King Charles the Bold. He grew up fighting the Danes, who made frequent incursions from their base in Mercia; and he had such a reputation as a warrior that he was chosen to succeed his elder brother, Aethelred I, in 871. Seven years later the Danes attacked again and defeated the Wessex army. For some months Alfred was a resistance fighter, hiding in the marshes of Athelney and making guerrilla attacks on the Danes. He rallied his forces, and decisively defeated the Danes under Guthrum at Edington, about fifteen miles from Chippenham. Guthrum agreed to withdraw his troops from Wessex, and he and his men became Christians. Alfred proved a generous conqueror: he stood as Guthrum's godfather at his baptism, and royally entertained his former foes.

When the Danes attacked again in 885, Alfred drove them out of southern England, and captured London. He became overlord of the English, though he never tried to encroach on the powers of the other English kings. He built a ring of fortified strongholds, named *burhs*, to keep the Danes within the Danelaw. He also built warships to keep the Danes from the coasts, and so is credited with being the founder of the British Navy.

Alfred is known as an enlightened legislator, a supporter of the Church, and a Christian scholar. His laws protected the weak against aggression, regularized the holding of folk-moots, and limited blood-feuds. He founded a monastery at Athelney for foreign monks, and a nunnery at Shaftesbury. Ealhswith, his wife, later founded another nunnery, Nun's Minster, at Winchester. He supervised seven scholars, including Werferth, bishop of Worcester, and Asser, bishop of Sherborne, who later became his biographer. They translated a number of books from Latin into Anglo-Saxon, including the *Pastoral Care* of *Pope Gregory the Great, Boethius' *The Consolations of Philosophy*, the works of *Bede, the *Soliloquies* of *Augustine of Hippo and the *Ancient History* of Orosius. Alfred personally added prefaces, notes and illustrations which reflect his own studies and the ideas of his time. Sir Frank Stenton makes the point that he was 'struggling with a refractory language'. Anglo-Saxon was a difficult medium for the expression of ideas, but Alfred believed that these books were 'the most necessary for all to know', the basis of civilized thought. In the preface to Augustine's *Soliloquies*, he compares himself to a man collecting timber in a wood – there is so much available, and he selects the best. This was the beginning of English prose literature.

In his preface to Gregory's *Cura Pastoralis*, he laments the illiteracy of the clergy, largely due to the devastation of the Danish wars and the burning of monasteries. Few of them understood the English equivalent of the Latin services they chanted, so that the Mass had become a kind of magical mumbo-jumbo rather than an expression of faith. Bishops were made responsible for training their clergy, and also for the education of free-born youths. Schools were set up where they were to become literate in Anglo-Saxon, and those who were to become clergy would also study Latin.

Alfred was king for twenty-eight years, during which his reforms were carried out throughout Wessex, then the largest of the southern kingdoms. He died on 26 October 899, and was buried at Winchester, his royal capital.

Asser, *Life of King Alfred*, various editions including a Penguin edition trans. and intro. Simon Keynes and Michael Lapidge (1983); A.S.C., pp. 67–93, 110–11. Modern Lives, Eleanor S. Duckett (1956); A. P. Smyth (1995). D.N.B., 1, pp. 152–61; Stenton, pp. 249–76.

28. Simon and Jude, Apostles   Festival

Simon is called 'the Canaanean' in the RSV, and 'a member of the Zealot party' in other translations (Matthew 10:4, Mark 3:19). In Luke 6:15 and Acts 1:13 he is referred to as 'Simon also called the Zealot'. In this way he is distinguished from *Simon Peter, Simon of Cyrene and other Simons. He may have been a member of the Zealot party, a strict and fanatical Jewish sect, before he joined the apostles. *Luke distinguishes Jude as 'Judas son of James' (Luke 6:16, Acts 1:13), though some translators have held that he was the brother of James rather than the son. Matthew 10:3 and Mark 3:18 mention Thaddeus as one of the Twelve, and this is thought to be another form of his name. *John calls him 'the other Judas, not Iscariot' (John 14:22) when he asks a question at the Last Supper.

The Letter of Jude is not helpful: though the writer identifies himself as 'Jude, the brother of James', the letter appears to have been written after the age of the apostles, and is thought to date from the years 70–80 or even later. In verse 17, the author says, 'But you, beloved, must remember the predictions of the apostles of our Lord Jesus Christ', which suggests that he was not one of them: if he had had apostolic authority, he would have used it in order to warn this group of Christians against false doctrine.

In the Eastern Church, Simon and Jude have separate feast days, and the Menology of *St Basil records that Simon died peacefully at Edessa; but a sixth-century tradition in the Western Church, based on an older cult, is that Simon preached in Egypt, then joined Jude, who had undertaken a mission to Mesopotamia. They went together to Persia, where they were both martyred.

• 'Grateful thanks to St Jude' may sometimes be seen in press notices, but there appears to be no historical reason why he has come to be regarded as the patron saint of lost causes. One explanation is that mediaeval Christians normally avoided invoking him because his name was too close to that of Judas Iscariot. It was only when they were desperate that they called on him as a last resort.

AA.SS., Oct., 12, pp. 421–67; N.C.E., 13, pp. 219–20 (Simon) and 8, pp. 16–18 (Jude); *Butler*, Oct., pp. 195–6.

29. James Hannington (1847–85)   [L.F.]

Born of a wealthy merchant family who lived in Hurstpierpoint, Sussex, James Hannington was twenty when he decided that he wanted to enter the Church. He went to St Mary's Hall, Oxford, but he did not know how to study, and the principal called him 'a gentleman at large'. He had a sizeable private income, and served a fairly unexacting curacy in Devon where he rode Exmoor on his pony, went shooting, and was well liked by the parishioners; but under a cheerful, extrovert front, he was searching desperately for his vocation. He wanted to save souls. He was searching for light, and praying very hard. He was twenty-nine when he wrote to a friend, 'I know now that Jesus Christ died for me, and that He is mine and I am His. I know that I *believe*. I do so little for Christ.'

He took Bible classes, learned to preach extempore, went to Temperance meetings and taught 'rough men' how to live without drink. He read Pascal and studied Jansenism. He married, and had a child; but he was being steadily pulled towards Africa. At meetings of the Church Missionary Society, he heard of the deaths of two missionaries in Central Africa, and he volunteered. His wife was 'more than brave about it, and she gave me to the Lord', he wrote.

His first missionary journey lasted from May 1882 to June 1883. His party went on foot overland, from Zanzibar north-west to Lake Victoria and the source of the Nile: a distance of over a thousand miles. The water in the wells was so foul that sometimes he did not drink at all for four days. He had tropical fever – not once, but repeatedly – and was plagued by dysentery; but these ailments did not 'take away the joy of the Lord'. For the last part of the journey, he had to be carried in a hammock. He reached Msalala, only about fifty miles from Lake Victoria, but he was 'a complete wreck', and was sent back, having to make the whole journey in reverse. 'I often think of poor Dr Livingstone,' he wrote in a letter.

He had an excellent constitution, and was soon well enough to address missionary meetings, which he did with energy and conviction. The CMS had a scheme for a bishop in Equatorial Africa, and on 24 June 1884, at the age of thirty-six, Hannington was consecrated as the first bishop by the archbishop of Canterbury. It was a post for a young man, and a brave one. His diocese would be based at the source of the Nile, in Buganda, the southern kingdom of Uganda. Then he set off again. 'Pray for us,' he wrote to his friends. He called Psalm 121 'my travelling Psalm': *I will lift up mine eyes unto the hills; from whence cometh my help.*

In January 1885 he was at Mombasa. This time, he was taking a different route, due west through Masai country. He did not know, and the British authorities in Zanzibar did not know, two key factors: first, that Mutesa, the *kabaka* or king of Buganda, who had been friendly to the missionaries, was dead, and his successor, Mwanga, was both vicious and unstable; second, that the land of the Masai was Buganda's 'locked back door', closed to foreigners. A letter from missionaries already in Buganda warning him not to take this route was never delivered.

The party's way to Lake Victoria was blocked by hostile Masai warriors. Bishop Hannington, with a complete disregard for danger, left the other missionaries and went on alone, with African porters carrying supplies for the missionaries in Buganda. He had a bad abscess on one leg and repeated attacks of fever, but he walked 170 miles in a week until he reached the source of the Nile at Ukassa, near to present-day Jinja. Then the war drums beat. He described in his diary, later recovered, how he was seized and imprisoned in a hut with 'rats and vermin ad lib. Fearfully shaken, strained in every limb; great pain, and consumed by thirst.'

He stayed there until 29 October, hoping that orders would come from Mwanga to release him. When he was taken out into an open space, and his porters were assembled, he must have thought that they were free to go; but the porters were killed on the spot by spear-thrust. Surrounded by their bodies, Bishop Hannington told the soldiers that he was about to die for the Baganda people, and that he was purchasing the road into Buganda with his life. Then he was shot, and his friend says, 'The noble spirit leapt forth from its broken house of clay.'

Four African porters managed to escape the massacre, and carried the news to the missionaries in Buganda. Fr Lourdel of the Catholic

White Fathers noted in his diary, 'Hannington murdered . . . Beginning of Mwanga's cruelties. Alas, it will not be the last.' The ordeal of the *Martyrs of Uganda was about to begin. There is a memorial to Bishop Hannington in the Anglican cathedral in Kampala.

E. C. Dawson, *James Hannington: First Bishop of Eastern Equatorial Africa* (1887); J. P. Thoonen, *Black Martyrs* (1941). D.N.B., 3, pp. 1191–2.

31. Martin Luther (1483–1546) [*Commem.*]

Martin Luther was born at Eisleben in Saxony. He came of peasant stock, and attended the University of Erfurt, where he was a cheerful, genial student who played the lute and got into arguments. After a terrifying experience in a storm, he entered the Augustinian cloister at Erfurt, where he endured deep spiritual and theological anguish. He was obsessed by a perception of the wrath of God, seeing human beings as 'miserable sinners eternally ruined by original sin'. Then he came to understand, through his reading of the Scriptures and the works of *St Augustine, that 'the justice of God' was not a threat but a gift, given freely to those who had faith. He began to understand *metanoia* (repentance), the grace of God operating on the human will.

In 1509 he was sent to Wittenberg, where he lectured in the university and was appointed official preacher in the parish church. He took his doctorate in Divinity in 1512, and became involved in theological controversy. He said, 'Theology goes to the kernel of the nut, and touches the bone and the flesh.' He was acutely conscious of the Church's failure to live up to its high calling, and in 1517, the abuse of indulgences moved him to open protest. The Dominican Friar Tetzel promised the people of Wittenberg remission of the pains of purgatory for relatives who had died: 'as soon as the money chinks in the box, the soul flies up to heaven'. On 22 February, Luther preached a sermon against this practice (which was used to fund the work of Michaelangelo and Raphael in St Peter's, Rome) and followed it with his famous Ninety-Five Theses which were nailed to the door of Wittenberg church. He denounced 'the wantonness and violence of the pardon-merchants' words', arguing that 'the pope can remit no guilt, but only declare that it has been remitted by God'. If the pope had the power to remit sins, he asked, 'why does he not empty purgatory for the sake of the most holy love and supreme need of souls?'

At the Heidelberg Disputations in April 1518, he developed his theology of the Cross: the merits of Jesus Christ were not a 'treasury' which popes could dip into at will: all Christians were called on to follow the way of the Cross. He was summoned to Rome, but he refused to go, and the Elector Frederick refused to hand him over to the papal authorities, though by this time Luther was being called 'a fanatical Hussite, heretical, seditious, insolent and rash'. He was condemned by the papal Bull *Exsurge Domine* of 15 June 1520.

Luther's response was to set out his Three Manifestos of 1520 'to the Christian nobility of the German nation'. He began, 'The time for silence is gone, and the time to speak has come.' He argued that God's power to remit sins was not delegated to *Peter alone but to the apostles as a group (John 20:23), and through them to the whole
• Christian community. He set out the doctrine of the priesthood of all believers, declared the pope 'an offence to Christendom', stated that only three sacraments – 'baptism, penance and the bread' – could be supported from Scripture, and proposed a married clergy. The papal nuncio, Jerome Aleander, noted that his picture was being sold in the streets embellished with a halo.

At the Diet of Worms in 1521, Luther was summoned before the assembled powers of Church and state – cardinals, bishops, emperor and princes. Copies of his books were set out on a table. He was ordered to reject everything that he had written. 'Here I stand, I can no other' was the spirit of his reply, though he may not have used the actual words. In the Edict of Worms, probably written by the nuncio, Luther's doctrines were described as 'a festering disease'. His books were to be burned, he was to be imprisoned, and his followers' goods were to be sequestrated. The papal Bull *Decretum Romanum* of January 1521 formally condemned and excommunicated him.

Luther escaped imprisonment with the aid of his supporters, including some of the German princes. In a state of nervous exhaustion and physical pain from chronic stomach trouble, he devoted himself to translating the New Testament into German and drafting his Longer and Shorter Catechisms. He married, and had five children. His letters give a picture of a very close and loving family life.

The Peasants' War in the German states seems to have had a very loose connection with Luther's doctrines: there had been sporadic risings over grievances for a century or more. In 1524, revolts broke out again: castles, monasteries and nunneries were pillaged, and bands of peasants with no very clear theological views terrorized the countryside. Luther did all he could to support the power of the princes in the interests of peace.

Luther was an outlaw and a proscribed heretic in the eyes of the Roman Church: he could not attend the Augsburg Confession in 1530, and it was his friend and colleague Philip Melanchthon who presented his statement. 'We are not heretics,' he wrote. 'Our trouble is with certain abuses which have crept into the Church without any clear authority . . . the ancient rites are clearly preserved among us.'

Luther died in 1546, when Lutheranism – not all of it derived from his beliefs – was already beginning to split much of northern Europe from the Roman Church. It was only at the time of the Second Vatican Council in 1962–3 that the full force of Luther's desire to maintain Christian unity was understood. In recent years, Catholic and Protestant scholars have found much room for agreement in his writings. 'For the true unity of the Church,' he wrote for the Confession of Augsburg, 'it suffices to agree together the teaching of the Gospel and the administration of the sacraments; it is not necessary that everywhere should exist similar traditions of men, or similar rites and ceremonies instituted by men.'

Contemporary documents ed. E. G. Rupp and R. Drewery (1970); *Luther, by himself*, trans. and ed. I. D. K. Sissons et al. (Edinburgh, 1972); post-Vatican II evaluations by J. M. Todd (1964); J. Atkinson (Pelican, 1967); R. D. Jones, *Erasmus and Luther*, (1968); G. Yule, ed., *Luther: Theologian for Catholics and Protestants* (1985, repr. 1986). K. Randall, *Luther and the German Reformation* (1988).

November

3. Richard Hooker (1553–1601) [L.F.]

Hooker was only six years old when the Elizabethan Settlement was introduced, so he was one of the first generation of Oxford scholars who learned to avoid theological extremes. He had a country living in Buckinghamshire for some years, but his reputation for learning and moderation was such that in 1583, Archbishop Whitgift appointed him to the influential post of master of the Temple. His rival for the post was a Puritan named Walter Travers, who had a lectureship at the Temple, and continued to preach there. It was said that 'while the forenoon spake Canterbury, the afternoon lecture spake Geneva'. Travers stirred up trouble and made allegations against Hooker, but Hooker was easily able to defend himself.

After eight years of controversy, weary of theological wrangling, Hooker accepted a living in the gift of the Crown, and became rector of Boscombe, near Salisbury. There he wrote the first four books of his *Ecclesiastical Polity*. The fifth book was published after his move to Bishopsbourne, near Canterbury, in 1600. He died in 1601 at the early age of forty-seven, and the last three volumes of the eight-volume work he had completed were published posthumously.

Ecclesiastical Polity is the first distinctively Anglican theological work, establishing a clear position between Roman Catholicism and Calvinism. While not accepting the jurisdiction of the pope, Hooker also refuted the view that everything necessary for salvation was contained in the Scriptures. The doctrines and structure of the Church must not deny scriptural injunctions, but human reason and natural law were also sources of insight and understanding. 'Where the Scriptures appointeth no certainty, the use of the people of God or the ordinances of our fathers must serve for a law.' He insisted on the continuity of the Church of England with the historical Church, and defended its rites and customs (regarded by the Calvinists as 'dregs of popery'. Episcopacy was 'a sacred structure, ordained of God'. 'The holy mysteries' of the Eucharist, he maintained, 'impart unto us, in true and real though mystical form the very Person of our Lord himself, whole, perfect and entire'.

Ecclesiastical Polity was intended as a work of reconciliation. It was very well received in Rome, where Pope Clement VIII was told that 'a poor obscure English priest' had written a work 'in a style which expressed so grave and so humble a majesty' that his informants had not 'met with any that exceeded him'. The pope himself subsequently declared that the work contained 'such seeds of eternity' that it would 'abide till the last fire shall consume all learning'.

In England, controversy was less easily stilled. Hooker despaired of the continuing bitterness, and wrote: 'There is no way left but this way: pray for the peace of Jerusalem'; but his eight volumes, written in clear and beautiful sixteenth-century English, with the simple aim of reconciliation, have remained as a masterly statement of Anglican principle.

L. S. Thornton (1924), *Richard Hooker and Contemporary Political Ideas* (1949); P. Munz, *The Place of Hooker in the History of Thought* (1952); *D.N.B.*, 9, pp. 1183–9; *Bridge Builders*, pp. 19–22. Works: 3 vols, ed. John Keble (1830); bk 1 and bk 8, with preface, ed. A. S. McGrade (1989).

Martin de Porres (1579–1639)   *[Commem.]*

The story of the Spanish invasion of Peru by Pisarro and his armies is told in great detail in Prescott's *History of the Conquest of Peru* (1847). One of the long-term social problems was the birth of despised *mulatto* children born of liaisons between the *conquistadores* and South American women. Martin was the son of Don Juan de Porres, a Spanish grandee, and Anna Velasquez, a freed black slave from Panama. He had his mother's colouring, and so could not pass as Spanish in racially conscious Spanish-Peruvian society: he was baptized as 'the child of an unknown father'.

However, his father took him to Ecuador to be educated, and secured a post for him as apprentice to a barber-surgeon. Martin learned many useful things: blood-letting, the treatment of wounds and fractures, and various kinds of medication. His mother was a recognized herbal practitioner, and her knowledge was also passed on to him. At the age of sixteen, he went to a Dominican priory in Lima to serve the brothers as a *donado*, a lay helper who received only food and lodging for his work. He became a Dominican Tertiary. His father urged the prior to make him a full member of the Order of Preachers, though there was a law forbidding the religious Orders to accept 'Indians, blacks and their descendants'. The prior said that he was prepared to evade the law, but that he had already offered Martin full status as a friar, and Martin had refused it, because he thought that he was unworthy. It was not until 1603, at the age of twenty-four, that Martin agreed to become a lay brother.

Martin suffered very much from the double stigma of illegitimacy and colour. The friars respected his spiritual qualities so highly that they went to him for direction and counsel, and a Spanish lawyer, Don Balthasar Canasco, asked if he might become his adopted son. 'Why do you want a *mulatto* for a father?' was Martin's reaction. Don Balthasar replied that he hoped Martin would be prepared to accept a Spaniard for a son.

Martin dealt with his problems by prayer and an all-embracing charity to others. Within the priory, he was barber, surgeon, infirmarian and master of the herb-garden. No post was too menial for him. He was instrumental in setting up a foundling hospital and other shelters for sick and poor people. He kept a home for stray cats and dogs. He even excused rats and mice for eating the corn: he said they were hungry, too.

When Martin died at the age of sixty, his funeral cortège included bishops and Spanish noblemen. The 'dog of a *mulatto*' as he called himself, had proved his value, and it was generously recognized in a society which had become anxious to heal the wounds of conquest. In South America, Martin is regarded as the patron saint of race relations and social justice.

AA.SS., Nov., 3, pp. 108–12 contains Martin's first biography by Bernardo de Medina; J. C. Kearns (1950); C. C. Martindale in *The Month*, April, 1920, pp. 300–13. *N.C.E.*, 11, pp. 595–6; *Butler*, Nov., pp. 18–20.

6. Leonard of Noblac (?sixth century)   [*Commem.*]

There is no early record of Leonard's life. He appears first in the *Historia* of Adhémar de Chabannes, an eleventh-century chronicler who specialized in unlikely marvels and miracles. In the sixteenth century, Cardinal Baronius included him in the Roman Martyrology, quoting *Bede as a source; but there is no mention of Leonard in Bede. In the seventeenth century, the Bollandists included his anonymous Life in the *Acta Sanctorum*, but described it as *fabularum plena*, full of fables.

There is evidence that Leonard is an historical character. The present town of Saint-Léonard in France was the site of the abbey of Noblac, of which Leonard was reputed to be the founder. The Crusaders came back to England from the First Crusade with a devotion to Leonard as the patron saint of prisoners; and there are some 117 church dedications to him in England, while a seaside resort in Sussex and a town in Roxburgh are named after him.

Leonard's story is given in the Life of *Remigius, bishop of Rheims. Shredded of accretions, the story of Leonard is that he was a Frankish nobleman in Clovis's reign (481–511). Remigius converted him, and Clovis was his godfather. He entered the monastery at Micy, near Orléans, but later refused Clovis's offer of a bishopric and became a hermit, living in a hut in the woods. Clovis was hunting with his court in the woods close by when his wife Clothilde, who was pregnant, suddenly went into labour. Leonard was present at the birth, praying for her safety and that of the child, and both lived. Clovis, in thanksgiving, made two promises to Leonard: he would give him as much land as he could ride round in a single night on a donkey; and he would release any prisoner whom Leonard visited. Leonard claimed his land, and called the place Nobiliacum, which became Noblac. There he set up an oratory, other monks came to join him, and the abbey of Noblac was built.

Leonard's link with prisoners is strengthened by the fact that in 1103, the abbey of Noblac was visited by Bohemond I, Prince of Antioch, a Norman Crusader who was a prisoner of the Saracens from 1100 to early in that year. He left with the abbey a gift of silver chains made on the pattern of the chains that he had worn in prison. Stonegrave Minster in North Yorkshire has the tomb of a Crusader, Sir Walter de Teyes, who was also a prisoner, and this lies at the door of a chapel dedicated to St Leonard.

AA.SS., Nov., 3, pp. 139–210; F. Arbellot, *Vie de S. Léonard* (Paris, 1863); A. Poncelet, 'Boémond et S. Léonard', *Anal.Boll.*, 31 (1912) pp. 24–44; *Butler*, Nov., pp. 45–6.

William Temple (1881–1944)   *[Commem.]*

William Temple was the son of Dr Frederick Temple, bishop of London. He was fifteen when his father became archbishop of Canterbury. His home life was happy and affectionate, with no apparent conflicts. He grew up in the Church of England and had a deep love for it; and he had a brilliant mind. In his schooldays at Rugby, he could do four hours' prep. in thirty minutes, to give himself time for reading, and he read widely. He became President of the Oxford Union, and his first class honours degree in 'Greats' (mostly classical studies and philosophy) was a foregone conclusion. He became a Fellow of Queen's College Oxford, then headmaster of Repton at the age of twenty-nine, rector of the fashionable church of St James's, Piccadilly at thirty-three, bishop of Manchester at thirty-nine, archbishop of York at forty-seven, and archbishop of Canterbury at sixty. He had a devoted wife, never suffered poverty, and never served in an ordinary parish. As many people commented, 'he never roughed it'. So how did he develop the passion for social justice which marked his life, and led many thousands, rich and poor, to mourn his passing at the age of sixty-three?

William Temple felt deeply that 'the personality of every man and woman is sacred'. There are many references in the biographies to his direct approach to people of all kinds, his tolerance, and his passionate desire to help those who lacked his own considerable advantages. Dean Iremonger tells how 'a boy called Billy Temple, more like Billy Bunter' was a favourite at the Rugby School Mission; how, as an undergraduate and a young academic, he spent much time at Oxford House, Bethnal Green, and the Bermondsey Mission, where there were bugs in his bed and he had 'a tin washbasin and a chair with three legs, on which he read Bosanquet's *Logic*'; and how he told the Governors during his time at Rugby that the public schools represented 'class divisions in an accentuated form'. He resigned from St James's Piccadilly after three years to devote himself to the 'Life and Liberty' movement for Church reform, writing and editing and tirelessly addressing meetings which led to the Enabling Act of 1919. That Act led to the setting up of the Church Assembly, forerunner of the General Synod, and gave the laity a voice in Church affairs for the first time.

Lloyd George proposed Temple as bishop of Manchester. He went to his diocese full of vitality and laughter, determined to seek 'the things which pertain to the Kingdom of God'. His priorities were the

University of Manchester, the Student Christian Movement, the ecumenical movement, contacts with industry, both employers and trade unions, and the Blackpool Mission, where he drew crowds of a thousand or more. He was a leader in COPEC, the movement for Christian Politics, Economics and Citizenship. When he undertook the Oxford Mission in 1931, undergraduates crowded into the church of St Mary the Virgin, even sitting on the pulpit steps; and he went to the women's colleges, where he commented that 'not even a treacle pudding could stop them discussing the Holy Ghost at luncheon'. In 1940, he acted as chairman and convenor for the great Malvern Conference on social reconstruction, attended not only by clergy but by distinguished Anglican laity including T. S. Eliot and Dorothy L. Sayers, planning the new society which would be set up after the war.

In that year, he went to Canterbury. He made many broadcasts and wrote for the Press, giving the general public guidance in the Christian attitude to the war against Nazism. He was involved in famine relief, and in work for Jewish refugees. The pace of his work was as taxing as ever. He was often exhausted and in pain, but he carried on with patience and good humour. In September 1944 he went on retreat at Pleshey, saying, 'I need this retreat.' In early October he was seriously ill, and on 26 October he died, after only two and a half years at Canterbury.

Dean Carpenter wrote of him, 'William Temple was a larger-than-life person – prodigal in his gifts, lavish in his generosity, wide in his interests, abundant in his energy, holy in his dedication . . . Temple had a unique place in world Christianity, not simply because of the offices he held, but because of what he was in himself.'

The most enduring of William Temple's many writings (more than forty books) are *Nature, Man and God* and the deeply devotional two-volume *Readings in St John's Gospel* (1939, 1940). Both are still on many theological book-lists.

F. A. Iremonger, *William Temple, Archbishop of Canterbury: his life and letters* (1948); John Kent (1992); *Cantuar*, pp. 466–86; *D.N.B. 1941–50*, pp. 869–73. Works include *Christus Veritas* (1929), *Nature, Man and God* (1934); *Readings in St John's Gospel* (1939); *Christianity and the Social Order* (1942); *Thoughts in War-Time* (1940); *The Church Looks Forward* (1944).

7. Willibrord of York (658–739)   [*Commem.*]

Willibrord is know as 'the apostle of Frisia', and he is the patron saint of the Netherlands. He was born in Yorkshire, where his father became a <u>hermit</u>. He was educated at Ripon under *Wilfrid, and went to Ireland, where he studied and became a priest. He was thus able to combine the Latin and Celtic traditions. On his return to England, he planned a mission for what is now a northern province of the Netherlands. In 690, he set out to work in territories conquered by the Frankish king, Pippin II, who gave him protection. He went to Rome in 692 to inform the pope, Sergius I, of the mission's work, and again in 695 carrying letters from Pippin recommending that he should be consecrated a bishop. He was consecrated as archbishop of the Frisians, and given a mission to develop a metropolitan see.

Willibrord built churches and monasteries, and consecrated bishops to work under his jurisdiction. In 698 he founded the monastery at Echternach, the largest and most famous of his foundations, in what is now Luxembourg. At one stage, he was driven out of Utrecht by Radbod, the pagan king of Frisia. Churches were burned and priests killed, but when the Frankish forces were again in control, he returned and built up the work again. On at least two occasions, he was in direct confrontation with the Frisians: on the island of Heligoland, he killed some cows to provide food for his followers against local taboos, and on the island of Walcheren, he destroyed an idol in front of the priest and worshippers.

For the most part, he worked under the protection of the secular authority. *Boniface worked with him for a time, and Willibrord hoped that Boniface would be his successor; but Boniface wanted to take missionary work into fresh areas.

*Alcuin describes Willibrord as 'venerable, gracious and full of joy'. He lived to the age of eighty-one, and was buried at Echternach, which became a centre of pilgrimage.

Alcuin's Life of Willibrord is in *AA.SS.*, Nov., 3, pp. 455–500. There is a translation in C. H. Talbot, *Anglo-Saxon Missionaries in Germany* (1953). See also A. Grieve (1923); K. Heerings (1940); C. Wampach (1953); *Butler*, Nov., pp. 52–4.

9. Margery Kempe (born *c.*1373)   [*Commem.*]

At twenty, Margery married John Kempe, a burgess of Lynn, now King's Lynn, and then a flourishing commercial port. She became pregnant almost immediately, and was very ill. She nearly died when her son was born. Thereafter she behaved very oddly, and respectable Lynn society was outraged.

For a time she saw devils, who 'cried upon her with great threatenings'. She slandered her husband, her friends and her own self, tore her skin, and bit her own hand so severely that she had a scar for life. She wore rich and extravagant clothes. She tried to set up in business – first to run a brewery, and then to manage a corn-mill. Both enterprises failed. She gave up vain-glory, and turned to God. She told John that she wanted to live apart from him, and that they had 'displeased God by their inordinate love'. She added that Christ had 'promised to slay her husband's lust'. John said, 'Ye are no good wife'; but he seems to have been kind and patient, 'ever having tenderness and compassion towards her'. After four years of her protests, he made a vow of chastity before the bishop of Lincoln. By this time, Margery was wearing a hair shirt, fasting and undertaking penances. She had many visions of Christ and the *Virgin Mary; she wanted to kiss lepers; and she cried constantly. Devout mediaeval people frequently wept when they prayed or meditated, but Margery's tears were not quiet and meditative. She speaks repeatedly of 'plenteous tears and boisterous sobbing', and this could go on for hours without pause. She was noisy, and people found her extremely irritating. On the occasion when she came back from the Holy Land by ship, her companions left her at Venice, swearing that they 'would not go with her further, not for an hundred pound'.

Margery made the three great Christian pilgrimages, to Jerusalem, to Rome and to Compostela, giving her money away and meditating on all that she saw. She wandered about England and the Continent, and was several times arrested on suspicion of being a Lollard (see *Wyclif). She defended herself spiritedly. When the archbishop of York told her, 'I hear it said that thou art a right wicked woman', she replied, 'I also hear it said that ye are a wicked man, and if ye be as wicked as men say, ye shall never come to heaven unless ye amend whilst ye be here.' The archbishop gave a man five shillings and told him to 'lead her fast out of the country'.

Many people, including the archbishop, could not endure her company, but it is remarkable how many strangers were kind to her. Friars consoled her, housewives fed and sheltered her, maidens slept in her room because she was afraid to sleep alone. It takes a real effort of imagination to get back into Margery's fourteenth-century world, where there were no relaxants or anti-depressants for someone with Margery's symptoms; in her world, unorthodox behaviour was categorized as either 'of God' or 'of the devil'. Margery chose God, and did the best she could with her severe physiological and psychological problems. She visited *Julian of Norwich. She read the lives and writings of the saints; and she left us her own Book – a unique record of middle-class life and perceptions of religion in the fourteenth century. If she was difficult to get on with, that was her burden; and it is to her credit that she pursued her faith with great honesty and remarkable courage.

The only source for Margery's life is her own account, *The Book of Margery Kempe*. The unique fourteenth-century copy is in the University of Cambridge Library. E.E.T.S. (1940): modern version by W. Butler-Bowdon (1936); *D.N.B.*, 10, pp. 1282–3.

10. Leo the Great (d. 461)   [L.F.]

Little is known about the background of Pope Leo I, but he was probably a Roman, possibly of Tuscan parentage. He became a papal adviser, corresponding with *Cyril of Alexandria and helping John Cassian with his treatise on the Incarnation, which Cassian dedicated to him. He was in Gaul in 440, negotiating with two rival Roman generals, when messengers arrived to tell him that he had been elected pope.

Leo's pontificate lasted twenty years. During that time, he twice defended the city of Rome from the invading barbarians, once when he persuaded the Huns, who had sacked Milan, to accept tribute instead of sacking Rome, and once when he met Genseric, leader of the Vandals, with a similar proposal; but Genseric plundered Rome for a fortnight, taking many captives and some ecclesiastical treasures.

As a theologian, Leo was able to provide an elegant, concise and exact formulation of the person of Christ for the Council of Chalcedon in 451. In a document known as the Tome, he described Christ's two natures, divine and human, as united 'unconfusedly, unchangeably, indivisibly and inseparably'. When the delegates heard this, they cried, 'Peter has spoken by the mouth of Leo', and the doctrine became the official teaching of the Church.

Leo's letters, of which 143 survive, are concerned with 'the care of all the churches'. He was a watchful and energetic pontiff, fully prepared to use papal authority to support his bishops, but able to reprove them when he thought that they were wrong, or had exceeded their authority. He continued to seek out and oppose doctrinal errors, such as those of Manichaeism (which held that good and evil were equal and opposing forces), Pelagianism (which denied the doctrine of original sin), and Monophysitism (which held that Christ had only one nature in which the human was subordinate to the divine). His writings also include ninety-six sermons.

Leo is one of only three popes who have been given the accolade of being known as 'the Great' in the Western Church, the other two being *Gregory I and Nicholas I.

AA.SS., April, 2, pp. 14–22; P.L., vols 54–6; N.P.N.F., 12; T. G. Jalland, *The Life and Times of St Leo the Great* (1941); *Letters*, trans. and ed. D. Feltoe (1896); D. M. Hope, *The Leonine Sacramentary* (1971); N.C.E., 8, pp. 637–9; *Butler*, Nov., pp. 75–9; *Later Christian Fathers*, pp. 278–80.

11. Martin of Tours (c.336–97)   [L.F.]

• Martin's charitable gesture when he cut his military cloak in two with his sword and gave half to a freezing beggar at Amiens is one of the great dramatic incidents of Christian history. There is a statue of him, wearing the remaining half of his cloak, in Henry VIII's chapel in Westminster Abbey, and stained glass commemorates the event at Tours, Chartres, Beauvais, Bourges and York. The story is vouched for by Sulpicius Severus, who was Martin's contemporary and knew him well.

Martin was born in Pannonia, now western Hungary; but his father was in the Roman army at the time, and was later posted to Pavia in Italy. Martin is said to have been attracted to Christianity from the age of ten, but his father insisted, as he had a right to do under Roman law, that he should follow him in a military career. He was a member of the Imperial Guard when he encountered the beggar at Amiens. After the campaign, the emperor Julian the Apostate sent for the

Imperial Guard, to reward them with a bounty. Martin refused the money, and asked to be relieved of his post, saying, 'I am a soldier of Christ, and it is not lawful for me to fight.' He was thrown into prison, declaring that he was prepared to face the enemy alone and unarmed; but when hostilities ended, he was released.

He became a disciple of *Hilary of Poitiers, was baptized, and began to preach. He returned to Pannonia for a time, spoke out against the Arians on the Adriatic coast, and was scourged before being driven out by an Arian bishop. He spent some time as a hermit on a small island in the gulf of Genoa, and when Hilary, who had also been exiled, was restored to his see in 360, went back to Poitiers. Hilary gave him land near the city where he could live as a hermit. Like many other hermits, he attracted so many other people who wanted to share his solitude that he developed a monastery, thought to be the first in Gaul. His fame became so great that the people of Tours demanded that he should be their bishop, and he was elected by acclamation in 372. It appears that some of the neighbouring bishops objected to this procedure on the grounds that this unkempt ascetic did not have the necessary presence. Martin always had his detractors, and one of them, Brice, became his successor.

Martin continued to live as a monk, occupying a small cell. He chose a deserted spot outside the city, where he founded the abbey of Marmoutiers, which soon had eighty monks. At this time, monasteries were usually in populated areas: the country-dwellers (*pagani*) had little opportunity to hear the Christian message; but Martin undertook energetic missionary work in the rural areas, travelling on foot, by donkey, and by boat along the Loire and its tributaries. Other monasteries were founded, and churches built. He attracted hostility by smashing idols and razing temples, actions which were illegal at the time; but he was never afraid to stand up for what he believed. He protested against the rigours of Roman law on several occasions, notably in the trial of Priscillian and his followers, Gnostics who were charged with heresy at Trier. Martin argued that heretics should not be put to death, and that they should be tried by the Church authorities, not the Imperial courts; but they were executed for the capital crime of sorcery. Martin was afterwards troubled by the thought that he had not done enough to save the lives of Priscillians who were being hunted in Spain.

Martin died on 8 November 397, and was buried in Tours three days later.

His life and work became known through the account of Sulpicius Severus, and the pilgrimage to his shrine at Tours was a very popular one in mediaeval times. Churches were dedicated in his honour across France, and in Germany, Italy, the Low Countries and England. The old Roman church in Canterbury which *Augustine and his followers used for worship when they first came to England in 597 had a dedication to St Martin. His memory will always be associated with that first impulsive gesture, the gift of half his cloak to the beggar of Amiens.

Life by Sulpicius Severus in *P.L.*, 71, pp. 911–1008. Eng. trans. in *Western Fathers*, pp. 5–44; Gregory of Tours, *History of the Franks*, trans. and ed. Lewis Thorpe (1974), pp. 91–7; *P.B.*, 13, pp. 312–37. Modern Lives by P. Monceaux (1926, Eng. trans. 1928); C. Stancliffe, *St Martin and his Hagiographer* (1983); Mayr-Harting, pp. 83–7, 97–8; *Butler*, Nov., pp. 83–7.

13. Charles Simeon (1759–1836)   [L.F.]

After going to Eton, Charles Simeon, the son of a wealthy Reading lawyer, went to King's College, Cambridge. He stayed there for the rest of his life. Both the University and the Church of England were suffering from spiritual indifference and sluggish administration At first, Charles behaved like many other students – going to the races, gambling and dancing; but when he was twenty, he had a powerful conversion experience. On Easter Day 1779, without advice or support from anyone, he was driven into aloneness with God. He had an overwhelming sense of guilt, and gave all his sins to Christ. He went back to Cambridge, prepared for ordination, and was made deacon by the bishop of Ely in 1782. He was very isolated until he met *John Venn, and found him a fellow-Evangelical. In the summer of that year, he preached a series of sermons at St Edward's, Cambridge, and they were so inspiring that when his father asked the bishop, whom he knew personally, to appoint Charles to the living of Holy Trinity, the bishop agreed, though Charles was still a deacon and had never served a curacy.

In the following year he was ordained priest, and he set about his ministry with great zeal. His sermons alarmed the well-to-do pew-holders: they locked their pews and stayed away. He preached to artisans and paupers. He acquired a barrel-organ, produced his own version of the psalms and hymns which matched its tunes, and set the congregation singing. At this time, music in church was almost unheard of. He wanted to instruct the poor in church on Sunday evenings, but the churchwardens locked the doors and refused to let him in. He started a system of group meetings not unlike *John Wesley's classes, and preached in poor villages.

He was a powerful preacher. His sermons came from many hours of Bible study, and were vehement. He began to publish his sermon outlines, culminating in the *Horae Homilectae* of 1832 – 2,536 outlines in twenty-one volumes. He sent a beautifully bound set to King William IV, one to each archbishop, one to every Cambridge college, and one to each of the chief libraries in Britain and the United States; and he made a considerable profit, which he gave to Evangelical societies.

He continued to live in college. The terms of his Fellowship precluded marriage, and he had no wish to leave. He acted for a time as Dean of Arts and later as Dean of Divinity, but he gave no lectures and tutored no students. His whole effort was directed towards conversion, and fostering vocations to the ministry. He was not popular either in his college or in the town. He was mocked for his affectations, his pedantic ways and his ponderous humour, called a Calvinist, criticized for lack of scholarship, and once pelted with rotten eggs; but he accepted obloquy: he thought of Simon of Cyrene, and carried the Cross.

As the Evangelical wing of the Church became stronger, his many followers called themselves 'Simeonites' or 'Sims'. When he preached, his 900-seat church was crowded. He was a very active member of the Church Missionary Society. He spent much time with ordinands and young clergy, urging them to go to the mission field, and even leaving his beloved Cambridge to see them and their families off at the docks. He had enormous energy, and once told a group, 'I am an eight-day clock. Now I am wound up for another week.' He lived a very ascetic life, fasting, praying and reading his Bible, and he drank no wine. It was a hallmark of the 'Simeonites' that they drank only tea. If he was never loved by the dissipated and extravagant element in King's, they came to accept him and respect him, calling him 'the Old Apostle'.

Charles Simeon was the founder of the Simeon Trust. He used his considerable wealth to acquire patronage, and used it to appoint clergy of Evangelical churchmanship. When he died in November 1836, more than eight hundred members of the University processed at his funeral. He is buried in King's College chapel, in a vault simply marked 'C.S., 1836'.

J. Tait, *Charles Simeon and his Trust* (1930); Hugh Evan Hopkins, *Charles Simeon of Cambridge* (1977); Donald Coggan, *These Were His Gifts* (1994); Marcus Loane, *Cambridge and the Evangelical Succession* (1952); A. Pollard and M. M. Hennell, eds, *Charles Simeon, 1759–1836: essays written in commemoration of his bicentenary* (1959); D.N.B., 18, pp. 255–7. Stock, ch. 6.

14. Samuel Seabury (1729–96)   [*Commem.*]

The American War of Independence left the Anglican clergy in the newly established United States in an anomalous position. Most of them had supported the British side, and they found themselves irretrievably cut off from the Church of England. The few clergy left in Connecticut held a secret meeting and elected one of their number, Samuel Seabury, as their first bishop. Seabury had been born in Connecticut, and was one of the early graduates from Yale. He had studied medicine in Scotland, then decided to take Holy Orders, and had been ordained in England in 1754 by the bishop of London. He had been a chaplain to the British army during the war. From the British point of view, his qualifications were impeccable, and he went to England to be consecrated.

However, there were difficulties on both sides of the Atlantic. Though the English bishops were willing to agree to his consecration, he could not, as an American citizen, take the oath of allegiance to the Crown; and from the American point of view, he was too closely allied with the British. The English difficulty was overcome: Seabury went back to Scotland where, as he knew from his student days, there was an Episcopal Church of non-juring bishops. After some discussion, the archbishop of Canterbury indicated that he did not disapprove, and Seabury was consecrated on 17 November 1784. The ceremony took place in the upper room of a house in Longacre, Aberdeen, and the bishops of Aberdeen, Moray and Ross, and Dunkeld and Dunblane took part. The Scottish Episcopalians were not popular in their own country, and could not build a church for fear of attack.

Seabury returned to the United States, consecrated as the first Episcopalian bishop in North America; but while he was away, there had been a counter-initiative. In May 1784, a meeting was held in Brunswick, New Jersey, attended by three delegates from each of the states of New York, Pennsylvania and New Jersey, with four laymen. The chairman was Dr William White, the rector of a church in

Philadelphia and the only Anglican cleric left in the state of Pennsylvania. From the American point of view, White's credentials were much better than Seabury's: he had been ordained in England, but he had openly joined the American cause at the outbreak of the war. George Washington was a regular attender at his church.

In September 1785, a General Convention met in Philadelphia, attended by sixteen clergy and twenty-five laymen. Samuel Seabury was back in Connecticut, but he refrained from attending. The members were prepared to admit that he had been validly consecrated, but they were not satisfied with the 'back door' method of his consecration: they wanted full recognition as an independent province from the Church of England. After a year's deliberation and discussion, three clergy, including Dr White, were nominated by the Convention, and the Anglican authorities agreed to their consecration. One was unable to make the journey, but on 4 February 1787, Dr White and Dr Samuel Provoost were consecrated in the chapel at Lambeth Palace by the archbishops of Canterbury and York and the bishops of Bath and Wells and Peterborough.

At the next Convention, Bishop Seabury 'took his seat among the bishops without any dissentient voice', and he and Bishop White, on opposite sides during the War of Independence, are said to have 'laboured together in perfect harmony'. Seabury died in 1796. His mitre is preserved in Trinity College, Hartfield, Connecticut.

W. Benham, *A Short History of the Episcopal Church in the United States* (1884); *Who was Who in America, 1607–1896* (Chicago, 1968) p. 471. Seabury's writings include *A Discourse on Several Important Subjects* (1798).

16. Margaret of Scotland (c.1046–93)

Margaret, the grand-daughter of Edmund Ironside, king of Wessex, was brought up in Hungary during the time of King Stephen I, having been exiled with her brother and sister from England by Canute. The Hungarian court was Christian, and under Benedictine influence. They returned to England on the accession of *Edward the Confessor, but were exiled again after the Norman Conquest. Their ship was blown off course, and they landed on the Scottish borders. There they fell into the hands of Malcolm Canmore (Malcolm III of Scotland) who was raiding Northumberland. Malcolm had a fearsome reputation as a pillager of churches and a slayer of captives, but he protected the exiles and married Margaret, who would have preferred to become a nun.

Malcolm's court was raucous and uncouth, but he seems to have been fascinated by Margaret's knowledge of a more civilized world. He was prepared to learn from her, and ensured that his courtiers did the same. The Danish Benedictine priest Turgot, who was Margaret's spiritual director and biographer, describes how there was no more drunken rioting or debauchery at court. Good manners were encouraged, particularly at meals, and colourful, fashionable clothes took the place of homespun garments. The courtiers 'appeared like a new race of beings'.

The king was devoted to his wife. Though he could not read, he would look at her books, turning the pages and kissing them. He had her favourite books bound in gold and silver. He never learned to read, and she could not stop him from making war, but she did teach him to pray. He did so often, with many groans and sighs, and greatly respected her gentle spirituality.

Margaret founded Holy Trinity Abbey in Dunfermline, and endowed it with many treasures. Her circle of ladies embroidered albs, stoles, cottas and altar frontals to beautify churches. She distributed alms freely to the poor people of Dunfermline, and would take the king's gold to give them – he pretended not to notice, and was amused. Every day, poor people were brought in to the palace, and Malcolm and Margaret waited on them personally with food and wine, he taking one side of the room while she took the other. Margaret ransomed Norman captives whenever she heard of them, and sent them home to England. She and Malcolm visited Iona and restored the monastery, devastated by the Norwegians. She built a hospice on each side of the Firth of Forth for pilgrims to St Andrew's, and had them transported by the Queen's Ferry.

She convinced Malcolm that the Church in Scotland was in need of reform. The monks, known as the Culdees, still followed the old Celtic rite, but most of them were unlettered, and the rite had deteriorated over the centuries. Turgot called it 'barbarous'. There were many irregularities in observance. They did not receive the sacrament, and some did not keep Easter. They kept the Sabbath on Saturday, and worked on Sunday. They stood in church instead of kneeling reverently. Malcolm called them together so that Margaret could address them, and he acted as her interpreter. The reforms were accepted, though whether this was a tribute to Margaret's diplomacy or their fear of Malcolm's anger if they refused, is not clear.

Margaret bore Malcolm six sons and two daughters, reared them all, and supervised their early education herself. Three of the sons – Edgar, Alexander and David – became kings of Scotland. William of Malmesbury writes of them: 'No history has recorded three kings and brothers who were of equal sanctity, or savoured so much of their mother's piety.' One daughter married Henry I of England, and the other married Eustace, count of Boulogne.

Malcolm was killed in the battle of Jedburgh in 1093, fighting against William Rufus. Margaret died soon after. The castle was besieged by Malcolm's brother Donald Ban or Donalbane, who claimed the Scottish throne. Her body was taken down the face of the Castle Rock under cover of a thick Scottish mist, and across by the Queen's Ferry to be interred at Dunfermline Abbey.

The cave near Dunfermline where Margaret went for prayer and meditation, and her ancient chapel on Castle Hill, Edinburgh, can still be visited. The arms of the Burgh of Queensferry are her personal coat of arms.

Turgot's Life (badly damaged by fire) is in the British Museum: (ms. Cotton Tiberius D III), and in *AA.SS.*, June, 2, pp. 316–35. For translations, see *L.S.S.*, pp. 159–82; and W. Forbes-Leith (Edinburgh, 1884). Margaret's Gospel Book is in the Bodleian Library at Oxford. Modern Lives by Lucy Menzies (1925, repr. 1947); T. Ratcliffe Barnett (1926); Margaret Gordon (1934); J. H. B. MacPhail (1947); D. M. Roberts (1960). *D.N.B.*, 12, pp. 1017–19.

Edmund Rich of Abingdon (?1170–1240)

Edmund Rich came of a very pious family. His father, also Edmund, entered a monastery when he was still young, and his mother, Mabel, brought up her six children on austere lines. They were taught not to eat on Sundays and festivals until they had sung all 150 Psalms in the Psalter, and to wear hair shirts or sackcloth. Edmund wrote 'Jesus of Nazareth' on his forehead every night before he went to sleep.

After Oxford, he was sent to study in Paris, where he stayed to lecture on the great classical courses of the *trivium* and the *quadrivium*. He was a gentle person of great kindness, and is said to have sold his books to give money to poor scholars. During this time, his austerities increased. He fasted constantly, and rarely slept except on his knees during his nightly vigils.

Some time after his mother's death, he had an experience in which she appeared to him, and drew three circles. He understood that these represented the Trinity, and that in future he must devote his life to the study of theology. Whether this was a dream or a vision or an unconscious prompting, he acted upon it. He turned to teaching Divinity about 1205, and was at Oxford from about 1214 to 1222. He left Oxford to become treasurer of Salisbury cathedral. In that capacity, he undertook much public preaching, and was involved in preaching the Sixth Crusade (1228–9).

In 1233, Pope Gregory IX appointed Edmund archbishop of Canterbury. It was not a happy appointment for an elderly scholar, for he was forced to intervene in many disputes between pope and king, king and barons. Within months of his consecration, he averted civil war by negotiation with the barons. He had a considerable influence on the rash young king and on the appointment of his ministers, particularly in his conflicts with Hubert de Burgh, and he negotiated a truce with Prince Llewellyn on the Welsh borders. At one point, he threatened Henry III with excommunication. The threat had been carried out in the time of Henry's father, King John, and all England placed under an Interdict, so it was an effective one. Henry was said to have heard three masses a day to retain the favour of God and his archbishop.

Edmund became renowned as a peace-maker and a mediator. He had a horror of bribery, and administered even-handed justice. He fought for the rights of the English Church, resisting papal exactions. He was on his way to Rome to counter a demand that three hundred livings should be surrendered to the Romans when he died at Pontigny. Henry III visited his shrine at Pontigny, as did his son Edward I, and Matthew Paris of St Alban's abbey wrote Edmund's biography, showing him as a revered exemplar to a turbulent and strife-ridden age. St Edmund's College, Oxford, long known as 'Teddy Hall', is named after him.

Matthew Paris, *The Mirror of St Edmund*, modern trans. by Francesca Steele (1905); M. R. Newbolt (1928); M. F. Bell (1933); C. H. Lawrence (1960); *D.N.B.*, 5, pp. 108–9; Powicke, pp. 47, 56–60, 119, 256n.

17. Hugh of Lincoln (*c.*1140–1200)   [L.F.]

This celebrated mediaeval bishop-statesman was born at Avalon, near Grenoble in France. He was educated at the Augustinian priory at Villard-Benoît, and became an Augustinian canon. He was in his early twenties when the prior took him on a visit to the great monastery of La Chartreuse above Grenoble founded by Abbot Bruno in 1084. He was much attracted by the austerity and silence of this mountain retreat, where the monks were virtually hermits.

He remained at La Grande Chartreuse, where he was procurator for ten years, until 1175, when he was called to England. *Archbishop Thomas Becket had been martyred in 1170. Part of King Henry II's penance was to set up the first Carthusian house in England at Witham in Somerset. Two previous priors had failed to launch this successfully, and the bishop of Bath was despatched to ask Hugh to take it over. He did so with great energy and intelligence. He discovered that the people whose property had been expropriated had not received due compensation, and insisted that the king should pay this in full. The house was organized, the Rule instituted, and some very able and spiritually minded monks came to join him.

In 1186 Henry II, who thought highly of his abilities, asked Hugh to become bishop of Lincoln. He did so only on condition that he could maintain his vow of obedience to La Grande Chartreuse. He had no desire to become the king's man, and in view of Becket's fate, this was a wise precaution. The bishopric had been empty for nearly eighteen years, during which time the king had appropriated the revenues.

Hugh found the diocese run-down, morale low, and the cathedral in ruins following an earthquake in 1185. He started the re-building of the cathedral, and used to go and help the builders himself. Though the re-building was not completed in his lifetime, the design was his. He gathered a group of committed clergy, revived learning so well that the Lincoln schools of theology were said bear comparison with the Paris schools, and travelled endlessly, preaching and inspiring his people. From time to time, he would retire back to Witham to find the silence and the time for meditation which he still longed for.

Hugh was a champion of the oppressed: he cared for lepers, who were then the most stigmatized people in European society; he righted injustices; he opposed some ugly outbursts of anti-Semitism, on three occasions facing a mob alone and unarmed to stop a persecution. He was also a diplomat: his relations with those three Angevin kings of uncertain temper, Henry II, Richard I and John were always good, though he would speak out fearlessly if he thought that they were acting unjustly. This had less effect on John than on the other two, but Hugh could always turn a difficult situation by humour.

After his accession, King John sent Hugh to witness the signing of the treaty of Le Goulet in France. He visited Cluny and Cîteaux, the older Benedictine and the newer Cistercian foundations, and revisited La Grande Chartreuse. On his way home, he went to pray at Thomas Becket's shrine. He became ill in London, and he died there on 16 November 1200. His body was taken in state to Lincoln. A great concourse of kings, princes, bishops and abbots attended his funeral, including King John, William the Lion, king of Scotland, and Prince Gruffydd ap Rees from Wales. Representatives of the Jewish community also attended, mourning the loss of 'a true servant of the great God'.

N.L.A., 2, pp. 41–52 contains the *Magna Vita S. Hugonis* by Hugh's contemporary, Adam. This is trans. and ed. by D. L. Douie and D. H. Farmer (1985) Gerard of Wales's *Life of Hugh of Avalon* is trans. and ed. by R. H. Loomis (1985) and *The Metrical Life of St Hugh* by C. Gorton (1986). Modern Lives by R. M. Woolley (1927); D. H. Farmer (1985); H. Mayr-Harting, ed. (1985); *Butler*, Nov., pp. 147–50. See also D. Knowles, *The Monastic Orders in England* (1963), pp. 375–91.

18. Elizabeth of Hungary (1207–31)   [L.F.]

Elizabeth, the daughter of King Andrew II of Hungary, was married to Ludwig (Louis) the Landgrave of Thuringia in central Germany when she was fourteen. What began as an arranged match developed into a deep love affair – so much so that the couple made a pact that if one died, the survivor would not remarry. They had three children. Elizabeth was warm-hearted, full of gaiety, and extremely generous. When there was a famine in 1225, she gave all her own stock of corn to the populace. When Ludwig was told, he said, 'Her charities will bring divine blessings. We shall not want as long as we let her relieve the poor as she does.' She started a hospice, and often went in to help the old and sick people under her care.

In 1227, Ludwig went to join the Emperor Frederick II on a new Crusade. He never reached the Holy Land, dying of plague in Otranto.

Elizabeth, who was still only twenty, had just given birth to their third child. When she was told that Ludwig was dead, she could not believe it, and thought that he must be imprisoned. When she finally realized the truth, she cried, 'The world is dead to me, and all that is joyous in the world.'

Her brother-in-law acted as regent for her infant son Hermann, who was the new Landgrave. She placed her two daughters with nuns, and became a Franciscan Tertiary. She went to live in a small house near Marburg with two ladies in waiting, one of whom had been with her since childhood. Her confessor was a former inquisitor, Conrad of Marburg, who became her mentor. He drew up a new and very severe régime for her, and sent away her ladies in waiting, substituting two 'harsh females' who were instructed to report on every aspect of her life, and her compliance or non-compliance with his orders. He would punish her with slaps on the face, or blows with a 'long, thick pole'. He was, as commentators have noted, a sadist, but Elizabeth accepted his cruelty with great docility. Perhaps she felt some irrational guilt for her husband's death; perhaps she really did not care what happened to her. Her self-imposed penance did not last long. Three years after Ludwig's death, she also died, at the age of twenty-four.

Elizabeth was very popular in Germany, and her shrine at Marburg became a place of pilgrimage until the Reformation, when a Lutheran Landgrave had it removed.

Near-contemporary Lives by Caesarius of Heisterbach, and by Dietrich of Apolda, ed. H. Canisius, in *Antiquae Lectiones*, 5, pp. 147–217; E. Horn (1902); J. Ancelet-Hustache (1946, Eng. trans. 1963); *Anal.Boll.*, 18 (1908), pp. 493–7 and 27 (1917), pp. 333–5; *O.D.S.*, p. 156; *Butler*, Nov., pp. 144–7.

19. Hilda of Whitby (614–80)   [L.F.]

Hilda was a relative of King Edwin of Northumbria. She grew up in his household, and when he became a Christian in 627, she was baptized. *Bede tells us that Hilda's life fell into two equal parts. Until she was thirty-three, she lived the normal life of a noblewoman. As a Christian, she probably carried out works of charity. Then she decided to live the religious life, and *Aidan, who had come from Iona to preach the gospel in the northern kingdom, persuaded her to stay in Northumbria rather than going to the royal nunnery at Chelles, near

Paris, where her sister was already a nun. She lived a secluded life with a few companions before becoming abbess of a small monastery at Heruten (Hartlepool) for some years. Aidan and other monks from Lindisfarne often visited the house, and were impressed by her 'innate wisdom and love of God'.

Hilda must have been in her early forties when she was appointed abbess of Streaneshalch – later called Whitby by the Danes – as superior of a double monastery. The monks were responsible for worship, while the nuns led an enclosed life focused on prayer and contemplation. Hilda was head of the whole establishment, which also included a large landed estate. The monks and nuns did not undertake manual work, and though there were still serfs in England, monasteries did not use their labour. Farm labourers, huntsmen, shepherds, butchers, fishermen, carpenters and wood carvers, blacksmiths and leather workers and other workers from the locality were employed. One of them was a cowherd named Caedmon, whom Hilda encouraged to study the Scriptures, become a monk and sing of the great Christian themes.

Hilda established a regular pattern of monastic life, and built up a library of manuscripts – all the New Testament and part of the Old Testament, which were then available in various translations, and had to be copied by hand on parchment or vellum. The learning and piety of her monastery were so celebrated that five of her monks became bishops. She became much respected as a wise woman, and many people came to her for counsel.

Streaneshalch, like all the religious houses in the north of England at the time, followed the practices of the Celtic Church. When the differences with the Roman practice brought to the south by *Augustine of Canterbury became acute, it was chosen as the meeting place for what is now known as the Synod of Whitby (664). When the final decision was taken to adopt the Roman system (largely on the representation of *Wilfrid), Hilda did so without question.

Bede tells us: 'In the year of our Lord 680, Hilda, abbess . . . a most religious servant of Christ, passed away to receive the reward of eternal life on the seventeenth of November at the age of sixty-six, after a life full of heavenly deeds.'

Bede, bk 3, ch. 24; bk 4, chs 25—34; Eddius Stephanus, chs 10, 54; A. Warren (1989). See also D.N.B., 9, pp. 832–3; N.C.E., 6, p. 1116; *Butler*, Nov., pp. 157–9.

Mechtild of Magdeburg (1210–98)   [*Commem.*]

Mechtild lived for thirty years in a community of Béguines, the devout laywomen of the Low Countries, who devoted their lives to serving poor and sick people. In her old age, when her sight was failing, she entered the abbey of Helfta in Saxony. Though the spiritual experience of the nuns of Helfta was largely shared, and she recorded some of the visions of Gertrude of Helfta, her own thought and writing are distinctive. There is no doubt that she was the author of her *Revelations*, subtitled *The Flowing Light of the Godhead*. She wrote in the vernacular of the Low Countries, and her spiritual director, Father Heinrich von Halle, later translated the work into Latin.

Mechtild describes how God gives all creatures the possibility of living according to their natures. Her own nature is to reject everything for God himself: he is her creator, her brother, her lover: she wants no-one and nothing else. One of the most memorable passages in her manuscript is a long dialogue between Love and the Soul. 'How can the Soul stand the fiery glory of the Godhead?' she cries, and the answer comes, 'It is what it was made for.'

> Fish cannot drown in the water
> Birds cannot sink in the air
> Gold cannot perish
> In the refiner's fire.
> This has God given to all creatures,
> To foster and seek their own nature.

There is a strand of visionary thought which seems to run from the neo-Platonists through Helfta to the Renaissance. Mechtild's vision is close to that of Plotinus and Pseudo-Dionysius. In another passage, she writes:

> Thou shalt love the naughting,
> And flee the self.
> Thou shalt stand alone
> Seeking help from none,
> That thy being may be quiet,
> Free from the bondage of all things.

It is doubtful whether Mechtild was directly acquainted with the thought of either Plotinus or Dionysius, since she was 'unlearned' and could not read Latin or Greek; but she would have learned of the thinking of the neo-Platonists through the more scholarly nuns of Helfta.

Mechtild's work seems to have influenced Dante. In Part III of her *Revelations*, she describes a journey into hell. In the deepest part of hell, she sees Christians who have failed their Master. In the middle part, where the torment is less, are the Jews; and in the highest part, with the least suffering, are the good heathen, according to their work. Dante, writing some years after her death, could have read of this early version of his *Inferno* in Heinrich von Halle's translation.

Dict. Spir., 10, cols 877–85; *The Revelations of Mechtild of Magdeburg, or the Flowing Light of the Godhead*, trans. and ed. Lucy Menzies (1955); Heinrich von Halle's Latin manuscript is now lodged in the University of Basle.

20. Edmund of East Anglia (841–69)   [L.F.]

Edmund was a young Christian king, said to be much loved by his people. The *Anglo-Saxon Chronicle* records how he did battle against a Viking invader named Ingvar, 'and that day Edmund fought against them, and the Danish men got the victory, and slew the king, and subdued all that land, and destroyed the monasteries they came to'.

The earliest Life of Edmund consists of the recollections of his armour-bearer, transmitted to *Archbishop Dunstan and written by Abbo of Fleury at the Benedictine monastery of Ramsey in the tenth century. According to this account, Ingvar demanded that Edmund should renounce the Christian faith, and offered to let him rule as a vassal under Danish jurisdiction. Edmund refused. He and his men were then pursued, he was captured, and Ingvar made the same offer again. Edward again refused, and was ritually killed, being scourged, shot with arrows to wound and not kill, and then beheaded.

His death may have taken place at Hoxne, Suffolk or Hellesdon, Norfolk: both the North-folk and the South-folk were anxious to claim him as their own afterwards. His body was later transferred to Bedricsworth, which became known as Bury St Edmunds. In 1020, Canute, the Danish king, who was a Christian, was anxious for reconciliation with his English subjects. He ordered a stone church to be built on the place of Edmund's burial.

More than sixty English churches bear dedications in St Edmund's name. His most famous representation is that in the Wilton Diptych, now at the National Gallery in London, where he appears with *Edward the Confessor as one of the two sponsors presenting Edward II to the Virgin and Child. His life is exceptionally well documented, and a cult grew up in his memory, based on the ideals of holiness, courage and resistance to the invader. He is said to have 'learned his psalter in the Saxon tongue', and the psalter was preserved at Bury St Edmunds until the dissolution of the monasteries. His relics are thought to have been secretly re-buried elsewhere to save them from desecration.

Abbo of Fleury's Life is in the J. P. Morgan Library in New York; an illustrated Life written somewhat later by John Lydgate, also a monk of Bury, is in the British Library (ms. Harley 2278). See also S. T. Ridyard, *Royal Saints of Anglo-Saxon England* (1988), pp. 211–33; N.C.E., 5, p. 108; Men.E.W., pp. 185–6, 236, 298 and n., 559–61; D.N.B., 6, pp. 400–1; O.D.S., pp. 147–8; Butler, Nov., pp. 173–5.

Priscilla Lydia Sellon (1831–76)

Lydia Sellon was the daughter of a commander in the Royal Navy. Her mother's family were connected with St Paul's cathedral, where her grandfather was receiver-general to the dean and chapter. When, in 1848, *Dr Pusey appealed to the bishops of the Church of England to establish religious houses for women, the only immediate response came from the bishop of Exeter, Henry Phillpott, who wanted Sisters to work in the dockland areas of Plymouth and Devonport. A small group were constituted Sisters of Mercy of the church of the Holy Trinity, Devonport, with Lydia Sellon as their superior, forming the first Anglican Sisterhood founded since the Reformation. Dr Pusey acted as their spiritual director.

In the early days there were people in Plymouth and Devonport who were not easily reconciled to the idea of Anglican nuns, and who were highly suspicious of their activities. The Sisters endured being pelted with potatoes and plates, and drenched with ale in the streets. When they founded an orphanage, there were allegations in the local press of cruelty toward the children. The bishop held a public inquiry, conceded that they had made some mistakes due to youth and inexperience, but ended by warmly commending their work. They proved to be devoted nurses during the cholera epidemic of 1854, and the later epidemics of 1866 and 1871. They set up schools and orphanages, and undertook housing work similar to that of *Octavia Hill, buying blocks of houses for poor tenants and making contracts with them so that they respected and improved the property. With her father's agreement, Mother Lydia was able to dispose of the property he planned for her to inherit, and added some thousands of pounds to the housing fund. She was sometimes criticized as being autocratic: the bishop of Exeter withdrew from acting as Visitor when she styled herself 'Spiritual Mother and Mother in Christ', and she moved from a relaxed Benedictine form of Rule to something much closer to the military discipline of *St Ignatius; but there was work to be done, and she organized her troops.

Seven of the Devonport Sisters with nursing experience accompanied *Florence Nightingale's party to the Crimea. In 1856, the community joined with the Holy Cross Sisters in a house at Ascot built with a legacy from *Dr Pusey's mother. Dr Pusey was closely associated with their development, and frequently spent the summer vacation from Oxford in working with them. Houses were established in many cities, and a missionary branch was started in 1864 for the Pacific.

T. J. Williams (2nd edn, 1965); H. P. Liddon, *Life of Edward Bouverie Pusey, D.D.*, 4, pp. 309–10, 341–3; *Far Above Rubies*, pp. 265–7; obituaries in *The Times*, 24 and 26 Nov. 1876.

22. Cecilia (?third century)   *[Commem.]*

All we really know about Cecilia comes from a legend, a tomb, a church with a remarkable late sixteenth-century statue, and her reputation as the patron saint of music. She is said to have been a girl of patrician family who was married without her consent to a pagan named Valerius in the time of Pope Urban I (222–30). She refused to consummate the marriage, saying that she had dedicated her life to God. Valerius did not denounce her to the authorities: he became a Christian also, as did his brother Tiburtius. The two men went about burying the bodies of Christian martyrs, which was forbidden on pain of death. They were arrested and executed together with an official called Maximus, who was converted by their witness. Cecilia buried both Valerius and Tiburtius, and was arrested in her turn. She refused to sacrifice to the Roman gods, and was also martyred.

This story is not mentioned by any of the well-known Christian writers of the fourth century with a special interest in virgin martyrs, such as *Ambrose, Pope Damasus I or *Jerome. There is a crypt dedicated to St Cecilia in the Catacombs of San Callisto, outside Rome. Her body is reputed to have lain there until 820, when it was discovered and moved to her church. The earliest Life of Cecilia dates from the fifth century, and at some time before it was written, a church in the Trastevere district of Rome had been founded by a Roman woman named Cecilia. She was probably a wealthy widow: under Roman law, widows were the only women who were allowed to dispose of their own property. It seems likely that the dedication was originally to her, and the legend of the virgin martyr was grafted on at a later date. The church of Santa Cecilia-in-Trastevere is reputed to have been built on the site of the martyrdom, but excavations into the foundations have revealed the remains of a house and a tannery, suggesting that the original Cecilia was more likely to have been a merchant's widow.

Part of the apse from the church re-built by Pope Paschal I (817–24) is still standing, and the church is enriched with a magnificent thirteenth-century fresco of the Last Judgement by Pietro Cavalli. In 1599, further partial re-building took place, and Cecilia's tomb was opened. The life-sized marble statue of a girl lying on her side, as if asleep, which stands in front of the high altar was completed by Stefano Maderno in the same year.

Cecilia has been the patron saint of music and musicians since at least the fifteenth century. The origin of this link lies in an antiphon from her fifth-century Life, which describes how, as the organs played at her wedding, she sang silently to the Lord, saying, 'Let my heart remain unsullied, so that I be not confounded.' She is one of the twenty-two virgins in the Byzantine frieze in the church of San Apollinare Nuevo in Ravenna, which dates from the sixth century, and she became patron of the Academy of Music in Rome and many other musical organizations. In stained glass windows, she is often shown with a lute.

Delehaye, pp. 72–96; 194–220; Quentin in *D.A.C.L.*, 2, cols. 2712–38; *N.C.E.*, 3, p. 360; *O.D.S.*, pp. 91–2; *Butler*, Nov., pp. 184–6.

23. Clement of Rome (d. *c.*101) [L.F.]

Clement I was probably the fourth bishop of Rome, following *Peter, Linus and Cletus. Papal lists give the dates of his pontificate as 91 to 101. He may have known the apostles *Peter and *Paul, and it has been conjectured that he may be the Clement mentioned as a fellow-worker in Paul's Letter to the Philippians. His own *Epistle to the Corinthians*, written about 95–8, is well authenticated, though other works attributed to him are probably spurious.

Clement gives details of Peter's residence in Rome, for which evidence is otherwise scanty, and of his martyrdom. His letter to the Church at Corinth is regarded as the first attempt of the Church in Rome to intervene in the affairs of churches elsewhere. Clement urges the Corinthians to reconciliation with Rome in the name of the traditions set by the apostles. This suggests that differences were already appearing; but his letter seems to have been received in a spirit of brotherhood, since it is recorded that it was read at the Liturgy in Corinth about the year 170, and it forms part of the *Codex Alexandrinus* to the New Testament.

Clement may have been martyred. There were sporadic persecutions in the time of the Emperor Trajan, and according to a fourth-century account he was deported to the Crimea, where he was forced to work in the mines and then killed by being thrown into the sea with an anchor round his neck. The ninth-century apostles to the Slavs, *Cyril and *Methodius, claimed that they had discovered his remains still attached to the anchor. The relics were taken to the church of San Clemente in Rome, though this was not a dedication to Pope Clement. The church is thought to have been built on the site of a house owned by a man named Clement, which became a centre for Christian worship in the third century.

Lightfoot, pp. 3–94 includes an English translation of Clement's *Epistle to the Corinthians*; J. A. Kleist, *The Epistles of St Clement of Rome and St Ignatius of Antioch* (1946); J. Colson, *Clément de Rome* (1994); Delehaye, pp. 45, 47, 96–116; *D.H.G.E.*, 12, cols.1089–95; *Butler*, Nov., pp. 188–9. For Clement's Letters, see *Late Christian Fathers.*, pp. 33–73.

25. Catherine of Alexandria (early fourth century) *[Commem.]*

Like *Margaret of Antioch, Catherine of Alexandria was a very popular saint in mediaeval England, and was named as one of the Fourteen Holy Helpers in the Rhineland; but her story rests on very shaky foundations. She was said to be a girl of noble birth who refused to marry the Emperor Maxentius. She disputed with fifty philosophers who tried to convince her of the errors of Christianity, and defeated them all in argument. She spoke out against the persecutions of Maxentius, and was tortured by being broken on a wheel before she was executed.

Maxentius, son of the Eastern emperor Maximian, carried out a coup d'état against his father in 306, and is known to have persecuted Christians. It is rare to hear of a young woman disputing with philosophers; but we know of at least one other learned woman in Alexandria later in the fourth century – Hypatia, who was killed by followers of *Cyril of Alexandria.

Catherine's story was brought back to Western Europe by the Crusaders. No doubt the story of how she was tortured by being broken on a wheel contributed to its spread: mediaeval stories of saints often contained horrific elements. Artists and craftsmen depicted her with the wheel, and the popularity of the 'Catherine wheel' in firework displays is a reminder of this practice. A wheel is a perfect circle, and so a very basic art form. She became the patron saint of wheelwrights, spinners and millers, as well as of young girls and students.

Mediaeval miracle plays were based on her life, including one recorded at Dunstable in 1110. Part or whole life-cycles in stained glass can still be seen in York Minster and Balliol College, Oxford, and there are many murals, including one in Winchester cathedral and another in Eton College Chapel. There are said to be at least 170 mediaeval bells which bear her name.

Golden Legend 2, pp. 232–3; O.D.S., pp. 88–9; N.C.E., 3, p. 253.

Isaac Watts (1674–1748)   *[Commem.]*

Even when he was at grammar school in Southampton, Isaac Watts wrote verses, in English and Latin. A wealthy physician of the town offered to send him to Oxford or Cambridge, but he declined, explaining that he would have been required to subscribe to the Thirty-Nine Articles, and saying that he 'preferred to take his place among the Dissenters'. He went to an dissenting academy in Stoke Newington instead. This decision closed many avenues of employment to him, and when he had finished his studies he became tutor to the son of a baronet. He attended an Independent meeting house in Stoke Newington, eventually became pastor there. He acquired patrons – Sir Thomas and Lady Abney of nearby Abney Park.

Watts devoted his whole life to writing, and wrote prolifically. His prose writing, on the whole, was undistinguished, but his hymns became very popular. A man of considerable learning and piety, he was highly regarded in London literary circles. *Dr Johnson greatly admired his work. His hymns, which are now found in almost every Christian hymnal, include 'O God, our help in ages past', 'Jesus shall reign where'er the sun', 'When I survey the wondrous Cross' and 'Come, let us join our cheerful songs'. The annual output of his *Hymns and Spiritual Songs* at the beginning of the twentieth century was over 50,000 copies. It sold widely in the United States, and was translated into Dutch and Welsh.

There has been some debate over whether Watts became a Unitarian in his later years. He certainly defended dissenters who were unwilling to subscribe to a belief in the Trinity, but it seems unlikely that the writer of 'When I survey the wondrous Cross' would lose his hold on the doctrine of the Atonement; and the evidence of friends who visited him when he was dying was that the belief that Christ died for his sins was one to which he held fast in his last hours.

The University of Edinburgh awarded Watts an honorary degree of Doctor of Divinity, and there is a monument to him in Westminster Abbey.

Thomas Milner (1834); N. R. Hood (1875); A. P. Davis (1943); *D.N.B.*, 20, pp. 978–81. There is a memoir in Thomas Gibbons' edition of the *Works* (1780), and another in Robert Southey's edition of the *Poems* (1880).

30. Andrew the Apostle   Festival

The facts given in the Gospels about the life of the apostle Andrew are limited, and this is probably why so many unsubstantiated stories have clustered about his name. We know that he was the brother of *Simon

Peter, and called with him. His name is repeatedly mentioned in the first four of the apostles, with Peter and *James and *John, the sons of Zebedee. Like them, he was a fisherman on the Lake of Galilee. He and Peter shared a boat, and the story of the healing of Peter's mother-in-law (Mark 1:29–31) suggests that he shared a house with Peter and his wife. The Gospels of *Matthew and *Mark say that they lived in Capernaum, and that Jesus called Peter and Andrew together when they were at work on their nets by the side of the lake (Mark 1:16–18; Matthew 4:18–20). *Luke mentions Peter as owning the boat which catches the miraculous draught of fishes (5:3–9), but does not include the story of the brothers' call, and does not mention Andrew until the following chapter, where he is listed as one of the Twelve (6:14). *John says that Peter and Andrew came from Bethsaida, which is a mile or two along the lake from Capernaum; that Andrew was a disciple of *John the Baptist, and witnessed the baptism of Jesus; that he and another man followed Jesus, and then he went to tell Peter, saying 'We have found the Messiah' (John 1:41). For this reason, Andrew is sometimes called the *Protoclete*, or 'first called'.

Andrew is present on a number of occasions in the ministry of Christ, perhaps somewhat overshadowed by his more out-going brother; but it is he who points to the small boy with five loaves and two small fishes at the feeding of the five thousand (John 6:8–9), and *Philip consults him about the Greeks who wish to see Jesus. The Greeks probably approached Philip because he was a Greek; Philip went to Andrew because he knew him well: he also came from Bethsaida. Andrew is in the upper room when Christ appears to the apostles (Acts 1:13) and takes part in the election of *Matthias to replace Judas.

Thereafter, there is no firm information about his ministry. In the fourth century, *Gregory Nazianzen and *Jerome say that he was martyred in Greece, while the historian Eusebius of Caesarea says that he went to Syria. An Old English poem, 'Andreas', once attributed to Cynewulf, is based on ancient legends which say that he was in Ethiopia. Many claims have been made both about his missionary work and the whereabouts of his relics, often as a counterbalance to the prestige of Rome, which claimed the relics of his brother Peter. Reputed relics were translated from Patras to Constantinople, where an early mediaeval forgery claimed him as the first bishop of Byzantium; the Crusaders took them to Italy; and the head, which had remained in the Vatican for five hundred years, was returned to

Constantinople in an ecumenical gesture by Pope Paul VI in the early 1960s.

An apocryphal account led to Andrew being recognized as one of the patron saints of Russia, and another to his adoption as the patron saint of Scotland. The legend of how St Regulus was told by an angel to travel 'towards the ends of the earth' and took Andrew's relics to the city now known as St Andrews on the east coast of Fife has a prominent place in Scottish mythology. It accounts for the presence of the cross of St Andrew on the Union Jack; but the saltire, or diagonal cross, was not used as an emblem of St Andrew until the tenth century, and did not become a popular representation of his martyrdom until the fourteenth.

Eusebius, *H.E.*, bk 3, chs 1, 25, 39; P. M. Peters, *Andrew, Brother of Simon Peter: his History and Legends*, supplement to *Novum Testamentum* 1 (1958); F. Dvornik, *The Idea of Apostolicity and the Legend of the Apostle Andrew* (1958); *L.S.S.*, pp. 436–40; *O.D.S.*, pp. 20–1; *Butler*, Nov., pp. 226–7.

December

1. Charles de Foucauld (1858–1916)   [*Commem.*]

Vicomte Charles Eugénie de Foucauld, Brother Marie-Albéric, Père de Foucauld, Brother Charles, the *marabout* or holy man of the Sahara: this strange and driven man had many names. He idled at the *Lycée*, just scraped into the military academy of Saint-Cyr, and developed a taste for gambling and girls. He joined the *Chasseurs d'Afrique* in 1880, proved an insubordinate junior officer, but was both disciplined and brave when a Moslem holy war started in Algeria.

Africa possessed his imagination. He left the army after two years and went back to North Africa as an explorer, travelling in Morocco, which was then virtually unknown. It was hostile country: he dared not travel as a Christian, and he could not pass as a Moslem, so he went disguised as a poor Jew, with a Jewish guide. When he finally returned to France, it was with a mass of geographical, military, political and cultural information, and he wrote two scholarly books which were well received. He was in a state of internal turmoil for some time, and then he came back to the faith he had been taught as a child, and had long abandoned. He went to the Holy Land; he visited four different religious Orders in France; and in 1890, on the advice of a wise priest, he became a Trappist. He needed the 'solitude and silence with God' which he had found in the desert.

He stayed with the Trappists at Notre-Dame-des-Neiges in the Ardèche as Brother Marie-Albéric for six years. The abbot said that he was 'like an angel, he wanted for nothing but wings'. He fasted, he kept vigils, he did hard manual labour, but somehow he did not fit in. He needed more solitude. In January 1896, he was dispensed from his preliminary vows. He noted, 'The new life that I am going to begin will be much more *hidden*.'

He went to Nazareth dressed like an Arab vagrant, without possessions. The abbess of the Poor Clares allowed him to live in a hut by the convent gate, to serve at Mass, and to run occasional errands for the nuns. He stayed there for most of three years, developing schemes. One of them was to buy the Mount of Beatitudes, but it was not for sale. He was drifting. The abbess finally persuaded him to go home and seek ordination, and he left the Holy Land in August 1900 with no possessions but a breviary and a basket of fruit.

In 1901, after his ordination, he went back to Morocco to begin his mission. He had sought the permission of Monsignor Guérin, the prefect apostolic for the Sahara, saying that he would live near a French garrison, act as its chaplain, and require no emoluments. He went to the oasis at Béni-Abbas, where he built a simple chapel and lived a life of silence, self-abasement and great austerity. Though he needed silence, he also hoped to build a community: he wrote to Monsignor Guérin on a number of occasions asking for 'slave relief work', staff for a shelter for travellers, Sisters to run an orphanage for abandoned Tuareg babies; but in spite of his many gifts, his religious superiors did not think his schemes practicable.

For a time, there was talk of Trappist brothers joining him, but none came. Monsignor Guérin wrote in perplexity to the abbot of Notre-Dame-des-Neiges: 'This very holy man . . . is absolutely alone in the midst of the savage Tuareg tribes, which he has succeeded in civilising, and to which he does the greatest good by the example of his life of extreme poverty, of charity unfailing, and of continual prayer'; but Charles wrote in a letter, 'I am still alone. I am not faithful enough for Jesus to give me a companion.'

He was still in contact with the *Chasseurs d'Afrique*, and would walk thirty miles to say Mass for them on a holy day; but he lived with the Tuaregs, made friends with the children, wrote back to France to get black hair dye for the women, who hated to go grey, and formed strong links of loyalty with the tribesmen – liars and robbers all, as he said, but steadfast friends. He spoke their language as well as they did. He did not try to convert them from Islam, thinking that they knew as little of that faith as any other, but spoke to them of natural law, of God's commandments, of contrition, and of charity. He moved to a small hermitage not far from Fort Motylinski. There he finished his French-Tuareg dictionary, and his translations of Tuareg poems.

During the First World War, the Turks stirred the tribesmen up to religious hatred of the French and British. The hermitage, where some French arms were stored, was captured by a group of fanatics, and Brother Charles was shot, almost casually, by one of them. The chief of the Hoggar Tuaregs wrote to his sister in France promising to hunt the assassins, and saying: 'All is dark to me. I wept, and I shed many tears, and I am in great mourning . . . may God have mercy on him, and may we all meet in Paradise.'

René F. Bazin, trans. P. Kerlan, *Charles de Foucauld: Hermit and Explorer* (1923); D. Hall, *The Priest of the Legion* (1947); R. V. C. Bodley, *Warrior Saint: Charles de Foucauld* (1954); M. Carronges, *Soldier of the Spirit* (1956); *Twentieth Century*, pp. 18–22; J. V. Taylor, *The Go-Between God* (1972). Works: *La reconnaissance au Maroc* (Paris, 1880); *Meditations of a Hermit*, trans. Charlotte Balfour (1930).

3. Francis Xavier (1506–52)   [*Commem.*]

The first members of the Society of Jesus, or Jesuits, led by *Ignatius of Loyola, made their vows of service to God in Paris in 1534. One of them was Francis Xavier, born in the castle of Xavier, near Pamplona. He was appointed apostolic nuncio in the East, and sailed for Goa in 1541 – a journey which took him and his small party thirteen months.

The Portuguese had founded a colony in Goa in 1510. Although the Church was already established there, it was confined to ministering to the settlers, many of whom were only nominal Catholics. Slavery was practised, and the worst kinds of colonial abuses were common. Francis started a mission to the Indians, working in the appalling prisons and hospitals, preaching in the open air, and celebrating Mass for the lepers. He taught the Catechism to children and slaves, and composed religious verses to be sung to popular tunes.

He went on to carry out missions to the Paravas, a low-caste population on the south-east coast of India. In all, he made the dangerous journey to this area thirteen times, learning their language and living as they lived, on rice and water, sleeping on the floor. His appeal was always to the poor and oppressed. He described their sufferings at the hands of both Portuguese and high-caste Indians as 'a permanent bruise on my soul'.

In 1545, he crossed the Indian Ocean to the Portuguese settlement of Malacca, which had been captured from the Malays in 1511. There he found a similar mixture of vice, lawlessness and oppression, and opposed it vehemently, converting and instructing many. He went on to other Portuguese settlements in 'the Spice Islands' (now Indonesia), and heard about Japan, which was then closed to all European influence. On his return to India, he began to make plans for a mission to Japan, and in 1549 he set sail with a small party. As he had learned the language of the Paravas, so he set himself to learn Japanese. He did not find Eastern languages easy (his own first language was Basque), but he made a basic translation of Christian teaching, and after a year in Kagoshima, where he landed, he had a hundred converts.

There was no general opposition to the mission: Christianity was a complete novelty to the Japanese at this time; but Francis soon learned that, though holy poverty brought him close to the poor of India, it did not impress the Japanese local rulers. He had to change tactics. He presented himself to the ruler of Miyako, well dressed and with the rest of his party acting as attendants, as the representative of the king of Portugal, presenting him with a musical box, a pair of spectacles and a clock. The ruler, delighted with these Western gifts, gave him an empty Buddhist monastery, where he baptized about two thousand people.

When he had consolidated his mission and left other priests and catechists in charge, he sailed back to India to deal with problems there, and then decided to undertake a mission to China. The Portuguese authorities in Malacca were obstructive, and the journey had to be undertaken in secret, because China was even more thoroughly sealed against the West than Japan. He finally crossed the China Sea in a convoy of merchant ships with only a young Chinese companion, Antony. They landed on the coast near Canton. Francis became ill, and had no support save that of one Portuguese ship which remained in the area. He was taken aboard the ship, but could not bear the motion of the vessel, so he was left on the sands in a state of delirium with only the faithful Antony in attendance. Antony put a lighted candle in his hand, and he died 'with the name of the Lord on his lips . . . with great repose and quietude'. He was forty-six years old. There were only four people to mourn him: Antony, a single Portuguese and two slaves.

Francis had spent his life in opening East Asia to the Christian faith, and in opposing the worst features of Portuguese colonialism. Other Jesuits followed him to southern India, Ceylon, Malacca and Japan. Many stories were to be told of his humility, his great powers of endurance, and his devotion to the poor and suffering. He is particularly venerated in Goa, where he was buried.

The major source for the life of Francis Xavier is the *Monumenta Xaveriana* (2 vols, 1899–1912), published in Madrid. See also George Schurhammer's definitive edition of the *Letters* (2 vols, 1943–4, with J. Wicki), and his *Francis Xavier: His Life, His Times*, trans. M. J. Costello (4 vols, 1973–82). Biographies by Edith A. Stewart (1917), with translations from letters by David Macdonald; and James Brodrick (1952).

4. John of Damascus (*c.*657–749)   *[Commem.]*

Born about five years after the death of Mohammed, John was baptized a Christian, and had a good Greek education, including logic and theology. He inherited from his father a hereditary post at the court of the Caliph. Some accounts describe him as a tax collector, but 'Grand Vizier' is probably a more appropriate description. Moslems respected Christ as a prophet, though they believed that Mohammed was a greater one. Christians were able to practise their faith unhindered until a new Caliph, Abdul Malik, began to introduce restrictions. John was probably in his forties when he gave away his wealth and went to join Mar Saba, an association of hermits, near Jerusalem.

Mar Saba was just beyond the frontiers of the jurisdiction of the Eastern emperor in Constantinople. At that time, the Iconoclasts were attacking the use of images in religious worship, tearing down pictures and statues of Christ and the saints. Mar Saba not only gave John the peace and quiet he needed for his writing, but provided him with a base from which he could attack both the Iconoclasts and the Moslems, who were equally opposed to pictures and images. Apart from one short period when he was called to Jerusalem by the patriarch, he lived the many remaining years of his long life there.

His writing covers doctrine, worship, biblical exegesis, liturgiology and other theological disciplines. It is based on scholarship and an encyclopaedic knowledge of the works of the early Fathers of the Church. His most celebrated works are his three treatises against the Iconoclasts, and *The Fount of Knowledge*.

In the treatises against the Iconoclasts, John argued that the saints were to be respected, their statues and pictures cherished, their lives recorded as a model for Christian living. They represented the Church Triumphant. He was particularly concerned that honour should be paid to images of Christ crucified and resurrected, and to those of the *Virgin Mary. He maintained a sacramental view of life. Matter and spirit could not be separated: Christ was not pure spirit, he took on a material form. The Holy Sepulchre, the Scriptures, the Eucharist were all matter. 'Do not despise matter, for it is not despicable. Nothing is that, which God has made.'

The Fount of Knowledge consists of three very long works, setting out the nature of the created world, an analysis of over a hundred heresies, and the tenets of the Christian faith. The third of these, *De Fide Orthodoxa*, consists of over a hundred chapters, and incorporates writings of other authorship. This was an acceptable practice in John's day. He was not attempting to develop new doctrine, but to analyse and evaluate the accumulated Christian literature of some five centuries in order to reveal the truth of the Gospels. Like the apostle *Paul, he describes how Christ came to fulfil the law and the prophets, and how at Pentecost the Church became Christ's body in the world, the source of love and peace. He writes, 'He who seeks God will find him, for God is in everything.'

In 753, some years after John's death, the Iconoclastic Council declared him to be 'anathema, the worshipper of images and falsehood', but his reputation survived, though for centuries his works were much better known in the Byzantine Church than in the West. *De Fide Orthodoxa* was not even translated into Latin until 1150, and his other works were not available in the West until the eighteenth century.

M. Jugie has a full and detailed analysis of the writings and doctrine of John of Damascus in *D.T.C.*, 8, pp. 693–751. Lives by J. H. Lupton (1883); M. Fortescue, *The Greek Fathers* (1908), pp. 202–48; J. Nasrallah (1950). Eng. trans. of *De Fide Orthodoxa* by S. D. F. Salmond, *N.P.N.F.*, 9 (1899), and of the *Apologia in Defence of Holy Images* by M. H. Allies (1898).

Nicholas Ferrar (1592–1636)   *[Commem.]*

In 1625, the Ferrar family left London for a remote and dilapidated house half-way between Huntingdon and Oundle. Nicholas had bought the Lordship of the Manor of Little Gidding, where he proceeded to set up a unique Christian community. With him went his mother, his sister Susanna and her husband John Collett and most of their children, his brother John with his wife and children, and several other relatives.

Nicholas, the son of a wealthy London merchant, had been a prodigy. He read very widely, and had an exceptionally retentive memory, being able to repeat the whole of the Psalms and chapters of the New Testament by heart when he was still very young. His tutor at Cambridge said that he learned more from teaching Nicholas than he could teach him. In 1613 Nicholas went abroad. On his travels, which lasted five years, he investigated the Anabaptists and Brownists in the Netherlands, learned German in Hamburg, toured Austria, Spain and Italy, and visited Tunis. In Spain, he ran out of money, walked many miles, and learned to soak his aching feet in a bowl of sherry sack. In Rome, he went incognito, to avoid the Roman Catholics: he regarded the Pope as Anti-Christ. He came home after five years with voluminous notes on religion, and a huge crate of books.

He returned to London in 1618 to find that his father, who was a prominent member of the Virginia Company, was ill, and wished to retire. Nicholas took his place. Though he was offered many other prominent positions, including an embassy and Clerk to the Privy Council, he regarded this as family duty. In the following year his father died, and Nicholas became his sole executor. His work for the Virginia Company, in which he became the chief executive, absorbed his abilities until 1624, when James I, who had become increasingly hostile to the Company, revoked its Royal Charter, probably under pressure from the Spanish ambassador. Virginia became a colony, and Nicholas's work came to an end.

The move to Little Gidding was probably accelerated by the plague which ravaged London in 1624–5: his first concern was to move all his family to safety. They were a very devout family. The bishop of Lincoln agreed that the tiny church could be licensed as a place of worship. Nicholas was made a deacon and took daily services, a priest coming once a month to celebrate the Eucharist. The women of the family furnished the church, which had been used as a pig sty and a hay barn, making the tapestries, hangings and carpets. The community developed gradually, the numbers varying as other relatives and friends came to stay, and they sometimes took paying guests. The household settled into a regular routine of prayer and worship, rising at 5.00 a.m., processing to church twice a day, attending a short service of prayer and Psalms every hour, and keeping night vigils. They are said to have recited the whole of the Psalter every day, and to have covered the whole of the four Gospels every month. During meals, there were readings from Protestant works such as John Foxe's *Book of Martyrs*. They lived very simply, and worked very hard, to be as self-sufficient as possible. They ran a school for their own children, of whom several were born there, taught the local children to recite the Psalms, founded an infirmary, and took in four poor widows.

After a time, this quiet community began to attract attention. *George Herbert, Richard Crashaw and *Isaac Watts were among the friends who came to stay, and *King Charles I visited Little Gidding en route from London to Scotland.

A particular feature of the community was 'The Academy', a regular meeting for religious study and discussion attended by an informal central council. Old Mrs Ferrar was known as 'The Founder' or 'The Mother', John Ferrar was 'The Guardian', and Susanna Collett 'The Moderator'. The daughters acquired such sobriquets as 'The Patient', 'The Affectionate' and 'The Obedient', and Nicholas was 'the Head'. They held learned discussions on many religious subjects, and produced and printed their own books, together with a massive biblical Concordance of which Charles I requested a copy.

Closed communities often excite suspicion in their immediate neighbourhood. As the king and parliament moved towards conflict, suspicion grew that the community's simple, pious way of life was a cloak for Roman Catholicism. The women of Little Gidding wore plain black dresses, and were accused of being nuns. There were many candles in the church because there was no other form of lighting, and they were suspected of celebrating Masses. When Nicholas burned some books – comedies and other works he regarded as trivial – the rumour went round the countryside that he practised black magic, and was burning his 'conjuring books'.

Nicholas died on 3 November 1636, and was buried under a plain unmarked tombstone. Ten years later, Little Gidding was raided by Puritan forces, and the remains of the community driven out. Most of their books were destroyed, and the house left in ruins. Today it has totally disappeared, leaving only the church which inspired T. S. Eliot's poem.

A. L. Maycock, *Nicholas Ferrar of Little Gidding* (1938); A. M. Williams, *Conversations at Little Gidding* (1970); T. S. Eliot, *Little Gidding* (one of the *Four Quartets)*. A transcript of John Ferrar's biography of his brother is in the Baker Mss. vol. 35 at Cambridge. Charles I's copy of the Concordance and three volumes of the original five *Story Books: Lives, Characters, Histories and Tales for Moral and Religious Instruction* written and produced at Little Gidding are in the British Library.

6. Nicholas of Myra (fourth century)   [L.F.]

The apparently mythical figure of Santa Claus has its origins in a real Christian bishop, Nicholas of Myra, in what is now southern Turkey. Nicholas was thrown into prison in the Diocletian persecutions in 303–5, but returned to his diocese after the accession of Constantine. He attended the great Council of Nicaea in 324–5, where the first version of the Nicene Creed was drafted, and Arianism was condemned. The Council had some stormy meetings. Nicholas was strongly opposed to Arius of Alexandria, and some of the Greek accounts say that he actually struck him during the debates, and was temporarily deprived of his office and imprisoned for doing so. He preached the doctrine of the Trinity tirelessly against both Arians and non-Christians. He is reported to have been a kind and generous man, with a great love of justice, and to have intervened on a number of occasions to save people who had been unjustly condemned.

He is thought to have died in Myra, and to have been buried in his cathedral, where there was a magnificent shrine; but his basilica is now in Bari, on the Adriatic coast of southern Italy, and he is sometimes known as 'Nicholas of Bari'. When the Saracens conquered Asia Minor in the eleventh century there was great anxiety about the fate of Christian relics. The fame of Nicholas was so great that cities in Italy contended for the honour of rescuing his remains. Venice claimed them; but it was finally decided that they should go to Bari, where there was a large Greek colony. The relics were secretly stolen in 1087, taken to Bari by merchant ship, and enshrined in the Norman basilica which still stands.

The earliest biographical account of Nicholas was written by Methodius, patriarch of Constantinople, some two hundred years after his death. Since then, he has been the subject of many accounts which have grown increasingly fanciful with the passage of time. He is reputed to have been the son of wealthy parents, and to have devoted his inheritance to works of charity. The best-known instance of his charitable works is the gift of three bags of gold to a man who had lost all his money, and whose three daughters were doomed to prostitution because there was no other future for them in a society where girls needed dowries in order to marry. A celebrated fifteenth-century painting by Crivelli, now in the Sainsbury Wing of the National Gallery in London, shows Nicholas at the window, the three bags of gold on the floor, and the three daughters sitting up in bed. This story is said to have been the origin of the pawnbroker's three golden balls.

Nicholas is the patron saint of sailors in the Eastern Orthodox Church. Sailors in the eastern Mediterranean traditionally invoked him with the prayer 'May St Nicholas hold the tiller'. In the Roman Catholic Church, he is the patron saint of children. The association with Christmas presents comes from neither of these sources, but from a Protestant custom in the Low Countries which the Dutch took to New Amsterdam before it became New York.

G. Anrich, *Hagios Nikolaos . . . in der griechischen Kirche* (2 vols, Leipzig, 1913–17) contains the Greek texts, with a full introduction and notes. K. Meisen, *Nikolauskult und Nikolausbrauch im Abendlande* (1931), has many pictorial illustrations. Modern studies in English include E. Crozier, *The Life and Legends of St Nicholas* (1949); A. D. de Groot, *St Nicholas: a psycho-analytic study of his history and myth* (Eng. trans. 1951); C. W. Jones, *St Nicholas of Myra, Bari and Manhattan* (New York, 1978); N.C.E., 10, p. 454. For legends, see *Golden Legend*, 1, pp. 21–6; Karl Young, *The Drama of the Mediaeval Church* (1933).

7. Ambrose of Milan (*c.*340–97) [L.F.]

Ambrose was a Christian, but he had not even been baptized when he was suddenly acclaimed bishop of Milan in 374. In his time, prominent people often delayed baptism until their old age or even until their death-beds, because their public position often required them to take actions of which they wished to be able to repent later. Ambrose was over forty years of age, and governor of the Italian regions of Liguria and Aemilia, with residence in Milan. The Church was still split by the Arian heresy, and when Auxentius, bishop of Milan, who was an Arian, died, there was rioting in the streets. Ambrose went to the church where the different factions were arguing over the succession, asking them to make their choice in a spirit of peace and harmony. They could not agree on a candidate, and someone – it is said to have been a child – shouted 'Ambrose for bishop!' The cry was taken up by the whole gathering. The emperor Valentinian agreed in order to settle the dispute, and within a week, Ambrose was baptized and consecrated.

He resolved to change his way of life completely. He gave away all his possessions: his considerable property in lands and estates went to the Church, his personal possessions to the poor. All that he kept was an income for his sister Marcellina. He began to study the Scriptures and the works of the early Fathers of the Church, taking instruction from a learned teacher, Simplician. He lived very simply, and devoted his life to writing and the care of his flock.

Marcellina, to whom Ambrose wrote letters which are still extant, became a consecrated virgin, and one of the most celebrated of his treatises is *De Virginibus*, in which he defended the right of women to take up the religious life. It is said that the mothers of Milan kept their daughters away from his sermons, lest they should be influenced and refuse to accept the marriages arranged for them. He also wrote *To Gratian, concerning the Faith*, a major treatise setting out Christian doctrine, and a number of hymns and poems.

Ambrose was involved in several power clashes with the Emperor Valentinian and his mother Justina, who was an Arian. In 386, a law was passed forbidding anyone to obstruct Arian assemblies or to prevent the Arians from taking over churches. On Palm Sunday, Ambrose preached a sermon stating that he would not cede a single church. His supporters, fearing for his life, barricaded themselves in the basilica with him. The Imperial troops surrounded the building and tried to starve them out. On Easter Day they were still there, singing hymns and defying the emperor; and the emperor gave way.

Ambrose insisted, 'The emperor is in the Church, and not over it.' Valentinian and his mother had to flee, and placed themselves under the authority of the Eastern emperor, Theodosius. Though Theodosius reinstated Valentinian, he insisted that he should cease to support the Arians, and that he should respect Ambrose. This Imperial support did not prevent Ambrose from making a stand against Theodosius. On one occasion, he defended some zealots who had pulled down a Jewish synagogue, confronting the emperor in church and refusing to celebrate Mass until he pardoned them. On the other, more acceptably to modern eyes, he protested vigorously against the massacre of seven thousand people, guilty and innocent alike, in reprisal for the death of the governor of Salonika. He demanded that the emperor should do public penance; and the emperor did so.

Ambrose was a strong defender of the rights and freedom of the Church. He was not afraid to rebuke emperors, and to insist that Christian morality applied as much to them as to others. He died on 4 April 397, which was Good Friday; but his feast has long been held on 6 December, the date of his consecration as bishop of Milan, to keep it clear of Easter. He is one of the four Latin Doctors of the Church, together with *Augustine, *Jerome and *Gregory the Great.

Contemporary materials for Ambrose's life in *P.L*, 14, pp. 65–114. Life by Paulinus in *Western Fathers*, pp. 147–90; J. R. Palanque, *S. Ambroise et l'empire romain* (1933); F. H. Dudden, *The Life and Times of St Ambrose* (1935). Both Palanque and Dudden contain full bibliographies. Works in *P.L.*, 14–17 and Eng. trans. in *N.P.N.F.*, 10. Poems with Eng. trans. in Helen Waddell, *More Latin Lyrics*, ed. Dame Felicitas Corrigan (1978), pp. 70–1. See also H. Spitzmüller, *Poésie Latine Chrétienne du Moyen Âge* (1971), pp. 39–54.

13. Lucy (d. *c*.304)   [L.F.]

An inscription dating from the fourth century which records that a girl named Euskia died on Lucy's feast day can still be seen in Syracuse, in Sicily. It is thought that Lucy was a native of that city, and that she died, like so many others, during the persecutions of the Emperor Diocletian in 303–5. There are various stories about the manner of her death. One account suggests that, like *Agnes, she was a Christian girl betrayed to the authorities by a suitor who wanted to marry her in order to obtain control of her wealth. Another tradition is that a man, usually identified as a Roman soldier, tried to rape her, and denounced her when she resisted. By the time of Cardinal Jacobus de Voragine's *Golden Legend*, the story included an account of how she had been ordered to be taken to a brothel to be violated, but how she became miraculously immovable, and escaped this fate. In many of these early stories about women, constant oral repetition for centuries before they were written down tended to add salacious and circumstantial detail.

Whatever the true story was, Lucy died for her faith, and was honoured by the Church as an illustrious virgin martyr. Her name is included in the canons of the Roman and Ambrosian rites, and many churches in Italy were dedicated to her. She is one of the twenty-two virgins on the sixth-century Byzantine mosaic frieze in the church of San Apollinare Nuovo in Ravenna. By the seventh century, her fame had spread to England, and *Aldhelm, bishop of Sherborne (born 639), wrote extensively about her in prose and verse, though he relied on some spurious sources.

Lucy's name has connotations of light and purity, and many artists have portrayed her as a typical virgin saint, including Titian and Fra Angelico. The song 'Santa Lucia' refers to her. Her feast day is often marked by special celebrations relating to virginity. Perhaps because it occurs near the winter solstice, it has frequently been celebrated as a festival of light. In Sweden, where there are few hours of light in

December, young girls dressed in white and crowned with lighted candles traditionally processed to church to honour Lucy.

Hieronymianum, p. 407; References in Aldhelm's treatise *De Virginitate*, in *Monumenta Germanicae Historica, Auctores Antiquissimi*, 15 (1919), pp. 293–4; *La Historia di Santa Lucia, Virgine e Martire* (verse, c.1550); D.A.C.L., 9, cols 2616–18; A. Beaugrand, *Sainte Lucie* (Paris, 1882); *Saints in Italy*, pp. 281–3; *Golden Legend*, pp. 27–9.

Samuel Johnson (1709–84)   [Commem.]

Dr Johnson, author, critic and man of letters, was the son of a Lichfield bookseller. He grew up reading voraciously, and with a remarkable verbal memory. He had to leave Oxford when his father's business failed, and for several years he led a precarious existence in London, contributing to the *Gentlemen's Magazine*, *The Rambler*, and *The Idler* – solid pieces of writing to suit the tastes of an age which took its literature seriously.

In 1747, he conceived his plan for a *Dictionary of the English Language*, finally published in 1755. The *Dictionary* was so extensive, and showed such a wealth of learning, that as it became known, fame and prosperity followed. In 1763, he met James Boswell, a Scottish man of letters who was to accompany him on his journey through the Highlands, and to provide a memorable portrait of him in his *Life of Dr Johnson* (1791). From Johnson's later years come his critical commentary on Shakespeare (eight volumes, 1765), and his *Lives of the Poets* (ten volumes, 1781). His strange gesticulations, his untidiness, his abrupt and often devastating speech, his wit and humour, his affection for his cat Hodge, were all part of an original and much loved personality.

Dr Johnson was a High Tory and a High Churchman, devoted to the Church of England and intolerant of both Roman Catholics and Dissenters; but he showed great depth and sincerity of religious belief in what was a lukewarm age. For many years, he was a regular communicant at St Clement Dane's in Fleet Street, and he loved the *Book of Common Prayer*. He said he owed his faith to *William Law's *Serious Call to a Devout and Holy Life* (1729). He wrote many prayers and sermons for the clergy, and was often pressed to take Holy Orders, with the offer of good livings; but he had his own vocation, and he was a city man: he would not have been either happy or effective in a country parish. His faith was austere: he saw the omnipotence and omniscience of God very clearly, and found it 'awe-ful' in the seventeenth-century sense of the term. He dreaded death and the coming Day of Judgement, for he had a great sense of sin.

Despite his High Tory views, he never lacked kindness to humbler people. He opposed the severity of the criminal law, and long before *William Wilberforce, he spoke out against slavery. He had known poverty himself, and thought it 'a great enemy to human happiness'. When he had money, he gave generously to anyone in need, and he would thrust pennies into the hands of neglected children as they slept in doorways.

For much of his life, Johnson lived in fear of losing his reason: a terrible prospect for a man who lived by rational thought and brought to it such a high art. He suffered in his later life from acute depression, and he would often sit up drinking tea until four o'clock in the morning with anyone who was sufficiently wide awake to keep him company.

He died on 13 December 1784, and was buried in Westminster Abbey. His continuing literary reputation rests less on his rounded prose and noble sentiments than on a respect for the man himself: as English and solid as the oak tree, a sturdy defender of the Church, a man of much learning and piety, and great humanity.

Boswell's *Life of Johnson, The Works of Dr Samuel Johnson,* and *The Letters of Dr Samuel Johnson* are all available in many editions. See also *D.N.B.,* 10, pp. 919–35; M. J. Quinlan, *Samuel Johnson: a Layman's Religion* (Madison, University of Wisconsin Press, 1964); J. P. Hardy, *Samuel Johnson: a critical study* (1979); C. F. Fisher, *The Religious Thought of Dr Johnson* (Ann Arbor, University of Michigan Press, 1968); C. F. Pierce, *The Religious Life of Samuel Johnson* (1983); Norman Page, ed., *Dr Johnson: Interviews and Recollections* (1987).

14. John of the Cross (1542–91)   [L.F.]

John was born in Fontiveros, near Avila in Spain. After the death of his father, the family lived in great hardship, and John was sent to an orphanage, later finding employment as a nursing assistant in a hospital. There he developed a devotion to the sick and the poor, and a capacity for cheerfully undertaking the most menial and unpleasant tasks. At seventeen, he was sent to the Jesuit College, where he studied

Latin and the humanities for four years, and developed a vocation for the monastic life. He became a Carmelite friar, and studied at the University of Salamanca, the outstanding centre of theology in Spain. He was ordained priest in 1567, and soon after met *Teresa of Avila, who was seeking friars to start a Reformed Carmelite community for men. John and Prior Antonio de Heredia were the first two. They set up a house at Duruelo, about five miles from Avila. In 1571, Teresa became prioress of the Carmelite convent at Avila, and she sent for John to be its spiritual director and confessor.

As the Reform movement developed, the unreformed Carmelites became increasingly hostile. Teresa was under the personal protection of King Philip II, but John was not. He was captured and imprisoned in 1575–6, and again in 1577, when he was immured for eight and a half months in the Carmelite priory in Toledo. Here he spent most of his time in total darkness in a tiny cell, freezing in winter and stifling in summer. He was treated with hatred and calumny. He was half-starved, verminous, and was regularly flogged in chapter to force him to reject the Reform movement: he bore the marks for the rest of his life. He was told that he would die in his cell, and he was afraid that he was being poisoned.

It was in these conditions of stress and privation that John developed a remarkable spiritual insight, and composed some of his finest poems. In August 1578, he managed to escape, climbing down the high walls of the priory by means of a rope made by tearing his rag rug into strips. He found his way, barefoot and exhausted, to the house of the Reformed nuns, who gave him shelter in their chapel.

Subsequently, John was sent as prior of the Reformed house of El Calvario, near Beas. He continued to write poems for some time. When asked how he received his inspiration, he said simply, 'Sometimes God gave me the words, and at other times I sought them.'

John carried a heavy burden of administrative duties. In 1579, he became head of the college at Baeza, and in 1581 he was appointed prior of Los Martires, near Granada, and deputy vicar-general of the Reform. His days were spent in setting up new friaries, in teaching and the pastoral care of his friars and nuns, and in his prose writings, *The Ascent of Mount Carmel*, *The Dark Night of the Soul*, *The Spiritual Canticle* and *The Living Flame of Love*, with little time for meditation or prayer.

After Teresa's death in 1582, John faced mounting opposition, even within the Reform movement. In 1591 he was stripped of all offices, and sent to the remote friary of La Peñuela by the vicar-general of the Reform. His days were spent in setting up new friaries,rner like an old kitchen cloth'. When he became ill, he went to the friary at Úbeda, where he was badly treated by a hostile and vindictive prior. He died there in the first few minutes of 14 December 1591, as the choir began to sing Matins.

John's poems are full of symbolic imagery – light and darkness, flames, wounding, suffering, pursuing, finding. Probably his best-known poem is 'Dark Night', which describes how the soul goes forth under cover of night to meet the Beloved. Many devout Christians have found this poem a source of spiritual enlightenment. John's prose works seem to have formed the basis of his lectures to the friars and nuns of the Reform, and they are written in the precise and formal language of the lecture room, very different from the visionary insights of the poetry. *The Ascent of Mount Carmel* and *The Dark Night of the Soul* together form one work, describing the path to union with God. The *Spiritual Canticle* and *Living Flame of Love* keep more closely to the structure of the poems, and treat of the love between the individual soul and God. All these have become spiritual classics.

Lives by Bruno de Jésus-Marie, *Saint Jean de la Croix* (1929, revised 1961, Eng. trans. 1932); E. Allison Peers, *Handbook to the Life and Times of St Teresa and St John of the Cross* (1954). Works: Crisógono de Jésus (Eng. trans. 1958); E. Allison Peers (3 vols, 1933, revised edn 1953); K. Kavanagh and O. Rodríguez (1966). The last two include translations of the Poems, which are also trans. by Roy Campbell ·(1951) and Kathleen Jones (1993). Commentaries: Thomas Merton, *The Ascent to Truth* (1951); L. Saggi, *Saints of Carmel*, trans. G. N. Pausback (1972), pp. 142–69, with a very full bibliography on pp. 169–72; *Carmelite Studies VI: John of the Cross* (1992).

17. Eglantine Jebb (1876–1928)   [Commem.]

When Eglantine Jebb wanted to go to Oxford, her father, a country landowner, said that a university education was only suitable for plain girls, and she was not plain; but plain or pretty, she went. She attended lectures by *Charles Gore, Henry Scott-Holland and William Morris, and visited Toynbee Hall. After taking an honours degree in Modern History at Lady Margaret Hall, she trained as a teacher; but her mother, now widowed, wanted her at home in Cambridge. There was little to use her talents and energies. She thought of taking part of a

Theology degree course, but found that 'religion is not much studied. They count up the words, and make minute researches in Greek and Hebrew'. She accompanied her mother on holidays in France, Italy, and Switzerland. She worked for the Charity Organisation Society, but became disillusioned with middle-class philanthropy: 'Case after case noted, stories of drunkenness and debt and disease . . . one goes on to the next tea-party.'

Her opportunity came just before the First World War. After the Balkan War of 1912, two well-known Liberals, C. R. Buxton and his brother Noel Buxton, had established a Macedonian Relief Fund. C. R. Buxton's wife was Eglantine's sister Dorothea. The two ladies were asked to go out and distribute relief both to the liberated Macedonians and the defeated Turks. There were terrible stories of atrocities, and many thousands of displaced people. Refugees were sheltering in outhouses, begging, starving and often dying by the roadside. Eglantine returned to England to start a campaign for relief work. Though she hated public speaking, she forced herself to describe conditions and to raise public awareness of them.

During the First World War, she worked for the Agricultural Organisation Society. In 1918, when there was starvation and disease in defeated Germany and Austria, she was involved in the Fight the Famine Council. This was set up in opposition to Lloyd George's policy of 'squeezing Germany till the pips squeak', and when she distributed pamphlets showing starving babies, she was arrested and charged under the censorship laws. She was fined £5, but the prosecuting counsel made a contribution to the fund. Eglantine became the honorary secretary of what was named the Save the Children Fund. It was supported by many politicians and prominent people, including thirteen bishops. At a meeting in the Albert Hall, the National Union of Miners pledged £10,000. She went to Rome, and had an audience with Pope Benedict XV, who published an encyclical directing all Roman Catholic churches to make collections. Anglicans, Orthodox and Free Churches followed suit, and the collections were taken, appropriately, on *Holy Innocents' Day.

There were many criticisms, chiefly on the grounds that the children the Fund was saving would grow up to be Britain's enemies in the next war; but George Bernard Shaw entered the debate, saying that he had no enemies under the age of seven; and the supporters of the Fund pointed out that 'disease has no frontiers'. Three hundred local Save the Children committees were formed in England alone. The movement spread to other countries, and a conference sponsored by the Red Cross in Geneva led to the formation of Save the Children International, based in that city. In 1923, Eglantine Jebb compiled the Declaration of Geneva – a short, simple statement of the rights of children to physical, mental and spiritual development which was adopted by the League of Nations and became the basis of subsequent human rights legislation.

The work expanded: the League of Nations High Commissioner for Refugees asked for food relief in Russia; there were a million Greek refugees expelled from Asia Minor by the Turks; there were famines in Africa, in China. There was never enough money, and there was always intolerable suffering. Eglantine dealt with all the complexities of relief administration – the daily feeding of hundreds of thousands of lost or orphaned children, the re-uniting of families, and the problems of setting up hospitals, schools, and specialized care for those left blind or physically disabled by war.

'Every generation of children offers mankind a new possibility of rebuilding the ruins of the world,' she wrote. She died in Geneva on 17 December 1928 at the age of 52 after a very strenuous life of travel and campaigning. A model village in Albania, Xheba (Jebb), commemorates her name, and has her statue.

Dorothea Buxton and Edward Fuller, *The White Flame* (1931); Edward Fuller, *The Rights of the Child* (1955) and *If Any Man Build: a history of the Save the Children Fund* (1965); *Far Above Rubies*, pp. 69–91. The account in *D.N.B.* 1922–30, pp. 451–2, contains some inaccuracies.

26. Stephen (c.34) [Festival]

The first Christian martyr was probably one of the Hellenists of the Dispersion – Jews from outside Palestine, who had their own synagogues in Jerusalem, where the Scriptures were read in Greek. In the Palestinian synagogues, the Scriptures were read in Hebrew. Stephen's name, *Stephanos*, is Greek, and means a king or a crown.

We learn in Acts 6:1–6 that there was a disagreement between the Hellenists and 'those who spoke the language of the Jews'. The Hellenists complained that their widows (which probably implies anyone in need) were being neglected when food was distributed daily. The apostles, who were all Hebrews, decided to appoint seven deacons to care for the Hellenist poor, and Stephen, 'a man full of faith and the Holy Spirit', is the first to be mentioned.

It seems that the Hellenist deacons also preached and baptized, and Stephen proclaimed the gospel with such vehemence that he aroused the enmity of the elders of a synagogue (Acts 6—7). He was charged with blasphemy, and brought before the Sanhedrin. He made an intelligent and learned defence, showing how God had guided Abraham and Jacob, Joseph and Moses, David and Solomon. He told them that though Solomon had built the Temple, God would not be confined to houses made by men. This attack on the Temple, which was a large complex of buildings forming the commercial, cultural and spiritual centre of Jerusalem, roused them to great anger. He ended by calling them 'murderers' for having killed the promised Messiah. We are told that 'they became enraged, and ground their teeth'.

Stephen was condemned to death by stoning, and dragged outside the city wall. It seems that this was a judicial execution, because there were official witnesses. A young man named Saul guarded their coats while it was carried out, and approved of what they were doing. Normally the Jews were not allowed to pronounce the death sentence – this was a prerogative of the Roman governor; but Stephen's death may have occurred during the period between the end of Pontius Pilate's tour of duty and the arrival of his successor.

Stephen cried out that he could see the glory of God, and Jesus standing at God's right hand; but his attackers shouted and stopped their ears. He prayed that Jesus would receive his spirit, and asked forgiveness for his attackers; then he died.

Immediately after his death, there was a violent persecution of the Christians. This seems to have been mainly directed against the incomers, the Hellenists, for the apostles stayed in Jerusalem and were not harmed. Saul went on working for the destruction of the Church until the day when he too met Christ on the road to Damascus. Stephen's witness may have been the first stage in the conversion of the man who became the apostle *Paul, and carried the gospel into the Hellenistic world.

L. Duchesne, *Christian Worship*, pp. 265–8; M. Simon, *St Stephen and the Hellenes in the Primitive Church* (1958); M. H. Scharleman, *Stephen: a Singular Saint* (1968); F. M. Abel, 'Étienne (saint)', *Dictionnaire biblique* (Paris), supplement 2, (1934), cols 1132–46; N.C.E., 13, pp. 691–4; O.D.S., p. 441.

27. John, Apostle and Evangelist [Festival]

John is traditionally identified as the son of Zebedee whom Christ called with his brother *James when they were mending their nets by the lake (Matthew 4:21-2). He is also thought to be 'the disciple whom Jesus loved', and the author of the Fourth Gospel, of three Epistles and of the Revelation of John. In England, as in Greek texts, he is often called 'the Divine', that is, the Theologian.

There has been much theological discussion as to whether all these traditions can possibly relate to one person, or whether a number of people are involved. The references in the Synoptic Gospels are clear enough: John the apostle was a young fisherman; Christ named him and his brother James *Boanerges*, 'sons of thunder', and he was of an impulsive disposition. When a Samaritan village refused Christ hospitality, it was John who said at once, 'Lord, may we call down fire from heaven to burn them up?' In mediaeval iconography, he is usually shown as the youngest of the apostles, and frequently given red hair, perhaps to indicate his temperament.

In the Gospel according to John, there is no mention of his name. 'The disciple whom Jesus loved' accompanies Jesus on his mission, and shows an intuitive and reflective understanding of his ministry. He is next to his Lord at the Last Supper, and asks who is the traitor among their number (13:23-6). He is with the group in the garden of Gethsemane, and may be the 'other disciple' who accompanies *Peter into Jerusalem – to hear Peter's denials before the cock crew (18:15-18, 25-27). He stands at the foot of the Cross. *Mary the mother of Jesus is committed into his care, and he takes her into his own home (19:26-7). On the day of the Resurrection, he hears from *Mary Magdalene that the tomb is empty, and runs to see for himself – perhaps with a touch of his old impetuosity. He easily outstrips the older and slower Peter – but defers to Peter by waiting outside the tomb so that the older man can enter first (20:2-6). He is present when Jesus appears in the upper room, and again on the shores of the Sea of Tiberias, when the apostles return from fishing to find their risen Lord standing on the shore (20:19-22; 21:7). The death of Peter is foretold, and Peter asks what will happen to this disciple. Jesus replies, 'If it is my will that he remain until I come, what is it to you?' (21: 22)

Some of the disciples thought that this meant that the beloved disciple would not die, but would live to see Christ return in glory.

John lived to a great age. His brother James died in Herod's persecution of the Church, but John settled in Ephesus. *Bishop Polycarp of
Smyrna, who had known John himself, told *Irenaeus of Lyons that he
lived at Ephesus until the time of the emperor Trajan. He is thought to
have died early in Trajan's reign, about the year 100, at the age of
ninety-four, having outlived all the other apostles. *Jerome, nearly
three hundred years later, tells of a tradition that when John was very
old and feeble, he would have himself carried down to the assembly of
the faithful, and say, 'My little children, love one another.' When he
was asked why he repeated this injunction, he said, 'Because it is the
word of the Lord, and if you keep it, you do enough.'

The Gospel according to John was in written form early in the
second century, perhaps earlier. The content suggests that the writer
and his immediate readers were already familiar with the accounts by
*Matthew, *Mark and *Luke. The basic account of the earthly life
and ministry of Jesus is not repeated. The Fourth Gospel is written for
those who already know the facts, to emphasize their theological
import. It ends with a subscript:

> This disciple is the one who vouches for these things and has written
> them down, and we know that his testimony is true. There were
> many other things that Jesus did: if all were written down, the world
> itself, I suppose, would not hold all the books that would have to be
> written.

This suggests, as *William Temple demonstrated, that John in his
old age, telling his story after much meditation, may have had a
younger man to act as a scribe. Possibly more than one person was
involved in transcribing and editing this precious and unique account.
There seems no real doubt that 'the disciple whom Jesus loved' was
John himself, humbly obscuring his own role in order to make his
Master plain; and that he was also the author of the Epistles, in which
the same message of 'Love one another' occurs repeatedly. There is the
imprint of a single personality on them all.

The authorship of the Revelation of John poses different problems.
In English translation the differences are not marked; but the Greek of
the Revelation is very different from the Greek of the Fourth Gospel.
The Gospel is written in correct Greek with a limited vocabulary. The
Revelation is an outpouring, ignoring the rules of style, grammar and
syntax, but with a much wider vocabulary. J. B. Phillips thought that it
was written by a man still under the influence of an almost unbearably

intense spiritual experience: his words come out chaotically, trying to express glory too great for human comprehension. Other commentators have argued that a scribe with a greater command of Greek was involved, or even for a completely separate authorship.

John's symbol is the eagle – representing the 'eagle in flight' who is the fourth of the living creatures about the throne of God (Revelation 4:7–8), or perhaps the soaring thought of the Prologue to his Gospel, which is the Gospel reading for Christmas Day.

F. L. Cross, ed., 'St John on Patmos', *New Testament Studies* 4 (1963), pp. 75–85; N.C.E., pp. 9, 1005–6 and 1080–8. On the liturgical aspects, see L. Duchesne, *Christian Worship*, trans. M. McClure, 5th edn (London, 1919), pp. 265–8. Modern studies of the Fourth Gospel include William Temple, *Readings in St John's Gospel* (1939); F. L. Cross, ed., (1957); C. H. Dodd (1953 and 1963); C. K. Barrett (1955); R. H. Lightfoot (ed. C. F. Evans, 1956); E. Malatesta, *St John's Gospel, 1920–65: a cumulative and classified bibliography* (1967); R. Schnackenberg (3 vols, Eng. trans. 1968–82); O.C.B., pp. 373–50. See also *The Book of Revelation*, trans. and ed. with commentary by J. B. Phillips (1957).

28. The Holy Innocents [Festival]

When the wise men or astrologers arrived from the East to find the child born to be king of the Jews, King Herod ordered them to tell him where the child was to be found; but they 'left for their own country by another road' (Matthew 2:1–12), and Herod commanded that all the male children under the age of two in or near Bethlehem should be put to death. *Joseph took *Mary and the infant Jesus to Egypt, and they remained there until Herod was dead (Matthew 2:16–23]. The account of the slaying of these children parallels the slaying of the Jewish first-born in Egypt on Pharaoh's orders after the birth of Moses (Exodus 1:15–22).

The children who were killed in Bethlehem became known as 'the Holy Innocents' or 'the Holy Children', and they rank as martyrs because they died not only for Christ, but in his place. Bethlehem was only a village, so there were probably not many children involved, and the ten or twelve small stone sarcophagi preserved in the cave next to that of *Jerome in Bethlehem (now accessible through St Catherine's church) are reputed to be theirs.

The Innocents are mentioned in many early Christian works, including those of *Irenaeus, *Gregory of Nazianzus and *John

Chrysostom. At the end of the fourth century, the poet Prudentius wrote verses to them in his *Hymn for Epiphany*, beginning *Salvete, flores martyrum*. These verses are sung in Bethlehem on the day of their feast. In England, the Innocents have been known since the sixth century, and *Bede wrote a long poem about them. Their feast day was formerly called Childermas.

Irenaeus, *Adversus Haereses*, 50; Cyprian, Epistle 56, 3, ch. 58; Gregory Nazianzen, Sermon 38 in *Nativity*; John Chrystosom, Homily 9 in *Matthew*. See also Duchesne, *Christian Worship*, trans. M. L. McClure (1927), p. 268; *The Poems of Prudentius*, trans. M. C. Eagan (1962), pp. 89–90; *D.A.C.L.*, 7, 1, cols 608–16.

29. Thomas Becket (1118–70)   [L.F.]

Thomas was the son of a burgess of London, and was educated by the Canons Regular at Merton Abbey in Surrey. He joined the household of Theobald, archbishop of Canterbury, at the age of twenty-four, and proved to be a very able diplomatist. He received minor Orders, and the archbishop favoured him with a number of benefices. In 1154 he was made deacon and nominated as archdeacon of Canterbury, which gave him precedence over all the clergy in England except for bishops and abbots. He was involved in a mission to Rome, to seek the approval of Pope Eugenius III for the succession of Henry of Anjou as Henry II in 1154.

In the following year, the new king appointed Thomas as his chancellor. They were on terms of close personal friendship, and Thomas openly enjoyed the magnificence of his new position. He had an elaborate personal retinue, and lived in a style of considerable grandeur. At this point in his life, though he was nominally a cleric, he carried arms and fought for Henry of England in France. Though he was reputed to be proud, impetuous and capable of violent action, he was always liberal to the poor, and he made retreats with the Canons Regular at Merton Abbey.

Thomas was an intelligent and highly competent statesman, and the post of chancellor suited him admirably; but six years after he took office Archbishop Theobald died, and Henry II, exasperated by long battles with the clergy over their rights and privileges, resolved to have his chancellor as archbishop. Thomas saw the dangers, and warned him that if he became archbishop, his first loyalty would be to God and not to the king. 'For several things you do in prejudice to the rights of the Church,' he told Henry II, 'make me fear that you would require of me what I could not agree to.'

He only agreed to be consecrated after the papal nuncio had pressed him to do so in the name of the pope. He changed his way of life completely, living in near-monastic simplicity, praying earnestly and celebrating or attending Mass daily. He opposed the king's depredations on the Church, refusing to pay a royal levy on ecclesiastical lands, and defending the jurisdiction of the ecclesiastical courts. In 1163, Henry II demanded his assent to the sixteen Constitutions of Clarendon, which decreed that no prelate should leave England without royal consent, that no tenant-in-chief should be excommunicated without the king's consent, that the revenue from vacant benefices should be held by the king, and that the ecclesiastical courts should be subject to the king's officers. 'By the Lord Almighty, no seal of mine shall be put to them!' was Thomas's response. He tried repeatedly to seek accommodation with the king, but Henry II was determined to break ecclesiastical power. Thomas managed to leave England secretly, and to have an audience with Pope Alexander III, who was in Sens in northern France at the time. He attempted to resign his office, but the pope called him back and reinstated him, insisting that he bear the brunt of the conflict.

Thomas stayed in France for six years during endless and fruitless negotiations. He knew that it would be dangerous to return to England, but he was eventually drawn back by a crisis. In 1170, at the king's command, Archbishop Roger of York, assisted by six bishops, crowned the heir to the throne, Prince Henry, to assure the succession. This was a clear contravention of the rights and authority of the archbishop of Canterbury, and Thomas knew that he must go back to England to defend his position.

He met Henry II in northern France, but the king was cold and unforgiving. Thomas told the bishop of Paris that he knew he was going home to die. Carrying letters of papal support, he returned to England, and served letters of suspension on the archbishop of York and the six bishops. On Christmas Day 1170, he publicly denounced them from the pulpit of Canterbury cathedral. The archbishop and two of the bishops went to the king in France to lay their complaints, and in a violent fit of rage, Henry II asked who would rid him of Thomas. His actual words are not known; but four knights, Reginald

FitzUrse, William de Tracy, Hugh de Morville and Richard le Breton, took them as permission to kill the archbishop, and set out for Canterbury.

Thomas was ready for martyrdom. There are eye-witness accounts of how he processed calmly to the church, refusing to have the doors closed against his attackers; of how the four rushed in crying 'Where is Thomas the traitor?' and he replied, 'Here I am. No traitor, but a priest of God.' He was hacked to death between the altar of *Our Lady and that of *St Benedict.

The assassination of an archbishop carrying papal authority in his own cathedral on the apparent orders of a king produced universal horror and condemnation, and Henry II paid dearly for it in penance. Two years later Pope Alexander solemnly canonized Thomas as a martyr. The Pilgrims' Way from London to Canterbury to venerate Thomas's shrine was well known in mediaeval England, and Chaucer used it as the basis for *The Canterbury Tales*. The route can still be traced, though the shrine was destroyed by Henry VIII's officials in 1538. The story of Thomas Becket's martyrdom has been told afresh in T. S. Eliot's *Murder in the Cathedral*, and it remains one of the most celebrated episodes in the history of the Church in England.

C. Robertson and J. B. Sheppard, *Materials for the History of Thomas Becket*, 7 vols (R. S. 67, 1875–85); Lives by A. Duggan (1952); David Knowles (1970); and F. Barlow (1986). For the conflict with Henry II, see D. Whitelock, M. Brett and C. N. L. Brooke, *Councils and Synods*, 1, pt 2 (1981), pp. 914–50; C. Duggan, *Canon Law in Mediaeval England* (1982); B. Smalley, *The Becket Conflict and the Schools* (1973); M. Brett, C. N. L. Brooke and M. Winterbottom, eds., 'The Primacy Dispute', in intro. to *Hugh the Chanter, The History of the Church of York* (1990).

31. John Wyclif (?1324–84)   [L.F.]

Wyclif (Wiclif, Wycliffe – the spellings vary) was born in or near Richmond, Yorkshire. There is some debate over whether he was related to the Wycliffes of Wycliffe Manor, and whether he was briefly master of Balliol College, Oxford; but he certainly lectured at Balliol, was ordained, and left to take college livings successively at Fillington, Ludgershall and Lutterworth. He must have been largely an absentee vicar or rector, because he spent much time at court, where he wrote documents, some of which were circulated as pamphlets, against ecclesiastical abuses and papal depredations on the English Church (a subject of frequent royal displeasure since Saxon times). At some point between 1366 and 1374, he represented King Edward III at a meeting with papal representatives at Bruges. He became a Doctor of Theology in 1372, and in 1376 he published *De Dominia Divina*, in which he argued that all authority, religious and secular, derived from divine grace, and could be forfeited by unjust rulers.

Pope Gregory XI, alarmed by his views, sent many papal Bulls to England requiring the king, the bishops and the university authorities to imprison Wyclif; but he remained free, expressing his views in writing and from his pulpit at Lutterworth. He taught that the Church did not need a pope or bishops, and that the clergy had no power of absolving sins. The latter claim was particularly alarming to Rome, because it put the whole framework of confession and penance and the lucrative trade in indulgences in doubt. By 1380 Wyclif was teaching against the doctrine of transubstantiation, arguing that the elements in the Eucharist continued to have the character of bread and wine. In the earlier stages of his career, he had written in Latin: now he wrote in the vernacular, appealing to the ordinary people of England. He and his assistants translated the whole of the Bible into the vernacular. He recruited 'poor priests', and sent them out as itinerant preachers, to carry his views through the kingdom.

It was a turbulent and distressed age. There were acute dynastic struggles in England, with a weak and inept monarch. The Black Death in 1349 (bubonic plague, brought from the East) had killed between a third and a half of the population. Those who survived were fearful and confused, and there was rural unrest which led to the Peasants' Revolt in 1381. The new movement was put down harshly. Wyclif's theses were condemned by a convocation at Oxford, and his followers – contemptuously named 'Lollards' from the Dutch verb *lollen*, to mumble – were imprisoned and tried for heresy. Wyclif escaped persecution, probably because he had the support of the king's powerful son, John of Gaunt.

Wyclif's movement died out in England, but John Hus, the Bohemian reformer who died at the stake, was deeply influenced by his writings; and his theology came back to England more than two centuries later through *Martin Luther, who learned from Hus.

K. B. MacFarlane, *John Wycliffe and the Beginnings of English Non-Conformity* (1952); G. M. Trevelyan, *The Age of Wycliffe* (1898); R. L. Poole, *Wycliffe and*

Movements for Reform (1889); D.N.B., 21, pp. 1117–38. *The English Works of Wiclif*, E.E.T.S. original series, no. 74; S. H. Fristedt, *The Wycliffe Bible* (Stockholm, 1953); W. W. Shirley, *Catalogue of the Extant Works of John Wycliffe* (1924).

Appendix:
Martyrologies and Calendars

Martyrologies began to be compiled in the very early days of the Christian Church. Many Christians died in the persecutions of the Roman emperors, particularly those of Diocletian in the years 303–5, which extended to the Eastern Empire, most of Europe and North Africa.

The decision that a particular person had lived a life of unusual merit through the operation of the Holy Spirit was made *e consensu gentium*, by popular acclaim; but it soon became necessary for the Church to keep official lists. The *Hieronymianum*, based on the work of *Jerome (Hieronymus), and compiled while he was secretary to Pope Damasus I, is one such list.

When the persecutions ceased, other names came to be added: those of men and women who had shown outstanding Christian virtues in their lives, though they were not martyred. Many of them were confessors – that is, teachers; and most of the women were virgins. The monastic life, with its rejection of worldly values, was regarded as the surest guarantee of a life worthy to be honoured. Lists of saints (known as synaxaries in the Byzantine Church and menologies in the Greek Church) were kept by archbishops or bishops. The bishops of North Africa and Constantinople were particularly resistant to suggestions of centralization; but from the time of Innocent III (1199–1216), the approval of sainthood was increasingly reserved to Rome. Papal commissions were set up to investigate the lives of those whose causes were promoted, though many local and some unofficial cults continued to flourish, and the procedure was not followed with any rigour. A number of Anglo-Saxon saints such as *Augustine of Canterbury, *Bede and *Wilfrid were never officially canonized, though *Edward the Confessor and *Thomas Becket were.

In the sixteenth century, the definitive Roman Martyrology was compiled by Cardinal Caesar Baronius, the Vatican Librarian (1538–1607). In the seventeenth century, the Society of Bollandists began their massive work on the *Acta Sanctorum*, or Lives of the Saints. Sixty-four volumes were published in Antwerp, Rome and Paris from 1643. The June volumes were not published until 1867, and the volumes for November and December are incomplete. The work of the Society continues in the monthly *Analecta Bollandiana*, from 1882.

The process for sanctification was laid down by Pope Urban VIII (1623–44) and refined by Pope Benedict XIV in his *De Servorum Dei beatificatione et beatorum canonizatione* in 1734–8. The procedure requires a searching examination of the candidate's life, proving the three theological virtues of faith, hope and charity and the four cardinal virtues of prudence, justice, fortitude and temperance 'to a heroic degree', and the establishment of miracles. Procedures for beatification (the first step in sainthood) and canonization were laid down.

A major reform of the Universal Roman Calendar was completed in 1969, following Vatican II. Many dubious cults were eliminated – including those of *Margaret of Antioch and *Catherine of Alexandria, and the *Curé d'Ars' favourite, St Philomena. Saints were selected for inclusion in the new Calendar from every century and from many different countries, thus reducing the over-representation of Italians (who were more visible from the Vatican than others) and cutting the number of popes included to fifteen. Since then, it has been regularly updated and national Calendars are also being prepared. That for England was published in 2000.

Other reforms are under discussion in Rome. There is particular concern about the excessive cost of promoting a cause, and the necessity of proving 'miracles' – which becomes increasingly difficult as medical and scientific knowledge progresses. To date, the list has consisted exclusively of Roman Catholics, but there are reports that Christians from other communions are now under consideration.

The main modern sources of information on saints in the Roman Calendars (both old and new) are the *Bibliotheca Sanctorum*, twelve volumes published in Rome in 1960–70 (in Italian), and *The New Catholic Encylopaedia* (fourteen volumes published in New York in 1967, with supplements). In England, *Butler's Lives of the Saints* is the most accessible source. Father Alban Butler published the first edition in twelve volumes, one for each month of the year, in 1756–9. A revised edition was published in 1954, and there have been several shorter editions. A new and fully updated twelve-volume edition was completed in May 2000. The December volume contains a comparison of the Revised Roman Calendar with the Anglican *Common Worship* Calendar and the Calendar of the Episcopal Church of America, which are now similar in many respects.

Traditionally, the date of celebration for an individual is the date of his or her death, where this is known, on Augustine of Hippo's principle that this is the date of entry into eternal life; but in the case of many early saints, the actual date of death is not known, and the date of consecration, ordination or the translation of relics to a new shrine may have been used instead. Calendar changes complicate the issue. Another factor in determining the date of celebration is the need to avoid having too many entries for the same day, and to keep clear the major Festivals, such as Christmas and Easter.

Both the Roman Calendars and the Anglican Calendars keep to the traditional Fifty-Year Rule: individuals are not added to the Calendar until at least fifty years after their death, except in special cases, such as those of martyrs.

Index

Dominic	8 August
Donne, John	31 March
Dunstan	19 May
Edmund of Abingdon	16 November
Edmund of East Anglia	20 November
Edward the Confessor	13 October
Elizabeth of Hungary	18 November
English Saints and Martyrs	*see* Reformation
Ephrem of Syria	9 June
Ethelburga	11 October
Etheldreda of Ely	23 June
Felicity	*see* Perpetua
Felix of Dunwich	8 March
Ferard, Elizabeth	18 July
Ferrar, Nicholas	4 December
Fisher, John	6 July
Foucauld, Charles de	1 December
Fox, George	13 January
Francis of Assisi	4 October
Francis de Sales	24 January
Fry, Elizabeth	12 October
Gardiner, Allan	6 September
George	23 April
Gilbert of Sempringham	4 February
Giles of Provence	1 September
Gilmore, Isabella	16 April
Gore, Charles	17 January
Gregory the Great	3 September
Gregory of Nazianzus	2 January
Gregory of Nyssa	19 July
Grosseteste, Robert	9 October
Hannington, James	29 October
Helena	21 May
Herbert, George	27 February
Hilary of Poitiers	13 January
Hilda of Whitby	19 November

Lanfranc	28 May
Latimer, Hugh	16 October
Laud, William	10 January
Laurence	10 August
Law, William	10 April
Lazarus	29 July
Leo the Great	10 November
Leonard of Noblac	6 November
Lowder, Charles Fuge	9 September
Lucy	13 December
Luke the Evangelist	18 October
Luther, Martin	31 October
Luwum, Janani	17 February
Macrina	19 July
Margaret of Antioch	20 July
Margaret of Scotland	16 November
Mark the Evangelist	25 April
Martha	29 July
Martin de Porres	3 November
Martin of Tours	11 November
Martyn, Henry	19 October
Mary Magdalene	22 July
Mary, Martha and Lazarus	29 July
Mary the Virgin	15 August
Matthew the Evangelist	21 September
Matthias the Apostle	14 May
Maurice, Frederick Denison	1 April
Mechtild of Magdeburg	19 November
Mellitus	24 April
Methodius	14 February
Mizeki, Bernard	18 June
Monica	27 August
Monsell, Harriet	26 March
More, Thomas	6 July
Mungo	*see* Kentigern
Nathanael	*see* Bartholomew
Neale, John Mason	7 August
Neri, Philip	26 May

Simon the Apostle (with Jude)	28 October
Singh, Sundar	19 June
Slessor, Mary	11 January
Stephen	26 December
Studdert Kennedy, Geoffrey	8 March
Sumner, Mary	9 August
Swithun	15 July
Taylor, Jeremy	13 August
Temple, William	6 November
Teresa of Avila	15 October
Theodore of Tarsus	19 September
Thomas the Apostle	3 July (or 21 Dec.)
Timothy, Companion of Paul	26 January
Titus, Companion of Paul	26 January
Traherne, Thomas	10 October
Tyndale, William	6 October
Uganda, Martyrs of	3 June
Underhill, Evelyn	15 June
Vedanayagam, Samuel Azariah	2 January
Valentine	14 February
Venn, Henry, John and Henry the Younger	1 July
Vianney, Jean-Baptiste	4 August
Vincent de Paul	27 September
Vincent of Saragossa	22 January
Watts, Isaac	25 November
Wesley, John and Charles	24 May
Westcott, Brooke Foss	27 July
Wilberforce, William	30 July
Wilfrid	12 October
William Tyndale	6 October
William of Ockham	10 April
Willibrord	7 November
Wulfstan	19 January
Wyclif, John	31 December
Xavier, Francis	3 December

Printed in the USA
CPSIA information can be obtained
at www.ICGtesting.com
LVHW021037020224
770700LV00003B/24